D0848959

ELEPHANT-HUNTING

IN

EAST EQUATORIAL AFRICA

Library of African Adventure
Mike Resnick, Series Editor

African Nature Notes and Reminscences
by Frederick Courtney Selous

King of the Wa-Kikuyu
by John Boyes

Elephant-Hunting in East Equatorial Africa
by Arthur H. Neumann

ELEPHANT-HUNTING

IN

EAST EQUATORIAL AFRICA

BEING AN ACCOUNT OF THREE YEARS' IVORY-HUNTING
UNDER MOUNT KENIA AND AMONG THE NDOROBO
SAVAGES OF THE LOROGI MOUNTAINS, IN-
CLUDING A TRIP TO THE NORTH
END OF LAKE RUDOLPH

BY

ARTHUR H. NEUMANN

WITH NUMEROUS ILLUSTRATIONS
BY J. G. MILLAIS, E. CALDWELL, AND G. E. LODGE

INTRODUCTION BY MIKE RESNICK, SERIES EDITOR
THE LIBRARY OF AFRICAN ADVENTURE

St. Martin's Press
NEW YORK

ELEPHANT-HUNTING IN EAST EQUATORIAL AFRICA,
LIBRARY OF AFRICAN ADVENTURE, VOL. 3.

Library of Congress Cataloging-in-Publication Data

Neumann, Arthur H.
Elephant hunting in East Equatorial Africa /
Arthur H. Neumann.
p. cm. — (Library of African adventure : v. 3)
Originally published: London : R. Ward, 1898.
ISBN 0-312-10458-8
1. Elephant hunting—Africa, East. I. Title. II. Series.
SK305.E3N4 1994
799.2'761'096—dc20   93-44525
CIP

First Edition: April 1994

10 9 8 7 6 5 4 3 2 1

TO

Macleod of Macleod

MY KIND FRIEND DURING MANY YEARS, WITH WHOM,
IN DAYS GONE BY, I PASSED SOME PERILOUS, THOUGH
PLEASANT, TIMES ON THE ZULU AND SWAZI BORDERS,
WHEN UNDER HIM IN THE GOVERNMENT SERVICE,
AND IN WHOSE HOME OF DUNVEGAN CASTLE THE
GREATER PART OF IT HAS BEEN WRITTEN, THIS LITTLE
ACCOUNT OF MY ELEPHANT-HUNTING ADVENTURES IS

AFFECTIONATELY DEDICATED

ELEPHANT-HUNTING

IN

EAST EQUATORIAL AFRICA

INTRODUCTION

WHEN they speak of the great elephant hunters, three names always come to the fore: Karamojo Bell, James Sutherland, and Arthur H. Neumann. There doesn't seem to be any question that Bell was the best shot, and killed the most elephants—well over a thousand. Sutherland lasted the longest. But I think the most interesting and least typical career belonged to Neumann.

Neumann was one of the last of the professional hunters, as opposed to a "white hunter". The former was self-employed and hunted for a livelihood; the latter organized safaris for employers and acted as guide and support gun to his clients. The switch-over seems to be the period between 1905 and 1910. Prior to that, there were enough elephants—and few enough regulations, a point not to be overlooked—for a man with a keen eye, a lust for adventure, an abundance of stamina, and a disdain for hardship to make a handsome living by the hunting of elephants. The last great herd was decimated in the Lado Enclave in 1909–1910, which just happened to coincide with the first of the great organized safaris, that of the former American president, Theodore Roosevelt. From that day forth, the paucity of legally obtainable ivory and the abundance of wealthy clients changed the entire picture of African hunting.

That wasn't an option for Neumann, who died in 1907.

Neumann was born in Bedfordshire in 1850, and moved to Natal in 1868 to work a coffee plantation. He spent the next decade alternately farming and prospecting for gold, during which time his father died and he became, if not wealthy, at least financially independent. It would not be unfair to say that his first twenty-eight years were completely undistinguished. The next fifteen weren't much different: He became Captain of a native contingent during the Zulu War of 1879, had the good fortune to miss the massacre at Islandlwana, later joined the 71st Highlanders, and spent the better part of the decade of the 1880s hunting and exploring along the great, green, greasy, gray Limpopo River.

By 1890 he had made his way up to Kenya, where he was hired to find a route for the "Lunatic Express," the informal name for the Mombasa–Uganda Railway. He took a spear in the arm while plotting out the course, but finished the job, then accepted a position back in South Africa as a magistrate of Zululand. The paperwork and physical inactivity palled on him, and in 1893 he returned to Kenya and organized the first of his elephant hunts, disappearing from civilization for three long years.

And it was there, in Kenya, between the years 1893 and 1906, that he wrote his name into the history of African hunting in large, indelible letters.

To begin with, Neumann held a minimalist, even Spartan, philosophy regarding safaris. Where most hunters would set out with 200 or more porters—all of whom were paid up front and most of whom would desert early on— Neumann preferred to take thirty or thirty-five that he knew and trusted, reasoning that if the hunt were successful he could always pick up more along the way. This allowed him to move faster and farther than any hunting expeditions that might be in competition with him. He frequently packed only a bedroll rather than a tent; and his one outfit was expected to last the duration of the hunt.

Most hunters needed an interpreter. Although he used a native named Mnyamiri to translate several of the more obscure dialects, Neumann soon learned the major languages. Most hunters were quick to use the whip as a method of discipline, and thought nothing of shooting an occasional recalcitrant porter as an object lesson for the others. Neumann didn't believe in corporal punishment, never killed a native, and as a result had the most motivated and loyal staff of any hunter in East Africa.

One telling incident occurred early in his career. Upon returning to camp after a long, exhausting day in the bush, with a tropical thunderstorm beating down on him, he discovered that his camp crew had neglected to gather any wood to make a fire, and the maize meal had been ruined by the rain. A Sutherland would have had the whip out instantly; Henry Stanley would have certainly have spilled somebody's blood. Neumann simply picked up an ax, split the dry hearts out of a few logs, started a fire, and shared the meat he had brought back with the camp staff. It was a show of consideration typical of the man, and one that was to pay off in the long run.

When he started out, Neumann was laughed at for not using a gun *larger* than a .577. He soon found that excessive use of a Martini-Henry .577/.450 military rifle was enough to numb his shoulder and blister his trigger finger, and before long he began using a Lee-Metford .303. (Alexander Lake, a long-time African hunter during the first half of this century, argued forcefully that his Lee-Enfield .303 was more than capable of killing any target he hit, and that the larger calibers, while they may have given hunters more confidence, couldn't kill an animal any deader, and had this annoying tendency to shatter both shoulders and eardrums. The greatest proponent of the light caliber rifle was Karamojo Bell, who downed most of his elephants with a .256, a caliber that called for pinpoint accuracy—but then Bell was one of the few men possessing just such accuracy.)

For all his success, Neumann, who once shot fourteen elephants in a single day, wasn't immune to failure, and he got himself into some of the damnedest scrapes—like this one, which occurred in the harsh, arid Northern Frontier District:

"I had just fired a shot . . . when Squareface called my attention to the noise made by another portion of the herd. Now, I am deaf in my right ear, and, owing to that, am unable to tell which direction a sound comes from; consequently, I have to trust chiefly to my attendants as to that. I ran towards the point indicated, as quickly as the zigzag, obstructed passages would allow. . . . I could see the bushes swaying, and a bit of an elephant here and there, as they crashed through, only a few yards beyond. I stood in the path, facing across it but a little toward the left, in which direction the elephants I was watching were running; and had just fired a snap-shot at one I got a chance at when, immediately, there was an ear-piercing, screaming trumpet, of the shrillest pitch, close to me. It sounded very angry, and I supposed it had been made by the animal I had just wounded, and I stood, still gazing in the same direction and trying to make out, among the dust and bending bushes, a mark for my second barrel, when I felt a clap on my back, just under my right shoulder. Turning my head, I found myself face to face with an elephant, its black head and gleaming tusks just above me. . . ."

That was an almost typical day for Neumann. He would bathe in a stream, and come out covered with leeches. He would fail to chase baboons out of his camp, and one of them would kill his pet terrier, Frolic. He could grab "something that looked like a toad beside my boot" and find himself holding onto the business end of a five-foot puff adder. His longtime gunbearer, a native he called Squareface, was taken from camp one night by a lion as Neumann fired futilely into the darkness, and his camp servant, Shebane, was killed by a crocodile while fetching water on New Year's Day of 1896.

And yet the same man who could complain in a letter to fellow hunter John G. Millais, after a visit to England, about "the failure of that old brute of a butler to bring me my early morning cup of tea in my bedroom . . . and being dragged off for a beastly walk on Sunday, when I would much rather have pottered round with you and Selous" was the man who could walk, uncomplaining, to Lake Rudolf (now Lake Turkana), where the average daily temperature topped 120 degrees Farenheit, and could sit with his back to a tree in a tropical storm, sharing handfuls of wet maize with his men. Neumann seemed to think hardship and African hunting were synonymous, and never complained about conditions manyfold worse than he would have tolerated in England.

Of course, he didn't come to those conclusions about the dangers and discomforts of hunting without ample cause, as this oft-quoted encounter with a cow elephant demonstrates:

"I stood to face her, and threw up my rifle to fire at her

head as she came on, at a quick run, without raising her trunk or uttering a sound. . . . The click of the striker was the only result of pulling the trigger. No cartridge had entered the barrel on my working the bolt after the last shot, though the empty case had flown out. . . . The enraged elephant was by this time within a few strides of me; the narrow path was walled in on each side with thick scrub. To turn and run down the path in an instinctive effort to escape was all I could do, the elephant overhauling me at every step. As I ran those few yards I made one spasmodic attempt to work the mechanism of the treacherous magazine, and, pointing the muzzle behind me without looking round, tried it again; but it was no go. She was now all but upon me. Dropping the gun, I sprang out of the path to the right and threw myself down among some brushwood in the vain hope that she might pass on. But she was too close; and, turning with me like a terrier after a rabbit, she was on top of me as soon as I was down. In falling I had turned over on my back, and lay with my feet toward the path, face upwards, my head being propped up by brushwood. Kneeling over me (but fortunately not touching me with her legs, which must, I suppose, have been on each side of mine), she made three distinct lunges at me, sending her left tusk through the biceps of my right arm and stabbing me between the right ribs, at the same time pounding my chest with her head. . . ."

Eventually the elephant lost interest, or perhaps thought him dead, and moved off. Almost unbelievably, her tusks missed his arteries and major organs.

At this point most hunters would have found themselves deserted by their natives for what little remained of their lives, but Neumann's treatment of his staff was repaid in kind, and they nursed him back to health, a long and difficult process. ("I had to be washed off amid clouds of mosquitos. . . . For weeks I hardly slept, and it was two months before I could lie in any position except on my back.")

As soon as he was strong enough—sooner, actually—he went back to hunting, but in his weakened condition he came down with fever and then dysentary. Unperturbed by anything except by his forced inactivity, he spent another two months in camp recuperating, and then the man who couldn't abide a lazy butler or a meaningless walk in the park went off a-hunting again.

He wrote the book you are holding in 1898, and this led him to meet another hunter-turned-author, John G. Millais (who later wrote what is considered to be the definitive biography of Frederick Courtney Selous). According to Millais, Neumann was "a man of extremely shy, hypersensitive nature, and subject to alternate fits of gaiety or depression, but when happy was of such a charming, lovable temperament that his society was a continuous pleasure. In later years he imagined that nearly everyone disliked him, and his obsession grew upon him to such an extent that he avoided all intercourse with people who were often most anxious to be kind to him."

After the book's publication, Neumann returned to South Africa in 1899 to spend the next three years serving in the Boer War, then returned to Mount Kenya. According to Denis D. Lyell in *The African Elephant and Its Hunters*, "After his mauling (by the cow elephant) he could no longer use his heavy black-powder weapons, so he killed some of the largest bulls he had ever secured with the .303." Eventually he settled on the .450 Rigby as the perfect compromise between his old .577 Gibbs and the .303 Lee-Metford. He also used a .256 Mannlicher for everything except elephants, but as a letter to Millais makes clear, that simply means he used the Mannlicher hardly at all:

"I take but damned little interest nowadays in shooting any other beast but the elephant; but him I worship. Nothing else thrills me, but the spell of the elephant is as potent as ever."

With the great herds being decimated—his 500-plus total hadn't slowed things down—Neumann was acutely aware of the tide of conservationism that was sweeping Europe, and of some of the criticism that had been leveled at his book on moral rather than literary grounds. His answer, also written to Millais:

"I wish some of those superior sportsmen who call one 'butcher' and 'slaughterer' and other pretty names when expressing opinions on such work could have tried it for once. I make no pretension to being anything but a humble hunter; I rather dislike the title of 'sportsman:' I never quite know what is meant by it. But as to *butchery,* one is just as likely to be made into sausage-meat as the poor little elephants. Several times I was trampled on. . . ."

Of course, the way Neumann hunted them, being partially deaf to start with and then chasing them into thick bush where he couldn't see them either, the elephants *did* have a chance, and they made the most of it on more than one occasion. Neumann remarked that "I always feel when I get back to camp, 'Safely through another day'." Probably because there were so many he didn't get through safely. ("I often think now," he wrote just prior to his death, "of the rash way in which I behaved in times gone by and wonder that I was not killed over and over again.")

He hunted in the north of Kenya through 1904, selling the ivory from his last safari for a princely sum of 4,500 pounds, but then the colonial government began strictly limiting the number of elephants any one hunter could kill, and though he was far from destitute, he discovered that his livelihood had ended overnight.

It was a difficult adjustment for him. Scarcely a decade prior the townspeople would line the main street and cheer when a safari returned with from 50 to 200 natives each carrying a tusk on his back, just the way Dodge City and Wichita used to turn out and cheer the cowboys driving the cattle through their streets, for it meant that civilization was on its way. Well, somehow, when no one—and least of all, Neumann—was looking, civilization arrived, and now everything had changed.

He left Mombasa for England in 1906, planning to return and establish an estate on the slopes of Mount Kenya (very near where the Mount Kenya Safari Club stands today), but while in England he developed a severe case of influenza. This kept him bedridden for a few months and sent him into a deep depression. There are conflicting reports, but it would seem that he also fell in love with a young lady at about the same time, proposed marriage, and was turned down, which certainly didn't help him overcome his depression. He killed himself in 1907, before he could return to his beloved Kenya.

Neumann was a loner, and while John Boyes, Frederick Selous, Karamojo Bell, and others turn up in literally dozens of hunters' and settlers' memoirs, first-hand references to Neumann are notably absent. His only friends, neither of them exceptionally close, seem to have been Millais and Selous, and so perhaps it is fitting to close with an appraisal of Arthur Neumann by Frederick Courtney Selous, perhaps the greatest hunter of them all:

"I shall never cease to regret his loss. I look upon him as the last of the real genuine hunters of African big game."

I think Neumann would have agreed—most bitterly—with that.

—Mike Resnick

PREFACE

THE experiences of other wandering hunters have always
had so much interest for me, that I have ventured,
perhaps presumptuously, to conclude that my own may
possibly be thought worthy of perusal by those with
similar savage tastes. Even then I should hardly have
made bold to wield so unaccustomed a weapon as the
pen, were it not that my elephant-hunting has been
done in regions hitherto unvisited by the hunter. This
circumstance, and the fact that my account is of quite
recent adventures, describing faithfully, to the best of
my ability, the country and game as they actually are
to-day—an important quality in the value of such matter
—may, I hope, tend to justify my present more daring
enterprise. For, although I have hunted in South Africa
while yet the "high veldt" was black with wildebeeste
and the "bush veldt" still teemed with wild beasts, is
not *A Hunter's Wanderings*—to go no farther back in
the classics of big game—too unapproachably fascinating
as a latest record of elephant-hunting there to admit of
rivals in that field? And for descriptions of a more
recent search for sport in the southern portion of the
continent, have we not the charming volume of Mr.
J. G. Millais, who to a facile pen adds the enormous

advantage of artistic talent, enabling him to illustrate his own works?

Of course, I am prepared to be denounced as cruel. I admit at once that I am. This trait is part and parcel of the barbaric tastes which caused me, in my earliest years, to be stigmatised as a "cruel boy," by tender-hearted members of the family, for my ardour in the pursuit of the harmless, necessary cat, in company with a couple of equally keen terriers, among the farmyards of the neighbourhood (though I am bound to say that the cats always escaped into trees or on the heights of inaccessible ricks). One cannot complain of the censure of kind-hearted people who object altogether to the taking of life—on the contrary, I respect them. But the attacks of such superior sportsmen as, while themselves giving us graphic accounts of their exploits in pursuit of the harmless eland, giraffe, and other defenceless creatures, write in horror of the cruelty of hunting elephants (having themselves not penetrated far enough into the wilderness to get the chance) are harder to bear. It is particularly cruel, they tell us, to hunt cow elephants (especially to the hunter, no doubt). I wish one of these gentlemen would come and show us how to shoot bulls only, in the dense cover in which elephants have to be sought in Equatorial Africa.

By all means let elephants and other wild animals be preserved as far as possible. But as, unfortunately, their continued existence is incompatible with the advance of civilisation, the only way to do so successfully is by making reserves in places where effective control can be exercised alike over natives and Europeans.

However, for those amiable sympathisers to whom the descriptions of how I killed elephants can have no interest, my account of how one of these animals very nearly killed me may afford pleasure ; and if that should be tempered by disappointment because it was not altogether successful, they may hope that vengeance may yet be consummated. Akin to the heathenish propensity of my early youth above alluded to, was an attempt I remember to have made to get out of sight of houses in a secluded part of a common and fancy myself in an uninhabited country ; and among the prophecies uttered at a later period by observant Kafirs, who noticed the development of my unquenchable thirst for prying further and further into remote wastes, was one to the effect that I should end by dying in a far wilderness, inhabited only by wild beasts, where no smoke could be seen the horizon round.

It remains only to express my thanks to the artists (their names are a pledge for good work), who have done their part so much better than I can hope to have succeeded in mine, for the painstaking way in which they have endeavoured to carry out my ideas—actuated, as these have been throughout, by a desire to represent every incident truthfully—to Dr. Geo. Kolb, Major Eric Smith, Mr. J. R. W. Pigott, and other friends for photographs much better than any of my own, and to Mr. Rowland Ward for his courteous co-operation. I am also indebted to Miss E. M. Bowdler Sharpe for arranging and describing my butterflies. Several articles of mine which appeared in the *Field* are incorporated in some of the earlier chapters.

I should add, by way of guarding against any misapprehension, that wherever I have used the term "Central Africa" in this book, it must be understood in its original and literal sense, and not as in any way connected with Nyassaland, which has been (rather confusingly), of late years, officially known by that title.

ARTHUR H. NEUMANN.

BATH.

CONTENTS

CHAPTER I

FIRST EXPEDITION FROM MOMBASA

Preliminary observations—First acquaintance with Mombasa—Enter service of I.B.E.A. Company—Description of Mombasa—My hunting weapons—Organise elephant-hunting expedition—My Swahili name—Our start—Desertions—Overland route adopted—Last outpost of civilisation—My terrier companion " Frolic " —Reach Laiju—A fertile district—Build a stockade—" Papa," an old Ndorobo —Hunting trip across Mackenzie River—The Ndorobo's idea of happiness— Expedition unsuccessful—Shoot zebra and oryx on return—Side-shot at rhinoceros—The rhino's death-waltz—My second rhinoceros—His death-charge— First sight of Waller's Gazelle—A rhino's close inspection—Shoot a giraffe—His peculiar fall—Stalking herd of oryx—Device for scaring vultures—The Ndorodo's one occupation—Ideal game country—Varieties of game—Return to camp— Disheartening news—Loss of pack-animals—Experimental visit to Embe district

CHAPTER II

ON THE JAMBENI RANGE

Over Embe hills to Mthara—Description of country—The natives : their appearance and habits—Their mode of killing elephants—Fruitless search for game—Sight bushbuck—Tempting chance of a rhino—Critical moment—Trumpetings heard —An obstinate guide—First encounter with elephants—Reputation as hunter at stake—A longed-for chance—My " cripple-stopper "—Three elephants shot— Change of camp—Friendly natives—Shoot an impala—Presents from natives— Holding a " shauri "—The request for tribute—" Blood-brotherhood "—An unpleasant ordeal—My elder brother " Ndaminuki "—Track elephant spoor— Native curiosity—Sight another herd—Their favourite cover—A satisfactory shot—A good day's work—Ivory trading a tedious process—Scarcity of impala —Kenia—A reason for making " shauri "—Visit native kraals

CHAPTER VII

SECOND EXPEDITION

CHAPTER VIII

EXCURSIONS FROM EL BOGOI

CHAPTER IX

EXCURSIONS FROM EL BOGOI (*continued*)

CHAPTER X

EXCURSIONS FROM EL BOGOI (*continued*)

CHAPTER XV

RETURN TO LAKE RUDOLPH (*continued*)

CHAPTER XVI

EN ROUTE FOR EL BOGOI

CHAPTER XVII

CAMPING AT EL BOGOI

CHAPTER XVIII

EL BOGOI TO MOMBASA

APPENDIX

LIST OF ILLUSTRATIONS

CHAPTER I

FIRST EXPEDITION FROM MOMBASA

AFRICA is a big country. Few people who have no personal acquaintance with more than one portion of the continent realise how big. Thus in South Africa anything outside of the various colonies and states that make up what is commonly included under that designation used to be "somewhere up about the Zambesi," though it might be a thousand or more miles beyond. Just so now the average idea of Central Africa held in this country is expressed in the query "anywhere near Buluwayo?" I would therefore ask you to kindly glance at a map of Africa and notice what a long way Mombasa is from Cape Town, and how far the equator is north of even the Zambesi.

Though Durban is now the handsomest and most up-to-

date seaport town in South Africa, when I first landed there
early in 1869 it was a comparatively primitive place. Nevertheless I always felt that I had come too late, and listened
with envy to the tales of those who were then old colonists
about elephants in the Berea [1] bush when they first were
"Jimmies" or newcomers. The elephants had been driven
far beyond the borders of the colony by the time my foot
first sank into the deep sand which served for streets then,
and I never overtook them in South Africa. The last buffalo
even Natal contained was killed a year or two after my arrival.
Not but what I did find my way, during the many years I
wandered in South-Eastern Africa, to where the latter were
still in possession—big herds of them ; and other game, of
every kind peculiar to the country with the one notable exception above mentioned, yet swarmed. Some of those old
days might be worth recalling at another time ; but they never
satisfied me thoroughly. I hankered after the untouched
wilds which I knew still existed in Equatorial Africa : where
the elephant yet roamed as in primeval times ; where one
would never see the wheel-mark of a Boer's waggon nor hear
the report of any gun but one's own.

But circumstances—largely connected with a certain
emptiness of the pocket—kept me back for something like
twenty years from attempting to penetrate into the interior
of the continent from another and more favourably situated
point. Even when in 1888 I made my first passing acquaintance with Mombasa (before the days of the Imperial British
East Africa Company), as well as other African ports, in the
course of a voyage up the east coast, I was deterred by the
heavy cost which such an expedition as was said to be necessary to enable one to go any distance inland would entail.
Two years later I was there (Mombasa) again ; but still the
difficulties in the way of making an independent trip after
elephants, and the lack of encouragement to undertake it in

[1] The Berea is the fashionable suburb overlooking the harbour.

any other way led me to take service under the East Africa Company for a time, that I might learn something of th, country and gain a knowledge of the management of a caravan and a smattering of the Swahili language. Of a little more than a year which I spent thus—first cutting a bush road up the Sabaki River and afterwards joining in an expedition to the interior—it is not my intention to write

ENTRANCE TO MOMBASA HARBOUR.
(From a Photograph by Major ERIC SMITH.)

now, though there may be something worth telling about the latter some day. I had also the opportunity of finding out during that trip that elephants were not more difficult to kill than other game, and resolved to devote myself to their pursuit. Then the offer of an appointment in Zululand took me south again, but only to find after a year that the monotony of the life was unsuited to me. So I reverted to my original plan.

Mombasa had always a great attraction for me. A sleepy, old-world place, with its narrow streets and listless, picturesque inhabitants, it was suggestive of primitive times. If, one thought, the very port is so remote and untouched by modern progressive influences, what mysteries enticing to the imagination may not the interior contain? This, surely, was the very country I had yearned for. The island had, moreover,

PORTION OF THE OLD FORT AT MOMBASA.
(From a Photograph by Major ERIC SMITH.)

beauties of its own, though these it is not my province to describe, such as a picturesque and interesting old fort, a fine harbour, and dreamy shady mango groves run wild producing luscious fruit nearly all the year round. I always enjoyed the time I was detained there. The prospect over the still water in the cool of early twilight or by moonlight was particularly soothing, with the quaint dhows at anchor and fishing canoes paddling in and out or gliding before the soft breeze, a loin-cloth hoisted between two upright wattles serving for sail. The island too was then unspoilt. Such toy tramways as had been laid down were for the most part overgrown with grass and tropical vegetation; overturned dolls' trucks, rotting in the jungle, but emphasised the supremacy of nature. Now, alas! the place is all railways, iron roofs, and regulations, a change decidedly not for the better from my point of view. Let those who like them describe such "improvements."

I make these preliminary observations mainly with a view to showing that I had had considerable African experience, all of which was directly or indirectly of the greatest use to me, before embarking on the expeditions I am about to describe. I had shot much big game in South-Eastern Africa ; had travelled many thousand miles, albeit with different means of transport ; and had acquired such bush and veldt knowledge as only a long apprenticeship can give—knowledge of the greatest value not only to help one over difficulties but to enable one to understand the varying conditions with which one may be surrounded.

So that I was no novice when, in the end of November 1893, I landed once more in Mombasa, this time prepared to at last carry out my long-cherished scheme for making an independent expedition with my own caravan into the interior, the main object of which should be elephant-hunting. I hoped by this means to recoup myself through the ivory for the outlay incurred in following my bent of wandering in the most remote wilds I could reach. My weapons were a double .577 (which I had already once had the opportunity of testing on elephants, with good results), a single .450—both these by Gibbs,—a .250 rook rifle, and a shot-gun. This last I afterwards discarded as unnecessary, while its cartridges were an encumbrance. To these I added a common Martini-Henry.

I know by experience that the routine of organising and fitting out an expedition, starting it from the coast, and even the

first part of the journey itself make uninteresting reading, and
anything that I may think worth mentioning on these subjects
I can more conveniently allude to elsewhere ; I will, therefore,
not worry my readers with tedious preliminaries of the kind
now, beyond saying that in one month I was ready with
about fifty men (all of whom I armed with Snider carbines)
and some twenty donkeys to start for the "bara" or interior,
with the intention of getting as far as I could and being away
as long as I liked.   That was, I consider, a short time to take
in all the preparations necessary.   Mombasa did not offer many
facilities for getting work done, and I had brought nothing but
my guns and cartridges with me ; but porters were plentiful,
and I was known to them, not unfavourably—my very Swahili
name, "Nyama Yangu" (my meat or my game), being
suggestive of good times.   My headman was not altogether
a happy selection.   He was a most polite, polished, and
picturesque Swahili gentleman of Arab descent, but not
very practical.   Plucky he was, as I afterwards found, but
somewhat procrastinating and over punctilious about strict
Mahomedan observances to be altogether suitable to the rough-
and-ready life we had to lead.   Owing partly to this not too
suitable appointment, some undesirable men got "written on"
as porters.   There are abuses in the manner of engaging these
men ; and if not very carefully looked after, the wily rupee
plays an important but indiscriminating part in their choice,
quite unconnected with any useful qualifications.   The result
became apparent pretty soon, but not, fortunately, on any very
serious scale.

Our start, two days before Christmas, was most smooth
and propitious.   The men all turned up, and never was
there a happier and more enthusiastic lot of porters nor,
for the most part, a finer.   Two or three desertions took
place a day or two after, causing a little temporary inconvenience, and one gentleman took the belt containing my
watch with him, which had been hung on a bush behind me

while I was seeing the caravan off in the dusk. But strange to say—whether because his conscience pricked him or that he could not sell what it was so apparent he must have stolen —he came back of his own accord, watch and all, a few days later. I forgave him, and he was a faithful and reliable man for the rest of the trip.

Having had long experience of both ways of travelling, I prefer on the whole the Central African system of a caravan of porters for a hunting trip to the ox-waggons of South Africa. Of course the latter means of transport have many advantages and the others their drawbacks, and probably many people would disagree with my conclusion. But with the "safari" one is more mobile, independent of roads, and never has those terrible "stickfasts"—so upsetting to plans and tempers—to which waggons are liable.

I have no intention of inflicting upon the reader a description of the wearisome details of caravan travelling. It is less monotonous to go through than to read about. The exercise keeps you in good health, as a rule, and there is always something to be done which prevents the afternoons hanging heavily upon your hands ; while the constant change, even from one disagreeable camp to another, makes variety of a kind—never so tedious as stagnation. One soon shakes down to the life, and finds one's tent as comfortable as any house, while in the former you can never become a nuisance to your neighbours. Breakfasting in the dark at 4 A.M. is trying to one when fresh from civilised habits, I admit ; but one has to and does get broken in even to that, and a most important thing for one's comfort during the march it is to be able to eat heartily at such unearthly hours.

I had decided to make Laiju—a district on the north side of the Tana, and close to the foot of the Njambeni or Jambeni range, which is a little east of Mount Kenia—my first objective point, and to get as much farther north in the direction of Lake Rudolph as I should be able, or as circumstances might seem to make desirable. I ventured to disregard advice to take the Tana River route—involving a sea voyage, a fresh organisation, and a journey through difficult and unhealthy "fly"-infested bush all the way, with little useful help from canoes (which could not take animals) against the stream—and elected for the overland one through Northern Ukambani. But I made the mistake of going round by Kibwezi on the Uganda road, instead of following the more direct and convenient path used by Swahili traders and Wakamba visiting the coast. At the little German mission station of Ikutha, where one enters Ukambani, I passed the last outpost of civilisation in this direction. I have reason to feel the greatest gratitude to its hospitable head (Mr. Sauberlich) for many kindnesses and ready assistance in various ways. Shortly after leaving there I met Mr. Chanler returning to the coast. I had already had the advantage of some talks with Lieutenant Von Hohnel (previously Count Teleki's companion) in Mombasa, who had been hurt by a rhinoceros while travelling in his company, and from both these gentlemen I received much useful information. I had long previously, though, heard of Laiju and the Ndorobo country beyond from Swahili traders as a good one for elephants, and resolved to make that direction my aim, and as much farther as I could attain. It had the special attraction for me that the country that way was least known, and I was not likely to be hampered by rival travellers, official or otherwise, there. Chanler gave me a little half-bred terrier, named "Frolic," which proved a charming little companion, and continued so until her sad death on another expedition.

There is nothing worth recording in the way of sport during all this part of the journey. The uninhabited (principally desert) country traversed previous to entering Ukambani has but little game, though here and there an odd head may be picked up,—a Coke's hartbeeste, impala or zebra,—and a few guinea-fowl sometimes help the pot.

But one animal, to which considerable interest attaches, deserves more particular mention. In some parts of the country to the left (or south) of the road between Duruma and Taita—as, for example, about Pika-Pika and Kisigau, and sometimes not far from Ndara—a gazelle is to be found about which naturalists seem somewhat confused, namely *G. petersi.*

Some authorities seem to regard this antelope as a mere local variety of *G. granti;* but I am strongly of opinion that it is quite distinct, and, while taking the place of the latter in the coast regions, may be regarded as almost intermediate between it and *G. thomsoni.* I am able to illustrate this by a photograph of a series of skulls of the three species in my possession. These have, I may explain, not been specially selected, but are some of those I have shot, which I happen to have kept.[1]

Gazella granti ♀.
Length of horn
on curve, 12 in.

Gazella petersi ♀.
Length of horn
on curve, 10⅝ in.

It will be seen that they form a regular gradation, the females corresponding exactly with the males in their peculiarities. I am sorry that I have not been able to figure a female Thomson's gazelle skull, as it appears there is not one in England, not even in the Museum. I have, however, been kindly given the photographs of two mounted heads (the only ones, so far as I can discover, in existence in this country), one of which is reproduced. It is a curious thing that the female of this last gazelle seems almost to be in a state of uncertainty as to whether it ought to bear horns or

[1] That of the female petersi has been kindly given me by a friend, as I had not one myself.

not. For, while many specimens, like that illustrated, have properly developed symmetrical horns, in some they are more or less imperfect, others again being hornless.

Through Ukambani there is no game—there are too many natives—and the march is not interesting. I will, therefore,

Gazella granti ♂.
Length of horn
on curve, 26¾ in.

Gazella petersi ♂.
Length of horn
on curve, 17¾ in.

Gazella thomsoni ♂.
Length of horn,
13¼ in.

skip this part of the journey, fly across the Tana with its wide shallow valley full of monotonous dense scrub, and land my reader at Laiju, about five weeks' caravan journey from the coast by the most direct route (though I did not reach there until 22nd February 1894), which may be considered as practically the commencement of the game country in this direction.

Arrived here the first thing to be done was to establish friendly relations with the natives of the district, and open up a food trade. This was not difficult, since Chanler had been on good terms with them, and had been careful to keep market prices for produce within reasonable bounds, for which I felt

THOMSON'S GAZELLE ♀ (*Gazella thomsoni*).

grateful to my predecessor. So the preliminary negotiations only lasted a couple of days, and on the third Baikenda, one of the leading men of the immediate neighbourhood—a weird-looking, wizened old savage, suffering from rheumatism—came with his retinue, bringing the sacrificial sheep, and we went through the ceremony of "eating blood" most solemnly and impressively. I then made their hearts white with presents, as their bodies with calico, and Baikenda and I became, as he put it, as if born of one mother, emphasising the relationship with expressive pantomime by squeezing suggestively his shrivelled old breast with his hand.

It is a fertile district, and food was to be had in fair abundance and considerable variety. Luscious bananas were plentiful and fine yams cheap and good. My cook used to make me what he called " smash-im-up " of the latter—a capital substitute for mashed potatoes : indeed, as regards vegetable products, I lived better while here than I ever did again, and often, when restricted for months and months together to porridge and cakes of coarse dry meal in the barren country farther north, did I think of those delicious bananas.

Intending to make this my headquarters for a while, and finding Chanler's boma too straggling to be a secure depot in which to leave my goods in charge of a few men (though I used it as a camp myself), I spent some time in building a strong little stockade for this purpose. Various circumstances, into the details of which it is not necessary to enter, prevented my making any extended hunting trip for a much longer time than I had intended to delay here. I was able to obtain meat easily enough, as game of one sort or another was generally to be found within a long walk of my camp—waterbuck and zebra being the most numerous—and the young natives were always pleased to accompany me, being keen for meat, though they had a curious prejudice against letting their womenkind see them with any.

Of my first small excursion in quest of elephants—although unsuccessful in that I did not get a sight of any—a short account may not be uninteresting, since I saw a good deal of other game, and had a certain amount of sport ; but elephant-hunting being the main object of my expedition—as it is to be the principal subject of this book—I will not dwell too much upon it. It occupied little more than a fortnight, and the farthest point I reached was probably not more than about forty miles as the crow flies away from my main camp. Laiju is about east-north-east of Kenia (which, by the way, the natives here call Kilimara), and the direction we took was nearly due east—but slightly to the south by compass—from the former place.

An old Ndorobo, to whom I had been introduced by Baikenda, and who, being too feeble to hunt, lived here generally as a sort of dependant of his—mainly on charity—had offered to show me where elephants were, within two or three days' journey; and, as I was not yet in a position to start on a long trip, I gladly accepted his offer, in hopes of putting in a little of the time I was obliged to wait pleasantly and perhaps profitably. The Ndorobos,[1] of whom I shall have more to say later on, are a kind of degraded Masai, living on game, honey, etc., in the bush, something after the style of the South African bushmen, the grand object of their desires being elephants. They live a more or less nomadic life in small communities scattered over a wide extent of East Equatorial Africa, where no settled inhabitants are. The wild region from here northward to Lake Rudolph is left entirely to them.

On my outward journey, although I saw plenty of game, I did not do more shooting than just to supply my men and self with meat, for which a zebra or two and one or two Grant's gazelles sufficed. I will go more into details in describing our return journey, as it was then that I did most shooting. But first, touching the elephants. We had crossed several beautiful streams—the head waters of a considerable tributary of the Tana, which Chanler and Von Hohnel have called the Mackenzie River—and got into a pretty dry country beyond, where there was hardly any game. All the way the bush was more or less open and easy to walk through, as we

---

[1] I purposely refrain from using the Swahili form of plural, Wa-ndorobo, because it is no more correct than our own as applied to the Masai or Ndorobo language. I believe the proper plural to be Londorobo, but am not sure.

avoided the thicker parts. Our old guide was rather tedious, insisting on our making short stages each day, having always some excuse, such as the next water being a long way ahead, or that we might come suddenly into the elephants' haunts and disturb them prematurely. In reality he was in no hurry; having plenty of meat he enjoyed himself dawdling along, camping early, and cooking and eating the rest of the day.

HIPPOPOTAMUS IN THE TANA RIVER.
(From a Photograph by Dr. KOLB.)

He was, however, such a nice old chap that I could never get wild with him; indeed, we were great chums, he was such a pleasant contrast to the uncouth natives of this district, who have no shadow of an idea of courtesy, while he, on the contrary, was a polite old gentleman, like a Masai. He called me Papa (with the accent, however, on the first syllable), and as he was a much older man than I—though with fewer gray hairs, I am bound to confess—I could not do less, regarding the old fellow quite affectionately as I did, than return the compliment; so we always called each other Papa.

Well, at last we did get elephant spoor. The first we found was two days old, but it proved the elephants were in the locality. Old Papa was quite moved with the sight, it was touching to see him. Holding up his hand toward the sky he prayed, "Ngai (God), give us elephants," looking so earnest the while one could not but sympathise with his feelings, even if I had not been myself equally anxious for success. A little farther on the old man was deeply affected by coming upon some droppings, taking one of the dry loaves of vegetable fibre fondly in his hands and breaking it open to see whether still moist inside, so as to judge its age. The elephant is clearly the acme of the Ndorobo's ideas of happiness. He would wish for unlimited elephants, just as you or I might for £10,000 a year. Elephant's fat, in particular, seems to be the summit of their desires. "Oh! if I could but feed on elephant's fat," said my old friend, "my wife would not know me when I went back, so sleek and plump should I become."

Where we first found this spoor was near a small spring at which we had slept, at the base of a rocky koppie. Here there was a deserted Ndorobo camp, where Papa's clan had been about a month before. He showed me which had been his hut. The huts were mere gipsy shelters. There was a good-sized collection of them here. They did not seem to have had much success in hunting, judging by the bones, which were but few, about; among them were those of a giraffe. Several times in this country we came upon little circular low screens of branches, close to what were, when there was rain, small "pools in the parched ground"; in these, Papa told me, the Ndorobo hunters watched by night for game.[1]

We were now taken on to a sandy stream bed, where our

---

[1] Farther north I saw nothing of this kind. Different clans, I found afterwards, have different methods of killing game.

guide said the elephants were in the habit of drinking, and in the neighbourhood of which he felt confident they then were. We kept silence on the march on this day. Except for an odd Waller's gazelle or two here and there, and occasionally a little giraffe spoor, the country now seemed gameless. We at length entered the dry bed of the watercourse, and after following it up for some distance came, to Papa's intense excitement, to where elephants (a few only) had dug in the sand for water the night before. We camped not far off to leeward and kept perfectly quiet, after sunset putting our fires out and neither speaking nor stirring. It was hardly dark when we heard the elephants farther up stream, fortunately to windward. They were evidently drinking.

I had, of course, great hopes of success now ; and next morning was ready, as soon as it was light enough, to follow the spoor. In this, however, poor old Papa failed, much to my astonishment. I had been told by Von Hohnel that Ndorobos were not good at spooring ; but could hardly believe but that he must have been mistaken. However, mine could not keep it in hard dry ground ; and after casting about all morning he was at length forced to confess that he was not able to spoor with certainty except after rain. The poor old fellow was so down-hearted, being much more disappointed than I myself, that I could not be put out with him, although he had led me all this dance and wasted so much of my time for nothing. At that time neither I nor my gun-bearers had had much experience at spooring elephants, the ground was very hard with no long grass, and, our guide having failed us, I thought it was useless now thinking more of elephants this time ; so next morning we marched back in the direction we had come from. How I wished for a couple of good South African natives to spoor for me ! I have never had bushmen with me, but some of the Tongas and Shanganes living in the game districts of South-Eastern Africa are good enough for me. Had I been able to follow these elephants in such easy bush to hunt in I might have had a splendid chance at them.

We took a more direct route returning, and the first day slept at the most easterly of the head streams of the Mackenzie ; my intention being to go on to the second next day and camp there for a few days to shoot meat to carry back partially dried to the " boma." On our way the first day, when within about a couple of hours' march of the stream, we passed through a beautiful open glade with short green grass. Here I had shot a couple of Grant's gazelle on our way out, and seen zebra, oryx, and ostriches ; so I expected to find game, and hoped to shoot something for the men if not for myself, as I had been unable to get a shot at a rhino I had seen during the morning.

As soon as we emerged from the bush we saw zebra ahead, so I made the men sit down while I went after them alone. I soon saw that they were not the common kind, by their wide ears, narrow stripes and much larger size, and became interested ; for any animal new to me always delights me. But while I was stalking those ahead of me, another lot I had not seen trotted out of the bush to my right and ran past me. But halting for a moment to look at the (to them) strange creature, they gave me a good chance, and one received a bullet, which I saw at once by the way he galloped off would be fatal ; and following to where he had disappeared I found him lying down as if alive, but in reality dead. I might have shot a second, but one was enough for our present needs. A beautiful creature he was ; far handsomer than Burchell's and its allies as well as much bigger. This was my first acquaintance with Grevy's magnificent zebra. I skinned his head for a trophy. I noticed too that the cry of this zebra (as I shall have occasion to notice more particularly later on) was quite different from the bark of all the small kinds (which are merely local varieties of Burchell's), being a very hoarse kind of grunt varied by something approaching to a whistle. This

is about the limit of the species ; there are none south of the
Tana nor farther up the river on this side.

The men (I had about a dozen with me) soon piled all the
meat on to the loads they were already carrying, and we went
on to the stream.   This one, just at the part where we struck
it, flows through lovely open meadows of soft green grass with
only scattered trees.   The formation here is limestone, generally
close to the surface, and where it is so the grass grows short
and soft ; and there having been plenty of rain that season it
was then beautifully green.   As we came out of the bush to
the edge of the open a herd of oryx were standing in the
meadow ; and as I had no meat for myself (besides which I
wanted oryx heads) I shot one, which proved a nice fat heifer.
We camped close by on the stream, within a hundred yards or
so of the antelope.   A delightful and most picturesque spot it
was, with the delicious brook of clear, cold water—so especially
precious in Equatorial Africa—rushing past.   My tent was
pitched under a spreading tree on its banks and but little
above its surface, for it had hardly any bed and the gently
sloping lawn came right down to the water.   The men caught
quantities of fish, and one kind—a sort of small perch—proved
a very sweet little fellow when fried fresh out of the water.
On some of these streams grows a plant which I take to be a
kind of lily, of which the root when thoroughly boiled is a
very good vegetable and a welcome addition to one's menu in
the bush.

Next morning we started to move on to the next stream,
where I knew there was abundance of game ; and as the
" boma " at Laiju could from there be reached in one good
day, it would be a suitable locality in which to shoot meat for
the purpose of being carried in.   But on the way, while it was
yet early, as we were traversing the comparatively open bush
that covers most of this particular part (though in places are
dense thickets of considerable extent) of the nearly level
country, we came suddenly in sight of a rhinoceros standing a

short way off. Being bent on "biltong" for exchanging with
the natives for meal, etc., I thought it a pity to lose this
chance; so I exchanged my single Metford, which it was then
my custom always to carry myself, for the double .577 with
my gunbearer behind me and ran up to a little bush quite
near the rhino.

Although very bad-sighted, these animals often seem
to get some inkling of one's proximity even when the wind
is right, either from the tick birds which generally accompany
them or, in their absence, by some other means—perhaps
hearing. This one knew I was there and began to shift
about uneasily; but as soon as I got up to the bush which
screened my approach I took the first chance he gave me
of a side shot and before he had made up his mind to
decamp. He immediately executed what I call the rhino's
death-waltz—a performance they very commonly go through
on getting a fatal shot. It is a curious habit, this dying dance,
and consists in spinning round and round like a top in one
place with a rocking-horse motion before starting off at a
gallop, which generally is only a short one, to be arrested after
a hundred yards or so by death. I imagine the cause of this
strange evolution is the animal's endeavour to find out the
cause of the sudden wound it has received—much on the same
principle as a dog chases his tail when anything irritates that
organ. Mine passed close to me after his dance, but I felt
so sure he was done that I refrained from giving him the
second barrel.

On another occasion, however, I lost a rhino through
placing faith in the "waltz" being a sign of immediately
impending death. I had given him a shot in about the right
place; but as he was somewhat inclined diagonally towards
me, the bullet must have gone too far back. He waltzed
round several times with only an ant-heap, about as tall as a
man and not much broader, between me and him, he being on
one side of it while I dodged him, as his dance sometimes

brought him half round it, on the other. On that occasion, however, my rhino galloped so far that I lost him through not putting in the second barrel as he passed.

Well, my victim of this morning (to return to him) galloped off and I followed him with confidence. But no sooner had I started in pursuit than I saw him—as I supposed—standing a couple of hundred yards on. I made towards this one ; but on the way passed *my* rhino already dead. Getting quite close up behind another small bush I shot this second one in the point of the shoulder, breaking it, though I did not feel certain at the time that the bullet had penetrated to his vitals. He plunged about, and on my tiny dog " Frolic " running in and barking, charged savagely at her, ploughing up the ground and carrying some of the soil between his horns. The charge brought him towards me, so I gave him my second barrel in front of the shoulder ; and after trying to stand on his head, squealing like a gigantic pig,—as he is in appearance too,—he subsided into a lying position on his stomach, and though his ears flapped and his little eyes blinked still, was dead. It turned out afterwards that the second was superfluous, as both bullets had gone through his heart.

Thus we had two rhinos dead, only about a hundred yards apart. There had been rain the night before, and pools of water stood in depressions in patches of bare red ground such as occur here and there in this bush ; so we camped by one of these which we found a short way off, for the convenience of cutting up and carrying the meat.

We remained here two days, the men cutting up and hanging the meat in festoons. As they had as much as they could deal with I did not attempt to shoot anything more there, though there were giraffe as well as other game about. Waller's gazelle are particularly fond of bush of this character, where there are these bare patches of hard red ground. I made the acquaintance of this queer-looking gazelle for the first time now, with its extraordinarily long neck giving it the appearance of a little giraffe. Among the flocks of vultures that congregated around were a few marabou storks, reminding me forcibly of the old days when I used to shoot on the Sabi and Crocodile rivers in South-Eastern Africa, while game yet teemed there, where there were always two or three of these quaint birds about whenever anything was killed ("elephant openers," as the native name for them in that country may be freely translated). One I shot here had the exquisite little white fluffy feathers under the tail in perfect order.

The day we moved our camp on to the stream—the pool being nearly dried up—I did not want to shoot anything except a Grant's gazelle, to provide some fresh meat for myself, as the men were busy carrying down the bundles of still heavy rhino biltong ; but I went out into a great open plain that extended for a considerable distance in the direction of Laiju to look out for messengers I had sent back to the boma, lest they should not find our new camp. I sat down here under a tree and amused myself by looking through my glasses in all directions at the game visible. I could see large herds of zebra in many parts, also numbers of Grant's gazelle ; a couple of giraffes were visible one way, and in the distance some ostriches. By and by, while we were skinning a gazelle I had shot, a family party of three rhinoceroses came into view not far off.

On our way back to camp, as they were in the direction we wanted to go, I went straight towards them out of curiosity, to see what they would do. My experience of these creatures has not been that they often charge viciously, though when a long caravan is passing and they wish to get through they can hardly avoid going for some one, but of course they do undoubtedly sometimes attack their enemies. I have always believed a cow with a calf to be more dangerous than any other—as is, of course, the case with other animals (it was one such, I believe, that hurt Lieutenant Von Hohnel)—and I was anxious to see how this one would behave, though as I had no wish to shoot any that day it was perhaps a foolish thing to do. The cow was leading, followed by her calf, the bull being some distance behind ; and when about one hundred yards from her I stood and examined her and her mate's horns through my glass, but decided they were not worth coveting.   When we got within about fifty yards, she started straight for us at a sharp trot.   I waited until she had come on to within about half the distance, and then, as she still made dead for me, who was in front, I confess I did not care to await passively the further progress of the experiment, so gave her a bullet in the face, which turned her off at a gallop.   I was really sorry to have to hurt her, but as the ground was perfectly open, with not a stick to dodge behind if she had run amuck among us, she might have got foul of some one (we were four) and done damage.   I don't know whether this was a *bonâ-fide* charge or not ; if I had waited longer she might have turned off of her own accord when she was satisfied what we really were, but I disliked so close an inspection.

Another day I came back to this plain to try to get a shot at the ostriches.   I failed to get near them, but, while trying, a giraffe came towards me — apparently not seeing me or mistaking me for something harmless ; so I sat still till it had walked a little past, some 150 yards off, so that the solid bullet I sent into its ribs from my little Gibbs .450 might travel forward.   It galloped violently for about 200 yards, and then, after staggering a little, plunged head first, its hind-quarters curiously standing up for a second or two after its neck was on the ground.   It is not often one has the chance of seeing a giraffe fall plainly, as they are generally shot among bush. More often they, like most animals, fall backwards when mortally wounded.

I left my men cutting up the giraffe, and carrying my two guns myself, like Robinson Crusoe (I can't say I admire his plan), I directed my steps towards camp, old Papa with a load of meat for himself alone following me.   But before arriving at the stream I saw a herd of oryx away to the right, grazing among some clumpy bushes on slightly rising ground. I wanted some oryx heads, and the meat would be useful too— for I had sent back to Laiju for porters to carry in the biltong, of which we could hardly have too much ; so I determined to go after them, especially as the ground was rather favourable for getting near.

Papa had gone on ahead towards camp, and was so taken up with his burden and absorbed in the happy thoughts it evoked that I could not attract his attention ; so I put my second rifle and sundry other impedimenta I had taken from my gun-bearer, such as glasses, etc., down—or, rather, hung them on a tree — and proceeded to stalk the herd. Taking advantage of the cover afforded by the bushy shrubs, and keeping my eyes fixed on such of the grazing herd as were from time to time visible between as I crept nearer— lying low now and again till the position of any member that seemed likely to discover me became favourable again—I got at last within shot. Then wriggling myself into a sitting position under cover of a bush, I edged out cautiously a little to one side, and waited till a good chance should be offered by the antelopes moving slowly about as they grazed—for I had succeeded so well that they were absolutely unconscious of my presence. It was not long before a favourable opportunity presented itself, of which I took advantage, getting in another satisfactory shot at a second immediately after, before the herd took to flight, and I felt certain that each had gone well home. Nor was I disappointed, for on going to see when the rest had decamped I found both lying dead not very far apart, in the track of the retreating herd.

I have for years adopted the device of hanging my handkerchief on a bush or stick beside the carcase of an animal I am obliged to leave by itself while men are called to skin and carry it to camp, to keep the vultures off, and have always found this plan effectual. I generally have two or three white cotton cloths for the purpose in a satchel my gun-bearer carries, but I had not any with me now, and as my handkerchief would only serve for one of the oryx I took off my vest of cotton web—all I wear under my little loose holland jumper—and hung it up to mount guard over the other. Papa had come on hearing the shots, and helped me to drag each under the shade of the nearest bush, the ensign being hung from it over the buck. Various modifications of this may be adopted as circumstances render convenient. Thus, a stick may be stuck into the ground beside a large animal which cannot be moved, or even into the bullet wound ; or if none is obtainable, the horns or leg of the beast itself may be made to serve the purpose, as is shown in the accompanying illustration (copied from a photograph of mine) of a Grant's gazelle, so disposed (the hind-foot wedged between the horns and the fore-leg round behind them) as to cause the horns to stick upright, conveniently for attaching the hand-kerchief. I took this photo specially for the benefit of any one who may not have hit upon the plan for himself. In the meantime I had skinned the heads, and we started for the camp ; and though it was not far, my wrist ached when I got there with one in my hand which I had to carry in addition to my rifles, etc., for old Papa could only manage one. The sly old fellow always pretended to be no good at carrying a load, unless it was something he specially wanted himself and could get no one to bring along for him ; but I fancy it was partly put on, lest we should expect him to carry something always.

I wanted to see something shot with a bow and arrow, as I had never yet witnessed such sport, and often tried to persuade my old friend to give me an exhibition of his skill ; but I could never prevail upon him to shoot at anything, though once or twice opportunities for close shots at antelopes presented themselves. My own opinion is that he knew he couldn't hit anything, and I doubt if many of the Ndorobos are much good with that weapon. The only one I have ever seen shoot at any unwounded animal missed clean a small buck standing still at only a few yards range. But there are some, no doubt, who do kill game occasionally by these means (the Wakamba certainly do), though I do not believe they are good shots unless at very close quarters. One thing I have always wondered at with regard to these people is that the children do not seem to practise for amusement—as Kafir boys do the

MODE OF PROTECTING GAME FROM VULTURES.

Grant's Gazelle (*Gazella granti*). (From a Photograph by the AUTHOR.)

use of the assegai by throwing pointed sticks at a pumpkin rolled down a hill—nor do they ever shoot at birds. It is a curious thing, too, that an Ndorobo would rather starve than eat a bird : he looks on a guinea-fowl even with aversion, the consequence being that the boys do not attempt to snare birds as other young natives are so fond of doing ; indeed their only idea of occupation seems to be to join in the everlasting hunt for honey.

I did not hunt much more here as we had already a large quantity of meat drying, and I wanted to get back to Laiju and lay my plans for a trip in another direction in quest of elephants. I shot one or two oryx, being anxious to get a finer specimen of this handsome, long-horned antelope, and a few of the smaller kinds. One oryx which I had hit rather low ran some distance, and when we finally came up with him after following the spoor showed fight, so that though already done it was necessary to use another cartridge to finish him. It is, of course, well known that it is very dangerous to lay hold of a wounded oryx or go within reach of its sharp, sweeping horns, and I have before experienced its dexterity with these formidable weapons ; but I do not remember to have noticed its angry voice under such circumstances : this one fairly growled when we went near it.

The neighbourhood of which I have been writing is quite an ideal game country, and very pleasant to camp and to shoot in. The drawback is the difficulty of getting there ; otherwise a very delightful time might be spent by a small party in the district. My camp there was by a little lakelet formed by the stream—a charming spot—my tent pitched under a spreading tree on the very water's edge. One day I shot a huge barber (as they are called in South Africa) in this pool with my rook rifle. I was sitting having my meal under the shade of the tree outside the tent door, and it came feeling about after scraps I threw in on the surface of the water close to the bank above which I sat, and I put the little bullet right through the centre of its nose—or rather where the nose ought to be in its wide ugly head—killing it instantly, to the delight of my Swahili retainers (to whom fish never comes amiss).

The varieties of game to be found in this district, not of course all in precisely the same locality, but in the neighbourhood round about, are :—rhinoceros, giraffe, oryx, waterbuck, lesser koodoo, Grant's gazelle, Waller's gazelle, impala, a few Coke's hartebeeste and the tiny " paa " (Kirkii) ; zebra of two kinds,

ostriches, lions and rarely warthogs.   Leopards may sometimes
be heard at night, and hyenas are, of course, numerous, though
these I regard as vermin.   Guinea-fowl, francolins, etc., are
plentiful in places.   There are also plenty of hippos in the Tana
and the lower reaches of its larger tributaries.   Impala (or pallah,
as it is sometimes written) are curiously scarce, even in parts that
seem thoroughly favourable to them ; it seems strange why,
seeing that the species is present, they should be so few here.   In
South-Eastern Africa they used to fairly teem in their favourite
resorts—a thousand in a troop being sometimes no exaggeration,
probably often an underestimate—whereas nowhere in Equatorial Africa have I seen anything approaching to such numbers.
Coke's hartebeeste is here on the very limit of its range.   I
saw a few near Laiju and between there and the Tana, but none
farther east, though there are more (as I afterwards found) in
the opposite direction (that is westwards, between the Jambeni
hills and the river)—northward it is entirely absent.

It will thus be seen that the main stream of the Mackenzie
River (though in itself little more than a good-sized brook in its
upper course) may be taken as the line of demarcation limiting
the ranges of both Coke's hartebeeste and Grevy's zebra, though
in opposite directions, at this point, which is continued on the
one hand by the Jambeni range to Kenia and on the other by
the Tana eastwards.   The giraffe here is the northern species :
of its peculiarities and range I shall have more to say later on.
Buffaloes are almost extinct since the great cattle plague[1] of
some years before, especially in this region ; the occasional
spoor of an odd one or two is all that is ever seen of them
now.   Elands (which also suffered) may still be met with,
though a little farther on.

On the arrival of the porters I had sent back for, the store
of biltong—by this time fairly dry—was lashed up into long

---

[1] This murrain swept through East Central Africa in the year 1891. It did not—as
under the name of rinderpest it is said to have done or to be doing now—destroy other
game than the kinds specified, at all events to any appreciable extent.

bundles and we returned to the " boma," reaching there on the morning of 14th April.

The news that awaited me was far from cheering. Although before I left many of my donkeys were already dead, I had hoped that when those that had suffered most from " fly " in passing through the Tana valley had succumbed, the remainder would keep healthy ; for I did not then know that Laiju was one of the most deadly places in Africa for domestic animals, not excepting the generally hardy ass. But on my return now I found that all were either dead, dying, or sick. This was a great blow, as I knew that without these useful pack animals it would be impossible to penetrate far into the uninhabited country stretching northward from the Jambeni range towards Lake Rudolph ; and though I had been encouraged by many promises to hope that we might obtain some from the Embe natives, not one had yet been offered for sale. However, I determined at all events to explore as much of the country as circumstances would allow of my reaching in directions where I had reason to believe elephants were numerous. Various matters, with which it is not necessary to trouble the reader in detail, caused another fortnight to slip by unprofitably—I paid a short experimental visit to the Embe district, on the top of the range ; and the heavy rains at this season being unfavourable to travelling, entailed further delay —but at length I was ready to start for another attempt.

CHAPTER II

ON THE JAMBENI RANGE

ON 30th April 1894 about 6 A.M. I started from my "boma" at Laiju with about twenty men, leaving the remainder of my caravan of fifty all told with the goods, prepared for a raid of some length on the elephants which I had been informed were on the other (northern) side of the Jambeni range. The guides, who had solemnly promised to come the day before, had not turned up, according to the usual custom, as it seems, of these natives to invariably break their word. Having become used to this, I was determined not to let their failure to keep their promise interfere with my arrangements, feeling sure that I could pick up others on the way. On passing the kraal of my "blood-brother" I looked in for a chat ; and he assured me that everything was peaceful for us ahead, which was satisfactory, as the Embe tribe, through whose country we had to pass, are a treacherous lot. We had a thunder-shower on our way after getting up among the hills, making it very unpleasant and soaking some of my things. The path was perfectly awful ; greasy to a degree ; overhung with dripping jungle, weighed down with the wet ; and, being steep and sidelong, made it very hard work for the porters. In consequence of the rain, and partly also to get a guide, we camped early at the first suitable place ; a nice open spot near a small wood with water not far off. It is important in these hills to camp, if possible, where firewood can be procured (which is not the case every-where), as the climate is cool and damp and the nights very cold and trying to the men without good fires, often bringing on serious illnesses. On this occasion I put down in my diary " cold and beastly." The natives here are great thieves, so that it is necessary to keep a careful watch over everything, and a good open space is desirable as camping ground for safety. I secured a new guide and one of those who had disappointed me turned up.

The next morning was chilly, misty, and drizzling, and the going abominably bad, but we started early in spite of it all. By and by, though, the sun came out and made things more cheerful and let us see about us. This must be a grand climate and, I should think, perfectly healthy. The early mornings are very cold, but lovely after the sun gets up ; the air crisp and as clear as crystal. I walked to the top of a hill ahead and was abundantly rewarded by a wonderfully extended view of the country beyond for an immense distance right up to a range I thought must overlook Baringo, as well as the Lorogis and other mountains, with a peep of the Gwaso Nyiro River shining between. Of Kenia (or Kilimara, as it is more correctly called) —quite near, to the south-west by west—only the immensely wide base and the extreme apex of precipitous black rock flecked with snow were visible, all its snowfields being covered with banks of cloud, below which appeared extensive forests on the lower slopes, except those on the northern side, which are quite bare. The general aspect of the country to the northward

thus spread out in panorama before me, seemed, from this
bird's-eye view, to be more or less open and fairly level, though
hills and ranges were also to be seen. Its yellow colour, denot-
ing dryness, contrasted strongly with the verdant hills we were
on ; but this almost untrodden wilderness, stretching away
to the far northern horizon where the tips of hazy peaks, just
visible, seemed to beckon one on, had a wonderful fascination
for me. I longed to pry into its mysteries. What especially
attracted me was the knowledge that, save for a few scattered
Ndorobos, it was uninhabited—an immense sanctuary still held
possession of, as in primeval ages, by the (to me) more interesting denizens of the animal world.

Embe is a beautiful and fertile country, though very broken.
Many kraals are dotted about and there is a good deal of
cultivation, particularly banana groves. On the steeper slopes
there are woods with some fine trees in which plantain eaters
call, while grotesque great hornbills sail across from cover to
cover, alternately flapping and gliding with peculiar switchback
flight, uttering their loud peevish plaint, the curiously characteristic cries of both harmonising exquisitely with the spirit of
their surroundings like appropriate music—so sympathetic a
composer is nature. But most of the hillsides are covered
with a sort of jungle of what I should describe as giant weeds,
where probably the timber has been cleared, the open valleys
between being carpeted with the most lovely short, thick,
springy turf, full of clover, than which nothing could be more
delightfully green and soft and sweet looking. It is real sward
from which you may cut a genuine tough sod—none of your
tufts of grass with bare spaces between,—in fact more like an
ideal English pasture than African veldt. Here the natives
graze their few cattle (little humped beasts) and donkeys, and
their more numerous goats and sheep : all very small but sleek
and fat. The area of grass and jungle respectively depends
upon the amount of stock : when cattle are numerous the pasture extends and the jungle is gradually conquered, but when

(as has of late years been the case through the great cattle plague of a few years ago) the live stock decreases, the jungle again encroaches upon these delightful lawns. The soil is volcanic; and owing to the loose way the lava rocks lie jumbled together, most of the water runs below the surface, to break out near the base of the mountains into the streams

A VIEW OF EMBE.
(From a Photograph by Dr. KOLB.)

forming the head waters of the branch of the Tana which Chanler and Von Hohnel had named the Mackenzie River.

The contrast between the country and its inhabitants is great and not in favour of the latter, whether in appearance, habits, or character. They are inexpressibly dirty and smell strongly of castor-oil—to our notions not the choicest of perfumes. In common with those of Laiju and other adjacent districts, they are much addicted to a habit of chewing the leaves of a certain shrub, indigenous to the country, but which they also cultivate for convenience.   Some of the old men are never without their mouths full of this green stuff.   They carry a quantity of the tender shoots in a dirty old skin satchel slung from their shoulders, together with bits of tobacco, bananas, and other treasures, and every now and then strip the bark and leaves from several of these soft twigs and, throwing away the woody interior, cram the handful into their capacious mouths.   This inelegant custom with its somewhat disgusting evidences about the lips does not add to the enjoyment of a long "shauri" with several such old gentlemen ; at least it did not to mine, though it was apparently indispensable to theirs.   These natives are very numerous and there is no game of any kind.

After winding about among the hills and crossing several little purling brooks which rise near the highest peak—the actual Njambeni—we bore to the west, keeping along the edge of the high land, and then gradually descended by a zigzag course towards the low country on the northern side of the range, passing on the way the kraals of some natives who had "eaten blood" with Chanler (that is, entered into the bonds of "blood brotherhood").   These people were very friendly and seemed really pleased to meet a white man.   They took me down the slopes and helped me to find a nice place to camp on the banks of a stream and just above open level country dotted with thorn trees.   There is a patch of bush here which the elephants sometimes haunt and from where they make raids at night on the natives' crops.   Some had lately been there, but the owners of the shambas (cultivated ground) had managed to drive them out though they had not succeeded in killing any. They are no hunters, and the only way they ever kill elephants is by setting traps consisting of javelins (poisoned) in heavy shafts suspended over their paths, with a cord to release the impending harpoon stretched across, so that when a large animal passes along it falls on its head or back after the manner of a school "booby trap."

I walked down into the flats to look for game in the afternoon and got a shot at a rhino, half facing me, through a bush; but he made off, and though I followed the blood spoor a long way I had to give it up and return empty-handed, having seen no other game. I have found the truth of Selous' rule, that when once a wounded rhino goes any considerable distance the chance of ever getting him is very small. I only remember to have once bagged one under such circumstances. In that instance the rhino was shot through the shoulder, but the bone did not break till it had galloped a mile or more, and I came upon him again accidentally, unable to go farther.

I was able to dry my things here, and made ready for an early start the next day in the direction of Mthara[1] (the next district to the westward, along the foot of the range) to look for elephant spoor. There was thunder and rain again in the night. The next morning I made an early start, leaving my little caravan encamped and taking five men besides my gun-bearer and a guide with me. On the way down to the flats I saw two pairs of bush buck, and had a good look at one, a fine handsome male, very red in colour. I did not interfere with them, but was afterwards rather sorry I had not shot this one as a specimen of the bush bucks of this part of Africa. They are very far from common, and I think I only saw one other (a female) on the whole trip. The country here, at the northern base of the range, is very different from that on the other side, no doubt owing to less rain falling. The grass is comparatively short, it is much healthier for stock, and more open and easier and pleasanter to get about in.

After walking for some distance through open grassy flats, sprinkled with thorn trees and studded here and there with koppies, many of which were clearly small craters, keeping parallel with the range, I saw a pair of rhino ahead, in very

---

[1] This name has been written Msara by German travellers, who cannot pronounce the "th," but the natives themselves sound those letters quite distinctly, just as we do in the words "that," "there," etc. In the same way the name of the river is really Thana, not Tana.

open ground, standing close to a rather bushy little low tree. As I wanted meat for my men I went after them. The wind being right I got the tree between me and them and approached. But I could see through the tree that they were disturbed (probably by the tick birds which are nearly always with rhinos and give them warning of approaching danger), so scuttled up to a tiny little bush, only about three feet high, growing some thirty or forty yards from where they stood, and sat down, meaning to wait till one should show itself from behind the tree and be ready for a steady shot. But just as I did so one came half out on one side, offering a perfect side-shot. Though I could see that it was but a smallish one and thought from what I could make out through the tree that the other was much larger, as I knew they would be off immediately I thought it a pity to lose so tempting a chance, so gave her (it was a female) a bullet from my .577 just in the right spot behind the shoulder. Instantly the male came out straight for me. I had no time for a careful aim ; he was almost on me before I fired as it was, and sitting on the ground is not the most desirable position in which to receive the charge of a rhinoceros. He was not more than six paces from me when he turned off and bespattered me and my gun with spots of mud from the wet ground. So sudden was it all that I could not say whether it was the second *before* my shot that he lowered his nose (as for a charge) or the second after (as it might be stumbling to the shock of the bullet) ; but I know he did so just before swerving off. He then galloped away, passing his dead mate (for she was already down not more than fifty yards from where she had stood) on his way. I did not follow him, but sent two men back to camp to call more to carry in the meat, leaving one at the carcase, and went on with the other two, together with my gun-bearer and the native.

We crossed a small stream where was a reedy swamp into which led the spoor of a single buffalo—the first I had seen this trip—and following a big elephant path, along which a large herd had passed a few days ago, turned up between some low foot-hills (still skirting the range) and down into a flat valley full of curious, straight, slim mimosas, some with red, others with white stems, giving an odd striped appearance to this part of the bush. Passing through these we found ourselves close to cultivated lands and could see large kraals on the bare hills near. Here I proposed turning back, as I could not believe elephants would be so near natives at mid-day; moreover, this was the tribe who had fought Chanler's expedition and I did not feel sure how they might treat us should we run among them. But our guide vehemently protested that we were leaving the elephants close by; and while I considered whether it were possible he could be leading us into a trap or whether we should be wise to go on, we heard elephants trumpeting not far ahead.

I had been suffering severely all the morning from blistered feet caused by foolishly putting on a pair of new boots. This had also disposed me to give up the search for to-day, as we had seen no fresh spoor; but of course the sound of elephantine voices at once did away with all other considerations and we pushed on towards a grove of tall mimosas of the kind called "fever trees" in South Africa (so called, I imagine, because they only grow in the low fever-haunted country, generally near water, though their pale, yellowish-green bark gives them a sickly appearance too, matching well with the name). My guide was a very obstinate fellow, refusing to be influenced by any suggestion of mine in any respect; and now he persisted in it that we must go round to the windward side of the bush where the elephants were. I was, however, determined not to have my chance spoilt in that way, so I left him, since he would not follow us. I found afterwards that he never would go near elephants.

We went on to leeward of where we had heard the elephants and got into a tall, leafy undergrowth, though not very dense, and soon came out into a swamp bordered by tall " fever " and other trees with a little open between : a very ideal elephant haunt. We were uncertain now of the exact whereabouts of the elephants, so proceeded very cautiously up wind towards where we supposed them to be ; and before we had got far into the jungle, after leaving the swamp, we made one out. I then took my double .577 and leaving the men, approached stealthily quite close to the one we had first seen, till there was nothing between me and it but a smallish tree (through the fork of which I looked) and a little thin jungle. Great colonies of weaver birds, thronging the bush, made a great din with both voices and wings, with a rather confusing effect. It was a cow ; a big one, though her tusks were not large. I could now make out two or three others (apparently also cows) beyond, and I knew there were pretty certain to be more I could not see ; but there was no possible chance of getting farther without disturbing the nearest, so I determined to shoot her if I could. I should mention that it was now fully four months since I started from the coast on this expedition, the expenses of which were heavy, and these were the first elephants I had come across, so I was not inclined to risk failure through trying to pick and choose. She was, however, facing me, her great ears stretched out or slowly flapping. I could only see her head and my object was to get a temple shot. I waited, I think, not less than a quarter of an hour for her to turn her head. Once I tried to sneak round farther, but she and another next to her started and I slunk back. I suppose an eddy of wind gave them a slight whiff of me, or they may have heard me moving ; probably the latter, as they were not sufficiently alarmed to move when I kept still again. I was not more than ten paces from the one in front of me, I should say, and meditated the advisability of putting my bullet right into her eye (which I felt sure I could do), but, being uncertain whether such a shot would be fatal from my position, and feeling that my reputation as a hunter, with both my own men and the natives of the country, would be blasted at the outset should I make a failure of my first chance at elephant, I waited till my arms ached again with holding my heavy gun at the ready. At last, however, she did give me the longed-for chance, and I instantly put a ball between the eye and the ear, dropping her like a stone. The others near, not having winded me and not knowing what was up, moved away only a short distance. Following carefully I came upon two ; the nearest facing me, her trunk up and chest exposed, the cover fortunately allowing me to see it. Knowing they would be off again I gave her a shot in the chest, and as she turned to run, the second barrel. Following again I saw her down not more than fifty yards on. Going round to her head she gave a slight struggle, so I thought it wise to give her a shot in the back from my "cripple-stopper" (as I call a Martini-Henry one of my men always carries for the purpose, so as to economise my own cartridges).

Pushing on again I came upon another standing at right angles, which I dropped under a tree with the temple shot, like the first. Ahead a little way again two or three more were soon seen. One, as I approached, came towards me in an aggressive way, having evidently become aware of my presence. I dared not wait, so close was she, so fired for her head, being unable to see her chest, when not more than six yards off. She fell to the shot, but somehow or other sideways on to me. I could see her dimly through the undergrowth between us, and make out for a second the outline of her head as she lay, not on her side but as it were kneeling down. I ought to have given her the second barrel then, knowing she could only be stunned ; but I was a little too slow, and she was up again and off without giving me another chance. She stood and screamed some sixty or seventy yards off, but the cover was so tall I could only see the top of her back and the top of her head. Following once more I was taken off her spoor by two small cows which ran past on my left, at one of which I got a snap shot but failed to kill. I ought not, perhaps, to have fired at these, but the ivory hunter is bound to endeavour to make as much hay as possible when he does get a little sunshine, and the jungle precluded running or seeing beyond a few yards. However, both these last got off, and the herd seemed to have cleared out.

It was now well into the afternoon, I was terribly footsore, we were far from camp, our guides had disappeared, and we could hear natives shouting. I knew these must be the people who had fought with Chanler, so all things considered decided to return. We went back to the dead elephants to cut off their tails and take a piece of one's trunk and heart (for myself) as well as some fat (first-rate for culinary purposes), and I had a look at their tusks, which there had been no time to do in passing. The ivory was all rather small, even for cow ; still it was not bad for a beginning, though I was sorry to have let off the one that went for me. We took a straighter course back to camp than the way we had come, and had a good elephant path all the way, so got there before sundown. The rhino meat had been carried in long ago. Swahilis have a stupid prejudice against eating elephant meat, and are foolish enough to prefer rhino. Some of my Embe friends of yesterday had come again and said there were more elephants in the neighbourhood. Altogether things looked more hopeful than they had done yet with me on this trip ; the only drawback being those awful sore heels from which I suffered agonies to-day ; for getting footsore just now (for the first time since leaving the coast) was a real calamity. I determined to move camp on to the little stream we had crossed on our way to the elephant bush, so as to be more handily situated to chop out the tusks and go in search of more elephants.

The next morning, though it was raining, I was up about
4 A.M., and by the time it was fairly light we had packed up
and were ready to start. I left my headman and half-a-dozen
porters at this camp, to try and trade some ivory. I had
brought him chiefly for the purpose of trading a lot of goods
I had hampered myself with unwisely, and found both a great
nuisance and very little use. I was glad to leave him behind,
as I did not like the way he conducted my negotiations with
the natives. My guide of yesterday (who had overtaken us
on the way back) and another native accompanied us. I went
to the spring of the little spruit we had crossed the day before
(seeing no game on the way), where was a very pleasant,
convenient, and picturesque spot for my camp, under a grand
old low-crowned thorn tree with wide-spreading horizontal
boughs, which grew on a little rise above the stream. The
tree gave shade ; its great limbs were most handy to put
things on—one, too, formed a comfortable seat ; it lent itself
exactly to the making of a capital boma of suitable size for
us by simply having thorny branches packed all round under
the drooping extremity of its umbrella-shaped crown ; and
altogether the camp was one of the nicest I ever had, the
country around being fairly open, and the grass short and at
that time green.

Leaving half my men in camp to build the "boma," I
went on with the rest to chop out the tusks of my three
elephants of the day before, intending also to go on to look
for others. On the way we met some natives from the kraals
near : they were most friendly in their greetings, hailing me
as a deliverer on account of my shooting the elephants, which
destroy their crops, and whose depredations they compare
to the Masai raids. This is the district called Mthara, the
tribe which fought with Chanler. Their experience of the
consequences of attacking the white man seemed to have
taught them to respect him, and to have inspired them with
a desire to make him their friend ; so they received me with

open arms.   We had a talk with them, and they told us that
the elephants were not far off, and went to get information as
to their whereabouts to-day from those who watched the crops
day and night.   Afterwards one of them met us again with
the news that there was one large elephant near, and five
others not far off.   We went on with him, past the swamp of
yesterday, and on to a second and larger one.   But a number
of natives had now come (having, no doubt, got word of the
white man's arrival), and were shouting all over the place, and,
of course, the elephants had decamped.

I was again suffering agonies from my feet, and as
it was by this time past noon, and the elephants had been
disturbed for that day, I decided to go back to camp.   On
the way back I saw a few impala, one of which I shot.   In
the evening some of my new friends of Mthara came, bringing
me presents of bananas, tobacco, and native beer.   We had
a satisfactory talk, and I promised to remain in camp the
following day to have a "shauri" with their head men and
become their "blood brother" if they wished it.   This rest
would also suit me on account of my chafed feet.   I, of course,
gave small presents to my visitors.

Accordingly, the next day I did not go out.   A number
of the Mthara "elders," as well as many young men, came,
bringing small offerings of food.   I had a great "shauri" with
them, and they seemed very well disposed.   Of course they
tried at first to get me to stump up something in the shape of
"hongo" or tribute, as Swahili traders are in the habit of paying
for the privilege of entering each district, though they do not
visit this particular part at all, on account of the bad name
the natives have ; but I told them distinctly I could not
consent to this, as it was not the white man's custom.   I said
that any presents I might give must be of my own free will ;
no demands could I entertain.   I wanted to shoot elephants :
if they wished to have them shot, I would be glad of their help
and guidance.   On the other hand, if they did not wish me to

shoot near their gardens, well and good ; there were elephants elsewhere, and natives anxious that I should go and shoot them : nothing would I pay for permission to hunt. They at once gave in, and said they would willingly guide me, and that the whole tribe—old men, young men, women, and children— were most anxious to make me their friend, and they would like to clinch the friendship by making "blood brotherhood" with me. I consented ; and after much parley it was agreed I should wait here the next day and go through the ceremony formally with them. The arrangement suited me, as I was quite unfit to hunt, and knew I should only lay myself up for a much longer time if I attempted to walk again before, at soonest, the day but one after. Altogether—though the delay was tantalising with elephants close by, as they were reported to be, and my getting footsore just at the very time when my luck seemed to have taken a favourable turn, after so long a period of patience and disappointment, was truly heart-breaking—things seemed turning out propitiously, and I had great hopes of favourable results in the near future.

The next day the great ceremony of "eating blood"[1] was performed. During the whole performance I had to sit in a swamp, sandwiched between two very unwashed savages, necessitating a bath and change directly it was over. It is a very unpleasant ordeal, but I went bravely through it, much to the satisfaction of the admiring crowds of savages. I gave small presents to many, and rather larger ones to my two new "brothers" (sons of the principal head men of the tribe), and received numerous calabashes of rather good though thick native beer, etc. These people always remained loyal to the bond, and my elder brother, "Ndaminuki," has been most

---

[1] I have not thought it necessary to describe in detail this rather disgusting rite—it has been done by others—but "eating blood" is literally a true definition of it. The principals have to eat a drop of each other's blood, taken from an incision in the chest, with which a bit of roasted meat (cut from the heart of an animal specially sacrificed with many curious superstitious observances) has been smeared.

NDAMINUKI (Author's Blood Brother).

(From a Photograph by Dr. KOLB.)

useful many times to me and mine, as well as subsequently, at my instigation, to a German traveller, Dr. Kolb. Everything went off satisfactorily, and it was arranged that I was to be shown the haunts of the elephants the following morning, a herd of which was said to be still in the bush adjoining the cultivated lands. My feet were still very sore, but I felt that I must walk somehow.

Having made an early start, then, the next day, some of the natives met us near the cultivation, close to where I had shot the three elephants. Some had been in the crops that night. We followed their spoor through the adjoining patch of forest, in which were the swamps we had seen before, and out into the shorter scrub beyond to the westward. They had gone in the direction of Kenia (which was only a comparatively short way off), evidently feeding. Unfortunately, I and my proceedings were a source of such interest to the inhabitants of the neighbourhood, few of whom had ever seen a white man, that numbers of them had followed us, and we gradually collected quite a gathering. They were a great nuisance, as they have little idea of hunting ; it was difficult to keep them quiet, and altogether they were very much in the way, but I had to put up with them.

After proceeding a considerable distance through scrub sufficiently open to be easily walked through, on coming near a small stream a single cow elephant was made out standing by it. On our side there was open ground, but across rather dense scrub. I made a circuit to get the wind right and to have cover. Fortunately, the bulk of the native onlookers had made for some rising ground some distance away, whence they could get a view over the scrub, to see if they could discover the whereabouts of the elephants, and the one or two who had kept with me I now left behind. After crossing the stream twice I got close up to the cow, which was standing in the water feeding on trees growing on the bank. She waded down towards me and I dropped her with a temple shot, and, as she stood up again, though apparently about to fall dead, I made sure by shooting her through the heart with the " cripple-stopper," and the stream, in which she lay, literally ran red.   Her tusks were about the same as those of the three previous ones.

No other elephants were in sight, but we could see the natives, who had taken up their position (as above mentioned) on a rise, excitedly beckoning to us, so we went towards them, unfortunately, as it turned out.   Before we reached them we saw what they were looking at, namely, a long line of elephants coming straight for the spot where I had just shot the first.   There was quite a crowd of natives collected on the rise watching them, quite regardless of the fact that they were directly to windward.   I made back as quickly as possible, but, the elephants having already got our wind, I was too late to intercept them, as they were going fast.   Had I only known and remained where I was, the whole herd must have passed right by me.   They were making straight back for their stronghold, the patch of forest near the " shambas " (cultivation), and we followed their spoor as quickly as possible.   It was not till they were close to thick cover, though, that we again sighted the tail of the herd.   I climbed a tree to get a view of them, and could see two or three standing in rather open ground, one a large cow with tusks that seemed long and much curved.   Making for this one, which stood sideways, offering a perfect shot, I was just getting up to it when a wretched native who had been following me rushed right to windward, in spite of my frantic beckonings, in order to get behind a thick bush he had spotted as a safe retreat, with the result, of course, that the elephants got his wind and made off before I could get a shot at the one I had chosen as my victim.   Running on, however, I could not resist giving her a stern shot ; and just ahead another stood sideways for a moment, about fifty yards off, apparently to see what was the matter with their rear, which I dropped on

the spot (temple shot).   This last had rather nice teeth for
" kalasha " (cow ivory).

After cutting off her tail we again followed the track of
the herd, which had now entered their favourite cover.   This
patch of forest consists of groves of very large " fever " trees
and other kinds (some of great size), with an undergrowth of
dense leafy jungle, in parts very tall and thick but shorter in
others, and with some more or less open spaces.   The spoor
led through some of the densest, darkest parts ; some places
were very bad, so that one could not see above a yard or two
and could only get through by struggling, stooping, and even
creeping along the track, the bushes closing in after the
elephants had passed.   I wondered they did not stop there,
but felt glad they had not.   It was a long time before we got
up to any again.   They had separated and rushed about the
bush in different directions, making the spoor confusing and
troublesome to follow sometimes.   At last, however, we got
sight of some again ; but before I could get a fair chance
they started off and I only got a snap shot at one, which,
though it staggered, went on ; but just ahead I got another
temple shot at a young bull, which I was lucky enough to kill
on the spot.   As it seemed not quite dead I gave it another
bullet in the head, though I think it was unnecessary ; it is
better though to make sure if there is the least doubt.

It was afternoon by this time ; but we followed again as the
elephants stuck to the forest (which was not of great extent).
They were scattered in small lots of a few together and kept
moving about and then standing and listening until disturbed
again.   At last, when I was thinking of giving it up and we were
close to the outside of the jungle, we heard the solemn rumbling
made by an elephant's inside ; and just after I caught sight of
one's forehead between two large bushy shrubs.   I advanced,
trying to get a view of the temple, to within a dozen yards or
a little more ; but, though I could not see enough of her, she
had her eye to the opening and could see me, for she suddenly

came straight out for me at a run, screaming, her trunk up. There was no time to waste ; so, as her chest was hidden by the low scrub between us, I let her have my right barrel in her head, instantly springing to one side and ducking, with the idea of dodging under the vegetation. But she was down, after getting within six paces (afterwards stepped) of where I stood. Remembering the former one getting off under similar circumstances and knowing she could only be stunned, I was

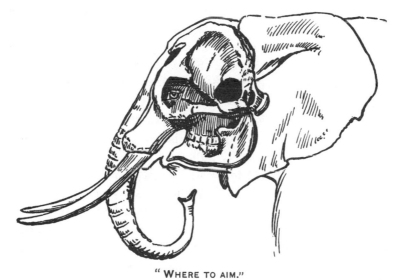

" WHERE TO AIM."

Skull with brain marked black, showing its position with respect to ear, eye, etc.

on the look-out this time, and as she rose (having slewed round in falling) I gave her my second barrel in the ear, before she was fairly on her feet, knocking her over plump and dead, her legs kicking up in the air as she rolled over while the blood poured out of her ear. This was the most satisfactory shot I had made ; and, under the circumstances, I felt excusably pleased with myself. She had longish curved tusks, crossing at the points (44 lbs. the pair). On examining her I found this was the elephant I had wounded from behind just before the herd entered the forest : no doubt that made her so vicious.

It being now late, I thought it a suitable time to knock off, so made tracks for camp. I afterwards regretted not having gone on as long as there was any daylight ; as I heard (what I did not know at the time) that a big bull, which I had been told was in the herd but had not seen, was caught sight of by a native with me just when I shot the last elephant. One ought never to give up while there is a chance of scoring another when hunting for ivory. Still I had not done so badly for that day : though my teeth were not large they were nice " kalashas," and a better average size than those I had got two days before. My men, too, were very pleased and jubilant that our luck had turned, and that we were at last really doing some good work. To make elephant-hunting pay in Eastern Equatorial Africa is no easy matter; the expenses of an expedition are so heavy, owing to the enormous cost of transport and the necessity of taking a large number of porters both for this purpose and also for safety ; the distances, too, are so great, and so much time is cut to waste in travelling and inevitable delays from various causes. The uncertainty of animal transport is sufficiently shown by the fact that I had only a single survivor (and it afterwards died) left out of upwards of twenty pack donkeys! As to trade, nowhere I have yet reached is there any profit to be made by a white man ; Swahili and Wakamba traders have spoilt it. Moreover, ivory trading is a tedious, pottering process, far better suited to the Swahili than the English temperament ; especially in a climate where activity is (in my experience) the great essential in preserving good health, while stagnation means fever.

The next day we cut out the tusks. Of course the elephants had cleared out. I tried to get information as to where the herd had gone to, and word was brought that it had gone down a stream that ran through the forest in which I had found it, in the direction of the Gwaso Nyiro River ; so I determined to go in search again on the morrow, notwithstanding that my feet were still very sore and that I was suffering from a touch of fever, brought on by the pain and consequent restless nights they caused me. On the way back to camp that day I shot another impala in the curious striped bush previously described. One of these bucks standing among the red-barked mimosa stems was very difficult to make out, so exactly did its colour match with these trees. The impalas in this part of Africa seem to have much wider-spreading horns than those of the south. They are nowhere anything like so numerous as they used to be in the parts of South-Eastern Africa I hunted in years ago. Along the Umbuluzi, lower Komati, Crocodile and Sabi rivers they were formerly to be met with in immense herds; but in Central Africa the herds are always comparatively small and these much fewer and farther between, though here they are very much freer from molestation. On the strength of the news that had been brought me as to the direction the elephants had retreated in, I took a long round next day through the low country in hopes of cutting their spoor ; but the report proved to be false, so I had my tramp for nothing except that I shot another impala for the benefit of some natives who were with me.

Though badly in want of a rest—both for the sake of my feet and general health—as a Mthara native had come to report elephants to be in another patch of forest, beyond the one where I had killed mine, and slept in camp on purpose to take me there, I made a very early start with him the next morning to look for them. The place was very similar to the other, though of less extent ; with, like it, a swamp in it. The elephants were not there though ; but the spoor of the day before showed our guide had not deceived us. We went a long way farther in search of them, leaving the next district (called Janjai) to our left, and got close to the foot-hills of Kenia. We found many recent spoors and at last some of the night before, but too late in the day to be worth following at such a distance from camp, as it was in open bush and they were therefore likely to lead us a long chase. However, I had

a good look at the country and gained information likely to be
of use.   I saw three giraffes with a small herd of zebras and a
couple of rhinos during the day, but did not attempt to shoot
anything (though one of the latter with a rather fine horn gave
me a tempting chance), as it was far from camp and I did not
want to be delayed by waiting for my men, who were in want
of meat, to skin and cut up an animal.   This was a long, hard
day and I felt I *must* take a rest, as my feet were very
painful in the night : so the following day I really did remain
in camp.

A great many of my Mthara friends came to my camp to
make shauri (*showery* it is pronounced), as the Swahili call a
palaver, corresponding to the South African " indaba."   The
shauri is a great institution in Central Africa, and I have known
white men to develop quite a passion for shauri making ; but
for my own part I find them a bore, though one cannot escape
them altogether.   One of these, in this instance, was about an
elephant (one wounded by me) which I had been informed had
been found : but it turned out it was a mistake, arising from
defective interpretation.   I had to promise to go to the kraals
the next day to call upon " my father " (that is the father of
my new " blood brother "), whither the young men were to
escort me.   In the afternoon, as a relief to the monotony of a
whole day in camp and partly to get away from these tedious
" shauris," I strolled out to look for impala, as I knew there
were some quite near and meat was wanted, and succeeded in
shooting three.

My visit to the kraals was not at all interesting.   The
huts are small, untidy, and dirty, as are the owners.   I had an
interview with a blind old man (my brother's father) and was
kept waiting a long time, while my relatives made their
inevitable " shauri," but was eventually given a sheep and a
promise of men to go with me to hunt under Kilimara, and
allowed to go my way.

As this escort was not to come till the day but one after,

and I thought it better to wait for it, so that I might be introduced by my friends to the adjoining tribe of Janjai (which I had been told was likely to be hostile to travellers), I decided to hunt for my men the next day and went out early for that purpose.   I followed the little stream that rose close to my camp down for some distance and then struck across towards some koppies, which like those on the other side of the range are small craters — some almost perfect.   But before getting far I saw three rhinos feeding in the open : a cow with a half-grown calf and a little way off a bull.   I got round to leeward of them and stalked the bull, keeping a tiny bush between us ; and then sat down and waited till he gave me a favourable chance, which he soon did, moving slowly across my position, when I gave him a shot behind the shoulder.   He ran for a short way and stood for a little, but blood coming from nose and mouth showed that he was done, and he soon went down.   As I wanted to get a good supply of meat to last my men some time (for they were only getting half rations of other food), and the rhinos were still unalarmed, I now turned my attention to the cow.   I followed similar tactics in her case, getting a baby thorn tree before me, and gave her a precisely similar shot with exactly the same result.   I wanted to let the young one go, as it was quite old enough to take care of itself; but as it would not run away and when we went forward seemed inclined to be pugnacious, and being as big as a large bullock could have made itself unpleasant, I shot it too.   I sent for all hands to carry in the meat, and as it was only a short way from camp none of it was wasted, and it gave my men a good store of biltong.   I didn't myself care then for any part of a rhino except the tongue, which is very good when thoroughly boiled ; but Swahilis consider the liver a great delicacy, and delight in the oily fat.   The latter I found useful, together with the elephant fat, of which I had now a good store, for my extemporised slush lamp (made out of a butter tin), as I was short of candles.

I climbed one of the koppies near to look over the country, and got a fine view all round.   It being very open I could see everything for a long distance and made out six or seven other rhinos in sight and a couple of giraffe, but no other game barring a very few Grant's gazelle.   On my way back to camp I met one of the Mthara natives coming to tell me that there were two or three elephants in the bush where I had shot the others.   It was too late, however, to go after them that day; so I arranged to start very early the next morning, and he promised to meet me on the way.

CHAPTER III

CAMPING AT MOUNT KENIA

A good rhino horn—A fresh campaign — Advantage of head shot — Exciting encounter — Attacked by bees—A red-letter day—Eleven elephants killed—The Kenia jungle—Wealth of butterflies—A crater lake—Hippos—Return to Mthara —Start for the Gwaso Nyiro River—Signs of elephants—A hunter's disappointment—Sufferings from thirst—Encounter with lions—Rhinos—Filial affection—Despatch of ivory—Return to Laiju—A hazardous undertaking—Hostile natives.

ACCORDINGLY I was off as soon as it was light ; but as the guide had not met us by the time we reached the first swamp, just inside the forest already described, I sat down to wait while one of my men went off to look him up in his shamba, which was not far off. As their cultivation was so near the elephants' haunt and the latter were so fond of making havoc of the crops by night, the owners were in the habit of sleeping there in huts built on very high stakes or in the branches of a big tree, whence they kept a look-out and tried by shouting to frighten away the depredators. We had to wait some time and as there was a cold wind blowing it was rather miserable so early ; but I amused myself by watching through my glasses the quaint behaviour of some baboons sitting in a row that were trying to warm themselves in the sun on the other side of the swamp, where its first rays had just reached. While so engaged one of my men drew my attention to a rhino cow with a half-grown calf on the hillside just above, where it was open with only scattered shrubs. As we could see she had a very fine horn I determined to occupy myself during the delay by going after her. I stalked up near, and getting a good opening gave her a shot in the usual place. She ran off but soon stood, and as I wanted to make sure of her I gave her the second barrel (though it was really not needed) also in the right spot. She then ran only a few yards farther and dropped. Her horn was far more magnificent even than I had thought when examining it through my glasses. It measured fully forty inches round the curve and was beautifully tapered and symmetrical. This was not only by far the longest I had ever shot but considerably longer than any (belonging to this species) I had had the opportunity of measuring, thirty-five inches being the best measurement I had, up to then, myself verified.[1] The latter had been a much straighter and thicker one, apparently of a male. I was no longer sorry for having been compelled to wait. As there seem to be some points with regard to the rhinos of this part of Africa on which differences of opinion exist (judging from letters that have at different times appeared in the *Field* on the subject and observations I have heard), I will, later on, endeavour to add my mite to the information on the subject as the result of my own personal experiences and observations.

But first let me finish the account of this day's work, which was to be an exceptionally lucky one. After sending back to camp for men to come and carry the meat, with orders that it was to be cut up and dried for future use, the guide having turned up we went on. It seemed that the elephants reported as being in this cover yesterday had not stopped, nor were any about now ; indeed it was hardly to be expected that these intelligent beasts would harbour here now

[1] This horn (I say advisedly the horn, for the animal which bore it was indistinguishable from any other of the numerous rhinoceroses of the district which differ in no respect from the typical *R. bicornis*) ought perhaps to be classed as *R. holmwoodi ;* but I have a shrewd suspicion that the range of that interesting species is limited to the bazaars of Zanzibar. I have since seen a more striking specimen still, with a double bend— first back, then forward—which measured 48¾ inches along the curve. A photograph in which the first-mentioned horn is shown, together with others, will be found on p. 353.

with the carcases of their fellows scattered here and there through the forest ; so we went on to the next patch, where there was another swamp. Having searched this through without finding any fresh spoor, I hesitated whether to persevere again to the Janjai valley or return to camp ; but one native being confident that we should find there to-day, we pushed on. As soon as we got over the intervening ridge, beyond which was another broad flat valley also with forest and scrub bordering a swamp, while on the far side were low open hills with kraals and cultivation at their base, elephants were seen in the bush below and close to its edge on our side.

I at once commenced the campaign, getting first to leeward and then cautiously advancing. I easily got close up, and could see several, as they were standing in a most favourable position by trees where there was a small space comparatively open, while I was hidden by a screen of tall undergrowth ; but as one was much larger than the rest (evidently a big bull, though I could not see his tusks), I waited till he gave me a chance at the temple, and was lucky enough to drop him dead, killing a cow alongside of him similarly with the second barrel. Loading quickly I had time to knock over another cow before they ran. When taken quite by surprise in this way, if one can only manage to drop the first on the spot, its companions frequently give one the chance, before making up their minds what is the matter, to get in a second shot ; and possibly even, as in this case, should that also be successful, yet another. That is one great advantage of the head shot. If shot through the heart an elephant immediately rushes off, though only for a short distance, of course scaring any others with it. I have found, however, that though one can make pretty sure of dropping a cow if one gets a fair chance, the brain of an old bull is by no means so easily reached. The bull I had just shot, though large (I measured him as accurately as I could the next day, and made out his height to be about ten feet six inches), was a comparatively young animal, with only (for a bull) moderate teeth weighing 55 lbs. apiece. I did not waste time in examining my prizes then though, hardly allowing myself even a glance at them, for we heard others close by, and going in the direction and climbing a tree I was able to see one.

The undergrowth was here very dense, tall, and leafy, but on getting a little nearer I could just make out a bit of the elephant I had seen from the tree, and was worming my way forward with the greatest care so as not to make any noise, my eyes fixed intently on it, when suddenly I heard something which made me look round quickly to the left, to behold another, which must have been within a few yards, though hidden by the thick high scrub, coming for me and almost on me. No time to aim ; all I could do was to bang off in its face, which was right over me, and throw myself down into the scrub behind me. I could just draw myself among the stems far enough to escape being trodden on, and only just in time, as she (it was a cow with small tusks) was where I had stood the instant before (for my shot did not stop her), and waited there apparently looking for me. She could easily have reached me with her trunk, which I could see moving about as if feeling for me, without stirring, and I momentarily expected to be hauled out by one of my legs, which I was unable to draw in farther on account of the close-growing scrub, and made an end of in some unpleasant fashion. As she stood there a second or two, screaming and wondering, as it seemed, what had become of me, I fired my second barrel as well as I could for her ear ; but I was in so awkward a position (a bit flustered, too, I confess) that I failed to get at her brain. However, she made off on receiving the shot. I now found that my cartridge pouch was not on me, and in the excitement of the moment forgot what had become of it, so rushed back to Squareface (as I called my gunbearer), who was a little way behind me, for more ammunition. We sought in vain for the belt and pouch where I had dropped my hat in avoiding the charge, and at last it turned out that an idiot of a Swahili (one of two or three I had following me), to whom I had given it to hold while I climbed the tree, had put it on himself instead of handing it back to me. I was not complimentary to him, as his stupidity, added to my own forgetfulness, might have cost me my life.

I began to follow up the spoor of this vicious cow, though there was not much blood on it, and I did not think she was badly wounded, for I felt rather vindictively inclined towards her; but before we had gone far another little clump of elephants was discovered not far off, towards which I accordingly made. Getting up to them I succeeded in flooring another cow with fine tusks, one of which grew right across the other (this skew tooth proved particularly long and solid, having scarcely any hollow at the base). The rest ran to the edge of the bush and stood on a slight rise among low scrub, just outside the tall forest patch. I followed, and getting a good view of them knocked over a right and left, and loading again was just about to repeat the performance, as the others still stood about apparently quite bewildered, when I was suddenly attacked by swarms of bees, whose tub was in the tree under which I stood. (It is the practice of the natives to stick these bee tubs up in trees here and there about the bush for the accommodation of the wild bees, which speedily take possession of such convenient quarters, by which simple means they secure a regular supply of honey for themselves.) They stung me round my eyes and all over my face, ears, neck, etc, compelling me to flee ignominiously and leave the elephants still standing! This was a sad stroke of bad luck and probably cost me a brace of elephants. I could hold my own with the elephants alone, but when reinforced by these fiery little allies I was instantly and helplessly put to flight. After retreating a little way, however, I managed to shake off the new enemy, and going round above the elephants returned to the attack, and was in time to get a shot at another; but they were now on the move, whilst I was somewhat upset by my discomfiture and numerous wounds by the bees, so that, though my next shot knocked down another cow, she was only wounded and got up again directly; with the second barrel, however, I felled her again and left her for dead. My rifle got quite hot after these five shots in quick succession.

I now sat down for a short rest and a drink of gruelly native beer (very refreshing and sustaining when one is hot

" The natives stick these tubs in trees for the accommodation of wild bees, by which simple means they secure a regular supply of honey."

and empty), while my gunbearer and I pulled the stings out of each other's face and neck, the second one meanwhile going to cut off the tails of the elephants I had just shot. The last one they could not find, and brought me word that it had gone; but as it had fallen just under the bee tree, I thought they had perhaps been afraid to venture to the right spot, and was not satisfied until I had once more run the gauntlet of the still furious insects and seen for myself that nothing but a pool of blood remained to show where she had fallen. I knew it was useless to follow her, as she had clearly been only stunned ; so, word having been brought me that some of the herd had just been seen on the far side of the valley, we made our way through the bush towards the open beyond. But just before emerging from the forest we came across another little lot, and, my luck still holding, I scored another right and left——the third to-day——at a young bull and a cow. Running on, I was able to get in another shot, at a big fellow, but bungled it somehow and he went off with the rest.

I now started with the man who had brought me word about some others he had seen ; but we were unable to find them, and after wasting some time we went towards some natives who were standing on a rise in the direction of their shambas, and whose gesticulations and beckonings seemed to indicate that they could see elephants. Sure enough, on reaching the high ground where they were, we found that a small herd was visible in a rather open part of the bush. But the wind was blowing towards them, and although I made a detour to avoid going down wind, they had already scented danger before I reached the place, and were retreating. I got a running shot, but the scrub was too high to allow a clear view, and there was no result. Following them up, and occasionally sending a man up a tree to survey the jungle, I soon found where some had halted once more. I climbed a tree myself to note their position, and made them out standing in a clump in a little opening. Having got up pretty close, and finding it impossible to see for the high scrub, I climbed the broken bough of a large tree which happened to lean at a convenient angle against the trunk, reaching to the ground at the end. Getting high up on to it, I got a good view of the elephants, and waited some time for the largest to give me a chance ; but he persistently kept behind the others, which were huddled together, and finally moved into tall scrub, where he went out of sight ; so I chose a cow with long and very straight tusks, which stood at the outside of the clump, giving me a fine chance at her temple, and had the satisfaction of seeing her throw up her trunk and fall dead to my shot.   I had now used all the .577 cartridges I had with me, as I had unluckily omitted to replenish my pouches before starting on the morning of this red-letter day ; so I fell back upon the Martini-Henry, which my men passed up to me, afterwards throwing me cartridges one by one.   The elephants were moving off, but, passing diagonally across my position, were still within shot. The cover was very high and dense, so that they were hidden even from my commanding perch ; but two stood with their heads in view long enough to give me another opportunity, and I succeeded in dropping both.   The last fell with its head resting on the other.   It proved to be a young one with very small teeth, unfortunately, but in such thick jungle it is impossible to pick and choose much.   I had now eleven elephants dead.

The sun by this time was low, so that it would take us all our time to reach camp by dark ; and as I did not feel sure how the natives here, against whom I had been warned, might be disposed towards the white intruder (though so far as I had seen they seemed friendly enough), I thought it prudent to go back without further delay.   I accordingly had the tails of the last five elephants cut off—getting a bit of a scare over one, which could not be found at first, but proved to be dead safe enough, to my relief—and tramped hard back to my boma, meeting before I got there some of my men, who, as it began to get dusk and I had not arrived, had started to see what had become of me.   I was, of course, well pleased with my success, though I considered I ought to have secured a couple more elephants, and particularly the big fellow I had wounded.   I had not been feeling very fit in the morning, but that had gone off, and at night I was as fresh as possible, my feet, luckily, being nearly all right again.   I had used in all just twenty cartridges.

I have perhaps described with tiresome minuteness every detail of this day's hunting ; but it was one of such exceptional opportunities that it seems worth while to give full particulars of all its incidents. I may add that, some time after, some natives found the large elephant which I had wounded, dead, and I eventually recovered the tusks (though not, unfortunately,

NATIVE GIRLS AND WOMEN OF TRIBES NEAR THE FOOT OF MOUNT KENIA.
(From a Photograph by Dr. KOLB.)

without rather serious trouble with them), which weighed between 80 and 90 lbs. apiece.

Next day I moved my camp to near the patch of forest where I had been so lucky, for the convenience of getting out the ivory (which my boys took two days to do), and afterwards to a stream close to the extreme base of Mount Kenia, in order to hunt in the extensive forest on its lower slopes. I was fortunate enough to shoot a giraffe at the stream, just at the place where I wanted to camp—one of the three which I found there on arriving ahead of my men, and stalked successfully

—thus obtaining without trouble a fresh supply of good meat.   With the exception of rhinoceros, of which there is a good sprinkling, there is hardly any game (besides elephants) in all the neighbourhood.

During the next fortnight I hunted perseveringly from this camp without any success.   Though I toiled hard almost every day, frequently from daylight to dark—having my breakfast before it was light and my dinner often late in the evening, with nothing between but a bit of biscuit and a drink of water or perhaps a banana—only once did I sight elephants, and in that case I bungled abominably a chance at two bulls, both getting away wounded, I regret to say.   I followed the spoor almost daily, but owing to the densely matted nature of the tall dark jungle in which the elephants here live, except during their nocturnal rambles, it is next to impossible, unless by a stroke of exceptional luck, to get a shot at them.   The labour is most arduous.   There are no open paths in this jungle ; the growth is so elastic that the passage of elephants leaves scarcely any opening, and one has to struggle, stoop, and crawl continually to get through at all.   The work is very exhausting ; and, to add to the drain on one's strength, poisonous caterpillar hairs and an irritating dust from the vegetation, through which one has to be always forcing one's way, cause a most annoying eruption on the body, the itching of which is a constant worry by day and prevents the refreshing sleep at night needed to recruit the strength daily expended.   A caterpillar down one's neck, for instance, causes intense itching, tingling, smarting, perhaps for days.   All such discomforts would, however, be lightly regarded by the elephant-hunter if he were rewarded by success in the pursuit of his quarry.   But such is the density of this Kenia jungle that though you may get within a few yards of your elephants it is impossible to see them, and they either scent or hear you ; and all the satisfaction you get, after hours of hard work, is to hear them crashing off.   So tall, too, is this cover and so leafy, that even from a tree (where there are any) nothing is visible, though the elephants may be close by. It is not to be wondered, then, that I got disheartened and came to the conclusion that I was wasting my time and strength, and after a thorough trial of the district gave up such a hopeless task.

The forest on the lower slopes of the mountain (I did not try the higher parts) is not all of the same nature as above described ; but in the comparatively open tree forest, where the undergrowth is scant, the elephants never harbour. The relief, after toiling through the jungle where their haunts are, to enter the pleasant shades of these cool woods, where one can walk with some comfort, is inexpressible. In parts of these, particularly near springs, the wealth of butterflies is wonderful ; sometimes I have seen the air filled with clouds of them of several beautiful and magnificent species. Birds of course there are ; but of mammals these forests seem almost destitute. Barring an occasional rhino and once in a way the spoor of an odd bushbuck, one finds no traces of game other than the elephants, which roam through them but are by no means always easy to locate. The mountain is very grand, with its almost perpendicular peak of black rock shown off by a setting of dazzling snow ; but its near vicinity is not without its drawbacks. The cold comes down at night and chills an old African uncomfortably ; while the heavy, almost frosty, dew on the long grass is disagreeable to plod through at dawn, saturating one's lower half with icy wet. It may be worth while, though, before leaving the foot of the great mountain, to give an account of a typical day or two's hunting on its lower slopes, including a visit to a lovely crater lake which I discovered there, called " Ngunga " by the natives.[1]

I took with me a blanket, etc., and a little food, so as to be prepared for sleeping out. We travelled along the edge of the

[1] I afterwards called this Lake Kolb, after Dr. George Kolb, who was with me there on a subsequent occasion and afterwards made an ascent of Mount Kenia, and mapped the district.

open country, which, as already explained, characterises the whole of the northern slopes, as far as I could see (including a high ridge running far out on the north side), keeping just outside the extensive jungles and forests which lay on our left as we ascended from the north-east. The crater itself is just within the forest, but we had little to go through in reaching it. Coming over the lower edge, which here has depressions with game roads worn by hundreds of generations of elephants, rhinoceroses, and buffaloes, the view is most enchanting. It is perfectly circular and surrounded by high, steep forest-clad walls ; below lies the placid lake occupying the whole of the wide interior, while from the high edge Kenia's jagged, snowy peaks are visible across, showing up sharply above the dark forest which clothes the opposite wall. Great beds of water-lilies with blue and lilac flowers and banks of water-grass or rushes cut up the glassy, clear water, which may be reached by the steep, stony paths above mentioned ; numbers of ducks, coots, geese, divers, etc., swim, fly, or flap about on the surface ; little water-hens with long toes run about on the lily leaves all the same as on a Japanese screen. Hippopotami, too, inhabit it (one wonders what instinct enabled them to find out so secluded a retreat), floundering clumsily about and eating roads through the beds of lilies with machine-like movement of their huge jaws, exposing the red interior of the mouth each time they are opened wide. A cow and calf came near the edge, while I watched, and stood in shoal water ; wild fowl gathered round them, perhaps getting food stirred up by the hippos. I watched the scene with delight ; and though my larder was empty I could not disturb this peaceful sanctuary even by the murder of a duck, so refrained from firing a single shot there.

I hid my camp away in a nook in the forest up on the edge, to avoid alarming elephants should any come down the path to water during the night, and made a circuit of the crater to look for spoor, but found none. Above it juniper forest begins, and I passed through some fine groves of tall, straight trees; but the ground is mostly all rock—broken-up lava, in fact. I did no more hunting that day, but spent the afternoon in watching the birds on the lake and bathing, and felt as if I should like to spend days pottering about in that way.

In the morning, after a very chilly night, though my guides (two natives of Janjai) were inclined to hang fire on account of the cold and heavy dew, we started pretty early.

NATIVES OF JANJAI DISTRICT.
(From a Photograph by Dr. KOLB.)

Keeping still along the edge of the grass country we ascended yet higher; and, after seeing a little eland and rhino spoor but no game, we came upon where a single bull elephant had passed the day before. Its tracks soon entered the cover. We persevered for a long time on its spoor through frightful jungle, and at last got that of the night before; but it kept steadily ascending towards Kilimara, and finally the guides refused to go farther and suggested striking back towards the cultivated grounds, far below, belonging to a tribe called Mnyithu (the same I afterwards had the difference with), where elephants had frequently been seen of late. The fact was we were not provisioned for a campaign in the bush, and they—and my own men too—were hungry ; so, as I had seen no game, I was constrained to consent. We had the most trying day imaginable, through the very densest, most abominable jungle it is possible to conceive. Our guides eventually lost themselves and us, and it was not till late in the afternoon that we at last struggled out into shambas. We had found no fresh spoor all day (except of a bushbuck) ; but I was rewarded for my toil by a wonderful display of gorgeous butterflies around a spring of crystal water in a valley, at which we rested while I caught a number of fine specimens.

After an uncomfortable and rather hungry night, I was shown the spoor of two bulls ; and I made another attempt to overcome the difficulties of these extensive thickets. But it was useless ; it is so leafy one cannot see a yard ; and after much crawling through tunnels, shoving one's way—bent double—or charging sideways between the meeting bushes, all the satisfaction I had was to find the bulls had winded us and gone. It seemed wonderful how such huge creatures could crash through and leave so small an opening after their passage. I followed for an hour or two all their windings, but, as they kept down wind, had to give in. We had still a great deal of this sort of leafy, elastic cover to overcome on our way toward camp, after relinquishing the pursuit, before we at length, to our infinite relief, got once more into the cool, pleasant forest. It was delightful to swing along its shady avenues, comparatively free from undergrowth, and seemed rest by comparison with the labour of tearing one's way through that dreadful jungle.

I felt that I had done all I could here, for the time, and that hunting elephants—dispersed as they seemed now to be—in this almost limitless, impassable tract, in whose depths they found a secure retreat, was waste of strength and energy. It was therefore with no regret that I returned to my "elephant camp" at Mthara.

From there I then made a short expedition in another direction—namely, northward, towards the Gwaso Nyiro River. My Mthara friends had offered to take me to a swamp, in whose neighbourhood they said elephants were sometimes to be found ; so I accepted their guidance, and on 31st May we started, in the lightest possible marching order, as I did not intend to be away more than a night or two from my camp. It was nearly noon before we got off, on account of the guides being late—rather to my disgust, as I am always for an early start even if the distance to be travelled is not great ;—but as we had only half a day's journey to go, with no heavy loads to carry, it did not much matter. We followed down a stream, which comes from Mthara, through very stony ground, until it spread out into a reedy swamp. The country was very open, with only scattered thorn-trees, and so far did not look at all likely for elephants ; nor did we see any spoor. On the way I saw no game but a few Grant's gazelles ; but near the swamp was a troop of Grevy's zebras, one of which I shot for my men. After choosing a place to camp close to the swamp, where, after some trouble, a spot fairly clear of stones was found, I went after some gazelle, which were close by, at the guides' request, and shot one for them, as they turned up their noses at zebra. But they then said they did not eat game at all, and only wanted the skin. The airs these natives give themselves, in imitation of Masai customs, are ridiculous. They own very little stock (a few sheep and goats and a very few cattle), but pretend they despise game, though in reality most of them will eat it on the sly. I have no patience with such nonsense, especially in the bush ; but as they counted themselves my brothers and had brought no food themselves, I gave them my only yam, resolving not to take them as guides again. Two or three ostriches were visible across the swamp, and an old rhino was pottering about near our camp. There were, too, great numbers of guinea fowl and large francolin along the stream.

At daybreak next morning a lion was roaring a little distance off, and as soon as it was light I went to look for him, as he was still to be heard every now and then ; but he probably heard me coming over the stones, for I saw him slinking away while yet a great way off. Then leaving most of the men where we had slept, we started and followed the stream down past another swamp, larger than the first, and on to a third and smaller one. Here we found fresh elephant spoor, a few cows having been there during the night. Having looked all round the swamp (the last of the series) and finding no other spoor, we followed this. The guides now said they were hungry and thirsty ; so, as I was rather disgusted with them for refusing good venison and had nothing else to give them, I told them they had better go home. This they did. The spoor now led us towards more bushy country. On the way we saw quantities of game. Looking across one broad open flat I saw a herd of giraffe (of which I counted forty-five) pass across one end, while in another part were some half-dozen rhino dotted about. Zebra and Grant's gazelle were in numbers everywhere, and in the opposite direction several ostriches and a few oryx. It was a wonderful and almost fabulous sight, such as " one reads about but very seldom sees." One herd of zebras, of mixed species, we watched pass within less than thirty yards of us while we stood concealed.

Persevering on the spoor, we came, after some considerable time, to country the surface of which was nothing but a mass of fragments of broken-up black lava. Strange to say, though many patches of this frightful ground, composed of hard lumps of rock without a suspicion of soil, were quite bare, where there were shrubs or grass the vegetation was much greener than else-where. Here we found many signs of elephants having fed yesterday, and soon after were cheered with the sight of freshly-broken and chewed bits of bark, wood, etc., still wet, also recently dropped dung. We followed the now quite fresh spoor eagerly though cautiously ; and after puzzling it out with the greatest care and no little trouble, owing to the abominably bad going, for some distance farther, we at length heard that solemn rumbling of the great animal's stomach which is more moving to the hunter's soul than the grandest organ peal. Leaving my men now, I picked my steps, with fearful anxiety, through the jagged, loose lumps of lava rock towards the spot whence the sound came, and caught sight of one of the great beasts, a little ahead, moving slowly to the right.

It was a still morning, the sun intensely hot, and the air stirred slightly, sometimes one way and sometimes another. As I approached nearer, with every effort to avoid being heard or seen, I noticed this elephant to have but small tusks, so refrained from shooting in hopes of getting a chance at a better ; but immediately it showed signs of alarm (having probably got a whiff of my wind) and began to make off. Looking ahead of it I saw two others standing by a large thorn-tree : one a fine, large female with nice teeth, the other smaller. I saw no time was to be lost, so hurried after the first, got near before the others had realised what was the matter, knocked over the big one, and then let the first have a shot in the back as she retreated, partly maiming her, with my second barrel. Reloading instantly, I, as she shuffled off, got a slanting shot at her head and dropped her dead. Noticing, as I ran past, the first still kicking on the ground, I thought it a wise precaution to give her another bullet right in the centre of the top of her head. Seeing the blood run from the hole just in the spot I intended, I left her for secure to follow the remaining cow. She turned and held up her head to discover the cause of alarm, standing diagonally with her head towards me. I think I had better perhaps have given her a body shot, as the ground was fairly open ; but thinking to reach her brain through the eye I aimed for that. With a shake of her head, however, she made off again. When my gunbearers came up we found a little blood on the spoor of the wounded elephant, but decided to go and cut off the tails of the two that were down before following it. Passing the second one I had shot, to go to the first and largest, to my intense chagrin I could not see it ; and, looking carefully, found where it had lain, but only a large pool of blood there now, no elephant! This is an instance of the disappointments a hunter has to bear, after days of hard toil and fatigue, just when he has the fruits within his grasp. We then took up the spoor of the large cow which I had left for dead. We followed it a good way (or what we believed to be its spoor, for there was some confusion of tracks owing to there being blood on the spoors of both this and the other I had wounded), and then heard the cry of an elephant ahead several times at intervals, and at last got so close as to hear its stomach rumbling once. The bush was here pretty thick, though the ground was as rocky as ever. I tried to get up to it, but it probably heard or winded me, for I only got a rather distant glimpse of the top of its back as it made off. We tried to follow, but the rocks made running almost impossible, and though I climbed a tree it was nowhere to be seen ; all I saw were two giraffes calmly browsing quite close by—much closer than one can ever get to them when you want to shoot one. We lost much time and also the spoor by this ; and when, after trying back, we did at last again pick up the latter, it was afternoon, we were all very fagged, thirsty and disappointed, and I decided to give it up.

The day had been excessively hot and sultry, the sun beating down upon and being reflected by the rocks with terrible power ; the going had been trying in the extreme, and the men had stupidly forgotten or neglected to fill the water bottles. I had done a lot of running, too, as far as it was possible to run among such a jumble of rocks ; but what made me the victim of thirst especially that day (for I do not commonly suffer in that way) was that I had drunk cocoa instead of tea that morning. So when at last, well on into the afternoon, we began to make back in the direction of the stream—the excitement being over and a good deal of annoyance at having so bunglingly allowed my best elephant to escape taking its place—the distance, which had not been noticed in passing it that morning, seemed now very long.   My men were probably suffering more from thirst even than myself, as they always eat quantities of meat, which tends to produce it, and never seem able to go far without wanting water.   Coming then upon a herd of zebras (Burchell's [1] and Grevy's mixed), I shot two, one of each kind, and, cutting them open, we drank the water out of their stomachs.   Zebras always have plenty, as they drink regularly, never being found very far from water ; and if you give the contents time to settle, it spouts out as clear as possible when an incision is made in the right place.   We did not wait for this though.   What we assuaged our thirst with was yellow, like weak tea with a strong flavour of vegetables ! But it was only grass after all ; and though we might have been looked on with disgust, imbibing the lukewarm fluid, by those who know not what thirst is, I certainly felt much refreshed by it, and trudged on more unconcernedly to the spruit and up it to camp past the swamps, arriving at dusk.   A wash in a bucket of hot water, followed by several of cold, freshens one up to enjoy a hearty dinner, with such an appetite as ensures against indigestion even though turning in directly after.

I was up again before daylight the next morning, feeling quite fresh again after a good sleep, and off before sunrise.   I struck straight across country, leaving the stream to the left, for the place where we had left the spoor of the wounded elephant, and found it without difficulty, as we had marked the spot.   I sent on two of the men to cut out the tusks of the one elephant that was really dead (they proved a little better than I had thought, though one was broken), while I and Square-face tried to take on the spoor again.   However, after puzzling

---

[1] I use this name to distinguish the small species, though the variety here is not the typical Burchell's zebra.

along for a while, it beat us and we turned back.   In vain I
looked out for vultures in the direction the elephant had been
going in ; but as a matter of fact they often do not collect
round the carcase of one of these animals (especially if in thick
bush, as it generally is) until a day or two after it has died.
There were plenty though to be seen all about where I had
shot the zebras, and as we came along in the morning we had
seen the trees near the place laden with them, as if with a heavy
crop of some curious great fruit ; so I now determined to pass
that way, though it was by this time almost too late to hope
to find lions at the carcases, as I knew would have been very
likely earlier.   I should have liked to go before, on the chance
of that ; but in elephant-hunting everything else has to give
way to the serious business.   On the way back I saw the remains
of a Grant's gazelle which had just been eaten by a lion ; and
just after, on coming out into the open, saw one making away
ahead, having clearly been disturbed from its prey by our
approach.   I tried to get a shot, but it would not wait, and
with an irritable swing or two round and up of its tail, and
sulky growls, made off into the bush before I could get near
enough for a running shot.

The place where the carcases of the zebras were was below
a little knoll—one of the ridges of lava, in fact.   We approached
from above ; and, just as we got near the brow, a lioness
appeared from behind a bush, having evidently just come up
from below, but noticing us began to slink away again.   I
immediately gave her a shot in the side with my .450, and
knocked her over.   She lay kicking and growling for a second
or two and then lay in a crouching attitude, her head towards
us.   I sat on a rock and gave her another bullet in the neck,
sending her sprawling again and biting savagely at the stones.
Hardly had I fired the second shot when another lioness came
up from beyond the first, apparently to see what was up.   She
stood erect after coming over the rise, with head up and neck
stretched out, looking intently our way and offering a lovely

shot at her chest. I did not neglect it. I had already taken my double .577 from Squareface and slipped in two hollow bullet cartridges (a most reliable way to be armed against lions) so I at once sent one of these smashing balls just into the junction of the neck and chest, dropping her stone dead. But the first lioness was not dead yet ; so, not wishing to waste more of my valuable cartridges, I took my " cripple-stopper " (as I call a Martini-Henry one of my men always carries for finishing off disabled elephants) and watched her a little while. To my surprise she stood up, and as she took a step I put a bullet into her shoulder, rolling her over again, growling and flinging her tail in the air. She now lay quite still for some time, so we went close up and I looked carefully at her with my glass at a distance of only some dozen yards. I could see her breathing regularly still, but as I felt sure she was helpless and at the point of death, we went round to inspect the other, which lay only a few yards on the far side of the first. We stood over this one, and were talking quite loud and considering whether we could get her under a tree to skin, when we heard the other lioness growl, and, looking round, I saw she had somewhat shifted her position. I at once gave her a raking shot from in front of and above her, finishing her tough life ; but before going right up to her and kicking her, I chucked a stone on to her head as a test.

It was a hot job skinning them in the sun among the lava. The lioness I had to give four bullets to was a very old one, though in good condition ; the other in her prime and very fat. The fat came in handy to add to my stock of rhino and elephant fat for my lamp. But before skinning them I looked across the green plain below us ; and there, on the far side, skirting just inside the scattered bush, I saw a whole troop of lions, led by a grand old male, the rest either females or immature males, evidently coming from the zebra carcases. I counted up to ten, and then, before I had finished, they got mixed up among the bushes ; but I am certain there were at the very least (to be quite on the safe side) three more, which, with my two, would make fifteen altogether. I never saw so many before at once.

We got back to camp in good time, but it took us till long after dark before the skins were cleaned and pegged out. On the way back I saw an enormous herd of zebras, numbering several hundred at least. No wonder there are so many lions here with such a wealth of prey. We saw no more fresh elephant spoor.

The next morning I made an early start again to search for it in other directions, as it was necessary to wait another day here for my lion skins to dry. We first followed our stream down a good way, some on each side, and then struck across towards some hills to the westward. We crossed two more streams on the way, near one of which we passed close to a rhino cow and calf lying asleep ; and I stood and had a good look at them and wished I had a camera, it was such a splendid chance for a photograph, and then went on, leaving them peacefully slumbering. We made a very long round but found no recent spoor, though during the last rains there had been a large troop of elephants about, as we could see by the mimosa bushes being broken all over the place in one part we passed through. On our return by another course we found we had three streams to cross instead of two ; the extra one a very strong torrent, running above ground only in places and then disappearing again. These brooks all come from the neighbourhood of Kenia, but many do not reach the Gwaso Nyiro with any surface water in their beds except during the rains. On the way back, seeing another rhino cow with a three parts grown calf lying under a tree, and noticing that she had a rather nice horn, I thought I might as well shoot her, as the meat would be welcome to my men ; so I went up to her, and when she stood up shot her in the chest, and she dropped after a short run. As usual when there are two in company, the young rhino would not run away at first,

and I was much amused by my men's cautious efforts to drive
it off, shouting and throwing stones at it from behind the
shelter of trees.   I am dead against shooting anything I do
not want unless forced to do so in self-defence.   The cow was
very fat, and my men (I had several with me) carried away
as much as they could stagger under.   As we were all hungry
I made a fire, while they skinned her, and we had a snack of
toasted liver.   Rhino liver is considered a great delicacy by
Swahilis ; they say it is like fowl's liver.

Farther on we passed among five more rhino—two cows,
each with a calf, and a bull—besides one or two more odd
ones I had seen in the distance during the day.   I also noticed
some giraffe and a good many oryx, some Grant's gazelle, and
a few impala ; but there was nothing like the quantity of game in
this direction as the other way, the veldt being drier.   We got
somewhat out of our course going back, owing to my men insisting on keeping more to the right than I was steering, and my
giving in to them in spite of my own strong opinion that I
was right, as it proved I had been ; so that we struck our
spruit a good deal too high up and did not reach camp till
dusk.   Altogether it had been a hard day ; for we had walked
fast almost continuously from daylight till dark : a good thirty
miles we must have covered, and under a very hot sun.   As
there were clearly no more elephants in the neighbourhood, I
returned to my " elephant camp " at Mthara the next day,
seeing several rhinos on the way.   When within less than an
hour's walk of camp, I passed near one with a young calf
lying in the open a little way to my left.   I stood and looked
at her, and, noticing she had a good horn, was considering
whether to go and shoot her, as it was within easy reach of
camp for sending to fetch the meat, but had not yet taken my
.577 double, which had been carried in its cover as I had no
intention of shooting that day, when she got up and made
straight for me.   Laying my single .450 down in front of me,
while my man hurriedly tore the other rifle out, I had just

time to ram in a couple of cartridges (as she had some distance to come) and fire a quick shot at her chest before she was upon me. She had her head up still when I fired first; but as she got within about a couple of strides she lowered it for a toss. Having taken my rifle from my shoulder after the first shot—expecting it to turn her, as I have always found happen in such cases—but she coming on straight for me as hard as she could go, I had not time to get it there again, so hastily threw up the butt with my right hand and pulled the left trigger with the muzzle pointing downwards on to her neck and instantly sprang to the right, just in time to let her pass where I had stood, within arm's reach of me, covering my .450 with dirt. But luckily, though she ran right over it, she did not step on it. She ran right on and I after her; I broke her shoulder with another shot and then put three Martini bullets into her in quick succession till she dropped. This was wasteful, as she would soon have been dead without any of these superfluous shots, but I was angry and would not wait to give her time to die lest she should escape.

It generally takes a few minutes for these animals to succumb to the effects of even a vital wound. My first shot had struck her a little low for the heart, going into her breast bone. The second barrel had entered the top of her neck just before the hump, and must have disabled her very soon, as it slanted downwards and penetrated deep. Her calf would not leave her for a long time. Twice it got its fore-quarters on its dead mother's back. Squareface and Juma (my gunbearers) threw stones at it, and at last it cleared out. It was old enough to shift for itself. This rhino had a very nice horn ($27\frac{1}{2}$ inches). Another (probably the male) stood not far off for a long while after all the fuss was over. I have noticed that in such family trios the male parent generally keeps at a respectful distance from the testy mother and her offspring; and I once witnessed a vigorous assault made by a cow upon her hapless mate, which she prodded unmercifully, apparently because he had unwarily approached too near her calf. I sent at once for men to carry in the meat, while we cut off the horns. On a neck between two hills which we passed through before descending into the valley where my camp was, we disturbed yet another rhino; and when close home, just before crossing the little spruit where we got our water, we came upon some impala and I shot a nice fat doe for my own larder.

I was very tired and glad to take a rest the next day, being rather unwell owing to the troublesome itching eruption one gets when hunting in this country, which brings on touches of fever. But in spite of these drawbacks I was very fond of this camp, and was sorry to leave it. It was necessary, though, to take my ivory back to my boma at Laiju; and before making another hunting trip I sent it off to the coast, in charge of my more ornamental than useful headman, as I had more men than I wanted here and was glad to reduce the monthly expenditure a little. I also took the opportunity of forwarding some specimens and despatching letters, the bearers of which were to return with my mail from Mombasa. By the time I got back to Laiju it was the second week in June, and I was not ready to start northwards in search of elephants again before the beginning of July.

One thing that delayed me was the necessity of making a second journey to the neighbourhood of Janjai, to recover the tusks of the bull elephant I have referred to as having been wounded by me and afterwards found by the natives of the next district beyond. This was a quick trip made for the above purpose only. It was a somewhat hazardous undertaking, as the natives refused to give up the ivory and I could only muster thirty-six men to take with me. We found ourselves amongst a dense and, unfortunately, unfriendly population, and spent a rather anxious night in the midst of them, camped in a small open space among banana groves and other cover without any boma to protect us. In spite of our endeavours to persuade them that we desired to discuss and arrange the matter amicably, they surrounded us and after dark began to shoot arrows at us, compelling us in self-defence to dislodge them with our rifles. In the morning we retired with the teeth without retaliating in any other way for their attack upon us than by preventing them from making any further attempt to interfere with us. I regretted very much having been forced into a quarrel ; but when, on a subsequent occasion, I visited their district, these natives had been transformed, by the lesson they had learnt, from enemies into enthusiastic friends. On passing through their country they welcomed us, entreated me to become their blood brother, acknowledging that our former little misunderstanding had been all their fault ; and as I was pleased to accede to their request and go through the ceremony of " eating blood "—in the midst of an admiring, crowded audience, who solemnly murmured earnest words of assent, after the manner of responses, to each sentence of the declaration of brotherhood between us, declaimed by the officiating performers of the rite which constitutes the bond—they are now, I am happy to say, among my firmest friends.

Apart from one's natural reluctance to be deprived of the hardly-earned reward of much arduous hunting and many blank days, I considered it a duty to make a point of retrieving these tusks after being returned a defiant answer to my civil message : a duty, I mean, not only to oneself, but to future travellers, to insist on the white man's property being respected. There is nothing I hate more than rows with the natives ; but when forced on one you must go through with them or lose all their respect. In all my dealings with the natives in Central Africa, one consideration I ever bear in mind is to try to make the country safe for other Europeans who may come after me.

CHAPTER IV

THE NDOROBO COUNTRY

IT was not, then, till the 3rd of July that I started once more
from Laiju for a more extended hunting trip into the region
to the northward, commonly called the Ndorobo country, but
which is practically uninhabited, in the ordinary sense of the
word, for hundreds of miles ; for the Ndorobos are only thinly
scattered in small communities, leading the life of pure savages
—that is they neither cultivate nor own stock, but live on what
they can pick up in the bush. Before I went among these
people I had always supposed, from what I had heard and
read about them, that they were all skilful hunters, living solely
on game. I have found, however, that this is by no means
the case, at least in the region of which I am writing. The
majority of them depend almost solely on honey and wild
fruit, roots, berries, etc., for their existence ; and, as may be
supposed in a country to which nature has been by no means
bountiful in edible products, they are usually in a state of semi-
starvation ; indeed it is a puzzle to me how they manage to
live at all. It is certainly not a country I should care to be
turned out to graze in after the manner of our first parents in

the Garden of Eden. There are only a few among their number having any skill at hunting, and even these are not what I should call expert hunters. They kill now and then an elephant or two or a rhinoceros, either by creeping up to and harpooning them or by trapping with a suspended javelin in a heavy shaft, on the " booby trap " principle, set in their paths, the weapon in either case being poisoned. In spite of the poison, however, the animal (at all events in the case of harpooning by hand) more often gets away wounded than is bagged, and frequently recovers from the wound, as I have myself shot elephants with old wounds on them, and in one we found the head of the weapon. Game of other kinds they seem hardly ever able to kill at all, except once in a way getting a giraffe in these traps. Their easiest victim is the rhino, which, on account of its sleepiness, is easily crept up to quite close ; and in consequence, in the neighbourhoods frequented by these savages, rhinos are scarce and the few there are rarely show themselves during daylight outside the thick bush.

To return from this anticipatory digression to my journey. I left this time only half-a-dozen men in charge of my goods at Laiju ; for I wanted all available porters to carry food for myself and those who were to stay with me in the wilderness, and my small, but strong stockade being by this time completed, a few were quite safe inside, in the event of any trouble with the neighbouring natives during my absence, and able to take care of my belongings. I will not give a detailed account of this journey from day to day, as it would be tedious. I travelled at first by a rather circuitous route round the eastern end of the Jambeni Range (the one always taken by Swahili ivory traders visiting the Ndorobo country), but instead of following the course upwards of the Gwaso Nyiro River, I crossed it and struck across country to a mountain called Gwargess, and thence to the foot of the Lorogi Mountains, where I formed a camp on a small stream called El Bogoi. There is a fair quantity of game in places along the route, chiefly oryx and Grant's gazelle, with zebra of both species, and a few rhinos where a sufficient supply of water is within reach, and here and there giraffe, while in suitable localities a sprinkling of waterbuck, impala and Waller's gazelle are to be found, and occasionally ostriches. I shot one of the last, a cock

SCENE ON GWASO NYIRO WITH WALLER'S GAZELLE (*Lithocranius walleri*) ♂ AND ♀ IN CHARACTERISTIC ATTITUDES.

in pretty good plumage, and was always able to kill sufficient game to provide meat for myself and men.

During the first two days twelve streams were crossed, all coming out of the Jambeni Range. These are the head waters of the branch of the Tana River called by Chanler and Von Hohnel the Mackenzie. I should add, with regard to the range so called on Von Hohnel's map, that the natives really apply that name only to the highest peak, and do not use it (nor any general title) to describe the whole range. On the third day we were fortunate enough to get water in a hole in the rocky bottom of a gully (which is often

quite dry), at a convenient distance from the last stream. I
found afterwards that by a more direct route this place may be
reached on the second day. Here I found the skull of a
greater koodoo, an antelope which must be exceedingly scarce
in this part of Africa, as I had never yet come across one.
While here two or three young Embe natives came to get
water to drink. I had one brought to camp, and questioned
him as to where they had been, as their own district is a
considerable distance away. He said a large party of them
had been to make a raid on the Ndorobos of Lorian but had
failed to find them. These Embe people are a cowardly, but
cruel race ; they are afraid to attack any other tribe, so harry
the unfortunate Ndorobos. I told him what I thought about
it, and put him in rather a fright ; and old " Papa " (who was
with me as on a former trip), when he heard that his relatives
were to have been attacked, immediately drew out of his
quiver, with a savage look, his two most villainous-looking
arrows. The wretched fellow was divided in his mind between
fear and thirst ; fidgeting, as if wanting to run away, and
drinking alternately, until I reassured him by bursting out
laughing at " Papa's " vengeful expression and let him go about
his business with advice to let the Ndorobos alone. In passing
round the end of the Jambeni Range the baobabs are left
behind. From the coast up their bloated trunks have been a
common feature, but here the last are seen.

The next camping place is by a very perfect crater. Of
this I wrote in my diary—" This is a curious place, but a
disagreeable camp. The crater is large and deep. There is a
small lake at the bottom whose shallow water is very strongly
impregnated with some mineral (natron ?) smelling and tasting
of ammonia. It is in large white crystals. There were crowds
of Embe women fishing quantities of this substance up from
the bottom of the shallow water and carrying it up the steep
path in huge loads on their backs. I lifted one. It weighed
not a bit less, I will undertake to say, than a hundred pounds.

There were also a few men with donkeys, which they packed with the mineral. It seems they trade it for goats with the Wakanda, who use it to mix with their tobacco. The drinking water (nastily brackish) is got out of one of several pits near the edge of the lake ; all the others produce (I was told) salt water. I looked down from the edge of the crater, but did not descend, as it is a long way down."

The country hereabouts and towards the Gwaso Nyiro is frightfully barren and very stony. In some places are great plains and ridges almost devoid of vegetation, consisting of black lava in rough fragments of all shapes and sizes. This makes very bad going for men carrying heavy loads, and is trying work for their feet even with hide sandals— the more so that we have now left all paths behind, except the fitful game tracks ;—it is terribly destructive, too, to one's boots. Fortunately the lava ceases at the Gwaso Nyiro River. The lava overlies limestone, and where the latter crops out, as it often does near the river, the water, which has been under-ground before, comes to the surface here and there in springs, some very large. One, on which I camped one day, was a good-sized stream where it rose, but disappeared again a little way below. It was, as these limestone springs often seem to be here, quite warm, and the water slightly brackish ; it was full of leeches, as I found to my cost on bathing in it for the first time. Quantities of game sometimes frequent these springs.

Some of the marches between the waters were rather long on the north side of the river, and, as it was very hot, tried the men a good deal. I saw some fresh elephant spoor once or twice, but, as the country is mostly very open, the elephants appear only to pass through it in the night, except, perhaps, during the rains. I had to wait two or three days at the river before going on, in order to send ahead to explore for water, as our guides had not an intimate knowledge of the country through which I wished to pass. While waiting I shot something every day to keep up the supply of beef for all hands, generally oryx.

The best head was 33 inches (female), the longest I had then got. From two of these, which were very fat, I got a good deal of milk, very rich and a great treat in one's tea. One can have no greater luxury in the "bara" than fresh milk, a very rare one in East Central Africa. I always use honey, which can generally be had from the natives, to replace sugar. The latter one learns to do without, like all the "necessaries" of civilised life, with the exception of salt, soap, and tea, of which I always try to carry sufficient. For other things, such as flour, one has to substitute whatever the country through which one passes produces. Old "Papa" used generally to go out with me to shoot. The Ndorobos are fond of the blood of freshly-killed animals, and on one being opened they will put their heads into the chest cavity and drink the warm blood or take up double handfuls of the congealing vital fluid, sucking in the clots with their mouths. On one occasion I made "Papa" stab a buck, which was not quite dead, in the breast, so as to kill it at once without injuring the scalp, as cutting the throat would do. The blood spouting out, he went down on his knees, put his mouth to the wound, and sucked it in with the keenest gusto. There are still a few elands left on the north side of the Gwaso Nyiro, survivors of the great cattle plague of a few years ago, and in one or two localities I have seen the spoor of a very few buffaloes. I shot a fine bull of the former, and on my return a cow, the only elands I bagged the whole trip. I never set eyes on a single buffalo.

The shooting of the former was on this wise. We had, after a long march, reached a rock pool in a small koppie near a dry sand stream called the Njangitomara (giraffe) by the Ndorobos. This, like many other places called after animals, is still obviously named appropriately, for the giraffes are abundant at the present day : a striking contrast to the rivers, etc., of the Transvaal, so commonly named after game of which nothing but the name survives. The country was open, except for a sprinkling of low mimosas ; but instead of grass, prickly

plants and shrubs covered the ground. I had climbed the
koppie with my glasses, and made out an ostrich and a rhino
with a big calf in the distance ; and, being anxious to get some
meat for my caravan, I went out with old " Papa " to shoot
something. I found the two rhinos lying down, and got close
up to them. I was just about to shoot the big one in the head
when she changed her position, and when I tried to get farther
round so as to obtain a side shot, she became aware in some
way of my proximity (perhaps she heard me—she could not
have scented me, as the wind was right) and suddenly jumped
up and faced me. I was very near indeed and did not care to
wait, so fired as well as I could for her throat ; for, owing to
the way she stood, her chest was not exposed. I was very
sorry afterwards I had fired, as she galloped right away, and,
though we followed the blood spoor a long distance, as usual
when a rhino once gets well away, she kept on for miles and
miles and we had to give it up. I was particularly disgusted
with this abominable bungle, as I hate wounding an animal
uselessly, and I was specially desirous of getting meat that day.

Sweeping round, on our return, towards the river-bed above
mentioned, I soon spied two elands among some thorn bushes.
I tried to stalk them, but they saw me and made off ; not,
however, straight away, and as they crossed me at a swinging
trot I gave the second (a big bull) a good shot, though a little
far back, with my .450 (solid bullet). I followed full split,
and, after a hard run downhill, caught up to him, very sick
and going dead slow. Creeping nearer I gave him a perfect
shot behind the shoulder, and he galloped into the river-bed
close by and collapsed—a splendid massive beast and fat.
The cow waited, and I could have shot her too, but thought
" enough," and let her go. While men were fetched to carry
the meat I skinned the head, a nice one. I had a hard job to
turn the eland over with only poor old " Papa's " weak help,
but managed it. I came back late by moonlight, pleased, the
loss of the rhino having after all turned out luckily. On our

way to camp we were charged by a rhino. I was obliged to give it a shot in self-defence, which turned it off. " Papa " scooted like lightning and then cried out, much to my amusement. He laughed as heartily himself afterwards, and used to imitate the way he had screamed and make fun of his own discomfiture. It is certainly unpleasant to be charged by a great snorting brute in the dark. My cook was gratified with a huge mass of fat from round the eland's heart, which kept his frying-pan supplied for some time.

As we neared the Lorogi Mountains the vegetation, which farther back had been parched, gradually became greener, and near the foot of the range was perfectly spring-like. The quantity of muddy water in the Seya River, too, showed that much rain was falling on the hills, and the summits were often capped with heavy clouds, some of the showers from which often reached the low country below. The air too felt quite different, a pleasant softness showing a moister atmosphere ; indeed, we seemed to have got into another and much pleasanter climate than the excessively dry one of the open country behind. I made my camp on the El Bogoi, a pleasant little clear stream, a few miles from the foot of the range, and at once sent back two-thirds of my men to fetch more food from Laiju, intending to wait here for their return (which I expected in about twenty days) and then push on to Donyo le Nyiro (Mt. Nyiro), near the south end of Lake Rudolph, which I had been informed was the best district for elephants. Without donkeys I knew I could not do any good farther north than that. I trusted to luck to my camp being pitched in a suitable neighbourhood ; and, though I did no good there at that time, it eventually proved to be about as advantageous a position as I could have chosen in the district.

It took us a couple of days to find the Ndorobos of this district, but I afterwards got to be great friends with them. They showed me where to look for game, as there was none close about, and if I shot more than I needed to eke out the half rations of my own men, it was always a windfall to these unthrifty but pleasant savages ; as, for instance, one day when I was lucky enough to kill a bull and cow giraffe, right and left, and gave them the former (which measured 16 feet[1] in height), while the cow provided me and my men with an ample supply of good meat, besides giving me the luxury of fresh milk, they bringing me presents of exquisite honey in acknowledgment. One is sometimes almost tempted to believe that these people possess some

AUTHOR'S DINING-TABLE IN BOWER.

peculiar faculty enabling them to divine the presence of meat in camp.   No sooner is game killed than they begin dropping in, for all the world like vultures.   It is not merely that they follow those birds (though they do so), for vultures under any circumstances are never absent from around the camp.   I have noticed the same thing amongst natives in South Africa.

Although there were elephants about and I went after them

---

[1] In my experience this is the height of a full-grown bull, whether in Central or Southern Africa ; 14 feet being the average of adult females.   I have read of 18 feet for a male, but have never seen one of such dimensions.

many times, I was invariably unlucky, and during the time I waited for the return of my men I never killed one ; I got chances two or three times, but in every case I failed to score for one reason or another. Twice I did get shots, though indifferent ones, but both got away. The bush is dense and thorny and of great extent, and the elephants are never found except in the thickest parts, while I and the Ndorobos had to get used to each other's ways and style of hunting. I also wasted much of my time in hunting for meat for my men, which kept me pretty hard worked, as game had to be sought a considerable distance away. To give an example : one day some of my Ndorobo friends brought me word that there were some elephants in a valley some distance to the north. I was off with them first thing next morning, taking some of my men to carry a few necessaries to enable me to sleep out, but no tent. On the way I shot at and broke the shoulder of an oryx, and my little dog brought it to bay ; but before I could get up to give it another shot she came back to me, letting it away, and it got into thick bush and was unfortunately lost. Farther on I killed a gazelle, though, which sufficed to keep the wolf from the door for that day.

After leaving the extra men with my things at a little spring at the head of the valley containing the bush where the elephants were said to be, I went on with the two Ndorobo guides and my gunbearers to look for them. We found the spoor of a small herd of cows and calves, and, after much trouble, at length got close to them. But the wind was fickle, and, as is so often the case in these dense bushes under the hills, came in provoking eddies, and before we could get up to them they had got our wind and were already in full retreat, and, though we followed some distance, all the satis-faction I got was a glimpse of them making off, without the chance of a shot, for the bush was too dense to allow of my running up to them. The next morning I was off again early, though feeling rather slack after a bad night, through the roughness of the ground on which I slept. We went a long tramp through thick bush, but found no fresh spoor, so in the afternoon I worked round to some open country in search of other game for meat. After being disappointed of getting a shot at a single giraffe which passed near me on the way there, I was successful on reaching the open, killing two oryx with as many shots, and an impala and a gazelle a little beyond with three more. I gave one oryx to my Ndorobo guides, and sent for my men to bring all my things to some small rock pools I knew of nearer at hand than our last night's camp, and to come on to carry the meat there.

In the meantime heavy rain with thunder came on, lasting an hour and a half, making things very uncomfortable and soaking us thoroughly. At last we got back to the water at dusk, very wet, tired, and empty, to find my wretched cook and boy standing shivering under the dripping bushes, waiting for matches, but never having thought to collect firewood or do anything towards making things ready. Of course no one had thought of turning a bucket upside down over our sack of meal to keep it dry. I was not long in packing them off to hunt up firewood, while I set to work to chop out some dry wood from the inside of the biggest sticks I could find and split it up into thin slips and shavings with my knife, and soon started a fire which by and by burned up to be the comfort of the whole camp and to roast every one's meat. Then I had to see meat divided, clean my rifles, which were very wet (work I always do myself), and have my hot sponge-down ; so that it was eleven o'clock before I got any dinner, and fully midnight by the time I got to bed. But in hunting one must take things as they come, one day with another. Fortunately the rain ceased by sundown, and I was comfortable enough in the end, in spite of adverse circumstances, and slept well till morning. It had been a hard day's work, but I was in good hard condition and robust health and thought nothing of it. Had I waited for my Swahili servants to make the fire, though, I might have gone hungry and cold to bed ; for they are perfect duffers at it when everything is wet, and will waste a box of matches pottering with a few wet sticks and never getting a light at all.

Of my stay in this district at that time, while I waited for the return of my food caravan, there is nothing else of particular interest to record, unless it be the measurements of a very fine stallion zebra of the larger species (grevyi), which I took very carefully immediately after death, as I was much struck with the powerful proportions of these very handsome animals. These were as follows : height at withers, 4 feet 11 inches *full* (or barely an inch under 15 hands) ; length from forelock to set on of tail, 6 feet 8¾ inches ; ditto to end of tail (without tuft), 8 feet 1 inch ; girth behind shoulder, 5 feet 9½ inches. It seems a pity such strong and useful-looking beasts should not be made use of in a country where there is such a difficulty about transport, and where all our domestic animals, including even the humble ass, are so subject to disease. It is curious that, although in their proportions, action, and the shape of their hoofs, these zebras are far more horselike than Burchell's, their ears are much larger, while the cry resembles that of the ass very much more.

As my men did not return when I expected them, I determined to waste no more time, but push on without them. Accordingly I built a hut in which to store what food I could not carry, and leaving two men in charge (whom I knew the Ndorobos would not molest), I started with ten for Mount Nyiro. It became visible the first day, far to the north by west. On the second day we left the bush veldt behind and entered quite open country, not, however, grassy, but covered with thorny and other plants, very verdant-looking and rather pleasant, the air being fragrant with the scent of flowers and aromatic herbs.[1] Water, though, is scarce, and the going rather bad, the ground being stony, with much white quartz. Where water was not

---

[1] I discovered a herb here, with a flavour resembling mint, which I found to be excellent for culinary purposes.

too far off, zebra (chiefly Grevy's here) were plentiful ; of one (a mare) which I shot for meat on our second day, I wrote : " A lovely creature, very fat, and as sleek as a well-groomed and well-fed, stabled pony." This part is called " Ongata Ndamez " [1] by the Ndorobos, that is, " Camel Veldt " ; and farther on, where are high level plains covered with short, sweet grass, they are known as " Ongata Barta "—" Horse pasture." These names are relics of a tribe owning such animals, which formerly frequented the district ; it is now quite un-inhabited. Between the two is a long, waterless stretch, which our old Ndorobo guide made longer by taking us a roundabout course. Considering that he admitted his knowledge of the country to be derived from a raiding expedition in which he had taken part as a young man, which must have been, to judge from his apparent age, from forty to fifty years ago, it was not surprising that he should get a little out of his reckon-ing in the night, especially as his eyesight seemed rather defective. From the course we were steering in reference to the position of the moon and my knowledge of the bearing of Mount Nyiro, I suspected some error in the navigation. Un-fortunately, our pilot, like natives in general, took no account of the points of the compass ; and, knowing the winding routes they adopt for various reasons (often sufficient ones), I refrained from speaking to the man at the wheel—for I had learnt by experience that to interfere may cause trouble. On discovering his mistake, the old idiot smilingly explained that he had been steering for the wrong hill, with as much unconcern as he had shown in starting from the last camp without any warning to us that it was a far cry to the next water. I found out now that the information I had been given as to the distances on this route, by the traveller I had met, were very misleading, and it proved, in fact, that he had not himself reached this country at all.

---

[1] This is a Masai or Ndorobo word, signifying open country, and is pronounced as spelt here. " Angata," as it is often written, is wrong, being the corrupt Swahili pronunciation.

Altogether, it took us a day and the greater part of the night to traverse this stage. The porters got a good deal distressed, and we had at last to leave the loads and get on to the water, which we reached just before dawn. It is not the first time that I have welcomed the croaking of frogs in Central Africa as the most delightful music, on approaching at length the longed-for " stream in the desert." After a long, weary march through waterless wilderness, how affectionately one regards the "reeds and rushes" about the pool or spring in the parched and thirsty land ! Here (Ongata Barta) were great herds of oryx and Grant's gazelle—both the quantity of game and the aspect of the country reminding me of the " high veldt " of the Transvaal in the old days. From there to the foot of the rugged mountain block called " Donyo le Nyiro," where is a clear, strong, cold stream rushing over a rocky bed through a deep gorge, is another long dry spell, rendered longer to us, like the last (though the distance was in this case less formidable), by our old guide getting wrong in the night.

This proved a fruitless and wholly disappointing trip. The country was open and dry, and quite devoid of elephants at that time, as far as I went. Farther I did not feel able to penetrate then, owing to our small supply of food. We failed to get into communication with the natives (Sambur) living in the mountain, as they were suspicious and did nothing but run away from us, with their cattle, up into the fortresses, when we tried to get near enough to shout to them. Consequently we could get no information from them ; and as we had seen some Wakamba at our previous camp, who had come from this neighbourhood, the prospect was very poor of finding the game we sought ; for those people, who live south of the Tana, hunt in large parties, scouring the country for long distances, and, wounding far more than they kill with their poisoned arrows, drive the elephants out of the whole district. Moreover I was anxious, now that I saw that this trip was a mistake, to stop my food caravan (which I had left word at El Bogoi was to follow me) from coming on ; so I only stayed two or three days before retracing my steps towards my camp at the last-named place.

While at Nyiro I found an ostrich's nest, when out hunting for meat, containing no less than twenty-eight eggs. It was a great sell to find them hard sat upon. I shot the male bird, but he was in poor plumage. On my return journey I had an easy chance to shoot a magnificent bull eland, as he came towards us, where we sat resting one day, attended by four cows, and walked to within short range before finding out what we were, the wind happening to be right. But as it was just in the middle of our longest march, and we could not have carried either the meat or his grand head, I refused to be tempted to harm him, though my cook pleaded that his department was out of fat. The game that I shot for meat on this trip consisted of giraffe, zebra, oryx, and Grant's gazelle. One male oryx which I shot had only one horn, giving it a curious resemblance to the unicorn of heraldry. The other must have been broken off at the base when it was young, as the skin had grown right over the place. I kept the skull, but unfortunately the scalp went bad, or it would have been a curiosity when mounted. On getting near the Lorogi mountains again I skirted along the foot of the range in hopes of finding elephants, but there was no fresh spoor there then.

Thus by the time I once more reached El Bogoi I had been two months away from my Laiju boma without bagging a single elephant — a not very hopeful look-out, truly, for paying the expenses of my rather large caravan, which were running on month after month, while the goods I had brought from the coast in the hope of trading some ivory to help towards covering its heavy cost were lying idle, and there seemed no chance of doing anything with them. However, I had at length come to a more favourable turning in my long lane, and during the ensuing month I had a fair amount of luck among the elephant in the district around El Bogoi. Of this hunting I will now endeavour to give some account.

CHAPTER V

NDOROBO ELEPHANT-HUNTING

ON getting back to my camp there, I was warmly welcomed by my Ndorobo friends, who told me (of course) that there had been no end of elephants in the neighbourhood during my absence, and (which was more to the point) that some still frequented the extensive jungle between there and the Seya River. I was very sorry, though, to hear of the death, while I was away, of one of the Ndorobo elephant-hunters whom I had got to know well. He came by it in this wise. He had gone out after some elephants; and, getting near them, had prepared for action by fixing a dart into the handle of his harpoon. I should explain though, first, that, when after elephants, an Ndorobo hunter carries a wooden harpoon handle (fairly heavy) and a large quiver containing a number of darts with iron heads as sharp as razors, the shafts of which fit into the handle. The darts are smeared with the deadly poison they obtain from a particular wood which grows in the mountains, and each is carefully wrapped up in a thin strip of skin prepared for the purpose. On getting near the game he takes out two of these darts, removes the skin wrapping, and, fixing one with the greatest nicety into the handle, carries it in his right hand while the spare one he takes in his left.   He then enters the bush perfectly naked, having divested himself of his skin cape, belt with hunting-knife [1] attached, and any- thing else he may have about him, which he leaves together with his quiver.   Creeping stealthily up, through the thicket, to within a few paces of the nearest elephant (or the one most

NDOROBO HUNTERS.
(From a Photograph by Dr. KOLB.)

favourably situated of those next him as he approaches up wind), he delivers his blow with all his strength, and instantly dives through the bush to avoid a possible charge.   The elephants having stampeded, he picks up his harpoon handle, inserts his spare dart, and follows up.   The most deadly spot to aim at with this weapon is the part of the stomach where lie the small intestines, about the flank.   In the present case

[1] A kind of long, heavy, spatula-shaped dagger, called a " simé," carried in a sheath.

my friend had gone in as described ; but not being able to get up to within striking distance of his game at once, had sat down to chew tobacco, putting his weapons down beside him. In taking them up again as he rose, one of the excessively sharp points scratched his leg, with the result that he was unable to leave the spot and died right away.

Perhaps I cannot do better than quote the account of my first success, after this long spell of bad luck, from my diary as entered at the time.   I had moved from my standing camp to a temporary one near to the part of the bush where the elephants were reported to be then.   " Ndorobo elephant-hunter came early and said a herd of elephants was in the bush.   I went with him soon after sunrise towards the foot of the range, where dense bush extends with hardly any break for miles.   Before long we came on lots of quite fresh spoor ; but, before following in the direction the elephants had taken, we worked round to leeward, and then struck in.   My guide kept frequently taking up dust from the ground and letting it trickle out of his fingers to test the air-currents, though for my own part I prefer to be ' still plucking the grass to try where sits the wind,' dry grass crumbled in the hand being more sensitive to the slightest breath.   We soon heard the elephants making their curious sounds, and again came on warm spoor, which we followed carefully.   After following only a very short way, the solemn intestinal rumblings were heard, which so often give warning that the game is close ahead though still hidden by the thick bush.   I stole on (having left my surplus followers), till the Ndorobo gave place to me to pass him. The bush, though a dense thorny scrub, is cut up by the elephants' paths into a check pattern.   Rounding a corner I came in view of three elephants only a few yards away standing in a little bare space.   The nearest (a large one) had its stern to me, and seemed to be amusing itself by picking up dust to throw over its back.   Two others stood opposite, sideways on ; one a small one with little ivory, the other a large fellow but

NDOROBO HUNTER HARPOONING AN ELEPHANT.

"Creeping stealthily up . . . he delivers his blow and instantly dives through the bush."

with only moderate tusks. The last was my mark. He appeared to see me and turned his head a little towards me, somewhat interfering with the perfection of the shot afforded. I did not like to wait more than a few seconds, though, lest the chance should be lost, so let him have a bullet in the temple in what seemed to me the right spot. He fell to the shot, but rose at once, staggering and dizzy. I was ready for him, and gave him the other barrel (the others had fled). He did not fall again, but staggered about, very dazed and groggy. I kept close by his side, and when he tried to move away gave him a couple more shots in the region of the heart. He once got my wind (I having incautiously gone on the wrong side of him) and made a short spurt, I after him, losing my hat and getting arms, face, and clothes torn by the thorns. I was so close all the time I could have put the muzzle of my rifle against him easily by moving a pace or two more ; and no doubt that was why he could not see me, as I was behind his line of sight, or he would have gone for me. But he could not go far and soon pulled up again, seemingly at his last gasp. He seemed once to try to come through a thick clump of scrub for me ; but his strength appeared to fail, and he subsided backwards into a quaint sitting posture, his hind legs thrust forward on each side of his huge belly, his forelegs straddled out in front, while his head was kept quite straight upright by one tusk being against a small tree which was between it and his trunk. One would not have known that he was dead, only that now the curious rumbling noises he had been making all the time had ceased. He was a big bull, but his tusks were small (about 40 lbs. apiece)."

I was pleased to have, as it were, broken the spell and at last killed an elephant again. Contrary to my usual custom I did not follow the rest of the herd again that day, as I was suffering from a touch of fever, and, having got the sun on my head (very powerful in the scrub) when I lost my hat, felt somewhat exhausted. My Ndorobo hunter was anxious to go and fetch his family to commence cutting up the meat. The whole community of Ndorobos now shifted their quarters and went and camped near the carcase, so that they might be near their work ; and for several days I could not get any of them to go out hunting with me, so much taken up were they with feasting and drying for future use strips of meat and even pieces of the skin. For when pushed by hunger, as very frequently happens, they are glad to fall back upon old bits of elephant or rhinoceros hide, which they cook and eat. It is

" One would not have known he was dead."

a curious sight to see a party of these people, men, women, and children, swarming around, upon, and inside the carcase of an elephant, like ants with a big beetle, fairly wallowing in gore and thoroughly enjoying themselves.

I was not myself averse to a couple of days' spell, having fever on me ; for though I am so thoroughly salted, from many bygone encounters with this enemy of African travellers during long years of wandering in unhealthy regions, as to be so far fever-proof that I am never laid up or incapacitated for any needful exertion, I still feel the attacks to the extent of their affecting my comfort and buoyancy, and upsetting the nerves, thus interfering with one's shooting. But I soon got tired of taking it easy, though I amused myself with my little .250 rook rifle (a much handier weapon in Africa than a shot-gun) by shooting pigeons which congregated in the trees every afternoon to drink at the pool where we got our water. These made a pleasant variety to one's bill of fare too, either in a stew with elephant's heart, which I dignified by the name of " pigeon pie," or roasted on a stick ; in the latter way, with a piece of elephant's fat skewered over them, they are excellent. Butter-flies, the search for which is a great resource at odd times as well as on the march, were at this time almost absent here. So on the third day I went out with only my gunbearers, the Ndorobo being still immovable. I took a round in a direction I thought it likely the elephants might have retired in, and climbed a high koppie to get a view over the country. Sitting on the top with my glasses, I was able to get a glimpse of two or three elephants some miles away in a valley close under the hills, as they passed through a small open space at its mouth. However, my luck did not bear me out in spite of this good beginning ; for the wind was most perverse, and though I eventually did get a glimpse of one's head, as it was almost a front view the chance was a poor one, and my shot had perhaps better not have been fired, as it did no good and I failed to get up to the elephants again. My experience is that a shot in the head, though it may not touch the brain, will almost always stun a cow, thus giving one time for another shot as she rises ; but a big bull is not so easily felled, his massive skull resisting the force of the blow better, nor is his brain so easily reached. In this dense scrub, however, one had to make the most of such glimpses as one could get, though, as I became more at home in it, I found it possible to manœuvre close up to the elephants and get better shots than I dare attempt before.

The following day I was off before sunrise. My hunter had not yet turned up again, so I first went to seek him at his new camp. I found another Ndorobo clan (also friends of mine) had just come to make their encampment close by, in order to be handy for future feasts should I have further successes in hunting. Not finding my man, I took a couple of young volunteers along with me. We struck right through the bush to a point at the foot of the hills beyond where I had found the day before, in order that we might cut the spoor should the herd have trekked. We found no track, however, and walked back along the base of the hills towards the valley above mentioned. On getting near it, we came upon plenty of quite fresh spoor where the elephants had been feeding that morning. Having brought it up to the little swampy spring where they had drunk, I sat down to have a bit of a spell, as it was by this time noon, and eat a snack by way of lunch. I never carry anything that could be called a meal, but something just to spoil one's appetite ; something sweet I find the best for the purpose, such as a few raisins or a bit of chocolate with a few fragments of biscuit, washed down with a drink of water.

Meanwhile I sent out my natives to find out which way the elephants had gone from there. I knew by this time they would be taking their mid-day siesta and must be standing somewhere in the bush not far off; and, sure enough, by the time I had finished my little repast, my scouts came running back to say they heard the elephants in the scrub quite near. I cautiously made off in the direction, the wind being right and, fortunately, steadier to-day, though gusty with lulls. My Ndorobo climbed a tree and saw a little bunch, and, having pointed out to me where they were, stayed behind and I crept on alone. With cat-like steps I advanced, caught a glimpse of one through the bush, and approached without making a sound or being seen to within ten yards of the nearest one, a large cow, of which I then suddenly, for the first time, came in full view, facing me. She also saw me, but apparently could not make out what I was, though she looked attentively and suspiciously at me. I always

wear clothes of a reddish-brown colour — often using a decoction of mimosa bark to stain them if too light — thus resembling the colour of many tree trunks ; and when standing
motionless (the wind being favourable) I think an elephant
takes one, so disguised, for a dry stump.   I waited anxiously
for her to give me a chance, at the same time noticing that two
or three others, which I could see indistinctly behind her,
seemed all smaller ; so that, though my *vis-à-vis'* tusks were not
large, I decided she must be my victim.   She once or twice
offered to approach me, and once actually came, head up, ears
stretched out, to within five or six yards at most.   I stood firm,
having inwardly sworn not to spoil this chance by hurried or
nervous shooting, and ready, should she come right on, to give
her a shot in the chest and jump aside, though my object in
waiting was the hope of getting a chance for a temple shot,
knowing that if I succeeded in that, dropping her dead on the
spot (as can only be done by a shot in the brain), the others
might probably stand and give me a chance with my second
barrel.   She, however, hesitated, her courage seeming to fail her
at the last moment, or she was not sure what I was ; anyway
she backed away again and I ventured, in spite of crackling
twigs, to go a step or two nearer.

The breeze there had been as I came up to them had died
entirely away, and there was a dead calm, with a suspicion of
eddies the wrong way.   The elephants felt for scent with their
trunks, and suddenly turned and ran the other way.   I was
after them instantly ; and, as my cow was the last and they
only got slowly through the jungle at first, in a few strides I
was within a few yards of her stern, meaning to give her a
shot in that quarter and try at least to cripple her.   But
before I could do so she suddenly rounded on me with a
scream, having clearly heard me following and meaning to
charge.   But before she was well round I had put a bullet in
her temple, which felled her, to my great relief and joy.   As
she struggled on the ground I gave her the other barrel in her

head again, and then, as she still thumped her head about, screaming loudly, I shot her in the chest, the bullet penetrating her heart and finishing her. Following the others, which seemed to have lost their leader and ran about backwards and forwards, standing at short intervals, I sighted them two or three times, but could not get a shot. They were all small females with thin tusks, but I did not then know there were any more near, so was bound to try and score all I could. Shortly after, I got sight of two of them standing, and, the breeze being just then favourable, I got up, waited till one turned her head right, and dropped her. Going on again, Juma (one of my men) spotted another from a tree I had sent him up. I got close up and found there were three or four standing together, larger than the others, and which had evidently not been disturbed. Opposite me again was a cow, similar to the first I had shot, with a calf by her. The calf saw me, but I heeded it not nor its mother, having caught sight of a much larger tusk than she possessed behind a thick clump of scrub to the right, only a few yards from where I stood. Determined to try for this fellow at all hazards, I moved round this clump of wattles. As I came in view he swung round preparatory to decamping. But I was too quick for him, and as his head went round from me I plugged him right in the ear, dropping him dead on the spot. He was a small bull, very short in stature, but with nice teeth.

I now went back to the small elephant to get some water, and foolishly stayed some time while more was fetched for the men. This delay, I think, certainly cost me at least another elephant. When I did follow up again, leaving Juma to get out the fat, etc., on coming over a rise we saw the whole herd (perhaps thirty strong, but apparently all cows) going up the other side of a little valley in front of us, some 300 or 400 yards ahead. I doubled after them—an open glade here allowing it,—but, on topping the next rise, they were already disappearing over another, getting away from us at a run.

Two were, however, behind, and had not yet crossed the gully, so I ran down to try to cut them off; but they put on a spurt and I only managed to get a stern shot at one. Being above her the bullet caught her in the back (as it afterwards turned out), and told loudly; but they went off, and we had to give up the chase, as it was getting late. This cow was, however, found a few days after by some Ndorobos, and I got the ivory all right.

On starting back for camp I sent one of my young Ndorobo companions to call the two headmen of their clans, and on reaching camp, about sundown, they met me. There being heaps of meat in the wind they made no delay or excuses. I am bound to say, though, that these people are far more reliable, as a rule, than most Central African savages. On giving them leave to take possession of the elephants (apportioning each tribe its share, to prevent any quarrelling), I told them they must bring me some honey. This they promised to do as soon as they had eaten the elephants. They fulfilled their promise loyally later on, bringing me a liberal supply of the most beautifully clear, luscious honey. I find that honey is almost a necessity in the " bara." It is the only sweet thing one gets, for sugar one cannot carry sufficient of to last; and when living on nothing but the simplest and coarsest food with meat, one has a craving for something sweet and does not feel satisfied or strong without it. The Ndorobos depend largely on it, especially for their children. It is a wonderful country for flowers, and seldom dries up near the Lorogi owing to the frequent mountain showers; and bees in consequence thrive and accumulate great stores. I found a kind of wild fruit or bean (something like acorns), which the natives eat, very good when thoroughly boiled and eaten with honey, and it was a great stand-by while I was in that part. My poor old Ndorobo follower whom I called " Papa " had cut his hand while cutting up the elephant shot previously, and the meat, being somewhat high, had poisoned his blood and quite spoilt the old chap's pleasure during these times of plenty, and he eventually lost half the wounded finger.

These were great times with the Ndorobos of the whole country-side. They all camped in the vicinity and in a few days got quite sleek and fat, so that I could hardly recognise my recently starved-looking neighbours. As, however, they had overrun the elephants' favourite haunts, there seemed no chance of more luck for me thereabouts for a time ; so I determined to move a little farther off again. I was sorry to leave my pleasant camp at El Bogoi, with its pure little stream of water and shady tree with a canopy of creepers under which I could sit and rest in the cool. I was pretty hard worked there though, for game had to be sought a considerable distance away to keep up the supply of meat, as my men had not yet overcome the stupid Swahili prejudice against eating elephant meat, though they did eventually when they got nothing else. I was much inclined to move up on to the Lorogi range, where there are extensive forests of the kind called by the Ndorobos "Subugo" (a name applied to all similar high, damp forest tracts), and several times told my native friends I wanted them to guide me there. They did not refuse, but always tried to dissuade me and evidently disliked the idea, their principal objections being the cold and wet. One headman and particular friend of mine expressed the hardship he would think it to have to go there, by asking—" If I had a donkey " (he did not add " what wouldn't go ") " would I take him to the Subugo ? " So, as during the whole of my stay in the district the mountains were almost continually enveloped in cloud, I concluded their advice was good ; for not only would the climate be extremely unpleasant, but the elephants only frequent these cool, swampy forests when, through drought, water is very scarce elsewhere. Moreover, I had already made one mistake, against their advice, in going to Nyiro mountain. I therefore only went across the Leseya (or Seya) River (one day's march) ; and I did but little good there, only once finding any elephants, on which occasion I came across four cows, three of which I killed. While there I was very nearly caught in one of the fall-traps we frequently came across in that part (the El Bogoi Ndorobos never set them). I was walking along a path, with my eyes on a spoor which led in that direction, when suddenly my forehead came in contact with a cord stretched across it, and, looking up, I saw the murderous harpoon in its heavy shaft hanging right above my head. Luckily the owners do not set them "tickle," lest the wind should set them off, and I had not pressed the string hard enough to release the impending javelin.

The little river Seya, which drains the Lorogi range, afforded clear proof of the quantity of rain that was falling on the tops, being very full all the time. It is curious that none of the water from all the country north of the Jambeni hills finds its way to the sea, but is poured into swamps or lakes, with no outlet. The Seya runs into such a swamp, near the Matthews range, called El Gereh.

I had a fair amount of success during the whole of this month ; but it would be tedious were I to recount all the details of every day's hunt. I will, however, add the particulars of the killing of one or two of my big bulls ; for I was lucky enough to get several fine old fellows with heavy tusks. I was back again in the neighbourhood of El Bogoi, the two headmen of that district (my particular friends) having come after me to report that another large herd had appeared ; and as I had had but indifferent success where I had gone after leaving there, I was ready to go with them at once. The first day I was un-successful, getting only an indifferent chance and failing to bag the elephant I shot at, though, oddly enough, I killed the same one on a subsequent occasion.

I was having my early breakfast the morning after this disappointing day, when three Ndorobo lads came to say one of them had heard elephants quite near. I got ready at once and went with them ; and we had only gone a comparatively short way from my temporary camp (which was then right under the mountain, in a little open valley, the wide expanse of scrub stretching away in all directions below) when we heard the elephants. The breeze being happily favourable for once, I got up close without much difficulty, and made out two or three enormous bulls standing together. One faced me, another, whose tusks (from the glimpse I got) seemed as good, stood broadside on. By great good luck I could see the vulnerable part of his ribs, just behind his shoulder, through a little opening among the leaves, etc., and was able to get a shot by kneeling. Following, as they disappeared instantly after I fired, there was just a colour of blood (a very spot or two only); and, though I felt positive my aim had been true, I began to fear another failure. But, just after, he was heard ahead, and a little way on we came up to him standing in a little bare place. I gave him two more shots and he toppled over. Rushing up, we cut off his tail, and I had just brushed past his hind legs and pointed out my first shot (right over the heart), when he got on to his legs again and we cleared out of his way sharp. Getting the " cripple-stopper," I gave him a couple more shots, but they were unnecessary ; for, though so huge a beast takes some time to die from a tiny pellet of a bullet, he could not move away from where he stood, and, after swaying and tottering some time, he fell over again with a great crash, fairly bounding up again on to his stern, like a ship going down with its bows in the air ; sitting up, as it were, for a moment, his huge head and tusks aloft, before collapsing to rise no more. A truly gigantic beast ! What a little pop-gun my rifle appeared to such monsters. The skin of his back was like the bark of some great tree : all hard, scaly lumps, as is that of a big old crocodile. I measured him as accurately as I could and copy the entry as follows :—" He measured fully 10 feet 8 or 9 inches high at shoulder by tape ; 14 feet long from root of trunk to root of tail; circumference of fore foot 5 feet; his body

5 feet 6 inches deep, from ground to highest part of side as he lay." [1]   His tusks were massive but not very long (they weighed between 70 and 80 lbs. apiece),—a well-earned reward for much hard work.   I followed the others (five or six monsters) and got near them once more, but the wind again baulked me, and I had to be satisfied for that day.

The following day I did not hunt, but went early to get the tusks of the bull out and carried to camp.   I often here left them for some days, when they would come out quite easily without chopping ; but, as I intended leaving soon, I chopped these out at once.   Though it was still quite early, the Ndorobos had already cut up the whole of the upper half of the huge mass.   They were swarming all around ; the bush was full of them and covered with meat cut into strips or piled in junks.   They had made fires all about ; and eating and work were going on everywhere.   The next day's hunt is the last of which I shall, at present, give a description; for any one who may have had sufficient endurance to follow my prowlings in the bush so far, must by this time have had enough of elephant-hunting for a while.

I was off again, then, at dawn as usual, with two Ndorobo youths as well as, of course, my usual attendants.   The latter are three : " Squareface," my principal gun-bearer, who carries the double .577 ; Juma, the second ditto, carrying the " cripple-stopper," and " Smiler " (properly Ismail or Ishmael), with an axe and sundry other trifles.   The last I always leave some distance behind when approaching game, as well as any surplus natives, and when going right up to my shot, the others wait too until I fire.   On the way towards the Bogoi valley we found fresh spoor, and the rolls of chewed fibre the elephants are always spitting out when on the feed.   That is to say, such is their habit in this part of the country, where their chief food is the plant called " mkongi " by the Swahili.   Being, unfortunately,

---

[1] This was immediately after death and before he had become distended by the gases generated in the stomach.

no botanist, I do not know what it really is ; but I call it
vegetable bayonets.   It is just like a bunch of green bayonets
springing out of the ground, with points as sharp as real ones
and capable of giving most painful wounds to any one who
unwarily runs against one slanting towards him.   The bush is
full of this plant, and the elephants chew it and reject the fibre ;
consequently the ground in their haunts is often strewn with it,
more or less dry according to the time that has elapsed since
its juice was partaken of.   When it is green and moist, and
smells quite sweet, it is freshly chewed ; after a little exposure
it gets sour.   The fibre of this plant is very strong, and makes
excellent cord or rope.   I have often thought that it might be
turned to profitable account in places where it grows in great
profusion near enough to the coast, as, for instance, on the
Sabaki River.

On reaching the edge of the broad, nearly level valley, we
ascended a little prominence to get a view over it.   A good
deal of this scrub is not very high, so that if one can get on to
a rise, or even sometimes into a tall tree (though such are not
many in this kind of cover), and look down upon the jungle, it
is often possible to see the tops of elephants' heads and backs,
which the owners make more conspicuous by throwing dust
from the red ground over them.   Sometimes, even though the
animals themselves may be invisible, a little cloud of red dust
may every now and then be seen, like a puff of smoke, issuing
from the bush.   In the present instance we were inspired with
hope by making out the raddled heads and slowly flapping
enormous ears of two big bulls in the jungle across by the valley.
Worming our way down through the dense thicket, we crossed
the little stream and followed up a little dry gully on the other
side, near which, farther up, one of the elephants (they were
some distance apart) was standing.   I got up to him beautifully,
without his knowing of my approach, as he stood fanning
himself with his windmill sails, as is their wont when resting.
I got a nice shot at his side at close quarters ; but, owing to

only a bit of him being visible and the necessity of making the best of such chances as it is possible to get in such thick cover, I was not able to put the bullet quite so close up behind the shoulder as it should be for an ideal shot.   For an elephant's stomach seems to me to come farther forward towards his chest cavity than does that of most animals ; so that, if the shot is a trifle too far back, not only the heart but the lungs may be easily missed.   However, I felt sure this was not so far aft as to allow the latter organs to escape.   The grunt he gave also sounded confirmatory of my belief, and this was borne out by a little frothy blood on his retreating spoor.   Feeling that he was sure to succumb soon to this wound, and being anxious to go after the second bull (both were huge beasts), I did not follow the spoor of the wounded one beyond a few steps, but, leaving him to be sought for afterwards, turned my attention to his mate.   I may add that I did recover him all right, though not that day.   He was found dead by my Ndorobo friends not far from my camp, straight towards which he had, curiously enough, made.   He had only one tusk.   Single tusks are commonly reported to be usually very large ; but this was no heavier than an ordinary large bull's tooth (weighing 75 lbs.). I examined the skull, and found he never had a second, as there was no socket on the other side.

But to come back to my day's hunt.   My Ndorobo lads were very lukewarm and disinclined to go on, their hearts being with the meat at their kraals ; and, finding the other bull had moved on, it was not without some persuasion that I got them to go on, though I was determined to follow, whether or no. However, they came, and I was glad of it, as they were useful, knowing the country intimately and being somewhat better spoorers and much quicker of hearing (an important qualification) than my own men.   On catching the faintest sound of an elephant blowing, or a slight rustling of branches, they will at once fix the exact place whence the sound, very likely inaudible to other ears, proceeds.   The second bull had gone over the rise bordering the valley on the north, and, on reaching the top, we turned off a little to the right of the spoor to ascend a small koppie. The bush was here too tall and leafy to allow of anything being seen ; but, after listening a little while, my Ndorobo companions heard him. Being too near the wind, we made back and came cautiously up it, after a circuit to the left, instead of following the spoor again. Having arrived near the spot where he had been heard, we waited again for another sign, and so long was it without his making a sound, that we almost came to the conclusion he must have winded us when on the koppie and gone on ; but I persisted in proceeding with the greatest care until we should again cut his spoor, and before we had advanced many steps farther we all heard him blow distinctly quite close ahead. Motioning my attendants to remain there, I picked my steps gingerly on, intensely on the look-out, but could not see him until I got within a very short distance, when a little open track in the bush showed me his huge hind-quarters towards me. This being the only opening to leeward, I came up behind him, and stood within a distance I had time to deliberately calculate to be no more than five paces from his tail. To the right I dared not go, on account of the wind ; to the left the jungle was dense. There was nothing for it but to wait.

Now there is a curious contrast in the aspect at close quarters presented respectively by the two ends of an elephant, apart from the obvious difference in the moral effect on the hunter according to which extremity is towards him. When viewed from the rear there is a comically clownish, baggy-breeched, knock-kneed look about his drooping hinder parts ; while a front view of his majestic head, armed with gleaming tusks and furnished with a far-reaching supple trunk, and set off by the grotesque great ears, outstretched as if to catch any suspicious sound—all raised aloft on colossal fore quarters, so that the top of his massive forehead may be not less than 11 feet from the ground—is as singularly impressive and awe-inspiring.   I had now an opportunity of observing these two effects.   The wind died away as I waited, hoping he would move of his own accord so as to give me a chance to shoot.   I silently plucked a bit of grass ; the fragments floated down with a tendency very near his direction.   Sure enough just after he got a whiff ; for he suddenly moved forward three or four yards across a little bare space ahead of him, wheeled round and stood facing diagonally half towards me, his head up, trunk raised and ears out, all on the alert, the opposite of his previous sleepy attitude.   I knew he would be off now, so instantly aimed at his chest, in front of his left shoulder, which was towards me, and pulled both triggers together.   I had made up my mind to try this the next chance I got at one of these huge bulls, after failing to stop the one that morning. The gun gave me a smart kick in the face, but the elephant went off with very suggestive grunts and I felt I had given him a good shot.   Following his track, we found a good deal of blood spattered about, and a very short way on one of my Ndorobo lads (who had come up with my gun-bearers after the shot) started to run for it, a sure sign he had caught sight of our elephant.

Advancing cautiously, I found him (the elephant) standing in a fairly open bit of straight path.   His position being just what it had been (as regards me) when I first fired at him, I gave him another similar shot, though only one barrel this time.   He did not move, except to slue a little more directly facing me.   I was considering whether to give him the left barrel in his eye, his head being a little inclined to one side, and for that purpose took another step forward, when—this movement of mine having no doubt enabled him to make me out—he suddenly rushed at me. As there were not more than ten yards between us and he came straight for me at a quick run, there was no time for hesitation.   There was luckily a little opening to my right ; into this I slipped, crouching to be less readily noticed.

" Squareface " was just behind me, and the elephant charged past me after him like a locomotive. He followed my example and dodged to one side into the bush, leaving Juma, who was clad in raiment " by way of being " white, in full view just in front of the enraged beast. (I never had to complain of my gun-carriers decamping in moments of emergency, as one so often hears travellers say their men do ; on the contrary, I had oftener to reprove them for persisting in sticking close behind me, when I wanted to go on alone.) Juma, it afterwards turned out, foolishly ran straight along the path we had approached by, the bull within a few yards of him ; but instantly the latter passed my retreat, I, having an eye over my shoulder and being only two or three yards off, had swung round and given him my left barrel in his ribs before he had got many yards beyond me. This, it would seem, changed his mind, or else his powers were becoming exhausted, for he turned back and retreated to a little farther than where he had stood before.

My men now came back to me, and I made Juma climb a little tree. He saw the bull, only some thirty yards off, standing in the jungle. I felt I must do something, but did not think myself bound to advance hurriedly upon him again in his present frame of mind, being sure he was dying. So I climbed the tree, in spite of thorns ; but these were straight, and, being so much accustomed to the villainous hooked kind, one gets to despise such as comparatively harmless. Getting near its slender top, I could see the elephant staggering ; and, while I looked, his hind legs gave ; he backed into the curious sitting posture they often fall into when about to collapse ; his head went up, and, throwing his trunk into the air, as it were in sign of defeat, he went over with a crash, and, after a few struggles, lay still. Going cautiously up, I found him dead. Another massive beast, hardly so colossal as the last, but with rather heavier ivory (84 lbs. and 70 lbs.). His back was not so rough as that of the other, and he was fatter; perhaps a somewhat younger animal. My three bullet-holes formed a triangle on his chest; two went through the heart.

By this time I and these artless Ndorobo savages had become fast friends, as was natural under the circumstances. We were mutually useful to each other; they showed me where to find elephants, and, when I killed any, they grew fat on the meat, and laid up stores of dried strips of flesh and of fat boiled out of the bones. Superstitious, like all Africans, it is not to be wondered at that they gave me credit for possessing something in the nature of magic, to aid me in the chase. I think my field-glasses may have added to the impression. I remember one day in particular, when, accompanied by two of them, I had made a long round over the foot-hills of the Lorogis, near where the Seya River comes through the southern extremity of the range, and, having failed to find any fresh indications of the presence of elephants in the neighbourhood, we were just about to give up the quest. Standing on a spur of the mountain, I was scanning the wide expanse of jungle, that stretched below us, with my glasses, when, by the greatest luck, I happened to catch a glimpse of some reddish objects, passing a slight gap among the trees, a couple of miles away. I knew these could be nothing but dusted elephants. No one else had seen them, and I could tell by their manner that my guides of the day, who had not hunted with me before, were incredulous. On reaching the part where I had seen the elephants, we could at first find no signs; and their smiles plainly told that the Ndorobos did not believe there were any in the neighbourhood. But I was confident I had not been mistaken, and determined to persevere. We had not gone quite far enough, it proved, and a little more search brought us to their fresh spoor in the dusty soil. The change in my friends' demeanour was marked, and as that was the occasion (already casually referred to) when I killed three, the feasting which ensued served to impress the inci dent on their memories and establish their confidence in my powers.

Among those of El Bogoi, Lesiat was the leading man and my especial confederate. I think an Ndorobo becomes the head of a community by being a slayer of elephants, etc., his following increasing in proportion to his success in the chase.

Lesiat had for long been bothering me to give him a charm to increase his power in this pursuit. My assurances that I had no such occult powers merely made him the more importunate. He regarded my objections as a refusal to help him, and a proof of unfriendliness to him. When I was about to leave he became more pressing, promised to keep ivory for me against my return, as an acknowledgment, should I consent, and assumed a hurt air at what he regarded as my unkind obstinacy. Squareface interceded for him, explaining to me that Swahilis always accede to such requests, the most approved charm being a verse of the Koran, written in Arabic on a slip of paper. Not wishing to appear unfeeling, and seeing that no harm could come of it at all events, it occurred to me that a line or two of Shakespeare would probably be quite as effective. Bearing in mind that the Ndorobo hunter owes his success—when he has any—mainly to the powerful poison with which his weapon is smeared, if he can only manage to introduce it, in the proper manner, into the animal's economy, it struck me that the following quotation would be appropriate ; and I accordingly wrote it on a slip of paper, illustrating it with a little sketch of an elephant :—

> I bought an unction of a mountebank,
> So mortal that, but dip a knife in it,
> Where it draws blood no cataplasm so rare,
> Collected from all simples that have virtue
> Under the moon, can save the thing from death
> That is but scratched withal ; I'll touch my point
> With this contagion, that, if I gall him slightly,
> It may be death.

In presenting this to Lesiat, I impressed upon him that the most I could hope to do was to give more power to his elbow. I disclaimed all pretensions to make an elephant-slayer of a duffer. Confidence, I told him, was the main thing, and particularly enjoined upon him the importance of getting close before striking. On my starting for the coast, we parted with mutual expressions of goodwill, and he most earnestly wished me God-speed and a safe return.

The men I had sent for, to Laiju, had not returned by the time I wanted to start, and I had to send fresh messengers after them. In the meantime we moved the ivory, etc., across the Seya, making several journeys, and camped at a large rock pool. We were nearly out of meal, and depending on meat alone for food, so the non-arrival of the expected porters caused me some anxiety. I had just made provision for some time by shooting two rhinos one morning, when the men arrived. They brought bad news. On the return journey of the party which had brought my last supply of meal, its members had disregarded my instructions, which were, first, to keep together, and secondly, to avoid passing through Embe, unless escorted by some of my Mthara friends—for I distrusted the natives of the former district. They had, instead, made a short cut over the hills, leaving Mthara to the right, had straggled about in twos and threes—or even one man alone—with the result that four had been murdered. The Embe people seemed to have imagined that some disaster must have overtaken us, that I was dead, and that these scattered remnants of the caravan—as they supposed them— would be an easy prey. This was a sad damper to my spirits, and I felt that I had a difficult and distasteful task imposed on me by this misfortune : come what might, it would be my duty to endeavour to avenge the murder of my men before returning to the coast. As for their companions, their grief was short-lived. When a comrade is killed, porters are dismayed at first, and appear overcome with dejection. The day after, they regain their spirits, and the camp is as cheerful as ever. "Amri ya Muungu" (It is God's will).

Leaving our up route far to the left, we made for the Gwaso Nyiro River, and followed it down for several days, till we reached where we had first struck it before. But I thought it advisable to cross higher up, as we were getting heavy rain nearly every afternoon or night, and I feared it might rise. It is always pleasant travelling along the banks of a river, and there are some particularly pretty bits on this one. One generally finds a shady grove to camp in on the banks; and an unlimited supply of fresh, running water is such a comfort. Game, too, is seldom scarce, and I was able to keep up the meat-supply pretty regularly. I saw one marvellous herd of giraffe, covering, in scattered formation, a whole ridge; I also noticed some fifteen eland in a troop (a rare sight since the cattle plague), and other game was pretty plentiful. Lions were often heard at night, but I never came across any. Speaking of giraffe, I saw one day what I had never before had the opportunity of observing in all my experience, whether in South or Central Africa; namely, several lying down. I had a good view of the herd through my glasses, and saw two of them get up. The last I watched for some time lying, before it rose, and distinctly saw it get upon its legs—first on to its knees, then its hind-quarters rose, and lastly its fore legs were made erect. I think this must be an uncommon sight, in the case of wild giraffes, because the natives with whom I have hunted them in South-East Africa declare that they never do lie down, and have a fiction that a giraffe sleeps standing, with its head in the fork of a tree. This attitude of repose I have certainly never seen; but I have noticed, when a herd is resting on an open ridge in the heat of the day, some of them standing drowsily with their heads lowered, the long necks bent over like a bow. I am told that in the "Zoo" they lie down every night; but then they know they are safe from lions there. It was on the banks of the Gwaso Nyiro, during

this journey, that I shot my record impala head, of which a
figure is given from a photograph.

One or two rhinos that I shot for meat on this journey were
in poor condition. Papa said it was because of the rain :
probably he was right. I daresay wet weather makes them
lean, as it does wild
pigs. In a part of
Swaziland where
wild pigs used to be
numerous, the Swazis
always accounted for
their being fat only
during the dry winter
there, by saying that
the fright, caused by
the thunder accom-
panying the summer
rains, made them thin.

Through crossing
the river high up we
got sooner among
the lava (which has
run down from Kenia
and Jambeni thus far,
while there is none
on the north bank),
and had the rough
ridges of its broken-
up streams to cross,

THE RECORD PALLAH HORNS.
(*Æpyceros melampus.*)

Length of horns on front curve	.	28 in.
Tip to tip	.	22¾ ,,
Girth	..	5¾ ,,

with wide plains of lava shingle between.

Here, as I have noted in other parts, alternate green and
dry belts were crossed ; the storms following particular lines
and painting the country in streaks. But on rounding the
point of the Jambeni Range it became apparent that a much
wetter climate had been suddenly reached. The sodden ground

and verdant vegetation proved much rain to have fallen, and
the heavy and frequent showers made the shelter of our huts
at the Laiju "boma" welcome.   Cloudy nights had been inconvenient, too, in another way.   My watch had gone wrong
ever since I had been so foolish as to exhibit its works to some
natives in Embc, and I had to time my getting up by the stars.
When they were invisible I could only guess, and sometimes I
made a bad shot and called the safari too soon, with uncomfortable results.   These were the early or lesser rains,—always to
be expected about that time of year.   We entered the " boma "
on 15th November, and were accorded an enthusiastic reception, with much drumming and many congratulations, by those
in charge.

CHAPTER VI

RETURN TO MOMBASA

My new Lee-Metford—Advantage of solid bullet—Observations on rhinos—A white companion—Bag a "Roi rhébok"—A punitive expedition—A land of plenty —Our Christmas camp—Tribes round Mount Kenia—A playful escapade—Stung by hornets—A tribe on the war-path—A solitary wanderer—Sport and science—Return to Mombasa—A pleasant change—Organise a new caravan—An earthquake shock.

A few days' rest in a cool and rain-proof shed, with such luxuries as fresh vegetables and baked bananas, was enjoyable. The surroundings, too, were pleasanter than formerly, the young grass being now short and green. Flowers—among them many pretty ground orchids—were not yet choked in rank herbage, and my boy could always procure a handsome variety to adorn my humble table.

My messengers were back from Mombasa with mails, etc., and what was of even more interest to me—a new rifle. This was an ordinary service Lee-Metford (mark IV.). I shall have more to say about this weapon later on. At first I could not make very good shooting with it ; for, besides having to become accustomed to its unfamiliar handling, it needed an emphatically "long pull and a strong pull" to fire it ; so long indeed, that I had sometimes, after feeling the trigger come an appreciable way, to start afresh before it would go off.[1] Moreover, it was awkward in the bush, as the least touch of a branch against

---

[1] On my return to Mombasa, before starting on my next expedition, I was able, through the kindness of a naval officer, to get this defect remedied.

the prominent bolt was sufficient to make the breech fly open. Nevertheless, I soon found that its shooting powers were marvellous, and I was, from the first, particularly successful with it against rhinoceroses, of which I killed several—mostly with a single bullet each—during the remainder of this trip, none of which ran more than a couple of hundred yards after receiving the shot.

Up to this time all my elephant and rhino shooting had been done with my double .577. I had been laughed at by many for starting on such a hunting trip with no larger rifle, but I always was an advocate of small bores, and I am bound to say that I believe I used fewer cartridges for the number of elephants killed with this weapon than any other I have ever tried. Since I got that rifle (a good many years ago) many changes and improvements have been made, both in firearms and ammunition ; I may say, however,—without presuming to lay down any rule for others,—that my experience, with regard to bullets, is decidedly in favour of solid, as compared with any (what I should call) fancy projectiles. Steel cores or points are unsatisfactory : the lead invariably strips in passing through any bone—even a rib,—leaving the light steel with little remaining momentum. Of course you can kill game with almost anything, when you get a favourable chance and make the most of it. I remember a native in South Africa showing me a rough, cylindrical piece of iron, of his own forging, with which he had killed several head of game, including buffalo. It fitted loosely into his gun—an old musket.

In view of the conflicting opinions one meets with on the subject of rhinos, perhaps the result of my observations may be worth adding here, towards their explanation. I believe that, as a general rule, the rhinoceros, like all wild animals, runs away from man when he can. Here and there an individual may be met with, which, under certain circumstances, will charge (and I think the circumstances have more to do with it than the individual), apparently without cause. When these animals are numerous, che chances of coming across a cantankerous specimen are of course increased in proportion ; and a large caravan is, I think, far more likely to give rise to the aggravating conditions than a few people passing would be. I imagine that, when a rhino is anxious to escape, a long string of porters is apt to give it the idea of being surrounded ; but there is no doubt that, apart from this, one is occasionally liable to be charged.   I have myself nowhere met with them in large numbers ; four is the most I have ever seen in one party, and about ten during a long day's hunt would be the limit seen in any one day, and that rarely.   Generally speaking, this kind of game is scattered thinly, in parties of two or three or singly, over the country ; but under certain conditions, such as scarcity of water, they may be collected in particular localities.

I have taken particular notice of their behaviour in every instance among the many opportunities I have had, and I have come to the conclusion that they never charge from scent, but only from sight.   My experience is that a rhino invariably runs away on winding human beings (as, I believe, generally speaking, do all animals).   I have very many times passed close to these creatures, and sometimes had to shout at them to make them get out of the way.   That they are excessively stupid there can be no doubt ; and I think it is partly their very stupidity that sometimes leads them to make an attack, through not realising what the intruder really is ; for they will on occasion go for any strange object that may approach them, —as, for instance, I have seen a large stone charged, which one of my men had thrown at a rhino that would not get out of our way.   A cow with a calf is, as might be expected, more likely to prove vicious than another.   I do not believe that they differ in disposition in different localities, nor do I believe that there is more than one species of (so-called) black rhinoceros in Africa.

As Mr. Selous demonstrated long ago, all the different patterns of horns may be found in the same district, and

I have myself shot a pair of which the female had the second horn much longer than the front one, while her mate carried the ordinary kind. I do not say that the animals may not vary slightly in size or shade of colour of the skin according to the country they inhabit, just as some species of antelopes (such as the bushbuck and, to a less extent, the duiker) have types agreeing with the character of their surroundings ; but length of horn is no more a distinction than long or short hair among ourselves. I merely record the conclusions I have arrived at as the result of my own personal experience, and as perhaps helping to explain the different opinions expressed by other travellers ; my own being that, take him all in all, there is no occasion to stand in much awe of " the armed rhinoceros."

There is one other observation that may be worth noting ; namely, as to the voice of this curious, old-fashioned-looking creature, as I have not seen it alluded to. As far as I know, there are three sounds which a rhino can make. When disturbed, he makes a snorting like a steam-engine as he runs. Sometimes a mortally wounded rhino cries, when dying ; the cry is in a high key, but hardly shrill enough to be called a squeal. The third is the natural call, used, I suppose, to its mate. This I have heard only at night, when all was still in camp. It seems to me most to resemble the bubbling of a camel, only in a lower key ; it also sometimes reminds one somewhat of the amorous grunting of impala rams. At one of my hunting-camps, which was in the midst of thick bush where rhinos were numerous, I heard it frequently. Rhinos are also found in very open country in Central Africa, and may often be seen apparently grazing ; though closer observation shows that it is not the grass itself, but certain plants among it, which they eat.

Among other news that awaited me on my return to Laiju I learned that a German gentleman (Dr. Kolb) was at the Tana unable to proceed owing to difficulties with his caravan, and the

insufficient number of men that remained with him.   I accordingly sent to invite him to join me here, which he was glad to
do, after having crossed the river, swollen by the rains, in a
canoe he had most cleverly constructed by covering a framework of wattles with the canvas " fly " of his tent.

He had, he told me, been a member of the abortive Freeland
Expedition ; and on the collapse of that chimerical scheme had
determined to see something of the country for himself.   As I
intended making another excursion to the foot of Kenia, which
he was anxious to see, and could be of some assistance to him
through my knowledge of the country and natives, while it
would not be safe for him to go on alone with so few men, and
those imperfectly armed (all mine had Snider carbines), it was
arranged that he should accompany me.   I, on the other hand,
should be glad of his companionship ; and, having explained
to him that the wanton murder of four of my men by the
natives of Embe imposed on me the duty of teaching that
tribe a lesson, he volunteered to help me, and his assistance in
that rather ticklish business was of the greatest value to me,
a white man being, under such circumstances, a host in himself
in Central Africa.

Owing to continued wet it was three weeks from the time
of my return before we got off once more.   I occupied myself
pleasantly during the fine portions of these days of detention
in butterfly-hunting, for which Laiju is a good locality.   And
altogether I think we both rather enjoyed the delay.

Just above the " boma " was one of the small crater koppies
already spoken of as occurring on both sides of the range.   I
had several times seen two or three " roi rhéboks " on this hill
—a buck with which I had been familiar in South Africa,
particularly in the Lobombo district of Zululand, where it is
plentiful—but foolishly had not attempted to obtain a specimen,
supposing it to be identical with the southern species, though
I had never noticed any before in Central Africa.   But one
day, while we were there together, one showed itself on the

slope above, and Dr. Kolb shot it from just outside the "boma."
I did not even then notice any difference in it from the "roi
rhéboks" of the south, but I have since learned that a specimen
which Mr. Chanler had taken home has been deemed new, and
named after him. But the curious thing about this buck is
that I have never seen it anywhere but on that particular
isolated crater koppie, and the natives there said there were
none elsewhere, as far as they knew. I do not assert that
there are none on any of the other hills, but it is a strange
thing that I never came across any, and they must, at all events,
be very rare.

Fortunately for us, we had not much more rain after we
started, and the moon, being at the full, was favourable to our
somewhat hazardous undertaking. It sounds presumptuous
to talk of going among a tribe numbering thousands with a
handful of men to exact retribution, but it is not to be shirked
if the country is to be safe for us, and I always aim at leaving
it so for the next traveller. The method we adopted to chastise
the inhabitants of the district where my men had been killed
was to seize a number of their sheep and goats, and these we
slaughtered and left in a heap among their burnt kraals. I
suggested this because I did not want them to think that
raiding, for the sake of plunder, was any part of our object,
though two or three cows and a few donkeys which we captured
we thought ourselves justified in keeping. They made no
determined attack upon us, thanks, I fancy, mainly to the awe
the wonderful powers of our long-range rifles inspired ; for we
could easily disperse any threatening body of warriors, collected
anywhere within sight, by firing one or two shots. The night
was an anxious and sleepless time ; but having taken every
possible precaution, it passed without any attempt to rush us.
In the morning we descended by a difficult defile, not without
dread of ambuscades, but not a native showed himself, and, the
day after, we camped at Mthara.

The result of this action showed I was right. After this,

my men could pass safely through the district, the guns and other trifles that had been taken from the murdered men were returned, and the "elders" sued for peace. I have already described this land of plenty. It was, at the time of this visit, being devastated by locusts; but so prolific is the soil that famine seems almost impossible. Every few months fresh crops of grain and beans ripen, while bananas, yams, and sweet potatoes are always in season. It is worth noticing that in districts where bananas are the staple food, the inhabitants do not depend on the ripe fruit, but cook the green bananas, either by steaming or roasting in the fire. No doubt coffee would flourish, too, in these fertile hills, though the natives have none there. This hill district is only of small extent; a man can walk through the whole extent of it, from Laiju on the one side to Mthara on the other, between sunrise and sunset.

I will not give a detailed account of this excursion, but, as we visited some country I had not before reached, a few remarks may not be altogether uninteresting.

We stayed a few days at what I called my "ivory camp" (the one under the wide-spreading tree). It was now made less comfortable by swarms of caterpillars, which dropped upon us with painfully irritating effect upon our skins. Dr. Kolb, especially, suffered much from this cause, being, as a newcomer, more susceptible to the poison than myself. Here I had the honour of introducing my companion to my esteemed brother Ndaminuki, and to the rhino, an animal whose acquaintance he had not yet made. He had shot hippos in the Tana, but felt rather desponding about his chances of bagging a "faro" (Swahili for rhino). However, I promised him he should have that satisfaction, and my pledge was fulfilled the first time he went out with me. After that he shot many. He was, I believe, a first-rate shot, though somewhat hampered in the bush by the necessity of wearing spectacles.

We spent our Christmas at the foot of Kenia, in sight, at all events, of snow, and had frequent splendid views of the great mountain under varying conditions.   One phenomenon puzzled me.   I have often noticed Kenia quite clear, while the much lower neighbouring range of Jambeni would be capped with cloud.

The entry in my diary, under date 25th December 1894, is as follows :—" I don't feel quite sure that this is really Christmas Day, though Kolb is confident his dates are right (there had

SUMMIT OF MOUNT KENIA.

(From a Photograph by Dr. KOLB.)

been a difference in our reckonings).   However, we kept it.   I made a 'duff' of the dark-coloured meal of the country, suet, and raisins, and it turned out better than I expected.   The roast beef (a baron of veal) was first-rate.   In the afternoon I set a gun for the 'fisi' (hyenas), which had made last night hideous with their bad language over the skull of Kolb's rhino. This gave us a little occupation, and considerable amusement in the evening, when it went off in the middle of a useful dinner, and we went out, between the courses, to find a hyena dead in front of the gun, it having acted perfectly. Another shot itself before I went to sleep. Before morning it went off a third time, but without result, as the bait had got loose. I have spent many much less contented Christmases. We gave our men a young bull, all to themselves, to celebrate the festival."

From here we moved farther round the base of the mountain towards the south-east, and ascended, before camping, to a height of perhaps 8000 or 9000 feet. Our camp here was above all the settlements and slightly below the untouched forest, and commanded an extensive view over the country below. Between Jambeni and Kenia is a broad valley, fertile and abundantly watered. I saw a good deal at one time and another of this part, as well as that about the foot of Kenia on its eastern and north-eastern sides. The lower slopes were probably all forest once, but much has been cleared, and a large proportion of the land is cultivated by the natives, who are numerous here, the tribes being those of Mnyithu and Katheri. All these people are akin to those of Kikuyu. But there is also a clan of Wakwavi (a branch of the Masai), living alongside of Katheri, and a community of Ndorobos, too ; thus three distinct races with different customs live side by side. The people of Katheri cultivate, and also own some stock ; the Wakwavi are purely pastoral ; while the Ndorobos (a very inferior sample of the race) live on what they can pick up in the forest or cadge from their neighbours, who tolerate them on the strength of an occasional tusk of ivory they may now and again get out of them.

These Wakwavi, who still own considerable herds of cattle, live in great dread of the Masai of Ndoro, on the western side of Kenia. Like many other tribes with whom I have made friendly leagues at different times, they now wanted us, after becoming their " brothers " by their own desire, to aid them in a war on their enemies ; but this invitation we of course declined, as is my invariable rule. I always explained, when importuned in this way, that I had come to shoot elephants, not men ; and that until attacked, or unless my friends should be so while I was with them, I desired peace with all.

There is nothing in the shape of a plateau, such as one sometimes reads of, at the foot of Kenia, though it has a broad base and the slopes are on a gentle gradient. Between the cultivation and the virgin forest is some beautiful pasture land, where the timber has evidently been cleared and the land cultivated and afterwards abandoned. It was here that we made our camp for about a week. Numerous little streams, cold and limpid, run down between the undulations. This is a charming bit of country ; but I could not keep warm at night, do what I would. Hoar frost was on the grass every morning, and the wood, though abundant, would not burn. The forest is very beautiful, and contains many fine timber trees. The trunk of one that I measured girthed about 15 feet and was straight as a dart for at least 60 feet. It was here that I met with the very handsome monkey with a white collar, which, it appears, has been named *Cercopithecus albotorquatus*, from a specimen the locality of which was unknown. A large yellow monkey, which I had seen on the slopes above our Christmas camp, but of which I was unable to obtain a specimen, seemed quite different from any I had ever met with, and may probably be new. To these latter I was attracted by their peculiar, rather musical, hooting cry— reminding me somewhat of the call (distinct from its bark) of the wild dog ;—but I failed to get a shot at one. In the forest were, as usual in such localities, many scarlet-winged plantain-eaters and big black and white hornbills. A pair of the latter had their nest in a hole high up the trunk of a large tree close to our camp. The male used to feed his mate (which must have been sitting) through the aperture —at least that is how I construed their behaviour. Among many rare butterflies that I obtained here, Miss Bowdler

Sharpe (who arranged my collection for me) found one quite new species.

We had no difficulties with the natives, and entered into friendly relations by " eating blood " with most of the tribes we passed through—indeed I and my African brothers form quite a good-sized family altogether, and Dr. Kolb, I think, could say the same.   But one night things looked decidedly threatening.

DR. KOLB MAKING BLOOD-BROTHERHOOD WITH WAKWAVI OF KATHERI.

Just as we were going to sleep, an old " brother " of ours came into camp and warned us that he had discovered that there was a plot to attack us during the night ; and no sooner had we heard this rather disturbing news than an arrow, freshly smeared with poison, was shot into our camp.   Immediately after—extra sentries having been posted and precautions taken —an unfortunate porter, who had foolishly gone outside without telling any one, was shot by one of the guards and died in half an hour.   We despatched the ancient relative, who had given us timely warning, to summon another "brother" who lived close by ; he came at once, and shared our watch.   There was, however, no further disturbance of the peace, and the whole alarm may have been caused by nothing more than the playful escapade of some young bloods having their little joke.   It was enough, though, to cause us another of those watchful and anxious nights which are so unpleasant, but we did not consider it of sufficient importance to interrupt the friendly relations existing between us and our neighbours, in spite of the affair having indirectly caused the death of one of our porters.

I found the same difficulty as before in getting at the Kenia elephants, and had no success with them ; in fact I only once even saw one ; and ivory I had been told of, and which I had hoped to buy, turned out a myth ; so we decided to keep on towards the Tana instead of returning by the way we had come.   Passing first through the populous and fertile valley already mentioned, we then struck for the river.   After getting out of the undulating country, where the ground was nearly all under cultivation—magnificent crops of millet just then ripening (the locusts having disappeared)—we descended gradually to the level uninhabited tract below.   We had now left the paths behind us, and our progress became more arduous, particularly on the steep sides of the ridges, owing to the long and thick grass.   While going down the slopes, the doctor came in contact with a hornet's nest—a paper-like construction attached to a spray—and we were both badly stung.   Being a hardened old stager, the pain soon passed off in my case, as on many similar occasions, but my friend's system, fresh from Europe, resented the poison, and he suffered considerably for some time, the parts swelling a good deal.

Getting away from the hills, at the foot of which are some beautiful bits of forest, we entered, first, open plains covered with rank grass, with here and there patches of wood—a land of many streams and dotted with pools and swamps (the leakage of the mountain and hills).   Game was plentiful here :

herds of the smaller zebra, numerous waterbucks, and many rhinos. I also saw a troop of Coke's hartebeeste, and in the larger pools were hippos.

On the way we fell in with a raiding party of some two hundred young warriors from Embe, on a kidnapping expedition, bound for Thaka (a district a little higher up the Tana). Their idea of "the war-path" is to carry off any women and children they may be able to surprise in outlying "shambas." They were very civil and respectful to us, and went about their business when I told them we preferred having nothing to do with them under the circumstances.

Farther on the country became gradually more bushy as we got nearer the river, till the thick Tana scrub was reached.

While Dr. Kolb went on to shoot hippos, I halted where I had seen a little elephant spoor. I found a single bull, which I killed. He was a solitary wanderer of the "herd-bull" type: his tusks—long and handsome, but thin—weighed 49 lbs. and 44 lbs. respectively, one being considerably thicker at the base than its fellow. Probably he had been ousted by a rival from the harem, and was sulking by himself. He was in poor condition and had two sores on his back. I was very pleased with this stroke of good luck, after so long an interval, and wrote in my diary: "This was a glorious bit of exciting success. Nothing in the world can touch the glow of satisfaction on flooring a fine elephant."

On reaching the river I found the doctor enjoying himself vastly among the hippos. He had been combining sport with scientific research, and, on coming across to see me, produced from his pocket a little red hippopotamus he had just acquired, about the size of a guinea-pig, in which he was deeply interested.

As I could find no signs of any more elephants, and had made up my mind to visit the coast, sell what ivory I had, and reorganise my caravan for another expedition, I returned to Laiju to make my arrangements. I had all my goods transported back to the outside kraals of Ukambani, across the

Tana, where I left them in charge of a civil and intelligent headman named Mtiya, and made the best of my way to Mombasa with a few men carrying my personal baggage ; leaving Abdulla—now promoted to be headman and in whom I had perfect confidence—to follow with the ivory.[1]

AUTHOR'S IVORY CARAVAN ARRIVING.
(From a Photograph by Mr. J. R. W. PIGOTT.)

I arrived at the beginning of March 1895, after an absence of fourteen months, the caravan getting in nearly a fortnight later.

[1] I had to bid adieu to Dr. Kolb, who was not returning direct to the coast just then.   He subsequently made another journey from Mombasa to Mount Kenia, when he succeeded in ascending the mountain, and did much careful geographical work in its neighbourhood.   An interesting account of this expedition has been published in Dr. A. Petermann's *Mitteilungen* (42. Band, 1896).

The two and a half months which I spent in Mombasa, now, were a pleasant change to me ; change of diet, manner of life, and surroundings, with the opportunity of speaking my native language and enjoying the hospitality of kind friends. But it was not an idle time, far from it, nor was the work of reorganising my caravan uninteresting to me, though I fear it would be so to the reader were I to go into many details about buying and packing the few goods I needed.   Beads were the

AUTHOR'S PORTERS DEPOSITING HIS TUSKS AT CUSTOM-HOUSE.
(From a Photograph by Mr. J. R. W. PIGOTT.)

principal item, as medium for barter in the interior, our small change in fact ; while, for myself, an ample supply of tea, salt, and soap were almost the only groceries I took.

Most of my best porters "wrote on" again, and the few new ones engaged were all accredited as first-class men : my servants were the same as before.   I kept down the number this time to thirty-five, all told.   It was a little party to start with, for so long a journey, and of course its weakness involved a certain amount of risk.   Formerly I had imagined a much larger number indispensable, and have heard even two hundred spoken of as insufficient to ensure safety ; but in neither of the instances in which I had come to blows with natives, during the last trip, had I more than about the number above mentioned (between thirty and forty) with me.   One can do a good deal with thirty-five good men armed with Sniders in Central Africa. Besides, I preferred the risk of hostilities to that of starvation ; and, as I had determined to reach Rudolph this time and knew the immense stretch of barren, foodless country I should have to pass through, but could not tell how long it might take to traverse, I felt it to be most important to keep the number of mouths to be fed in the wilderness within the narrowest possible limits.

One of the first steps to be taken was to procure a fresh troop of good donkeys.   For this purpose I sent Abdulla to the neighbourhood of Pangani, and he was successful in buying me a very useful lot.   Another most important question was that of pack-saddles.   On my former journey I had used a kind similar to those in vogue among gold prospectors in South Africa.   I had noticed that Swahili donkeys always had sore backs, and blamed the method of packing.   I now found that the Arab " sogi," which they use, is much better adapted to the purpose than any hard frame.   It is a kind of soft panniers, resting on a large pad.   Through the kindness of the officers of a steamer that happened to be undergoing repair in the port, I was able to get some canvas ones made ; and so well sewn and satisfactory were they that they lasted the whole trip, and returned, much patched, through damage caused by thorns and rocks, to the coast.   I found that with proper care, and attention to the pads and the packing of the animals, there was no reason why they should get sore backs at all : mine never did. It is only the carelessness and want of feeling of Swahilis that causes these in their animals, through their neglect to take the trouble needed to keep the gear in proper order, added often to cruel overloading.   I have witnessed the most revolting

AUCTION SALE OF AUTHOR'S IVORY IN MOMBASA CUSTOM-HOUSE.

sights of this kind ; donkeys with horrible, reeking sores, penetrating to the backbone and even full of maggots, still made to carry loads.

Fortunately I was in Mombasa just during the wettest part of the rainy season, so that I avoided the inconvenience of travelling during its continuance. My preparations were finally completed on 13th May ; but, just as I was starting off the caravan on the morning of the 14th, it came on to rain heavily, and the loads had to be brought in again and our departure put off. At daybreak the next morning (about 5.30 of the 15th), before it was fully light, there was a severe shock of earthquake, followed by several slighter ones. I ran out into the street and saw my neighbours opposite and next door— missionaries with their wives—just coming out of their doors. It was a curious and rather amusing situation, meeting thus in deshabille in the street at so early an hour, and somewhat embarrassing to a shy man, as the sensation had been too impressive and suggestive of catastrophe to allow of even ladies waiting for the exigencies of the toilet. Fortunately no serious damage was done, though many walls were cracked. Rain came on again and prevented my starting yet another day ; but on the 16th we got off in good time.

CHAPTER VII

SECOND EXPEDITION

A CHANGE had been made in the rifles with which I was
equipped for this trip. Through an accident, my trusty .577
had become crippled, and I had replaced it by a hurriedly procured 10-bore by Holland. I was never in favour of big bores ;
and this one, though doubtless a first-rate weapon of its kind,
convinced me still more that they are a mistake. I had also
(as already mentioned) a Lee-Metford magazine rifle of the
ordinary military pattern, which I, personally, prefer to a
" sporting " stock.

The personnel of the safari being practically the same as
before, every one knew his work, so there was no confusion or
worry ; neither did I have a single desertion, and everything
worked smoothly from the first. I had still my little bitch
" Frolic," and a small fox-terrier pup, which I christened " Pice,"
had been given me.

On the fourth day out we reached Samburu, and from there,
turning off to the right from the main Uganda path, struck
across for the junction of the Tsavo and Athi rivers. I hate
main roads and was glad to get off this one, though there are

certain drawbacks to be put up with on by-paths, such as their
narrowness and windings, and the overhanging, sometimes
meeting, branches.   The country is similar to that commonly
known as the Taro desert ; an arid, level, scrub-covered tract
with a barren brick-dust soil and very little water.   This part
of the route is impassable in very dry seasons, owing to the
little water there ever is drying up.

It is especially troublesome watering donkeys where water
has to be dug for and scooped out by cupfuls from a hole into
which it trickles slowly ; for, before they are accustomed to
travelling, they are most exasperatingly stupid about drinking,
even when thirsty.   Some will not drink out of a bucket, at
first ; while others, that have lived where water is only in wells,
cannot be induced to drink except out of a utensil of some
sort.   Indeed, I have found, somewhat to my surprise, that
the obtuseness proverbially attributed to the humble ass is not
a libel.

It is curious to watch the change a good drink makes in
thirsty donkeys.   They come down with hanging ears and
hollow sides, looking dejected and thin, not a kick or bray in
the most vicious of them—and what more vicious than a bad-
tempered donkey stallion ?   But as they drink their sides swell
out visibly, and ribs become less prominent.   After about a
bucketful, up goes the head, the ears are pricked, the tail begins
to rise, and your lately limp and inoffensive "punda" begins
to look about quite cheekily again, as who should say, " Now
come on, you beggars ; if I don't make it hot for some of you,
never believe me again."

The distances here are very long, between water and water,
as much as forty miles sometimes, necessitating what is called
"telekeza" (literally "to make to pour in," signifying that
water has to be carried in gourds), which means cooking and
eating before starting, sleeping anywhere, and reaching the
next pool—often horribly foul—some time next day.   This
sort of travelling in such a country—tramping hour after hour

WATERING DONKEYS.

through the dry scrub under a burning sun—is monotonous and hard work. Still the very desert itself has its charms and even its advantages. It cuts off the back country and discourages communication, so that one feels fairly launched into the wilderness almost from the time of leaving the coast.

Of game there is little, as might be expected in so waterless a district. A few Waller's gazelle—an antelope which seems independent of water—may occasionally be seen, and I shot a lesser koodoo—perhaps a wanderer from the Sabaki, my first buck for the trip and welcome for the pot, being excellent meat—while the tiny " paa " (Kirk's antelope) is not uncommon ; I also saw a giraffe. After striking the Sabaki (or Athi, as it is called above its junction with the Tsavo), the path follows the river for three or four days. It is pleasant to get on the banks of this river (for which I always retain an affection) with its green willows and fresh scent, and its wide, though shallow and rather muddy, stream, and to have an unstinted supply of good sweet water. It was an old friend of mine, for I had done some road-cutting here in 1890 for the I.B.E.A. Co. ; and it was a comfort, after the narrow, overhung path we had been traversing, to find mine still quite open, with the exception of a branch here and there or a fallen tree. When I cut this path first, I was told the stumps ought to be dug up ; but, having had some experience in South African road pioneering, I merely cut the trees and bushes close to the ground, and the result proved I was right, for they almost all died ; whereas, had I dug up the soil, it would have had the effect of cultivation to encourage the growth of rank vegetation.

The river runs through the same barren, scrub-covered country—in some parts gravelly ridges, in others sandy flats bordering its banks. There are quartz veins in places, but I could never get a colour of gold, though I have tried. One thing that always strikes me about this country is the scarcity of game ; for even along the banks of the river there is marvellously little—a very few waterbuck at intervals, an

occasional lesser koodoo or two, a little lot of impala, sometimes, at one particular point, and rarely an odd bushbuck, are
all that is seen, without counting the diminutive paa, and now
and again a rhino, giraffe, or hippo spoor.   Formerly there
was a sprinkling of buffalo in small herds ; but these the
cattle plague swept off.   The other game, however, was always
scarce.   It is easy to say that the conditions are not suited to
its requirements—too much scrub and too little grass—but
one cannot help wondering why some species have not become

VULTURINES AND DOG.

adapted to the land.   Here are great stretches of uninhabited
bush country with a perennial river running through it, and
hardly any animals, though plenty of birds and of "fly"
(tetse).

On the Athi are three varieties of guinea-fowl.   Towards
the coast the small, delicate, little crested species, living in
thick bush, is found—the tenderest of all on the table.   In its
middle course large flocks of the large and beautiful vulturine
guinea-fowl are met with ; while higher up again comes the
common horned kind.   The second, though very wild and hard
to get a shot at without a dog, becomes the veriest idiot when

one is present. While one member of the flock is chased, the rest stand in a ruck on the ground close by, gaping with craned necks in stupid amazement at the apparition, and may be mown down for the pot if needed and a shot-gun is used. I once killed thirteen in a few minutes out of a large flock, using nine cartridges. The first shot killed five on the ground, in the manner described ; the rest were picked off in ones and twos from the trees into which they had flown, and where they sat watching my little dog below. But except the very young ones, these handsome birds are not so good for the table as the common sort, though in size and appearance, with their light-blue breasts and pheasant-like tails, they surpass all the other members of the genus.

After crossing and leaving the river, two or three days' march takes us to the commencement of Ukambani, where we join our former path at Ikutha (the German mission). Up to this point (a fortnight's journey) we had to depend upon what we had carried on donkeys from the coast ; but here food may be bought, and, through the kind assistance of my friend Mr. Sauberlich, we readily obtained a good supply.

The first part of Ukambani on this route is but sparsely peopled, and the country is, except where cultivated, for the most part covered with bush and badly watered. As one travels northwards it rises and becomes more open and hilly, and a good deal of it is densely populated. Here we get among granite hills, bare of wood, and even firewood is scarce ; what bush there may in former times have been, having been used up. But water is now plentiful. The Wakamba are an enterprising, but unprepossessing, people. On our way up we had been constantly meeting large parties of them taking cattle, sheep, and goats, and an odd tusk or two of ivory for sale in Mombasa, or returning with the proceeds in the shape of goods. Though peaceable enough in their own country, they are inclined, when not themselves raided by the Masai, to harass their weaker neighbours.

I may here notice the method of carrying burdens adopted by these people. The load is suspended by a strap passing across the forehead, and lies on the back of the bearer, who walks in a stooping attitude. This practice has evidently originated in a bush country, where it is most awkward to get along, under overhanging branches, with a burden on the head (as one sees exemplified in one's own porters' difficulties). On the other hand, close to the coast and in the far interior, where the country is for the most part more open, the natives carry on the head. As might be expected, the consequence is that the Wakamba and kindred races do not hold themselves nearly so well as those tribes who are forced, by their mode of carrying, to stand erect. This stooping attitude, induced by a similar cause, may be observed in parts of Scotland, where the women carry peats in a basket slung on the back.

The Wakamba are most assiduous bee-keepers. Their " bee-tubs " may be seen in the bush at immense distances from their kraals. The big baobabs are favourite trees for the purpose, and their huge, soft trunks have frequently a row of pegs, driven in at intervals, to serve as steps, by which a man may mount to the higher branches. The honey is used to make a kind of mead, on which they commonly get intoxicated. They also make a similar drink of the juice of pounded sugar-cane. The extraction of this syrup is a sort of festival. A party of them, each with a pole, may be seen dancing and singing round a huge mortar, keeping time to the tune by plunging their long pestles alternately into the pulp.

A rather curious custom of the Wakamba women is to take pet lambs or sheep (sometimes two or three) about with them. The object is, I imagine, to fatten these creatures, which follow their owners about while they work in their fields, and find pickings or are given food which they would not get if grazing with the flock. Once I met a little damsel, on the path, followed by three chickens. On meeting me the latter ran into the grass, and it was touching to see their little mistress stop and alternately coax and scold them till they came out and followed her again. I suppose she had no lamb to make a pet of, so she did the best her circumstances would allow to emulate her elders.

In Ukambani the women milk the cows. They do it in an awkward manner, as if cattle-owning was not their natural pursuit. One hand only is used to milk with, while the vessel is held in the other, the operator standing the while. A clumsier method of milking I never saw.

Mtiya's are the last villages of Ukambani towards the Tana, on this route, and some thirty miles south of the river. It is about a month's caravan journey from Mombasa hither; and, having been delayed two or three days to buy food on the road, we did not arrive till 20th June.

I was disappointed, though not surprised, to hear, on reaching Mtiya's, that the Tana was still too full to cross. I determined, however, to go on and camp on its banks myself, while Abdulla remained to buy a large supply of food, to be taken with us whenever we might be able to proceed. I was delayed a week, making "shauris" about market prices and various other matters—all such diplomatic treating is matter of time in Africa—and making all other preparations and arrangements needed in connection with our further progress, before parting with Abdulla. My plan was to have all our loads carried by the porters to the river, while I waited there, in order that, when the time came for crossing, we might get our donkeys through this "fly" belt as quickly as possible.

Having finished sorting and arranging the loads and seen the food trade fairly started and in full swing, I started on for the Tana, on 27th June, with the bulk of the caravan, carrying as many loads as they could take, and left Abdulla with two or three men in charge of the remainder of the goods and the donkeys. From Mtiya's to the river is a good thirty miles, through dense scrub without any water: a tiresome and most uninteresting tramp. We started about 1 P.M. and bivouacked for the night at sundown. In the morning we started on again with the first streaks of dawn, about five o'clock, which was as early as it was possible to proceed, there being no moon; for though the path here is, during the dry season when the river is low, well worn, it was now a good deal overgrown and consequently impracticable in the dark. I went ahead, leaving the caravan to follow at its own pace to the river. On the way I came upon signs showing that a herd of elephants had been about: the trees were broken down in many places, and sometimes the path was obstructed by branches they had thrown down; I noticed, too, that these evidences were of various ages, some quite recent, others older.

When getting towards the river, my little dog "Frolic" chased a troop of baboons in her usual playful way—as I could tell by their cries, though the bush was too thick for me to see—and I heard her give a yelp. She then came running back to me, and I found she had been severely bitten in the neck, at which I felt much indignation. But, though my poor little favourite seemed dejected, I thought the wounds were only skin deep, at first.

I got to the river by ten o'clock, and, turning off to the right through some little open flats bordering the banks, was making for a nice spot I knew of a little farther down, where was a shady tree to camp under, when I met a wart-hog sow with a nearly grown-up family, and had just time to give her a shot as she was starting to make off, knocking her over. One of the young ones came back towards me, quite close up; but I let them alone, as I had more than enough meat for my own larder in the one I had shot, and, as my men would not eat pig, I had no use for more.

The Tana is at this point divided by several islands (one or two of them of some extent) into a number of channels.

The principal of these is a roaring rapid, and never fordable ; but, when the river is low, it can be spanned by a rough bridge (or rather two bridges) of poles, at a point where its waters—confined in a narrow trough—rush down as a foaming cataract between opposing rocks. The other channels may then be forded. The water was now surging over these rocky buttresses, and far too high to permit of bridging, even if the other channels could have been afterwards crossed.

Having shown my gun-bearers where to pitch my tent by the tree in the small open flat with nice short grass, I went down to the river-bank to try to secure some meat for my party, as I knew there were always hippos close by. I shot a small one, which, on getting the bullet under the ear, dropped its ears for a second and then rolled over twice, feet in the air. But we never found it, the river being too full and the current too strong to allow the carcase to remain where shot until it would float. I noticed that elephants had been drinking quite lately (within a few days) near my camp. The vicinity smelt quite strongly of waterbuck, a small party of which I knew well by experience always frequented these little grassy flats. Different kinds of game have their distinctive odours, and one may often be warned by scent of the neighbourhood of certain animals : waterbuck are among the most perfumed ; so are giraffes, particularly the bulls. In the afternoon a rhino came close to camp, but it had made off by the time I could get hold of a rifle.

My men were all in by about one o'clock. No fear of them dawdling more than they could help until reaching the water. After a long, dry march like this, I always send my attendants back, carrying water, to meet the caravan and give the thirsty porters a drink.

The next morning I went down the river to look for elephant spoor, and soon found that some had drunk in the night quite close (*too* close, in fact) to camp. I followed until noon, but they had never fed nor even halted, and from the way they had meandered about in the night I felt sure they had scented our camp and were scared, so at last I had to give it up and return, getting back to camp during the afternoon, tired and disappointed, but feeling I had done all I could. It was *very* hot ; and following the traces of travelling elephants, hour after hour, through the dry, monotonous, thorny scrub, is weary work, especially when one seems to get no nearer to the game. The bush is not so dense as to be very difficult to get through, in most parts, but it is thick enough to make it a continual struggle and to shut out all view ; so that, with no encouragement to lead one on, it becomes extremely tiresome work. The only game I had seen the whole day was a couple of waterbuck, just after starting in the morning, at which, however, I did not get a shot.

I found by observations that the river, though still far too full to think of getting across for some time, was gradually falling, and hoped that, if this kept on, it might by and by become passable.

" Frolic " had become very bad, and was evidently suffering much pain. I felt anxious and depressed, and not very well ; and, having sent most of my men back to fetch more loads, I stayed about camp the next two days, doing all I could for the relief of my little favourite. She became rapidly worse, however, and by the third day from being hurt she could no longer move, seeming paralysed, the vertebræ being probably injured, and could hardly even drink. The next day I felt sure that she was dying. I had now to pour water into the corner of her mouth to enable her to drink a little. As, however, I could do no good by remaining in camp and it was most distressing to me to see her, I went out to look for elephant spoor, starting as soon as there was a little light.

On the way down the river I shot a hippo, but as usual it was carried away by the water. Some distance farther we found where elephants had drunk in the night, and, following the spoor, which did not take us very far from the river this time, came at length where it scattered and wound about with signs of feeding. This was encouraging, though the spoor was more difficult to follow now that the herd had spread out, the ground being dry and hard. We, however, stuck to that of one or two bulls, which seemed now to be alone—indeed I fancy had not really been with those we had followed from the river at all. It puzzled us a good deal, as they had sauntered along, making little impression on the baked soil ; but while rather at fault, we heard branches breaking ahead, giving us timely warning of the whereabouts of one at any rate. It was a still, cloudy day, with hardly any wind stirring ; but what there was seemed for the moment right. I advanced, stupidly allowing Squareface to follow—instead of proceeding alone, as was my usual custom on getting so close under similar ticklish conditions —and went in too hurriedly. The noise we made on the dry leaves in the still air alarmed the elephant (a single bull), just as I got the first glimpse of his head towering up among the bushes which concealed the rest of his huge form, and he made off at a run, screened by thick cover from me, giving me no chance for a shot. He ran close past my other gun-bearer, who had stopped a little behind, and he got a good view of him and told me he was a monster. Of course. This was terribly disappointing, and, though we tried afterwards to follow the others, the one that we had scared joined them and made them travel ; and, though we got warm dung several times, we had to give it up in the end, and got back late in the afternoon, tired and defeated, to find my dear little companion gone to where all the elephants and other game one shoots go, I suppose, and where I might follow her any day. How sad and lonely I felt I cannot attempt to express. I had had sorrowful losses before of favourites, both dogs and horses, but this was even sadder and more trying. She had been the companion of my travels for the last eighteen months : never apart were we, day

or night, unless I left her tied in camp while I went hunting.
She had the greatest confidence in me, and we never fell out.
Faithful, lovable little dog! I don't think I could have felt the
loss of a human companion more. I felt at least that her life
with me had been a happy one. I buried her with my own
hands by moonlight; and as I laid her in her little grave I
almost wished I could rest beside her in the quiet bush by the
roaring, cool river. A sad, sad day.

Thinking it best to go out and take my thoughts away from
my great loss, I was up again at 4 A.M. next morning, and off
as soon as it was light enough to see. We found the spoor of
a troop of cows, that had drunk not so far away as that of
yesterday, but it led us a long, long tedious chase, and it was
afternoon before we were able to hear the elephants. They had
crossed and recrossed a dry gully, and we had some difficulty
in keeping to their true course. However, at last we got on
terms with them, and I sneaked right up to within nice range,
but could not see to get a shot at either of the two small cows,
which were the only ones visible. One, the nearest, was facing
me—it had poor teeth; the other was behind and broadside
on, but I could only see a bit of her, and was waiting, trying
to make her out, when suddenly the one next me gave a shrill
trumpet (having evidently got my wind), and they instantly both
wheeled round and disappeared. I fired a snap-shot, but with
no apparent result; and, as we could find no blood, and as the
elephants here—owing to the proximity of the Wakamba, who
are constantly harrying them—when once disturbed go right
away, it was useless following them so late in the day. Another
disappointment; through the treacherous breeze, to-day. We
did not get back to camp till long after dark, having sat down
only once, for about a quarter of an hour, the whole day. On
the way back, after having struck the river again and while
following along its bank, we came upon some hippos, which
were very close to the shore; and one, which had a small calf,
charged towards me twice, in shallow water. But I would not

shoot, as it was too far from camp and there was always such a chance of losing them in this river, and it stopped when within a few yards of me. Of course I should have had to fire if it had come any nearer, but I thought it would not come right on and felt quite safe with my double rifle ready in my hand.

The porters having come again from Mtiya's with more loads, I decided to keep two or three more with me and try to make a " dug-out " to ferry us over ; for the river had not fallen at all during the last three days, and I did not feel inclined to simply wait an indefinite time. I felt the more impatient to get on since I seemed destined to have no luck with the elephants here, and was keen to proceed to my old hunting-grounds near the Lorogi Mountains.

Accordingly I selected a baobab tree of suitable size, not far from the bank of the river, and felled it ; afterwards cutting off the top part and leaving a fairly straight and even trunk. This kind of tree is very soft and spongy, and consequently can be worked easily and expeditiously. I had no knowledge as to its suitability for the purpose of making a canoe, but felt pretty sure it would serve our turn, if we could only make a decent job of it (for neither I nor my men had had any experience in naval architecture). We managed, by the aid of levers, to get it into a suitable position for working at. At first we were very clumsy with the axes, and I much regretted not having an adze ; but we improved with practice, and found a sharpened spade answered admirably to scoop out the inside, the soft wood working almost as easily as so much cheese. In four days we had so far completed it that we thought it would do, and began our preparations for launching our vessel, cutting rollers to put under it, and making paddles.

During the progress of this work I sometimes strolled a little way along the banks of the river to get something for the pot, and shot one or two of Kirk's tiny antelope, of which there were plenty, with my rook rifle. I saw the waterbuck once or

MAKING DUG-OUT CANOE.

(From a Photograph by the AUTHOR.)

twice, but never got one. As for the hippos, I had given up molesting them, since it was impossible to get one out of the water, even if killed dead, though I saw one, which I had shot before, stuck against a snag or bank in the middle of the river. There was practically no other game in the neighbourhood, and I was too much absorbed in my shipbuilding to go in search of elephants again till that was finished.

My caravan came in again, opportunely, the day that we cleared a road to the river ; and, in spite of a severe attack of fever, brought on by getting the sun (extremely powerful in this valley) on my back while working at the canoe, I worked hard to get it dragged down by the help of the porters. It is difficult to get natives to exert themselves and pull together. When a number are employed at lifting or pushing any heavy object, each thinks it unnecessary to put much strain on his own muscles. So it proved slow work, the dug-out being heavy and awkward to handle, and we only got it half-way that day. The next morning we got on better, and reached the water of the branch channel, and partly floated, partly dragged it down into the main stream, below the islands.

Now came the crucial test ; could we paddle it across ? It was a clumsy craft and the current was strong, but some of my men knew well how to use a paddle, being natives of the coast and accustomed to navigating canoes in the sea. So I started them off, with exhortations to ply their paddles with all their might so as to avoid being carried too far down by the current ; for, unless they hit the opposite bank within a reasonable distance, it would be impossible to land. I stood watching the trial trip with keen anxiety. The canoe shot out into the stream, but as soon as it got near the middle of the river, where the current was very strong and the water rather rough and full of eddies from the meeting of the two branches of the river just above, it swung right round and the crew had to bring it back to our side. They reached the shore, of course, far below where they started from, and had then to get out into the water and drag the clumsy craft up against the stream. We then made another pair of paddles and desisted for that day, hoping for better luck on the morrow.

In the morning we were at it again, this time pulling our canoe by hand over to the lowest island (having found that the channel was just fordable), and then up under the bank on the other side of it some distance, so as to get a good start. On trying again in this way, the paddlers succeeded in getting right across ; but, the current being very swift under the opposite bank, they were not able to land, and came back, being carried far down again, and we had all the work of dragging up over again. In the afternoon we made another attempt, and the voyage was so far successful that they got across nicely and landed, but when coming back, later, were carried a long way down again. It was disappointing work, and difficult to get the men to exert themselves in the water at dragging the canoe back up stream. I had been having another go at the hippos, in hopes of getting some meat to cheer them up, and the men who had crossed in the canoe saw two dying on the far side, but were not able to get at them. The next day I sent the bulk of the men back again to the kraals with orders to Abdulla to wait until he heard from me, as I did not want to use up our food supplies here, and a few always work better than a large number. We then set to work to improve our dug-out, lightening her fore and aft, as the ends were too solid and made her unwieldy and hard to steer. We then tried her again, and were at length rewarded by a perfectly successful voyage both ways. One of yesterday's hippos was found under the opposite bank, and cut up and the meat brought back in the canoe. It was in good condition, and the fat was a windfall. I also shot a goose.

We now began to ferry over the loads, first four, afterwards six at a time. We were only able to make five trips the first day, the men wasted so much time. Africans are slow in brain and action, never ready, and can seldom do anything in the nick of time. Their intelligence is of a low order; but one has to make the best of them and be patient. But though our progress was slow, I was pleased that I had at length made a success of my canoe.

The next day we got on much better, the men being quicker and wasting less time, and we got all the remaining loads across, with the exception of my tent and personal effects. I then went over myself and piled the loads properly, and prepared camping-ground ready for pitching my tent the following day. The only thing that bothered me now was how we were going to get the donkeys across; but fortunately the river was falling again, and was altogether about 2 feet lower than when we first arrived.

The following morning I struck my tent, and sent it and my kit across; but, with the incomprehensible stupidity peculiar to the negro, the men this time allowed the canoe to be carried down and nearly wrecked on a rocky promontory where the stream was very rapid. However, after much annoying delay they got back and took the boys across, I afterwards crossing myself, and finally the other men were fetched. Owing to the unnecessary delay caused by the careless apathy at the first voyage, it was noon by the time I got over. Then, after pitching my tent and putting things in order, I went to the drift, which was some distance up stream, at the far end of the islands, to see if it would be possible to cross the donkeys there. Juma, my second gun-bearer, being a good swimmer, made the attempt first, and got on to the island all right without getting out of his depth, though the water in the first narrow channel was very strong. I found we could get over to the island, and that it would be possible to pull the donkeys through the big channel (as we had done on my previous journey) with the rope. Besides, the river was now falling every day, and, though this troublesome and ticklish business was yet to come, I felt greatly relieved that our goods and chattels

were now all safely ferried over, for it was anxious work
watching each boat-load being paddled hard through the rough
and rushing water.   Some of our meal got wet, for the
water used to come in over the weather-side as the men plied
their paddles with all their might, but nothing was seriously
damaged.   In the afternoon I saw a rhinoceros drinking on
the opposite bank.

On the morrow, having sent word to Abdulla to send the
caravan on and follow the day after with the donkeys, I went
out to look for elephant spoor, starting early and following the
river down.   But though we went farther than we had ever
reached in our hunts on the other bank, we found no fresh and
very little old spoor.   This was probably owing to the bush
being generally more open on this side in that direction, and
for the same reason there was more game of other kinds here,
namely a good many waterbuck, some walleri, and a few lesser
koodoo.   I also saw a pair of the larger and handsomer kind
of jackal.   Hippos were numerous, of course, and I shot one
which I came upon lying in shallow water at the mouth of a
small tributary.   Though I had not molested any of the other
game we saw, I did not let this chance slip, because it was in
such an easy position to get at, and, as I succeeded in shooting
it in the brain with my Lee-Metford, it remained where it was.
Unfortunately it proved to be in very low condition, so that it
was not of much use.   I also saw the carcase of one, which I
had shot before but failed to find, close to the bank on the
other side, being eaten by crocodiles.   Some were tugging at
it in the water, while many of the hideous and repulsive brutes
lay basking, open-mouthed, on banks or snags near by.   At
some points on the banks, in this part of the Tana, are little
patches of dense leafy thicket growing by the water's edge.   I
looked wistfully at these shady retreats, which seemed so
enticing, in the burning heat, to one suffering from fever
(as I was then); and I sometimes felt as if I should like
to take up my abode in one of them, within arm's reach

of the cool, inexhaustible flood, instead of facing the toil-
some journey before me through the parched and thirsty tracts
ahead.

It struck me now that I had not made the most of my
opportunities on the south bank of the river; but as there
seemed little chance of finding elephants on this side, and it
was now too late to return to hunt on the other, I set to work,
while waiting for my caravan, to weigh and adjust the donkey-
loads, it being most important to have each pair (one for each
pannier) exactly the same weight. While doing this rather
trying work in the burning sun, on an empty stomach (a bad
thing), I got a fresh touch of fever. However, I could not
afford to be ill now; so, though feeling fit for nothing and my
head very painful, I disregarded the attack and worked it off.
The morning my men were to arrive, I went up stream a little
way to shoot a hippo for them. My first shot passed just over
one's head, but the second got it, as I could see by the way it
turned over. So, returning to camp, I kept a look-out, and in
two or three hours I saw it coming floating down. Singing
out to the men, several of them plunged into the river with a
rope to meet it, and, before it got far past the landing-place,
succeeded in making fast to it; but in trying to haul it in the
rope broke. Luckily, though, it got stranded in shallow water
near the bank a little lower down; and, being a fat cow, it
came in particularly handy; for my men from Mtiya's had just
arrived opposite, so that, on their being ferried over later on,
all hands were made happy.

It only now remained to cross the donkeys, which arrived
next day. We, on our side, made our way over to the top
island, to do which we had to ford several channels. The first,
where the current was very strong, we crossed by the aid of a
rope stretched across and made fast at each end (even then it
was no easy matter, as the bottom was all boulders); another
was up to our necks, but with hardly any current and a better
bottom. Having arrived on the bank of the main channel, the

PULLING DONKEYS THROUGH THE TANA RIVER.

men with the donkeys being ready opposite, a light cord with
a stone at the end (the other being attached to a stronger rope)
is thrown from the last boulder and caught by those on the far
side with a pole.   It is just as much as we can do to get it
over.   Having got hold of it they haul the rope through till
they have enough to make fast to a donkey's neck, we on our
side keeping hold of our end.   A noose, neither too tight nor
too loose, has to be tied, so that it does not choke the animal
and yet will not let its head through, while the knot must be
one that will not slip and can be readily undone.   Then I give
the word : the donkey is thrust by main force into the torrent,
and, as soon as it is launched out of its depth, we haul away,
hand over hand.   For the first few yards it swims with its head
above water ; but, as soon as it gets fairly into the rapid, the
boiling water forces it under, and we pull away might and main
to get it through as quickly as possible.   In a few seconds it
reappears close to our bank and is got out, with all despatch,
among the rocks, none the worse for its ducking.   So we go
on, working hard, until, one after another, we get them all
through.   In this we succeed without mishap this time ; though
on a former occasion, the last donkey, finding himself alone,
had plunged in, without the rope, to try and swim over to his
companions, and was carried down the rapids to the cataract
below and never seen again.   Then they had to be got through
the other channels, which also entailed much trouble and hard
work ; for donkeys unaccustomed to travelling will not face
water at all, though they get used to it in time, and after some
practice will cross rivers with little trouble.   As with oxen,
there is generally one among them that usually takes the lead ;
and, with a herd of seasoned travellers, on this one being taken
through, the others follow.   It took us the whole day before
we finally got all safely over to the far side and down to
our camp.   The animals were mostly looking fat and well,
though one or two were evidently sick.   Two or three had
already died, but I had calculated on losing some, as, what

with " fly " and other risks, some deaths are always to be expected. I felt thankful that we were at last ready to trek once more. It having now served our turn, we sent our good ship adrift, knowing that it would be rotten before we returned.

We did not get off very early the next morning, having so many pack-donkeys with new pads and " sogis " to load for the first time ; but it did not matter, as the stage was only a shor one to the first of several small rivers—tributaries of the Tana, from the Jambeni hills—that have to be crossed. They are all fordable, but the loads have mostly to be carried over by the men, to avoid getting them wet. I found that I had, luckily, calculated almost to a pound the quantity of food we should require ; and, on starting from the river, all hands had ten days' rations, while of the twenty donkeys seventeen carried food.

It takes a long time packing a lot of donkeys, and it is a bad plan to start the caravan before they are all ready. I found it took about an hour and a half from the time the men were called till we could actually get off ; so I used to blow my cartridge-case[1] at 3.30 or 4 A.M., according to the nature of the country. Under the equator, the dawn first begins perceptibly about 5, and if the going was fairly passable I used to start then ; but in very rough and bushy ground a little more light is necessary, in which case 5.30 is early enough. With a morning moon, and in decent ground or on a path, one may start at any hour. It is most important to get off as early as possible ; for in the cool of the morning the men do not feel the work, while after 11 o'clock the sun gets very powerful, and every half-hour then tells on them more than an extra hour before sunrise.

I had intended taking a path used by Wakamba hunting

---

[1] An empty cartridge-case (I found a long .450 the best) is the most handy and serviceable call you can use in the " bara," whether to arouse the camp in the morning or to signal to your gun-bearers in the bush. It is easily carried, can be replaced if lost, may be heard a long way, and does not alarm game.

and trading parties, which strikes direct for the northern extremity of the Jambeni range and so down to the Gwaso Nyiro River, avoiding the detour by Laiju, and we tried to follow it. It leaves the other at one of the rivers already mentioned. On coming down towards this stream, I saw a giraffe, actually in our camping-ground on the other side; but it made off before I could get within shot. Barring a few waterbuck, one sees little game about here—the bush is too thick,—though there are plenty of rhinos, and occasionally elephant spoor may be seen. Our attempt to follow the new route was a failure, and lost us a day. The path had not been used for a long time, and, except where now and again a cut twig showed that human beings had passed at some former time, was indistinguishable from the game-tracks. Eventually we lost it, and had to retrace our steps. This was annoying, particularly as " fly " is very numerous here, so that for the sake of my animals I was anxious to get through as quickly as possible. But the great thing is to bear all mishaps philosophically in Africa; so I made the best of it and had to go *via* Laiju again. The latter is a very disagreeable route; for, though the bush gets thinner as the hills are approached, the grass becomes very rank and troublesome to get through. I couldn't help thinking what marvellous ingenuity seems to have been employed in devising all manner of disagreeable products, in endless variety, apparently designed for the express purpose of making one uncomfortable. Burrs and spiky seeds, of the most wonderfully insidious kinds, some like small bristles with tiny barbed arrow-heads, warranted to penetrate through anything; ticks and all kinds of abominations, not to mention the grass itself, which is covered with irritating rasping hair. " Truly," I wrote in my diary, " this country is prolific in means of torturing the traveller."

However, I will not weary my kind reader with more details of these uninteresting marches. The number of my donkeys was reduced somewhat, as one by one they succumbed to the effects of the " fly " we had come through; the numerous streams, too, caused much delay and trouble with the pack-animals; but, when once the point of the Jambeni hills is weathered, the country becomes more open and the grass less rank, and from there onward it is healthy for them.   It is also less tiresome to travel through, though the marching is rendered very arduous by the rough lava rock which strews the ground.   It would be quite impossible for the porters to carry their heavy loads over such ground with bare feet, for even one's own get sore ; but with sandals of game hide, and travelling slowly, they do not suffer.   In some parts, too, game is plentiful now, and I was able to get meat for the caravan.   Between the last of the streams and the end of the range especially, I saw great quantities of game.   Here the grass had been burnt in the open plains, which was a great comfort for walking, though the air was often filled with smuts, making one's eyes sore.   In places the young green grass was springing, and this had attracted the game.   The smaller zebra were in hundreds, and I saw a good-sized troop of elands, perhaps thirty—a sight I had not seen for years and a pleasant one ; I also saw a little lot of giraffe, and counted eight rhino within quite a short distance.   There were a few Grant's gazelle, too, one of which I shot.   As this was a waterless march, though, I did not attempt to kill more meat for the men, as it only makes them thirsty under such circumstances.   It is rather hard to say why the rhino should collect in the burnt ground : perhaps they find roots or bulbs to eat, or it may be merely for the sake of company that they follow the other game. Lions were to be heard at night, as a consequence of the abundance of zebra.

I had some anxiety now about my donkeys, fearing lest they might all, or nearly all, die, and so upset again my plan for visiting Rudolph.   But I comforted myself with my favourite motto—" Whatever is, is best,"—feeling that I had done all I could, though it was heart-rending to see them dropping off one

by one. " My beautiful ' pundas ' [1] are looking so well too," I
wrote, " sleek and fat, and not one touched on the back ! It is
too cruel to lose them like this, after all my care." However,
I did not lose many more, and, when they once stopped dying,
I felt hopeful, as I knew all that had not become inoculated
with the " fly " poison were now safe.

This time I went down into the crater, already mentioned
in connection with the previous journey as being one of the
camping-places on this route. We pitched our camp in the
wide road—like an artificial cutting through its edge—by
which it is entered, and I descended into the great cup-like
interior. The pool had plenty of water in it now, and, by
digging out a little spring in the mud close to its edge, a good
supply of fresh water could be obtained. On our return
journey, though, after a long dry spell, the pool was nearly
dry, and what water was left in it was red, as if mixed with
blood. The spring then gave out but a feeble trickle, and
would, I should suspect, fail altogether if the drought continued.
There is always a gale blowing here, and as pegs cannot be
driven, one's tent ropes have to be weighted with many heavy
boulders to make it stand securely. Even at the bottom of
the deep circular crater, where one would think no breath of
wind could reach, tremendous gusts and eddies sweep round,
now one way and now another, carrying away one's clothes if
you should have undressed for your bath there in order to save
the men the toil of carrying so much water up the long, steep
ascent. Baboons seem the only creatures that inhabit the basin,
though I saw what I took to be a klipspringer on the top of the
high rim.

I again, after crossing the Gwaso Nyiro, took the route
through the pass under the mountain called Gwargess (at the
southern end of the Mathews range) in the hope of getting
news of elephants in that district. But they had already left
the neighbourhood, which they only frequent during the rains ;

---

[1] Swahili for donkey.

so we passed on, after getting out of the gorge (not without considerable trouble with the pack-animals, owing to steep paths and thick bush), towards my favourite preserve under the Lorogis.

We found the country less dry than usual this year, owing to the rains having been exceptionally heavy. This is, of course, an advantage, in that the water difficulty becomes somewhat abated ; but the rank growth of grass induced by a copious rainfall makes walking very much harder work, particularly for those in front, and thus renders travelling in a pathless country—as this region is, practically, from Laiju northward to Reshiat—much more tedious. Game is by no means plentiful everywhere, in this part of Africa. It is generally much scattered, and sometimes long stretches hold hardly any. But here and there one comes on a patch where it is abundant, being attracted by young grass or some such favourable conditions. Thus in one place, where there was young green grass, we passed through thousands of zebra, chiefly Grevy's, and also saw a herd of giraffes and a few elands, as well as one or two rhinos, in the same neighbourhood, and heard the zebra crying all night. I had at this time a fit of bad shooting, such as sometimes attacks me. It is very much a matter of health, as affecting one's nerves, I think ; and the cause of the bad shots is generally a tendency to flinch. In this way, I am ashamed to say, I lost several wounded animals at this time, among them a rhino, entirely through bad shooting.

One day, while on the march, one of these blustering beasts came unpleasantly near me while I was, for once, un-armed—my boy at the time carrying my rifle. It charged up to within two or three yards of me, but stood then,—I stooping the while behind a bit of a shrub, ready to dodge,—and Shebane (my boy), who was some distance behind, chucked down everything, including my magazine rifle, and bolted. The rhino, however, after pausing a moment on the other side of my tuft of bush, turned off, much to my relief; for a butterfly - net is not an altogether satisfactory weapon with which to receive the onslaught of an evil-tempered rhinoceros. Luckily my rifle was not hurt, but a piece was knocked out of the stock of Shebane's own carbine.   After this I broke the spell by killing, with a long shot, a Grant's gazelle, after a difficult stalk, which was especially satisfactory as I was feeling tired and unwell at the time.   I thus regained my confidence, which is everything.

As on my former journey, the country got greener and the climate more humid as we neared the Lorogi Mountains.   We found the little river Seya flowing strongly with muddy water ; and a thunder-shower, on the afternoon of the day we crossed it, showed that the weather we had experienced the year before near the range was no exception, but that the climate is really damper there than elsewhere.   A short march from the Seya took us to my old hunting-camp at the little stream of El Bogoi.   On the way we were delayed about an hour by a stroke of luck.   While marching, in the early morning, through cactus tree bush,—the thick grass still laden with moisture, and the dewdrops shining in the newly-risen sun,—we came suddenly right upon a pair of rhinos.   The breeze was in our faces, so they had not scented us, while the low sun, being on our backs, prevented such purblind creatures from seeing us. I had previously warned the men to be quiet, on the chance of seeing game (though it was giraffe I had in my mind), as I was particularly anxious to get meat for them at the end of this stage of our journey.   So, being meat hungry, they had made no noise, and the rhinos, still intent on feeding, did not hear our approach.   I had only got a glimpse of them, round the corner of a clump of bush, before I drew back and held up my hand for the porters (who understood the meaning of the gesture) to stand still, while I seized my Lee-Metford and sneaked forward.   I shot one, knocking him down on the spot ; but I gave him two more bullets to make sure, being anxious, after recent failures, not to risk any chance of his getting off. This most opportune supply I regarded as a happy omen, and the men were joyful, carrying off almost every scrap of meat on the top of their loads, for the beast was fat.   I also saw some giraffe not far from my camp, but was satisfied with what the gods had already sent us.

FROLIC'S GRAVE.

CHAPTER VIII

EXCURSIONS FROM EL BOGOI

Comfortable quarters—Among old Ndorobo friends—A favourite elephant haunt
—Bag a giraffe—Lost in the bush—A deceitful guide—A grateful recompense
—Native jealousy—Travelling elephants—A pair of lovers—Camp by the
Seya River—The Mathews range—Kill five elephants—A malarious climate—
Up the Barasaloi River—A marvellous sight—Abundance of elephants—An
exciting hunt—A narrow escape—A good day's work.

I FELT in great spirits at getting back to my old, jolly camp
in this most interesting country, and very hopeful of success
among the elephants again this year. We had passed, on our
way, two or three pretty recent trails of herds, though we saw
no signs of feeding. The vegetation was, as usual here, quite
green, and the weather evidently very wet on the mountains.
My camp was much overgrown; the shade tree, with its
canopy of creepers, more verdant than ever; and the skeleton
of my old shed was covered with beans in pod, which had
sprung up where some, which we had stored in it, had been
spilt, and crept all over its framework. I soon had the place
cleaned up, and made things comfortable in this favourite
camp of mine; and Shebane laid my table, decorated with a
bowl of flowers picked from the brooklet's banks, in the cool
and pleasant bower that formed my dining-room. I decided
to send the bulk of my caravan, under Abdulla, back to
Mthara (near Kenia) for more food, while I hunted the district;
but they were to halt one day here, first, to rest their feet and
run up a new shed and make a boma for the donkeys, which

were to remain here.   All hands were satisfied and as cheerful as possible.   During the afternoon an Ndorobo turned up and told us where my old friends were camped.

The first thing to do now was to get hold of my old Ndorobo friends, so I sent Squareface, my gun-bearer and interpreter, to hunt them up, while the shed was building for storing my goods.   It being very nearly completed, the second day I sent off Abdulla, with most of the men (keeping only twelve with me), for Mthara, to buy and bring on as much food as they could carry.   I also hoped he might manage to buy a few more donkeys, to replace those that had died ; for I had only fifteen left now, the last of the sick ones having just succumbed.   I had hoped that this one would have recovered, but now every one that had showed symptoms of being " fly-stuck" was dead.   I calculated that Abdulla could not get back here under a month, and I meant to employ my time in hunting during his absence.

The day the caravan started, Squareface returned with Lorgete, one of my Ndorobo friends, but Lesiat (the most important one) did not come, his camp being in another direction.   Lorgete said that he and his people were, as usual, starving, and he had not even any honey to bring me.   He had killed no elephants since I was here, though Lesiat, he informed me, had slain two ; but he said that there was a herd of bulls still about.   I arranged with him that I would meet him the day but one after, at one of my old hunting-camps, which was in the direction in which he said the elephants were, and that in the meantime he was to get precise news of their present whereabouts.   So, after finishing the thatching of the shed and storing my goods in it, I moved on there, leaving two or three men in charge of the stores and donkeys.

After pitching camp in the same spot whence I had done some hunting the year before, I took a stroll in the afternoon in the hopes of seeing giraffe.   But though I searched in what had been a favourite haunt the year before, they seemed to have deserted it now, for I could not even find any spoor.   I thought it strange that there was still no news from Lesiat, and began to suspect that Lorgete had not really sent him word, as he had promised to do, of my arrival.   I, however, took no further steps then to ascertain ; and, on Lorgete coming in the morning to show me his elephants—though not what I call early (by which I mean before it is fully light)—we went out. He took me a long tramp, more towards the Seya River than I had ever known elephants to be before, and we found none to-day.   We saw a little spoor of odd ones, but did not follow it, as we were hoping to find the herd.   It seldom pays to follow single elephants, as they go on, as a rule, till they find their friends, it may be far away.

In the afternoon we saw some giraffe towards the river, on a lower level than we were, standing in a peculiar kind of jungle, composed, not of thorny bushes, but of spreading clumps of a sort of shrub with long, thin interlacing stems. I managed, with considerable difficulty, to stalk to within fair shot of them, having to descend a stony, scrubby hillside ; but the jungle was high enough to cover the greater part of their bodies, so that I could not see the vital spots.   I was particularly anxious to get meat for the sake of my guides, for though I had given Lorgete some food to take home for his children, he and his companions said they were hungry, and that they had not strength to go after elephants until they had had a good feed of meat.   They always do say that.   So I tried to shoot one, but, to my disgust, only succeeded in wounding it, on account of the difficulty of judging through the foliage where the proper spot to shoot at was.   In long jungle it is generally best to shoot a giraffe in the neck ; as, if the bullet strikes the vertebræ, it of course drops on the spot.   Unhappily, I did not do that in this case, and the giraffe went off badly hit.   I hoped still to bag it, though ; but following a little way, without, however, sighting the wounded beast again, we suddenly came upon one in thick scrub, quite close.   At first I supposed it to be the one we were following, but on killing it—dropping it at once with two shots in quick succession—I found it was another, as it had no other wound. The two .303 bullets were found under the skin on the far side, having passed through diagonally, and either would have been fatal.

As the giraffe was very fat, my men were keen to cut it all up, and I got tired of waiting for them and had hard work to get them away at all. By the time we did start, carrying as much meat as we could and leaving more to be fetched the next day, it was late in the afternoon, and we had far to go ; so that, when we reached a hill near which Lorgete was living at the time, it was already dusk. He wanted to turn off home here, but I objected, feeling sure we should get wrong in the dark, as it was all dense bush, and we did not know that part of the country well, though we could keep our course well enough by daylight. However, Squareface was so confident of finding the way all right, that I foolishly yielded and allowed the Ndorobo to go his way. The result was, that, as soon as it got dark, we very quickly lost ourselves. Now there was a very deep, narrow gully, with precipitous sides, which we had to cross, and it wound about and had many ramifications, the bush being particularly dense all about it. We failed to hit the right crossing-place in the dark, and then, having, with great labour, struggled through, found ourselves, apparently, hopelessly entangled in a maze of deep dongas ; whichever way we tried, we came upon an impassable chasm, looking most appalling in the dark. It ended in our having to cross and recross, with much struggling and scrambling, several such ; and, after tearing our clothes and selves to pieces, and messing about half the night saturated with the cold dew, we at last got to camp, draggled, tired and worried, about midnight. After cleaning my rifles as usual, and having a bath, I had a little dinner about 1 A.M.

I found that one of my men had come over from El Bogoi bringing with him one of Lesiat's Ndorobos. This man told me that Lesiat had not heard of my arrival ; he also said that there were lots of elephants not far from El Bogoi, and many too now at Barasaloi. This was news indeed, and revealed the whole of Lorgete's little game. He had been deliberately humbugging me, in order that I might shoot meat for him alone, and get nothing whatever myself. On the strength of this information I at once decided not to go out again, as had been arranged with Lorgete, but to send at once for Lesiat. So I despatched Squareface early to fetch him, while Juma went with the rest to fetch the remainder of their giraffe meat ; and, when Lorgete came, I told him I was going to move the next day to near Lesiat's. Towards evening, Squareface returned alone. Lesiat and his people were away in the bush looking for two elephants which had been wounded by his men a couple of days before. His wife said she would send him word that I had come back, and that he was sure to come as soon as he heard. It was truly provoking that, all through the greedy jealousy of that humbug Lorgete, the elephants had now been disturbed, while I was already in the neighbourhood.

After considering what was best to be done, I decided to move, the day following, back to El Bogoi, but higher up the stream than my permanent camp. So in the morning I moved to a place I had spotted the year before as a nice and convenient one to camp at, near where I had shot a giraffe ; and, just after we got there, Lesiat and his pal turned up, having gone to our just vacated camp and followed our spoor thence. He told me that there were lots of elephants all through from there to Seya, but he wanted to go home first and send out men to prospect. I was impatient to hunt, though, so he agreed to stay himself to go out with me in the morning, and I made him happy with lots of my giraffe meat. I spent the afternoon in talking to him, as I was unwell and feverish. He told me that he had killed one bull and two cows since I left, and had kept the ivory for me. He afterwards faithfully delivered over the teeth of the bull (a fine pair) and of one cow, though I never asked for them. This was the result of the charm he had forced me to give him, which had clearly given him every satisfaction. I may here say, that if any aspirant would like me to use my art as a magician to enable him to become a successful elephant-hunter, I shall be pleased to do business on similar terms. I, however, made it up to my honest friend in other ways ; indeed I gave him far more in the end than he would have got from Swahili traders for the ivory.

Early next morning I went out with Lesiat and his chum, who had slept in my camp, going up stream in the direction of the range. But I soon found, from my old friend's manner, that he knew the herd (all old bulls) had left this part, and that he had been only gassing yesterday. So we sat down and had the inevitable "shauri," with the result that I let him go home to send out search parties in various directions, with the object of obtaining authentic information as to the present whereabouts of the game we sought. He also promised to keep me supplied with men every day to accompany me hunting. It is always a great advantage to have one or two of these people with one, as they know every inch of the country, and are better up to spooring, etc., than one's own followers. On the way back I took a short round across the stream, but saw no spoor newer than the night but one before, and that only of a few travellers. I felt most uncharitably disposed towards Lorgete ; for it was too disappointing that, when the conditions were so favourable, everything should have been upset all through his jealousy in keeping the news of my arrival from Lesiat, while at the same time making me believe that he had sent him word. There was nothing for it now but patience, anyway for a day or two. In the meantime I made arrangements with Lesiat's son-in-law (Baithai by name) to send to the Barasaloi in search of elephants, and, failing to find there, down the Seya towards El Gereh, and to bring me back the news.

In spite of being very unwell, with fever hanging about me, I could not rest, so went out again the following day, starting early as usual, and met Lesiat, by appointment, at the foot of a koppie where we had parted yesterday. We had crossed the spoor of a single elephant not far from camp, but not fresh ; and farther on had seen what we took to be the fresh spoor of two or three others, in the dewy grass. We went back to inspect the latter, but only to find that it was rhino spoor. We then went on again, striking straight through the dense bush which stretches for miles and miles along the foot of the mountains, and covers all the flat country towards the Seya. After a time we struck the last night's spoor of a few travelling elephants. We followed it a long way, but, as they showed no signs of feeding, I at last turned campwards —for I was feeling very unwell and hardly able to drag one leg after another,—telling Lesiat to send me news the next day.

This sort of thing went on for two or three days more. I hunted assiduously, but the only spoor we could find was that of travelling stragglers, the following of which resulted in nothing but profitless fatigue, for they never fed nor halted. So I became convinced that there was no herd near now ; the elephants had evidently been thoroughly scared and had left the neighbourhood, and it seemed folly to go on toiling about, tearing ourselves to pieces every day and all for nothing. For I had never even been near an elephant yet. As the promised news from Barasaloi had never come, I sent Squareface and Smiler to another Ndorobo camp I knew of, at the foot of the Murkeben hill, which is in the same direction, to make inquiries there ; for I was determined to move somewhere, since I was merely wasting my time where I was. They reported that they had found only an old man in the kraal, all the rest of the community being away in the bush, where they had just killed two giraffe. My men heard, though, that there were two young fellows there who had been sent by Baithai to get me news, and who were coming on to my camp the following day. I hardly believed that they would be able to tear themselves away while any of the giraffe meat remained ; but, true enough, they turned up as promised.   They told me that there were lots of elephants on the Barasaloi, and down the Seya towards El Gereh.   This sounded hopeful ; besides, I wanted to go and see the country in that direction, so I at once returned to my head camp and set about making preparations for an excursion of some length, being only too glad to get away from where I had wasted so much time fruitlessly.

I may mention, in passing, that one night before I returned to my main camp, about 2 A.M., a rhinoceros (probably there were a pair) was making the most curious noises near us, which I described in my diary as "just such exaggerated gruntings and bass squeakings as one might expect from a magnified pig."   I had heard bubbling noises before, but not in combination with the other piggish sounds.   I suppose this rhino must have been love-making.

That these blank days have been uninteresting to my reader I make no doubt.   I can only say, so were they to me : but, as my object is to give a true account of elephant-hunting, the many weary days of disappointment cannot be altogether left out.   But I was soon to have compensation for this bad luck.

After spending more than a fortnight, since my arrival at El Bogoi, as described, without any success, I started again from my camp there on 27th August 1895, taking my usual hunting outfit and two donkeys carrying food for my men, two or three young Ndorobo natives accompanying us as guides. Our direction was now east-north-east.   We camped that day at a good-sized " kurunga " or rock pool, in high open country, having emerged, after several hours' tramp, from the thick bush. We did not see much game, but a good deal of spoor of rhinoceros, zebra, etc.   The next morning we soon came to the edge of a pretty deep valley, through which we could see the little river Seya winding with patches of green jungle and thorn-trees along its banks, a pleasant sight in Africa, where running water is scarce. It was a long, steep, stony descent to get down to it, and took us till well on in the morning. There was a good deal of water in the river at this time, and I noted that it was at this point about 30 yards broad or nearly so, very rapid and perhaps an average of 18 inches deep, running towards the north now. I camped, though it was early, in order to go ahead and prospect, as I did not know exactly how near elephants might be found.

During the afternoon I walked a long way down parallel with the river. I found the valley similar to where we had entered it ; not wide, but pretty straight and even. The river was fringed, for the most part, with belts of thick forest or dense jungle, of varying width, sometimes on one bank, at others on both ; outside this the ground was open, with short grass only, and very dry. I saw a few Grevy's zebra, oryx, and Grant's gazelle, but could not get within shot, though I tried hard. On the way back I entered the thick bush bordering the river. It was very difficult to get about in, for though the trees, of good size, were not close together, there was a dense undergrowth, mostly over one's head, through which it was hard to force one's way, even in the game-paths. I saw and got near a giraffe in this forest, but the covert was so tall at that part that I could not see to get a shot, and I then lost sight of it. Just after this a rhino came suddenly into view in a little opening just ahead of me, and, for a second, gave a splendid chance, but he had already scented me and ran just as I raised my rifle, disappearing instantly in the thicket before I had time to fire. Finally I caught sight of the head of the giraffe again, and fired at it, but missed. On rejoining Squareface, whom I had left behind when going after the giraffe, he told me that three rhinos had passed close to him while I was away. We also saw plenty of spoor, so that there seemed to be lots of them there. We got back to camp at dusk, feeling rather disappointed, as I wanted meat badly for all hands and especially for my Ndorobo youths, whom, in its absence, I was obliged to feed on our own store of grain, which we could ill spare. Though very tired, I could not sleep much that night for the mosquitoes. They came swarming up from stagnant swamps lower down the river, which breed them both numerous and powerful. I noticed flocks of vulturine guinea-fowl again here.

The next morning we moved on again down the valley. I kept, purposely, somewhat ahead of my little party, on the look-out for game ; and soon, as I came over a rise overlooking one of the numerous little side valleys we had to cross, I caught sight of several Grevy's zebra straggling slowly along through small patches of cover towards the river. Watching my opportunity when they were for the moment hidden from sight, I ran quickly down so as to cut them off, and got within range by the time the leading one came out into view again ; when, getting a good chance, I shot it, and after a short rush it came down in a cloud of dust. It was fat, and most useful as a meat supply ; for my Ndorobo boys were a tax on my commissariat, the proportions of which were so exceedingly limited. After this, of course, I got easy chances at oryx and Grant's gazelle, when I no longer needed them. Cutting up the meat delayed us an hour, and, being now so heavily laden, we camped again, early, beside the river ; for, as it was near us all the way, we could choose our time for halting. "What a blessed thing," I put down in my diary, "a running stream is!" During this day's march we had seen some pretty recent elephant-dung on the game-path we had been following. This looked hopeful.

So far there was little change in the character or direction of the valley. The Barasaloi was said to join but a short way ahead now. As to El Gereh, which I had always understood to be the name of the swamp in which the Seya ends, the guides assured me that we had already reached it, that name being applied by the Ndorobos to the whole of this swampy valley, from here onward. We had now got pretty close under the Mathews range, which towered up to a considerable height across the valley on our right, and also ahead, where it seemed to shut it in. Continuing on our way down, parallel with the river, the following morning (30th August 1895), after about three hours' marching we stopped for a short rest ; and, shortly after proceeding again, we had arrived at a part of the valley where the bottom consisted of a wide, damp flat, covered with a tall and dense growth of reedy swamp grass, with here and there patches of jungle and thorn-trees and an occasional stagnant pool, while the river wound through all, sometimes approaching the opposite hills, at others near those on our side. I kept my eyes on this, as a likely harbour for the game I was in quest of ; and, sure enough, on topping a little rise which gave me a good view over it, a great black car caught my eye, among the tops of the thick brake, waving gently with a sinuous kind of motion reminding one of the lazy movement of the fin or tail of a fish lying sleepily poised in the water. I at once halted my little party in a hollow under the stony hills which enclose the valley, and the base of which we had been skirting. Fortunately the wind was right.

Leaving the other men with the loads and donkeys, with orders to keep absolutely still, I took my three gun-bearers and two Ndorobo lads, and, making a circuit round to leeward, crossed the river, struggled through the dense brake, and reached the steep bare stony hill on the far side, close to where the elephants had been. I say elephants, for, though only one (or rather a bit of one) had been visible, I felt sure there were more. It was no easy matter making our way through this formidable cover. The height of the grass may be inferred from the fact that, even from the coign of vantage whence I scanned it, only an elephant's ear could be made out ; while it was so dense as to be quite impassable except by the paths made by elephants and rhinos, and even then only with difficulty, as the heavy grass often drooped over the

In this drawing of the elephant's carcase (which is from a sketch made on the spot) it will be observed that the curve of the tusks is inwards. In the conventional representations of elephants commonly met with in pictures, the tusks are wrongly shown with an *outward* curve. With such it would be impossible for the animal to get through the bush.

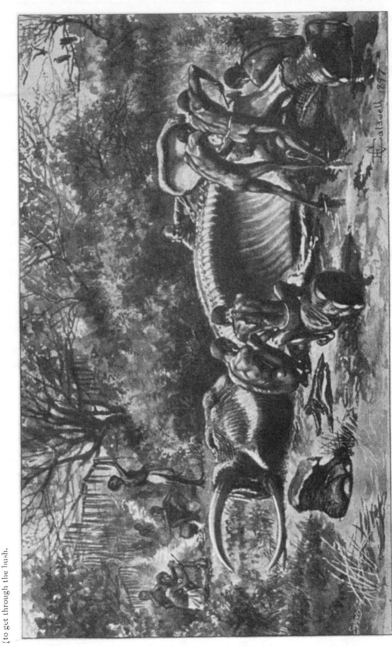

"Though it was still quite early, the Ndorobos had already cut up the whole of the upper half of the huge mass. They were swarming all around : the bush was full of them and covered with meat cut into strips or piled in junks. They had made fires all about ; and eating and track, and it was as much as one could do to push aside its stiff stems and rasping blades, while sometimes it was a case of creeping through low tunnels. I was pleasantly surprised to find that the surface of the ground was mostly dry and sandy, the water nourishing the rank growth being evidently below, though in places were shallow pools and wet mud, churned up and pitted with elephant tracks. On climbing cautiously a little way up the hillside, so as to get a view over the flat, we found that the elephant had moved from where we had first seen it ; but we soon spotted it again, a little farther on, standing under a tree. Then, while we watched, it moved into a clump of thorn-trees a little lower down, where the grass was not so thick, and we could now see that there were several. They were, however, on the other side of the river ; that is, the side we had come from, for it made a sweep, from where we had crossed it, over to the foot of the hills on the eastern side of the valley, and the elephants were in the bend. It was therefore necessary for us to recross.

We accordingly forded the shallow stream again, and forced our way cautiously through the giant grass towards where we had last seen them. The direction of the wind being up the valley, we still had it in our faces. Getting to where the growth was less uniformly luxuriant, we came in sight of two or three, through openings in the grass, some thirty yards ahead ; but, before I could get a shot, a treacherous eddy of air gave them a whiff of our scent, and they started off. Luckily they ran diagonally across our position, and, the ground being sufficiently open to give me a chance, I was able to give one a shot fairly behind the shoulder, with the 10-bore, as she passed. Following, I heard the grumblings and rumblings a dying elephant makes, and, approaching cautiously (as is necessary in such dangerous ground), though at first I could not make her out, after peering about a little I found her lying dead among some bushes. Then, forgetting my usual cautious tactics in the excitement of our first success for the trip, I foolishly talked exultingly to my men, who had come up, and again alarmed the others, which had been standing close by, though hidden from us, and thus lost our second splendid chance. Following, however, in their wake, we got close up again to them, standing in the grass jungle. One faced me, and as I tried to get into a position to shoot from, it approached. I waited for it to halt or give me a chance at its chest; but, instead of stopping, it came on quicker, while its chest was covered by the tall reedy grass, and, when within five or six paces, I felt constrained to fire in its face, and try to get out of sight among the stems of the brake. Luckily the shot turned it. Blood showed on the grass, but we did not follow it at once, going after others instead. I felt it to be unpleasantly risky work in this tangle of tall swamp grass. Impenetrable out of the elephant tracks, and often difficultly so even in them, it was high enough to conceal an elephant entirely unless very very close, and seldom allowed more than the head to be seen even then. Fortunately the wind, which kept pretty steadily in one quarter, came in stiff gusts now and then, drowning the noise one made in forcing one's way through the rustling grass, which also, by its waving about, helped to obscure one's movements. Taking advantage of one of these gusts, I crept in near, once more, to a clump of elephants, and succeeded in knocking over a couple more, like ninepins, with the head shot.[1]

As the elephants seemed now to have moved back up the valley, that is down wind, we struck across for the foot of the hills on the west side, so as to get round to leeward

[1] I am afraid this abrupt way of putting it sounds rather like bragging. But these sentences are mostly copied, word for word, out of my diary, in which I jotted down at the time, in as terse a manner as possible, my impression of the incidents, for the purpose of calling the circumstances to mind at any future time ; and they seem to give a truer idea of the occurrences than any more elaborate description, written at this distance, could.

again, and at the same time find out their exact whereabouts. Having made our way to the edge of the jungle, we went along, outside, back to where the caravan was left ; and the men told us that the elephants had passed quite near them, and were just ahead. Feruzi, my cook, was in a great state of excitement, and amused me much by the ardent interest he took in the chase.   I got round to leeward of them again ; then went in, and, making the most, as before, of the opportunities when the wind blew strongly, got up to them and dropped one more in the same way, giving another a shot in the ribs as they started off.   We now crossed over to the opposite hill again, whence we could get a better view over the whole of the valley bottom, and saw some moving about in the brake.   Once three came near enough, below our perch on the steep hillside, to give me a chance for a shot with the Lee-Metford ; but while I waited to get the glasses, in order to make out which had the best tusks, they moved away again.   Climbing down and following up once more, we got near, but could not see anything for the jungle, which was particularly impracticable at that part, while the wind had died away ; and to creep through a low tunnel in the tangled reedy growth to right under an elephant's nose, when it, being on the look-out, is bound to hear you coming, is not pleasant nor likely to be always healthy.   So I hesitated, and they went off again before I could get a shot. In looking for them afterwards, in the direction we had been in before, we came upon another dead elephant, which I had not seen fall, evidently the one I had fired at last.

It was now near sundown, so I returned to the caravan and determined to pitch camp.   On going back over the rise, for that purpose, whence we had first seen the elephant in the morning, we could make out two or three still visible ; but these were on the far side of the swamp, and in a very dense part, so I let them alone.   I thought they were cows with calves, which was a good reason for not attacking them ; but

I am afraid I was really inclined to shirk it, thinking it not
advisable to tempt fate too far.   Squareface wanted me to go
after them, but I decided to be content with the day's work,
though I fear Feruzi was a bit disappointed with me.   But,
for my part, I felt very pleased with this return of luck, after
our want of success at El Bogoi, and hoped this would prove
the commencement of good fortune for the trip.   I also felt
satisfied with my shooting ; I had five elephants down, and
only one had gone away wounded ; and I had wasted very few
cartridges, though I used one or two more, perhaps, than
absolutely necessary in finishing off, or rather making sure of,
elephants that had dropped ; but that is the safer plan.

As already stated, my rifles were now a Lee-Metford and a
10-bore Holland.   Both had done their work well enough to-
day ; but I had not yet acquired thorough confidence in the
former, and the discharge of the other was something of a
shock, which, though its rubber heelplate prevented from
hurting the shoulder, made one's head ache, and knocked one's
fingers about cruelly.   The volumes of smoke emitted, too,
were appalling, and a source of danger ; but its worst defect
was that the breech invariably jammed, and the empty cases
stuck, so that they had to be knocked out with a stick.
Altogether, I found my prejudices against big guns in no way
removed, and regretted more than ever the accident to my
trusty and equally effective .577.

I found a passably good place to camp, just at the edge of
the swamp (I call it so, for want of a better name, though it
was not really wet), at a point where the river was close to the
western side, and just at the foot of the stony, dry hills.   Not
an ideal spot, but neither was it a bad one, a thorn-tree or two
giving fair shade.   It is a most important consideration to get
suitable camping-ground, close to the water, where one can
rest in comfort.   I sent at once for some tit-bits and fat from
one of the elephants, so as to get it fresh, while I pitched the
tent and set things in order myself.   I was glad when all was

ready, and I could bathe and rest, for it had been intensely
hot work in the dense brake, under a broiling sun, and I was
tired.   In the evening I arranged for two of my Ndorobo
companions to go back with all speed the next day, to call
their friends and send word to Lesiat and his clan to come and
eat the elephants, that the meat might not be wasted.

This was the most interesting country I had yet been in.
It was perfectly wild—not even any signs of Ndorobo natives
about—and quite new, that is, no white man had ever been
into the district.   In these respects it satisfied my craving
for absolutely untouched nature.   Ahead, the berg—a part
of the Mathews range—loomed up imposingly.   It seemed
really a big mountain, much higher than I had thought, often
cloud-capped, and apparently with "subugo" forest on the
top.   This mysterious El Gereh swamp, too, which absorbs
all these streams, had always had an attractive interest for me.
The contrast between the green, damp valley and the dry,
barren hills enclosing it is very marked and curious.   What
crops of bananas and sugar-cane these moist alluvial flats
might produce, I could not help thinking, if there were only
cultivators!   But the climate is trying—excessively hot and
very malarious—and I myself was by no means in the robust
health I had enjoyed during the whole of my previous trip.
I only wished that I felt better up to the work I made no
doubt was before me ; but my appetite was indifferent, and
I did not sleep comfortably, and so, of course, my strength
suffered.

I did not get off quite so early as usual the morning after
(31st August), not intending to go far, but merely to prospect
the country ahead a bit.   I took one Ndorobo boy with me,
while the other was to remain to show my men yesterday's
elephants, for them to take the fat out of (to be used for
purposes of light, etc.), the remaining two lads having already
started to carry the news of the harvest of meat to their friends.
We followed the spoor of the retreating herd of yesterday, up

the Barasaloi, which joins the Seya just below where we were camped, here a dry, sandy channel (and nothing can look more desperately parched than a dry stream-bed). Its valley was here narrow, enclosed by steep rocky hills, the bottom of the trough having been evidently filled up with alluvial deposit, forming a level surface between the opposing rocky slopes and crags, under which the water which comes from the Lorogi range must pass, though probably at a considerable depth ; for the stream is too strong just under those mountains, and disappears too suddenly, to be wholly accounted for by evaporation, powerful though that is in Africa.

The valley was lined with patches of mimosa, the trees of considerable size, but without much underwood. As we tramped steadily along on the spoor, we occasionally disturbed a giraffe, which had been browsing on the thorn-trees, or a few oryx, with here and there two or three walleri. These last, when standing with the head up, look singularly like miniature giraffe, but, on commencing to run, the resemblance at once ceases. The head is then lowered, and the long neck stretched out straight in front ; and these, with its lanky legs and slender body, give the animal a very curious appearance as it starts off at a quick trot.[1] It is a very wary animal, and one which seldom offers an easy shot. After a time we sat down, for a spell, and considered whether it would be worth while to go farther. My belief was that the herd was trekking for the Lorogi Mountains, for there appeared to be no cover to hold elephants that had been alarmed, besides which I doubted there being any water in this spruit nearer than the foot of the range. However, noticing some big hills ahead, I decided to follow up as far as their base, where, if anywhere, the water would be likely to reach the surface. Plodding on again we came to where the valley curved to the left, and here and there we noticed signs of moisture. Soon after, we entered a rocky

---

[1] These gazelles have been faithfully represented by the artist, from my descriptions, in the illustration on page 81.

gorge, just above which we found the first pool.   Two or three
of the elephants had drunk here, but not all.   We stopped
again, too, for a drink and another rest.   We had now been
walking about four hours, and I was still doubtful whether to
go farther or return to camp.   But my Ndorobo boy was
confident we should overtake our game if we persevered ; my
gun-bearers, too, were keen to go on, and I thought after
coming so far it was a pity not to keep on as long as there was
any hope of coming up with the herd, so we continued our
course up stream.

Beyond this narrow gorge, which was shut in by high cliffs
of red rock, the valley opened out wider, but the hillsides were
still of the same bare, dry, stony character.   Pursuing our
explorations still further, we came to a salt swamp, full of
jungle, which, though naturally thick, was mauled, broken
down, and trampled by elephants, and cut up by their paths.
Hereabouts, too, was plenty of fresh spoor—not merely that of
our travellers of yesterday's acquaintance, but of others, which,
it was apparent, had been merely wandering at will.   As we
advanced, the prospect became more and more encouraging,
and I felt glad I had not been so foolish as to turn back.   On
the sandy bed now ran a shallow stream ; the swampy jungle
bordering it was of much greater extent and denser than
hitherto, and where the flats (here much wider) were dry, they
were covered with mimosa forest.   These, except the large
trees, were broken down and wrecked by the elephants, while
the bushes and shrubs were distorted and crippled ; in fact,
the condition of the bush in this great elephant haunt can only
be described as " rack and ruin."

Still following up the stream, as we turned a corner and
came into view of a long, straight reach, bordered on one side
by mimosa forest, and on the other by thick leafy scrub of
suaki and other bushes, suddenly I descried two or three
elephants a long way ahead, standing in the bed of the stream,
close to a grove of large mimosa trees.   As the wind was

blowing up stream and so with us, we at once turned off to
the left, and climbed the rugged stony hills in order to make
a long detour over them, and so get round above the elephants.
As soon as we got on to the first ridge, so as to be able to look
down over the valley from its elevation, a marvellous sight met
our view.

Stretched below was a large patch of thorn forest, fairly
open, simply filled with elephants standing, mostly in clumps,
here and there all through it.   These seemed, unluckily, to be
mostly cows (some with calves) or young bulls, but the massive
forms of one or two big bulls could be distinguished among
them.   I stood and gazed at this magnificent scene.   I had
never seen anything like it before, all my experience of
elephants having been in dense wood, where it was seldom
possible to see more than two or three at a time.   Then
they began to move slowly about, and we hurried on, over the
rough, rocky hills, until we got opposite a part of the valley
beyond the herd.   It was now about noon, or somewhat past.
Having got right round, we descended, and, entering the thorn
forest, advanced cautiously towards where we had last seen the
elephants (of course we could see them no longer), having the
wind now in our faces.   But they had slowly strolled up
towards us, and, as soon as we got near the spruit, we saw a
large herd standing about, some in the stream, some on the
banks, loitering and resting.   Such a sight I never beheld.   It
reminded me of pictures in ancient books on South African
hunting.   In the foreground were some Grant's gazelles and
a large Grevy's zebra ; the bush seemed full of vulturine guinea-
fowls and francolins; " paa " (kirkii) were everywhere, and here
and there one caught sight of a walleri or two making off,
while small birds were in clouds.   All the teeming life in this
oasis was due to the life-giving moisture from the little stream.

The mimosa trees, at this part, were large and wide-spreading, pleasantly shading the ground, which was here free from
underwood, and the grass, though thin and scattered, was

green. As I paused, some of the elephants moved nearer to me in the shallow, sandy stream, drinking and playing with the water. One pair, a cow and a large bull, were evidently making love. The bull fondled his mate with his trunk, and then, standing side by side, they crossed trunks and put the tips into each other's mouths; an undoubted elephantine kiss. This rather put me off, and I hesitated so long that my gun-bearer crept up to my elbow, as I crouched behind a tree, and whispered, "Bwana, pika" (Master, strike). Indeed, that was what I had come for; and since I had left the coast (between three and four months ago), I had had no success until now. I was about fifty yards from those nearest me, and, though the ground was quite open between, I daresay I might have got nearer, but some of the elephants were now moving into the dense bush across the stream, so I singled out a bull with beautifully symmetrical and fairly long, though not massive, tusks, and fired at him with my heavy rifle, aiming just behind the shoulder. At the shot he started off, throwing a quantity of water out of his mouth, and I gave him the second barrel before he reached the cover, both, as I thought, about the right spot. Then, seizing the magazine rifle, I gave another elephant a shot just as it was entering the bush. By this time all but one cow had disappeared into the opposite jungle; she stood some distance off on the far bank, apparently undecided what to do. Though a longer range than I had ever shot an elephant at before, I gave her a bullet (Lee-Metford) about the shoulder-joint; she staggered, and a second laid her low.

I will not attempt to give a detailed account of all the incidents of this exciting afternoon's work. I could not remember every particular, even the day after, when I made my entry for this great day in my diary; moreover, I don't think it would be worth while to put each one down if I could. I had, however, one adventure, which I must describe, that can only be called miraculous; though whether or not it was what can be classed as "a narrow escape" (a thing I do not care to cultivate), I know not. We rushed about from then (about I P.M.) till sundown, always following clumps of the enormous herd from one part of the bush to another, mostly in the dense scrub where the ground was wet and often muddy and it was only possible to get about by following the network of paths. The elephants, broken up into small parties, kept moving about, sometimes standing for a little and then dashing off again, but not all leaving the neighbourhood, so that we never had to go very far from where I commenced the attack. Most of the shots were running ones, and I fired a great many more cartridges than necessary—though I doubt if any elephants went away wounded, as it was mostly at those already hit that I wasted my ammunition. I confess I got too excited that day (contrary to my general practice), and have no doubt that, had I kept cooler, I should have killed more elephants and used fewer cartridges.

Well, in the midst of this very warm work—the crashing of elephants, stampeding through the thicket, sounding now in one direction and now in another—I had just fired a shot (a good one I believed) at one which passed near me full split, as I ran to try to cut it off along a path, when Squareface called my attention to the noise made by another portion of the herd, forcing its way through the thick jungle on the other side of us. Now, I am deaf of my right ear, and, owing to that, am unable to tell which direction a sound comes from; consequently, I have to trust chiefly to my attendants as to that. I ran towards the point indicated, as quickly as the zigzag, obstructed passages would allow, ducking sometimes under overhanging boughs, at others jumping over broken branches. I had just come out into a more open narrow path, which ran at right angles to the way I had been coming, as some of the elephants were tearing through the bush just beyond, in a direction parallel with the path I had just got into. I could see the bushes swaying, and a bit of an elephant here and there, as they crashed through, only a few yards beyond. I stood in the path, facing across it but a little towards the left, in which direction the elephants I was watching were running ; and had just fired a snap-shot at one I got a chance at, when, immediately, there was an ear-piercing, screaming trumpet, of the shrillest pitch, close to me. It sounded very angry, and I supposed it to be made by the animal I had just wounded, and stood, still gazing in the same direction and trying to make out, among the dust and bending bushes, a mark for my second barrel, when I felt a clap on my back, just under my right shoulder. Turning my head, I found myself face to face with an elephant, its black head and gleaming tusks just above me. It must have been running along the path I stood in ; screamed on seeing me in its way ; and, apparently, gave me a tap with its trunk to find out what I was, before making hay or pulp of me : but when I turned my head and looked it in the face, it seems to have become suddenly disconcerted ; for, as I threw up my rifle (and myself back, at the same moment), it sheered off, and, breaking through the bush, tore away after the others. I was not hurt at all, and that is why I conclude it was with its trunk, and not its tusk, that it gave me the pat.

We had not been able to follow up each elephant I hit at the time. I had got into a hot corner, and had to make the most of it while it lasted. But some we had seen fall, and others we came upon dead while following up the herd.

Late in the afternoon I killed three big bulls, well ; two of which, together with a smaller one, lay, almost on top of each other, in the mud, where we could hardly get to them without being bogged ; while the third, which had been crossing the stream, fell, to the second shot, just as it got on to the far bank. By sundown we had seen twelve lying dead ; but I had used all my cartridges. We had, however, not found the first bull I had fired at, though I felt sure it must be dead somewhere near. I wanted to find this bull, as it had very handsome tusks, and we spread out to look through the part of the

jungle near where I had shot it.   In doing so, I came upon
two or three elephants standing in a thick place, and had to
retreat and go round, leaving them so, for I had not another
cartridge for either of the rifles.

It being now dusk, we started on our long tramp back to
camp, without having found my first bull.   I did not consider
I had done as well as I ought to have (even allowing for one
or two elephants we had not found), considering the amount of
ammunition expended and the wonderful chance I had had at
this great herd in (for Central Africa) comparatively easy
ground.   But I excused myself, to a certain extent, in that I
was out of health, having fever on me and being overwrought,
as I never now got a refreshing night nor had a healthy
appetite ; and, if it had not been that we kept crossing and
recrossing the stream and so could get water frequently, I
think the great exertion in the fierce heat would have told on
me more than it did ; as it was, I had not felt it much, the
excitement, no doubt, helping to keep me up.   Moreover, the
difficulty of opening my double 10-bore after each discharge
and of extracting the empty cartridges, hampered me greatly ;
and the annoyance and even danger entailed by one's rifle
jamming in a hot corner, with elephants getting up all round,
may be imagined.

We had a good five hours' hard walk before us.   Luckily
it was full moon.   I kept swinging mechanically along at a
fast pace, though I felt pretty fagged ; but I knew it was
better not to rest.   We heard elephants in one patch of bush
that we passed on our way.   When we were getting near
camp, our Ndorobo made a mistake about the path.   Just in
the apex where the two valleys join is a little koppie, connected
with the rest of the hills by a low neck.   In the morning we
had cut this corner, but in the darkness we passed the turn off,
went right round the base of the koppie, and then went over
the neck by the same way we had gone in the morning, thus
getting back into the branch valley again, where we had already

passed.   On the top of the rise we met a single prowling
elephant, quite in the open.   It spread its ears and bore down
straight for us at a run, looking very weird in the moonlight.
No doubt it had got our wind and was really running away ;
but it came dead for where we were, and it was not a pleasant
idea to be run over by an elephant, even by mistake ; so, not
having a single cartridge left, as soon as my men started to
run for it, I felt constrained to follow suit, and, turning tail,
legged it with the best of them.   These mishaps lost us
perhaps an hour and a half, and added much to my fatigue ;
indeed, they were the last straw to my endurance ; so that,
when at last we did reach camp at 1 A.M., I felt dead beat.
But it was cheering to find a good camp fire burning, and the
iron bucket of water for my bath still boiling away, while my
boy and the cook were anxiously looking out for us.   I did
not, even then, shirk what I always considered my first duty
after a hunt, namely, to clean my rifles.   Then I had a dip
in the river, a swill down with hot water, another dip, and then
some soup—I couldn't eat—and turned in about 3 A.M.   But I
was past getting the sleep of the just.   We had been hard at
it for over eighteen hours, with a lot of running thrown in.

CHAPTER IX

EXCURSIONS FROM EL BOGOI (*continued*)

A well-earned rest—An Ndorobo harvest—Keen faculty of natives—A cool retreat —A large rhino—Fourteen elephants in a day's hunt—Distinctive character of tusks—Trek with ivory to El Bogoi—Resemblance to Robinson Crusoe— Experience as donkey-driver—An unexpected stroke of luck—Overloaded with ivory—Stalking Gazelle—A fictitious report—A handsome pair of tusks—A picturesque group—Welcome at El Bogoi.

As we had only been in bed for about two hours by the time the day dawned, and were all very tired, I decided we had better rest that day ; in fact we were not equal to the long journey to the scene of our yesterday's exploits again so soon. For myself I felt really ill ; for, having had fever on me for some days, I now felt thoroughly used up and sore all over. It is hard lines to be able to get nothing one can face in the food line, when a bit out of sorts ; but Swahili cooking is scarcely such as to tempt a sick man. Besides, good old Feruzi, who always did his best, was put to it for materials, as I was quite unprovided with anything in the shape of "medical comforts."

That evening a lot of my Ndorobo friends from near El Bogoi turned up, so I arranged for Squareface to go with them the day after, to show them our elephants and see if any more dead ones could be found. Accordingly, in the morning, he went off early with them. I was very unwell indeed, and obliged to stay in camp. In the afternoon I took a stroll down to the junction of the Barasaloi with our river, and sat on a hill overlooking the valley beyond, where it bends round to the eastward.   Just before coming back, I heard elephants trumpeting, away down stream, where there was extensive scrub ; but it was already sundown and too late to go after them.

Elephants are often noisy ; and the Ndorobo hunters say that they cannot keep quiet for long.   The sounds they make are a great help in approaching them in dense cover, and are taken advantage of by these people when in quest of them, so as to avoid following the spoor if the wind is unfavourable. An Ndorobo, when in the neighbourhood of the game, will listen, with his attention on the strain, till he catches the sound of a puff—as the beast blows through its trunk—a low rumble of its intestines, or a snapping branch—sounds perhaps inaudible to any one else,—and point, with expressive gesture and every silent indication of suppressed excitement and nervous tension, in the direction ; fixing with unerring decision the exact spot in the jungle whence the sound emanates.   But the loud cries which are often uttered, and which may be heard a long way off, are the voices of the females and young (more often, probably, of the calves) ; the old bulls, which keep apart, are more silent, and do not give vent, spontaneously, to such undignified noises.   The latter are, for this reason, sometimes more difficult to locate.

Numbers of Ndorobo women and children passed during the day, following the men of yesterday to the harvest of elephant meat.   One poor old blind woman was led by a stick, held by the one in front of her.   It was wonderful how she could walk over this rough, stony country.   Squareface returned in the evening, having found only one more dead elephant, which turned out to be the big bull I had first shot at, and which I had felt so confident would be found.   We had now accounted for thirteen elephants, mostly bulls, killed during that day's hunt up the Barasaloi.

I was feeling so ill the next morning that I sent Juma and another man off to my El Bogoi camp for my medicine chest (with which title I dignified a cigar-box which contained the few simple drugs I carried with me in my expeditions), as I had no more quinine with me.   Notwithstanding this, however, I went out to look for elephants down stream.   We found spoor of the night before at the junction of the valleys, and, seeing no more lower down, returned and followed it up the Barasaloi.   There was only a small lot (probably a portion of the big herd), consisting of small cows and calves, and they appeared to be travelling ; so I did not follow very far— indeed, I was quite unequal to a long tramp—but returned to camp about mid-day.

The heat in this confined valley was exceedingly sultry now, and trying to one when weak and out of health ; more- over, I could not tackle the coarse fare of elephant and insipid porridge, so that I was not able to throw off the attack so quickly as I usually did a bout of familiar fever.   Juma, too, was away longer than I had expected ; but I got so far better, even without the medicine, and so tired of two or three days about camp, that I determined to move on down the valley whether he came or not.   Luckily, he turned up the evening before I had arranged to start, so that I was able to take my tent, which otherwise we should have been unable to carry. He explained that the cause of his delay was, that, the night he got to El Bogoi, a rhinoceros had charged the donkey kraal, and he had waited to help hunt up and collect the scattered animals.   During his absence we had got out the teeth of the five elephants I had killed the first day, near where my camp was, and buried them.

Then we moved on down the main valley.   We travelled on, following the river as much as possible, during the morning, but our progress was but slow.   The hills closed in more, and got more rugged as we proceeded ; indeed the valley was now, practically, a gorge in the Mathews range, and the tops of the mountains towered up to a height of probably 3000 feet above the river.   But the floor of the valley was still flat and of some width, and was covered, for the most part, with dense, low scrub of a kind peculiar to salt swampy ground. It is composed of a very green, small-leaved shrub, which forms the densest thickets, utterly impenetrable for anything but an elephant, its branches, though thornless, being intertwined and matted together, and presenting a compact, green, wall-like barrier. Even the elephant paths are passable only with difficulty ; for they are often mere tunnels, and everywhere stiff, springy branches stick out across them and encumber the ground, tripping one up and making locomotion most arduous and uncomfortable. Elephants do not appear to feed on this kind of bush, and only use these jungles as a retreat when alarmed. We found no fresh spoor, nor even much old ; nor was there any bush of the kind likely to harbour elephants under ordinary circumstances. Indeed the country seemed so unpromising, that about noon, feeling fatigued even with this short march, I decided to camp and send Squareface on ahead to spy out the land before going farther myself ; for it seemed useless to push on, with no prospect of finding elephants, while we were, perhaps, leaving them behind us. I was so much out of health that I could not shoot a bit, and had missed two Waller's gazelle during the morning. A few of these were all the game we had seen, besides " paa " (Kirk's antelope), which were plentiful.

As the heat was excessive, I was anxious to find a shady spot to camp in, and, noticing a thick clump of trees and bushes close above the river-bank, I crept in, with my Ndorobo guide, to examine it, with a view to camping inside. While we stood surveying this nice cool retreat, my companion spied a rhino lying asleep close by—it having chosen the same pleasant shade to rest in that had attracted us. As the meat would be most useful to us and enable us to economise our small supply of meal, and as the beast was, as it were, delivered into our hands, so opportunely, on the very spot where we intended pitching our camp, I shot it at once, giving it two solid bullets in the head from my Metford .450 which I was carrying. And, as it floundered about still, and I was determined not to let it move from the spot, if possible to prevent it, I finished up with a couple of shots in the lungs. It was a very big old bull, in poor condition.[1] Its measurements were : total length over back from tip of upper lip to root of tail, 11 feet ; total length in straight line opposite side, 10 feet ; total length over back from tip of upper lip to end of tail, 13 feet 4 inches ; perpendicular height in straight line at shoulder, 5 feet 3 inches. These were carefully taken just after it was shot, and entered accurately at once in my notebook. I sent on Squareface and the Ndorobo at once, to prospect the country ahead, while we formed a snug camp in the spinney (where there was but little undergrowth that needed cutting away to make room for my tent), within a few steps of the carcase, so that the men could conveniently cut up the meat.

On his return in the evening, Squareface reported that, though they had gone a long way down the valley, they found no spoor nor any sign of elephants whatever, nor even suitable bush. So, seeing no chance of doing any good by going farther in this direction, I retraced my steps the following morning (8th September) to the camp I had started from the day before. I had hoped to reach the end of the Seya River : but there can be no doubt whatever that its water does not reach beyond the Mathews Mountains ; for not only did all the natives I questioned assure me that farther there was no water, but Swahili traders who had travelled by a route to the eastward of those mountains told me they crossed no such river there. This is not surprising in Africa, where the evaporation is so enormous and the soil so porous, while the rainfall is very fickle, for, on my return journey, I found the Seya with no running water in its bed, even much nearer the Lorogi Mountains, in which its sources lie.

---

[1] This was a large rhinoceros for Equatorial Africa. In Southern Africa they may possibly run larger. On Lake Rudolph they are much smaller.

After getting back to my ivory camp, I had a fruitless search for what turned out to be an imaginary elephant, which one of my men said had passed up on the other side of the stream while he was fetching water. Luckily I was getting quite strong again by that time, and so the extra exertion in that most exhausting cover did me no harm. I felt sure that if I had not been so unwell during the few days succeeding my great onslaught on the big herd, I might have picked up a few more, for some stragglers often hang about a neighbourhood for a couple of days after the main body's retreat. By this time, though, I feared they must all have cleared out of the district. I had entertained great hopes of finding more down the river valley, but, as often happens in such cases, my visions of teeming preserves in that direction proved illusory.

The next morning I sent off two men to fetch a couple more donkeys from El Bogoi, to enable us to carry all the ivory with us on our return thither. I also despatched Squareface, with the rest of the porters, for Barasaloi, to bring as much of the ivory from the elephants I had shot there as they could manage, as by this time the tusks would slip out without any chopping, owing to decomposition. Meanwhile, I sent a couple of Ndorobos to look for spoor up the valley of a small tributary stream coming out of the mountains, while I kept only Smiler to potter about with me, and amused myself shooting a few doves and a guinea-fowl or two, for the pot, with my rook rifle. There were numbers of both (the latter of the vulturine as well as the common kind) frequenting the mimosa groves near the river. The Ndorobos found no signs of elephants being about, but picked up a pair of tiny tusks of a calf which had died long ago, and brought them as an offering to me. Squareface and his men got back late at night, with the tusks of seven of the best elephants I had killed on 31st August.

The ivory proved better than I had expected. Three of the bulls had tusks of about 50 lbs. apiece, which is about the

limit of a full-sized "herd-bull's" teeth.[1]   The rest they had
extracted and put together ready to be fetched.   The Ndorobos
who were up there, eating and curing the meat of those
elephants, had found one more, making fourteen in all as the
total bag for that day.   The one found by Squareface, when
he went back the day but one after our shoot, was clearly the
first bull I had shot at, as I recognised the teeth, without

A GOOD DAY'S WORK WITH ELEPHANTS.
(From a Photograph by the AUTHOR.)

doubt, by their shape and general appearance.   There is a
great deal of character and individuality in tusks; and I
always find I can tell which elephant, of several I may have
shot, any pair that is afterwards recovered belonged to.   I
afterwards photographed, with my hand camera, the results in
ivory of my Barasaloi day, piled in front of my tent.

As Squareface reported that he had seen the spoor of a
few elephants coming down the Barasaloi valley, I went with

[1] By "herd-bulls" I mean the breeding males, such as are found consorting with the
herds of cows.   The old fellows, with heavier ivory, associate with their peers in separate
herds.   I infer from these facts that a bull elephant is in his prime when his tusks
weigh about 50 lbs. apiece.

him the next day to look for them, while the other men went again to bring in the smaller ivory, which had been left the day before.   But the spoor proved to be two days old, and it returned up the valley again : he had apparently mistaken some of it for fresh, in the dark, so our search was fruitless. Fortunately I had now recovered my health and was beginning to feel quite my old springiness ; and a great blessing it was to feel well and strong and to enjoy one's grub once more.   I had been beginning to fear ill health would spoil my trip, and so was the more pleased to find I was getting back to my old form again.   My cook, good old Feruzi, had comforted me considerably by concocting a sort of thin gruel for me in place of the everlasting tea, of which one gets so particularly sick when suffering from fever, and which it is, I think, by no means wholesome to be continually drinking.

I was getting impatient to move now, so was very glad when, the following evening, the men I had sent to El Bogoi turned up with two more donkeys and my spring balance. Except when in real need of rest, hanging about camp does not suit me at all, especially in so warm a spot as this was ; for, paradoxical as it may sound, excessive heat is far more trying when you are doing nothing than while marching or hunting.   So I set to work at once to pack up the loads, which I could not do satisfactorily till the arrival of the scale enabled them to be adjusted evenly ; and in the morning we started with all our ivory, which was just as much as we could carry, to trek back towards El Bogoi.   The party of Ndorobos who had been here, too, were now ready to return to their own district near the Lorogi, and trekked at the same time, all laden with as much dried meat as they could stagger under. My plan was to take some of them with me to hunt in the Lorogi Mountains (after depositing my ivory at my main camp), where I hoped to find a herd of old bulls.

It took some time to tie up the donkey-loads, so that it was about nine o'clock, on the 12th of September, before we

at length got off. Two donkeys carried, each, two 80 lb. loads
of the smaller ivory, one my tent on one side and bedding, etc.,
on the other, and the fourth our meal, cartridges, etc., while all
the men were loaded up with the larger tusks. I was afraid
the ivory loads on the donkeys would be very troublesome, as
there had not been time to lash it properly, as it should be, with
hide—put on wet and dried on—but to my agreeable surprise
it travelled capitally. All hands being heavily laden, I had to
help to drive the donkeys myself, Squareface, carrying a big
tusk, going before them. Donkeys always require a man in
front of them, whom they follow. I felt quite like Robinson
Crusoe, as I had to carry two rifles—my .450 slung from my
shoulder and the rook rifle in one hand, while in the other I
held a switch to drive the donkeys with ; and, to make the
resemblance complete, I had what I call Crusoe sandals over
my boots. These are inventions of my own, and are most
useful in saving one's boots in the interior. They are made
of game hide (eland or koodoo is about the best), and, if
properly made, are not at all uncomfortable, while they make
a pair of boots last quite twice or three times as long' as they
would without their protection. In driving donkeys the great
thing is to make plenty of noise. It is worse than useless to
strike them, and should never be allowed. They are quite
different from oxen in that way. The use of the switch is to
strike the load or saddle, to frighten the donkey, but never
the animal itself. I have, in former years, driven my own
waggon hundreds of miles, and I know a good deal about trek
oxen and their ways. As an old Boer once said to me when
I was a novice at waggon travelling, " You must give them
plenty strips " ; but with the patient ass it is different. It is
only since I have been elephant-hunting in Central Africa that
I have learnt his peculiarities, and the result of my experiences
as a donkey-driver is that you should never hit him.

As the place where we had to leave the river was too far
to reach in one day—and it is the greatest mistake to attempt

too long a march with heavy loads—I wished to do only about half the distance; and so, about mid-day, I began to look out for a suitable spot to camp.   The river here ran through a wide strip of forest, and could not be seen from outside; so, halting my little caravan, I entered the bush to see how far away the water would be if we stopped where we were.   The river proved to be farther away than I thought, but I soon found something that interested me much more, namely, quite fresh elephant dung.   The bush, too, was extensive and most likely looking, so I was filled with hope for another successful hunt.   I went back at once, trekked some way farther, and then, finding a suitable spot on a little rise in the open, with a tree or two for shade and the river close by, camped.   It was by this time fully one o'clock, and as I had to see things put straight, etc., and believed that, with due caution, there would be no fear of disturbing the elephants where we were, I decided to leave them till the next morning, so as to have the whole day before me for the hunt.

The Ndorobo party had luckily camped farther back, at a rock pool away from the river.   In the afternoon I went out into the open country towards the hills, and shot a Grant's gazelle for meat.   As I have said, outside the forest, dense jungle, and rank swamp growth, which, in varying proportions, clothed the flat alluvial floor of the valley immediately bordering the river, the country was perfectly open, and the transition from the one to the other was quite sudden.   At this part there were stony slopes and comparatively level ridges between the flats and the steep hills enclosing the valley. The ground being so open, and covered only with short dry grass, it was not easy to get within shot of game; so that it was only by making a careful stalk after a long circuit—not forgetting, of course, the direction of the wind—and creeping down a narrow gully that I was able to bag my buck.   But that is just what gives interest to such shooting.   Having reached a point opposite where I had noticed the little herd of gazelles feeding, I crept out cautiously on to the stony ridge, and was able to get my shot at easy range before they took the alarm, and to knock over my victim successfully. I returned to my tent very pleased, and hopeful for the morrow. It was extremely lucky my happening upon signs of elephants here ; and, as I was now enjoying the blessings of health again, and feeling quite strong and up to my work, I was in the best of spirits.

As soon as it was light next morning I started out to hunt, attended, as usual when after elephant, by my three faithfuls, Squareface, Juma, and Smiler. Skirting the edge of the bush for a little way, before entering the wide part near where I had found the tracks yesterday, we passed round the edge of a slimy-looking, evil-smelling, salt lagoon, from which a slight steamy-looking exhalation (strongly suggestive of malaria) was rising in the still air of the early morning, and which had sent us its contribution of - mosquitoes during the night. Little water-hens swam nodding about in it, and sacred ibises stood solemnly on the mud. We then cut straight across the valley bottom, passing through the dense cover with which the flats bordering the stream were clad, to see if the elephants had passed up during the night. Inside, the bush was tunnelled with their paths, the soft ground being, in many places, worn into deep grooves. Sometimes we came upon regular caverns in the forest, the thicket being, as it were, hollowed out by their trampling into shady cloisters, where they had evidently been accustomed to rest and stand about, for the ground was covered with their droppings. In other parts were grassy little openings and passages—the soft, thick grass laid by their sweeping tread. We found that they had passed during the night ; but, before following the spoor, we went through to the edge of the bush on the far side of the valley to make sure that they had not returned. Having assured ourselves on this point, we followed their tracks up stream. At one point, not far from our camp, some of them had skirted the edge of the forest on our side, and it seemed there as if they had been inclined to turn down again ; but possibly they had got our wind, for they entered the bush again and continued up the valley.

After a time we came to a place where the river spread into a number of channels, meandering and interlacing in a bewildering manner, and all between was a horrible quagmire, full of half-dead, tangled jungle, battered and broken down, while below was stagnant water and fetid, black mud—a dismal, forbidding swamp. In some of the deep pools were quantities of fish, showing that they never dry up. We soon found it impossible to penetrate this fastness, and all we could do was to skirt round it on the far side. I feared the elephants might be in this impenetrable stronghold, and that we should pass them ; but luckily we struck off the spoor again, higher up, just outside. We followed it again, with sundry checks, a long way ; and, when nearly opposite where we had first struck the river when coming from El Bogoi, we found that we had overrun the scent. Then, suddenly, we heard elephants singing out quite close in our rear. It was fortunate that we had thus got beyond them, for the wind was, as usual, blowing up the valley, and consequently had been with us. It was now about 3 P.M., for we had had many delays, and at one time, believing the elephants to be near, had unluckily waited for a spell, in hopes of hearing them, so as to avoid inadvertently running into them *with* the wind, thus wasting much valuable time. Going round a bit farther, in order to get well to leeward of the herd, we then advanced cautiously, hearing the elephants at intervals, but farther off, as they were moving —but now in the opposite (down stream) direction. The cover here was rather open forest, with an undergrowth of dense jungle (but at this part not very high), so that, though it was rather troublesome to get through, I could see over it. After following slowly some little distance, and when beginning to fear that they must have got our wind, while we were passing up, and were now retreating, I suddenly saw ahead the tops of the ears and heads of several, standing in a cluster under a tree. Creeping on, big gun in hand, a few paces farther, I was able to see them well, apparently all cows. One bulky but short old cow stood nearest me, but I could not see her tusks at first, and, as she was partly facing towards me, she did not offer a very good shot. Still she seemed to be the biggest and was also the one I could see best, the others being more or less hidden behind each other.

I waited, deliberating whether to try a head shot, and with this idea took the Lee-Metford from my gun-bearer, who stood silently behind me. But she then gave her head a lift and showed me a fine long pair of " kalashes," crossed at the tips. This decided me not to risk the doubtful chance of reaching her brain from that position, so, taking the 10-bore rifle again, I waited till she let me see the spot just behind the shoulder, and fired for it (though, considering the way she was standing, I ought to have aimed at the shoulder itself). While the others were turning rather slowly to retreat in the opposite direction, I got in a good second barrel on the shoulder of one. The first went on with the rest, but the other could not move away, and in a minute was over and dying. Then Squareface saw some run back away to our left. We rushed to try and cut them off, but the jungle was too dense to let us get through quickly enough, and they passed before we got near. Returning, we followed the spoor, and found blood sprinkled over the jungle, evidently blown either from the trunk or through the wound. A little farther we got puzzled, the blood spoor seeming to return on itself ; but while looking about to make out which way it led, I heard, close ahead, the rumbling made by a hard-hit elephant. These are the most intensely exciting moments of the chase. The nerves are tightly strung, but the tension is so great that, when it has been repeatedly indulged in, one is rendered ever after incapable of excitement : the capacity for it becomes exhausted.

Gliding cautiously nearer, with set teeth, I saw my big cow

standing, very sick, with another by her.   I finished the former off with a Lee-Metford bullet in the brain, dropping her dead, and knocked over the other alongside of her in a similar way. The latter, though, plunged about, rising partially and falling again several times, while I fired two or three more shots into her head as she swung it about.   Then she kept down, but still struggled.   There were two half-grown ones, which I had not noticed before, standing by their prostrate friends ; I could not harm them, and, as I wanted to go up to finish securely the second cow, I told Squareface to shout at them.   This had the desired effect of making them run away.

Perhaps I should have gone on in the hope of finding others standing not far off, but it was getting near sundown, and I was tired (my strength not being yet fully returned after my recent spell of illness), and we had left Smiler at the first elephant.   So we went back to it, cut out the heart and fat, taking also a piece of the trunk and a foot, and started to make our way out of the bush.   By the time we got out (on our own side) it was sundown.   We had gone but a few steps along the open, skirting the edge of the forest, when we heard an elephant scream close by, just inside a patch of some of the densest kind of jungle I know of—namely, that matted green growth, such as I have lately described, found in damp, sandy situations where the soil is salt.   I do not much like going into these places under such circumstances, but the hopes of another elephant overcame my hesitation, and I entered the dark maze by a narrow path.   Then, as I rounded a corner, an elephant, which was just crossing ahead, halted for a moment in the path, and gave me a peep at its shoulder.   I aimed quickly for just behind it and fired.   It gave a loud grunt as the shot struck it, and plunged into the cover.   Then the herd dashed across beyond, making an appalling crashing and cracking as they tore a great road through in their first rush of frenzy, but it was impossible to distinguish any mark in the confused mass, crossing so narrow a gap.   We followed a little way farther, but the path soon became almost impassable, and I decided it would be foolhardy to go on where escape would be impossible and one might be trampled to death without any malicious intention on the part of the elephants. Besides, it was getting dusk ; so, as we could see nothing of my wounded elephant, I made for camp. I had an instinctive confidence that this elephant was mortally hit, and felt no doubt but that I should secure his short thick tusks (of which I had caught a clear enough view to show that they were those of a young bull). It took us till quite eight o'clock to reach camp, going hard through the open. After cleaning my rifles and the usual bath I got some dinner about ten and turned in by eleven, well pleased with this extra stroke of luck— an unexpected one, as I had supposed all the elephants to have already cleared out of the whole valley. We had no Ndorobo natives with us, so had to rely entirely on our own spooring on this hunt, nor did any turn up at all that day.

As we had been already loaded up to the last pound almost we could possibly carry, with the additional ivory now obtained it would be beyond the capacity of my little party to transport all at once. So, first thing on the morning after the hunt just described, I sent off four porters with loads of ivory for El Bogoi camp, in charge of Fundi, one of my responsible men. The porters were to return at once, after depositing the ivory, and should, I calculated, get back on the third day. The tusks were, as usual, to be buried at once, for greater security, and particularly as a precaution against fire ; for ivory is said to burn like a candle, and the grass huts in which one stores one's goods are particularly inflammable and liable to catch fire through the carelessness of the men in charge.

Soon after despatching them, I started again, to see if any elephants were still to be found in the neighbourhood. Cutting across the valley again, to find out if the herd had come this way in the night, we found spoor at once, close to camp. We wasted a lot of time puzzling it out, before we could get fairly away with it in the direction the elephants had finally taken. After manœuvring about they had gone down stream, in which course they steadily kept on, and evidently meant trekking. After patiently following the tracks all down the valley again, we got at last into that awful jungle of giant swamp grass just above our old camp. The spoor led through the most impracticable part of this forbidding fastness. The grass was high enough to hide the biggest elephant; its stems were like canes, and the paths inside were mere tunnels, often obstructed by masses of the thick, heavy crop being laid across them. It was with the greatest labour that we could make any progress through the tangle, and in places it was well-nigh impenetrable, while anywhere but in these tunnels it was as absolutely so as a solid wall. Moreover, owing to the paths being covered with dry litter, it was impossible to keep the spoor. Nor would it have been possible to do anything with them if the elephants had been inside (though my belief was that they had gone right on); for one could hardly see a yard ahead, even in the path, and, as they must have heard us coming and there would be no possibility of escape if they charged, the danger was excessive. So we wormed our way out, and I was not a little relieved to emerge, about three in the afternoon, from the stifling heat and stiff rasping stems of the brake into the open air, where one could stand erect and walk with comfort.

On the way back I got a chance to stalk some Grant's gazelle, which had been feeding on some short green grass growing in a damp hollow near the edge of the lagoon but moved away at our approach, and succeeded, by crawling up a stony ridge under cover of the crest, in shooting a couple to keep up our supply of fresh meat. One of these ran some distance; but feeling confident it was mortally wounded, I sent Juma after it, and he retrieved it and met us farther on with it on his shoulders, Smiler bringing on the other, while Squareface and I carried all the guns and other odds and ends. We reached

camp about sundown after another hard day. I found two of my
Ndorobo friends in camp.   Doubtless they had heard the firing
yesterday and surmised that there would be more elephants to
feast on.   I told them they deserved no more meat, because they
had brought me no honey.   It was always the understanding
that when they were living on my elephants they should keep
me supplied with this wholesome luxury.   But they protested
they could find none here, and I believe they spoke the truth,
for I always found them liberally inclined when they had any ;
so I said they were welcome to go the next day and cut up
the elephants I had killed, on condition that they would search
for the one I had shot in the evening, which I felt convinced
could not go far.   They were not slow to accept my offer, and
turned up in force before it was properly light in the morning,
on the strength of another feast being on the board.   They
brought me a little honey; all they had, they said.   It was
but a tiny portion, but an acceptable addition to my rather
monotonous fare.   Feeling a bit tired myself, and as there did
not seem much chance of finding any more elephants about
now, I sent Squareface and Juma with them to try and find
my lost elephant of the last day's hunt ; but they returned in
the evening without having found it.

In consequence of Squareface having brought a report that
on his way back he had seen the fresh spoor of a herd going
down stream, I was off again as soon as light and tramped
straight down to our lower camp on the chance that it might
have stopped somewhere in that neighbourhood.   However, I
could discover no fresh spoor at all, and though on the way
back we cut through the bush backwards and forwards at
intervals, crossing and recrossing the stream in all six times,
until we reached the locality of our camp again, we could find
no recent traces of elephants nor any spoor fresher than that
we had followed two days before.   The same evening my men
returned from El Bogoi, but they brought no news of my
caravan, which I was now beginning to expect back from

Mthara with stores of food, nor any at all except that another donkey was dead.

Being determined not to move away while there was the least possibility of our leaving elephants behind us in this neighbourhood, I started early again the next morning (17th September) to work up stream in the same way as we had done from below the day before; sending two men meanwhile to get out and bring back the tusks of the dead elephants, so that we might be ready to trek the following day and have no further delay on the way. But we found no fresh signs, and it became clear that the yarn Squareface had brought me was a "cock and bull" one, hatched more out of his head than resulting from any careful investigation. I then went to the dead elephants, and learned, to my great satisfaction, that my Ndorobo friends had found the other quite near to where I had fired at it. It was, as I had thought, a young bull; and I recognised its teeth (weighing 50 lbs. the pair) at once. For I always remember the tusks of an elephant I have shot, even though I only get a glance at them. The tusks of the big cow looked splendid now they were out. I guessed them to weigh about 36 lbs. apiece, but they really scaled 38 lbs. and 39 lbs., and still weigh, now they are thoroughly dry (for I have kept this pair), about what I had estimated them at. This is the heaviest pair of cow teeth I have ever shot, by a great deal. The other two were also good cows, but one had unfortunately broken her tusk in plunging about, digging it into the ground when falling; and, though we picked up one piece, the tip could never be found, notwithstanding that we dug up the ground all about in our search, in which we were helped by the Ndorobos. These, with their women and children, were enjoying themselves immensely, notwithstanding that the game was, to say the least, a shade high, to our ideas. They were in great glee over the old cow with the heavy teeth, as she was excessively fat, which made them grin with delight as they described their satisfaction at such a windfall. I, too, was well pleased as I returned to camp with the ivory. I then set to work, after weighing it, to make it up into loads. We had now again, besides the four loads carried by the donkeys, four loads for porters ; making, with the four already sent to El Bogoi, twelve loads as the result of the present little excursion.

The next day we marched to the top camp on the river, I again driving two donkeys and carrying two rifles, and the morning following, while yet cool, we climbed the long steep stony ascent out of the valley, and halted during the heat of the day at the rock pool on the heights. It was a relief to get out of the hot valley and beyond the reach of the fetid odours exhaled by its pestiferous swamps, with their salt lagoons and reeking black slime, breeding fevers and swarms of mosquitoes—though even these unwholesome pools are not without their redeeming features, to wit, interesting birds (Egyptian geese, ibises, cranes, etc.). There was plenty of edible green stuff, too, to be had along the river, which Feruzi (my cook) always looked out for, and boiled as a vegetable for me ; while my donkeys did themselves well, there. On the tops—probably at least 1500 feet above the river—the air was cooler and fresher and there had been a good shower, reviving the grass and filling the pool with sweet water. While I rested under my "fly"—which had been pitched, without the tent, to give me shade, as there were no trees beyond a scraggy thorn or two,—I could see several elands, a pair of rhinos, and a herd of zebras [1] (Burchell's with a few of Grevy's), forming a picturesque group in a valley not more than half a mile away. One bull eland stood under a tree, apparently within shot of a gully ; and, by going a long way round and getting into the gully higher up and then following it down, I could probably have stalked it. Baithai, a pleasant Ndorobo and a great chum of mine, who

---

[1] I call them Burchell's, but they are really one of the allied varieties of the smaller zebras—all closely related—(possibly Grant's).

GREVY'S ZEBRA (*Equus grevyi*), SHOWING MODE OF PROTECTING FROM VULTURES.

(From a Photograph by the AUTHOR.)

had met me here with a skin bag of exquisitely fragrant honey (a great blessing, as I was almost out of that necessary of the " bara "), wanted me to go and shoot it or a rhino. But, though the meat would have been useful to me, as I had none to take to El Bogoi (where game had to be sought far), I was disinclined to incur the delay, being anxious to continue my journey. After all the elephants they had had (more than even they could cope with), too, I felt under no obligation to hunt for them just then ; so reserved my strength for the rather hard work this style of travelling entailed. I accordingly made another move about 4 P.M., bivouacked at dusk for the night, and arrived at my El Bogoi camp before noon next day, not sorry to be relieved of my donkey-driving duty and load of rifles when the men in charge there, hearing our shouts of encouragement to the pack-animals, came running, with pleasant smiles of welcome, to meet us.

CHAPTER X

EXCURSIONS FROM EL BOGOI (*continued*)

A native duel—An offended guide—Camp by Mreya spring—Signs of elephants—A wrong action—Dearth of water—Deemed a benefactor—Lions disturbed—A chance lost—Spot for a mission station—Replenishing the larder—Back to El Bogoi—A faithful headman—A remorse of conscience—A great disappointment —An Ndorobo camp—News of an elephant preserve—Starvation times—Man-eating lions.

IT was agreeable to get back to my comfortable homelike camp here, with its pleasant shade and little cool stream ; especially as I had run out of salt while away, and did not find the saline deposit I got off the dried-up mud about the salt marshes a satisfactory substitute—it tasted more like Epsom salts ! There was no news of Abdulla and the caravan yet. They had been gone now about forty days ; and, though I did not exactly feel anxious, I wished I could know they were safe. Baithai had accompanied me back and had brought a young fellow with him who had received some nasty spear-wounds in a fight with a friend. I doctored his gashes, and he told me, in the cheeriest way, that he had killed his antagonist. They did not seem to think this a matter of any moment. Another Ndorobo was sent to take word to Lesiat of my return.

I was pretty well occupied, the day after my return, weighing and entering in my note-book all the ivory, and burying it in a big hole close to the door of the hut in which the goods were stored, and with other matters that had to be attended to. A day in camp was not unwelcome ; for I was suffering from nasty wounds on my fingers, made by the 10-bore rifle, which, with its ten drams of powder, kicked like a mule; and, from constant exposure to a scorching sun, the sores had festered badly. As no one had come from Lesiat's, I sent Squareface, on the 22nd, to look him up, while I went out to the open country to try for meat. I saw some oryx, but they were wild; and I did not particularly care for zebra, so left them alone. Then, after managing to miss some Grant's gazelle, I was on my way back, having given up hopes of getting anything, when I came upon some more and killed two with the next two shots, for which success I was very thankful as I was quite out of meat, and it was a long way to where game is to be found from El Bogoi.

Lesiat had not been found, and I now learned that he had gone with his clan to camp in the "subugo" forest on the top of the Lorogi Mountains. This seemed strange, and I came to the conclusion that he was piqued at my going away to hunt at El Gereh. But Baithai had now, with my permission, pitched his camp not far from mine, and he was really about the most sensible Ndorobo I had come across; so I availed myself of his services. One of his men, who came with him the next morning, brought word that there were elephants in the vicinity of a spring at the foot of the range towards the north; so we packed up at once and moved again to a small rock pool, from whence I could hunt that district. This informant described the length of a bull's spoor he had seen by laying one arm on the ground and grasping it with the other hand a third of the way up from the elbow to the shoulder, thus indicating the measurement of the diameter of the footprint. We had some trouble in getting through the old game-track that led towards the water, for it was very much overgrown with thorns; and when we got there we found the hollow in the rock almost dry, so that I had to send to another some distance off for more.

I was off, as usual, betimes on the 24th September, and

made straight for the neighbourhood of a spring called Mreya. Our route led us along the foot of the range, still going north, and in and out of amphitheatres formed by the mouths of valleys running down from the mountains. All the country at their base and for some distance back from them was covered with dense scrub. We found spoor in the vicinity of the spring, but wasted a good deal of time in trying to puzzle out its ultimate direction, as the elephants had been strolling about backwards and forwards. Then I decided to do what we ought to have done at first ; namely, go to the water. There we found the spoor of two small lots, but, as far as I could make out, all cows ; and I could not discover the phenomenal footprint that had been described to me. One of the lots seemed to have gone back in the direction of El Bogoi, the other ahead. We followed the latter. It was slow work, for there were quite a few elephants and the tracks were often difficult to follow. They had been sauntering along, feeding here and there, as the chewed rolls of fibre of the mkongi plant (which they spit out) testified. Occasionally fresh droppings were on the spoor, but we had not found any warm yet ; and though, as is customary when elephants are known to be not far off, we stopped now and then to listen, no sound indicating their close proximity had reached our ears.

We were thus moving along on the spoor without any immediate expectation of coming up with our game, though as a matter of course we were proceeding in the cautious and careful manner which becomes instinctive habit, threading our way silently through the narrow and more or less obstructed winding alleys which permeate these dense and thorny jungles and testing the wind now and again, when we came suddenly close upon them. I could see several at once, for, just where they were standing, the bush was not quite so thick. I stole up yet nearer, and stood surveying the position. Luckily the breeze was favourable and held steady. Two cows were close on my right, heads towards me, and prevented my getting into a better position for a shot at another a little farther off, which appeared the biggest, standing diagonally, head away, rather more than three-parts turned from me. She was standing under a kind of euphorbia or cactus tree and had a piece of a branch she had broken from it in her mouth, off which she was chewing the bark, the bare white end protruding on one side. The thick milky juice of this tree is excessively pungent, the least spurt of it in the eyes causing intense irritation. I should imagine the effect of swallowing any on the human stomach would be very serious ; but an elephant's mucous membrane must be less sensitive.

I waited a little ; but as they did not seem inclined to move at all, and fearing the two cows next me (which were very close) might get my wind if I delayed longer, I took a steady shot at the ribs of the big cow, calculating my aim so that the bullet, driving forward, would get her heart, and fired. She gave a tremendous grunting cry as she received the ball. As they began to stampede I got a snap at one of the others with the second barrel. Immediately after, the first appeared again for a second standing close by, after the rest had passed, and, with a scream, fell over. Looking round in hopes of discovering the second, I saw a rhinoceros standing close by, which, as it afterwards appeared, some of my men, who had been just behind and now came up, thought was a fallen elephant.

Not wishing to waste more time, I followed up the spoor of the rest, and very soon came to where they had stood again. Possibly, if I had come on immediately after the collapse of the first, I might have got another chance here. Going on, we heard them rumbling, and soon sighted two, standing in a comparatively open space (as bush goes here). To be able to see elephants at all means that you are already pretty near, and a few quick, but stealthy, steps brought me quite close up to these. But, before I could get a chance to shoot, one came walking straight for me ; and as I could not well get out of the way, owing to the thick and thorny scrub, I fired in her face when only a few paces off, not knowing what else to do and not caring to wait to test her intentions by allowing her to reach me — though I do not believe they were evil, but rather suppose she did not know I was there at all. I afterwards, in thinking over the situation (one which has occurred to me more than once before), came to the conclusion that I ought to have shouted at her, to make her halt or turn her broadside. I did not want to shoot at her as she came on ; for not only was it well-nigh impossible to give her a fatal shot in that position, but behind her was one with larger tusks. Her chest was covered by the undergrowth as well as by her trunk, which was down, and to reach her brain through the thick part of the latter and the whole length of her head, as I looked up at her, was barely possible even if the aim happened to be right—at all events with the 10-bore I had in my hands, though no doubt a .303 has sufficient penetration. Jumping aside into the thorns the instant I had pulled the trigger, and before the voluminous smoke from the big charge of black powder allowed me to see what she was doing, I was too late to give her a second shot as she turned off, as I might have been able to do had I stood firm. But, in the momentary glance I got at her the second after I fired, I distinctly saw the bullet-wound in the centre of the thick part of her trunk and the blood coming from it.

Following again, we soon came upon the two once more, but this time in a very thick place. I could only see one ; she was standing awkwardly, nearly facing me, and in the shadow of the bush, and before I could get a better view they moved on. Probably the old cow which I had killed had been their leader, and her loss was the cause of their delaying so much ; for the wounded one was not badly enough hurt to prevent their going right away, and they were of course thoroughly alarmed. We found blood, though only a little, on the spoor ; but we never sighted them again, though we persevered and heard them close to us several times, for the bush was dense and the wind shifty and they kept on the move.

At length, well on in the afternoon, I gave up and retraced our steps towards where I had first encountered the elephants. Squareface and Juma maintained that there were two elephants down there, but I felt convinced that what they had taken for a second was a rhino; for I could not believe I was mistaken about it, having distinctly seen its horn. Nevertheless, I could not help entertaining a lingering hope that they might be right. On reaching the spot, however, there was neither elephant nor rhino to be seen, so that there could no longer be the least doubt that I had been correct; for, though we searched well all about, the only elephant we could find was the old cow I had first shot at and which we had seen fall. It was curious that the rhino should have stood close by while I shot and the elephants shouted and stampeded. This instance proves, too, that there is not necessarily any antagonism between these animals. The dead elephant was a very old cow, with a wizened face and unusually skinny throat, and both her tusks were very much worn down, though of fair thickness for "kalasha" ivory. We took out her heart, and found that my bullet had gone through the very centre of it. I returned to my camp at the rock hole, rather disappointed with the day's hunt; but I entertained a hope that possibly the other wounded elephant (both shots were at the same) might yet be found.

I got back after dark a good deal torn and scratched by thorns, and my finger, which had been sore so long from repeated wounds inflicted by the trigger-guard of the heavy rifle, very painful. On getting to camp I was not a little annoyed to find there was no water for my gun-bearers; as it appeared even the second pit had run dry, some of the Ndorobo women belonging to Baithai's party, who had followed me and camped close by, having emptied it. Under these circumstances I told the Ndorobo who had been with me that day to summon Baithai himself to a consultation the first thing in the morning.

He, however, hearing that I was annoyed, sensibly came at once ; so we had our council of war by the fire and I was mollified.

It was decided that we should move camp in the morning to a larger rock pool, which I was assured was full of water, beyond where we had just been hunting ; the little Ndorobo community, consisting of two or three women and a few

AUTHOR'S CHEF EXERCISING HIS ART.
(From a Photograph.)

children belonging to Baithai and one or two of his mates, following.   Baithai assured me there was a very favourite haunt of elephants farther on (still along the foot of the Lorogi), where a stream ran out of a gorge in the mountains, and said he thought we were almost sure to find some about there. Failing that, we were to climb the range and hunt in the " subugo " forest on the top.   He told me he had sent all through the El Bogoi bush and southward along the foot of the mountains as far as another spring where I had shot some elephants the previous trip, and that there was not a spoor to be seen anywhere in that direction.   It was pretty late before I had done my gun-cleaning, bathed, and dined.   My dinner consisted of broiled kabobs of fat elephant heart and Grant's gazelle fillet spitted alternately on a stick—a really delicious dish.

I did not intend to do anything but move camp on the following day and we had not far to go, so for once in a way I slept till broad daylight and then had breakfast quietly and comfortably before starting.   Baithai accompanied me and we were followed by his belongings—women, children and all, their household gods (not very extensive) on the women's backs. These Ndorobos are pleasant people when you have won their confidence.   They looked on me as a benefactor, and always greeted me with friendly smiles.   Shaking hands with them (a custom of their own) is rather a trial sometimes, when they have been busy about the carcase of an elephant that has been dead several days (elephant meat does not keep well), or handling some hoarded bones with a powerful aroma, it is true ; but I like such cordial manifestations of confidence in one.

I found the rock pit a good-sized one and full of curious-looking water, very green and opaque, but not bad tasted.   No doubt its colour was caused by some kind of minute growth in it ; though why this particular pool should differ in this way from other similar ones puzzled me.   It was on a rocky little spur of an outlying hill near the foot of the main range, and I found a picturesque spot to camp in, half-way up the side, where there was just enough fairly level ground to pitch my tent under a convenient tree.   Being pretty high here, my camp commanded a magnificent view over the country north-wards right up to Mount Nyiro (near the south end of Lake Rudolph), which loomed up big and dark in the distance.   I spent a rather pleasant, lazy day after the short march, making things snug, writing up my diary and pottering about. Baithai and Co. had made their camp near by, but most of them were away all day cutting up yesterday's elephant, which was not far from here, and some slept by the carcase.

The next morning, feeling thoroughly refreshed and fit after my easy day, I was off before sunrise with Baithai and my usual gun-bearers. We went along the very edge of the valleys lying under the mountains, keeping close under the latter, where there were, at this part, frequent little open glades which enabled us to get along more freely and comfortably than when threading the thorny mazes of the jungle which stretched away on our right. While it was still early we passed over a rather steep and stony shoulder (the foot, in fact, of a buttress of the mountain) and into the valley which contained the stream, issuing from a kloof or gorge in the mountains, for which we were making, and where Baithai hoped to find signs of elephants.

While descending by a very rough game-track overlooking this valley, which the rising sun was just lighting up, I noticed that a large white thorn-tree, growing near the edge of some thick bush, beside a grassy glade which it overlooked, was laden with vultures. Going, as is my invariable custom under such circumstances, to see what might be the cause of this gathering, with thoughts of my wounded elephant of two days before in my mind, we disturbed about half-a-dozen maneless lions or lionesses from the carcase of a large bull giraffe they had apparently killed the day before but were still eating. When after elephants I do not carry a rifle myself except when getting close to them ; and to-day I had, with unpardonable carelessness, not yet loaded any, as we had not seen any fresh spoor and I had no idea of going after any other game. The consequence was that I lost this chance, or I might anyway have got one of the lions, which stood before clearing out. I did not care particularly though, as I hoped to find elephants, and should not have liked to spend the time needed to skin a

lion.   However, as it turned out, we might just as well have
spent the day in skinning lions, for we could find no traces of
elephants.

There was here a beautiful stream of clear, cold water,
running strongly for some little distance after issuing from the
ravine before it disappeared in a little swamp in the flat, and
some pleasant grassy meadows bordered it.   It struck me as
a pity such a suitable spot could not be utilised—say, for a
mission station,—with its adaptability for irrigation.   Baithai
said that if elephants were anywhere in the neighbourhood they
would certainly resort to this stream to drink ; so, having
searched its banks in vain for any indication of their recent
visits, there was nothing for it but to turn back.   I returned
then to the carcase of the giraffe, in hopes of finding the lions
there again, but they had not gone back to it nor could we find
them anywhere about.   I then took a round through the more
open country to the eastward, in hopes of getting some fresh
meat, but missed a chance at zebra through the sight of my
Lee-Metford (which required careful adjustment, as it was
incorrectly regulated) having got wrong, and got back to
camp empty-handed and rather disgusted with this unlucky
day.

I had a talk with Baithai about further plans, and it was
agreed that he was to send off two lads on the morrow to
prospect for elephants still farther on than we had yet been.
They were to return at once if they found spoor, but otherwise
would not be back till the day but one after.   I sent Juma to
El Bogoi, the morning after, to fetch some more supplies ready
for an expedition on to the mountains which I had in view, and
instructed him, should he find the caravan there (as I thought
very probable), to tell Abdulla (my headman) to come back
with him.   I went out to try for meat, making for some open
country which could be seen out on the flats.   But, while
passing through the broad belt of thick bush which separated
us from it, we cut the fresh spoor of two or three cow elephants,

and I thought it my duty to follow it. However, it proved labour in vain. They were travellers making straight, evidently, for the Barasaloi, where that stream comes out of the mountains, which was a very long way off, and not feeding nor delaying, so we had to give it up and come back.

A shower we had had in the afternoon made it delightfully fresh the next morning as I turned my steps early once more towards the "Ongata," or open country, with a view to replenishing the larder, though the glistening drops studding each spray made it rather damp work getting through the intervening jungle. No sooner had we reached the grass land, which here had been recently burned and was springing green, than I saw some Grant's gazelle. At first they saw me and ran ; but, as I sat down and kept still and they did not get my wind (the breeze being in my face), curiosity made them come back to see what I was (I had left my attendants behind), and I shot two, buck and doe. Perhaps the glint of the rifle-barrel in the early morning sun fascinated them, as a revolving mirror attracts larks. The Grant's gazelle seemed to be mostly thin here at this time (September). I think most of the does must have had young fawns, though none were to be seen ; for, when quite young, they are left lying alone, while the mothers graze, and it is only when accidentally come upon that one is noticed. Having accomplished my object, I went back early to camp, my men carrying the two gazelles.

Soon after my return, Abdulla and several of his men arrived, along with Juma. I was indeed pleased and thankful to see them seemingly in first-rate form and spirits, and to hear that the whole caravan was safe and well. They had got to El Bogoi camp yesterday, Abdulla told me, and all his news was satisfactory, and he had had no mishaps. He had stayed so long (this was 28th September and they had left me on 13th August) in order to buy donkeys, having had my permission to do so, and had got five. He had brought twenty-four loads of beans, which he had been able to buy quickly without any difficulty. He had done one thing, though, I did not approve of, as it was risky; he had been to Laiju, attended by only two men, passing over the Jambeni range, which is inhabited by the Embe tribe, the same treacherous people who had murdered four of my men on my former expedition, and whom I had been obliged to punish for that crime. He had a spear thrown at him, which he brought along; but he made light of this, which he said was the act of some turbulent young fellow, and declared that it was quite safe now for one man to pass through alone, as there was no hostility shown by the people generally.

After discussion and consideration I decided it would be best to send once more to Mthara, so that we might accumulate ample supplies of food for our long journey through the wilderness, with margin for possible hunting by the way. This would give me a little more time in this region, so that I might carry out my plan for hunting in the "subugo" before trekking on. Abdulla also reported that Ndaminuki, my "blood brother," to whom he had been the bearer of presents from me, had behaved in the most friendly and obliging way and done all he could to help him.

Late in the evening Baithai brought word that his messengers had returned from the Barasaloi "subugo" and reported that they had found no fresh spoor anywhere, nor could they hear any news of elephants being in that neighbourhood now from Ndorobos belonging to that part whom they had met there. In consequence of this I decided to return to El Bogoi the next day with Abdulla, so as to arrange everything there with regard to their second trip to Mthara, and then make a fresh start from there myself for the mountains. In the evening some guinea-fowl perched in a tree close to camp and I took toll of one with my rook rifle. The tusks of the old cow had been brought in to-day. I guessed the pair to weigh about 30 lbs., and this subsequently proved correct to a fraction.

In the morning we trekked back to El Bogoi by a different and more open route than we had come by. On the way I

shot another gazelle.   Had I known, I might have got an
oryx, as there were two close by, but I did not see them till I
had shot the other buck, and they had got well away.   I found
my men all as cheerful as possible and looking very fit.   They
were quite contented to go again to Mthara, as they got good
living there, but seemed to be looking forward eagerly to the
onward move towards the lake, which they were as keen as I
was to visit.   Abdulla's new donkeys were fine strong ones, in
good condition, and would be a great help on our journey to
the north.   My other donkeys had also improved with their
rest here.

I was altogether very pleased with the way Abdulla had
done his duty on this trip, and told him so ; for he had carried
out my wishes most zealously and faithfully.   He was a headman after my own heart.   I arranged everything for him to
start again the following day, and told him to be back, if
possible, in twenty days, by which time I meant to be quite
ready to make a final start for Reshiat.   Though anxious to
go on, I was glad to get a little more time here first, as I
particularly wanted to go over the Lorogi Mountains, under
which I had done so much hunting ; it was as well, too, to
secure an abundant supply of food before plunging into the
desert ahead, for there is nothing like having an ample provision
for the future.   In the meantime, I hoped to get a little more
ivory.

The porters had come to me in the afternoon and asked
me to give them another day to rest here, to which I willingly
assented ; so I went out the next morning to try and get some
meat, but saw not a living thing.   Baithai, who had made his
camp not far from mine again, came and said he had sent men
to prospect the " subugo " (that is, the forest on the mountains)
far and wide for elephants ; he also told me that Lesiat had
come back with his clan, and was encamped under the range
near one of my old hunting-camps, whence I had shot several
elephants last year.   But what sounded less hopeful was the

news he brought that Lesiat's party had killed one or two elephants in the mountain forest ; however, he seemed confident there would still be some about.   The weather was much drier and consequently more favourable for visiting the high "subugo" than when I had been here the year before, for now it seldom rained even on the range.   Another Ndorobo friend of mine, the head of the community who had been to El Gereh with me and feasted on my elephants there, also came to see me, and said he had a small tusk he wished to give me.   Of course such gifts entail return presents, and are really often more costly in this way than if bought ; so that my general motto with most natives is " timeo Danaos et dona ferentes " ; but these people are not nearly so grasping and insatiable as the average African, and I do not grudge treating them liberally.

On 1st October Abdulla left for Mthara once more.   I was still waiting for news about elephants, and thought it best not to go to the "subugo" till I had got some.   My old friend Lesiat came to see me.   He tried to conceal his success at the elephants this time, and declared that he, at all events, had only killed a very little one himself.   He had brought me some most beautiful honeycomb, as white as snow almost, and the honey as clear as crystal.   As usual he stayed all night in my camp, where he knew he always got a hearty welcome and a hearty feed.   But when in the evening, after I had done my dinner, he came to sit by the log fire in front of my tent to have our customary chat, with Squareface as interpreter, I noticed that there was a certain unwonted constraint in his manner.   He seemed to think he had not treated me quite well in scaring the elephants while I was away, for he knew I had taken particular pains to let him know when I killed mine : and I, on my part, pretended to be angry with him.   But the fact was, he had been too lazy to go as far as El Gereh, which was beyond his beat, and yet he did not like my going without him.   He declared he had no news of elephants anywhere

now. Juma, whom I had sent off the day before in the opposite
direction to that in which I had been lately hunting—that is, to
the southward in the district of the upper Seya—returned,
bringing with him two Ndorobo youths from that part. They
had nothing to impart, though, as they said there had been no
elephants in their neighbourhood since Lesiat drove out the
big herd just after my arrival. Juma, however, declared that he
had seen fresh spoor on his way back, in a part where I had
hunted formerly. Taking all things into consideration, I
decided to go that way first, leaving the mountains till I had
definite news as to what part of the range I should be likely
to find in.

But before starting next morning I gave Lesiat as much
beans as his wife could carry, the greater part of a big loaf
of tobacco (which Abdulla had brought me for the purpose of
giving my Ndorobo friends, who prize it more than anything),
and six Grant's gazelle skins. This made him smile again.
The skins (which they are very fond of to sew into cloaks) he
would not take then, as he did not want his friends to see
them lest they should beg some from him, so he told me to
put them away till he had an opportunity of smuggling them
home on the quiet.

We then packed up as quickly as we could, and went south
to a place about the same distance from the range, where there
was a pool of very hard and rather nasty water impregnated
with some kind of salt mineral, and I sent for Lorgete (the
Ndorobo who had behaved rather badly on my first arrival this
trip). When he came he had a great many words to say,
first, about our quarrel, trying to make out that he was the
aggrieved party. I listened patiently and answered him
quietly, pointing out how he had deceived me in order to
prevent Lesiat hearing of my arrival, in consequence of which
the latter had disturbed the elephants, while he could show me
none, so that my chance of getting any was spoilt—through
his selfish jealousy. At last he consented to come back to

elephant news. He told me then that there was a small troop of bulls about, and that they had been seen yesterday not far from here. He slept at my camp, so as to be ready to go out early with me on the morrow. By sunrise we were well on the way towards the part where he thought the herd might probably be, as he was familiar, from life-long experience, with their favourite haunts when in the neighbourhood.

Before long fresh spoor showed that he was right in his calculations. We did not, however, follow it, but made for a high rocky koppie not far off, which we proceeded to climb. As I reached the summit, Lorgete, who had preceded me, beckoned me to follow him on to a rock free from bushes. I could see by his smile of satisfaction and the excited look in his eyes that he had already made out elephants, and on reaching his side I too saw at once—without the help of his eager clutch of my arm and demonstrative pointing—the tops of the heads and backs, and the upper parts of the slowly flapping ears, of several elephants, visible, from our point of vantage, among the bush a little beyond. Our perch on the top of this abrupt, conical hill completely overlooked the dense jungle, which lay spread below us in all directions, for some distance. The greater part of it was thorny scrub, some ten or twelve feet in height, but in some places were clumps of bushy thorn-trees through which we could not see.

As I carefully scanned the bush all about and beyond the elephants I had first caught sight of, gradually another and another became defined as it waved its huge ears or moved out of the shadow of a tree with which its dusky form had been blended. I thus made out eight, all big bulls as their broad foreheads and massive outlines made at once apparent. "Kitok" (big), whispered Lorgete, with tremendous emphasis on the last syllable,—holding out his spear to indicate exaggerated length, and then putting his hands, spread, in the position of grasping, wide apart on each side of his thigh, by way of suggesting fabulous bulk, the while grimacing notes of admiration to further accentuate his pantomimic description of the enormous size of their tusks according to his opinion. I watched for some time. They seemed to have ceased feeding. Five moved on ahead ; another was some way off apart, the other two remained standing quite near our koppie.

While we sat on the top, the wind, though light, kept steadily in our faces ; but on descending, for the purpose of approaching these last two elephants, it became puffy and shifty, and, as I advanced through the dense cover, I felt almost certain it would betray me. Oh for a good stiff breeze ! However, I decided to go on and chance it, and picking my way with every caution, I got near enough to see them through the narrow opening in the bush left by the path which I was following. One mighty fellow stood among thick scrub, head on to me, the other was behind him. I approached close, but could not possibly get a shot. I wanted to go back and try from another direction, but he seemed to see me and I feared if I moved he would go—or come. In this suspense I stood for a considerable time, face to face with the great beast. He was a huge brute, with magnificent long and thick tusks, which I guessed to weigh not less than 90 lbs. apiece. My heart sank as I felt the wind lull and veer, and then a gentle breath on my back. I knew it was all up, as I could not possibly shoot him in his present position, but trusted to a possible chance as he turned. Up went his trunk and round he swung and was off at a run in a moment. I fired a snap-shot, but could not see to aim for the thick cover. Nor were there any traces of blood on the spoor. We followed their windings for hours in this vast stronghold, but at last had to give it up, as they had turned down wind in the afternoon. I returned to camp heavy at heart. It was a truly heart-breaking disappointment that, of the first big bulls I had seen this trip, I had failed to get even one. One must bear such, though, in a hunter's life ; and the only thing I could hope, as I had

not killed my elephant, was that I had missed it altogether.
But oh, those heavy tusks!

Though I had but slight hopes of finding again so soon
after scaring our game, I was out again the next morning and
met Lorgete at a spot in the bush by arrangement. As I had
feared, the elephants had cleared out, and there was no fresh
spoor to be found. Lorgete was an unsatisfactory man to
hunt with, and always annoyed me a good deal. He was too
excitable, and had far too much to say, and a habit of halting
every now and then to unburden himself of many irrelevant
words, which is particularly vexing when one is intent upon
the search for game. To-day he disgusted me with his
constant humbug, so much so that I thought he must have
been drinking mead. He showed plainly, too, that he was
eaten up with jealousy of my much stauncher and more reliable
friend Lesiat; so I was rather glad to get rid of him and
return early to camp, especially as Squareface was lame and
had foolishly followed me without telling me about it. Later
in the day his son, who had just returned from Lesiat's, told
me that he had seen the spoor of our yesterday's herd going
towards El Bogoi. Under these circumstances I decided to
move back in that direction.

We accordingly shifted our quarters again, but, instead of
returning to the main camp, struck across to a point higher up
the stream, near to which I knew Baithai's family was now
encamped. A newly used path from the water showed us the
way to the den—stinking like a hyena's lair—quite near. It
is extraordinary what miserable places these Ndorobo camps
are; huts hardly deserving the name—put to shame by many
birds' nests—just stuck down in the uncleared scrub without
even a shady tree or open space. Baithai and his companions
and their women came in just after we got there, the women
laden with rotting elephant bones and putrid meat. It seemed
he had found a small elephant dead, undoubtedly the one I
had shot with my second barrel (and afterwards hit again) the

day I killed the old cow at Mreya. The tusks, which he loyally gave up to me quite cheerfully, were small. I would not have shot it if I had known ; but it was a snap-shot in the bush, and the only one I got a chance at. This one made up my total so far for this trip to twenty-five. He said his messengers had found lots of spoor in the "subugo," but he thought there were also some elephants in the gorge of the El Bogoi, just under the mountains, and promised to come in the morning to hunt with me. Our search there was fruitless. We followed up the El Bogoi, carefully examining its banks all the way, to the head of the ravine, but not a spoor could we see. This proved there could be no elephants in the neighbourhood of the stream. We accordingly came back to camp early.

In the afternoon I was visited by quite a crowd of Ndorobos, composed of Lesiat's people and some of a clan living farther along the mountains at their highest part (which is that properly called Lorogi, though the name is often used to denote the whole range). These latter were, with their headman—a nice old gentleman—on a visit to Lesiat's tribe, with whom they were friendly. I was glad to make their acquaintance, as I hoped some day to hunt in their district. I had an interesting chat with the old man, who had brought me a little honey, and gave him a present. He described their part of the country as a renowned elephant preserve, and said truly, as I knew from what I had heard elsewhere, that it had always been celebrated as such. After these interviews Lesiat's young bloods danced for me. Their dances are similar to those of the Masai, consisting mainly of jumping up and down accompanied by singing. The music is, of course, of a barbaric and primitive kind, but rather tuneful. I was very sorry I had no meat to give my visitors ; but, as a matter of fact, I had not a scrap for myself or I would have shared it with them, as they knew well. Indeed I was having rather starvation times just then, and felt a bit stale, as the result of constant hard exercise with little that is wholesome or satisfying in the way of food; an unsuitable combination. I had rarely been out of meat before on hunting expeditions; but luck was against me now, for though I went out on purpose to shoot some the next day, I returned unsuccessful. I saw game—oryx, giraffe, etc.—but the wind was unfavourable, so I had to come back empty-handed to starve again. Lesiat came again, in hopes, no doubt, that I should have killed something; for he knew by experience that I would share my last morsel with him. He had no encouraging news to give me: however, in the evening one of his men brought word that elephants were in the part of the bush not far from his present camp. Cheered by this, I decided to put off my journey on to the mountain, for which I had made preparations, another day.

It is unnecessary to weary the reader with a detailed description of the next day's hunt, as it was an exact repetition of my recent experience with Lorgete. The scrub was of the densest; the wind any way—when there was a breath at all—and Lesiat rather fussy and irritating. The bull I came up to stood directly facing me in a narrow, hardly passable track, in the midst of impenetrable thicket which covered it even in front, so that I could not possibly get in a shot at its chest. Of course it got my wind, and disappeared instantly with a sudden rush. Lesiat was disheartened, I nearly heart-broken, and camp a long weary way off. So I gave up and tramped back, tired and discomfited. The glimpse I had got of its load-apiece tusks did not lessen the chagrin I felt.

Lesiat showed no inclination to accompany me to the "subugo" (as the elevated forest tracts are called by the Masai and Ndorobo tribes). The word is often mistaken for the name of a locality, and appears as such in many maps; but in reality it denotes the character of the forest—a kind found on high mountain ranges and plateaux of considerable altitude in many parts of East Central Africa. The most characteristic tree of the majority of these true forests, which are nurtured by the comparative moisture of such cool heights, is the juniper, a conifer with foliage reminding one strongly of that of the "arbor vitæ" though much less dense.   Lesiat said that if I killed any elephants, not too far away, he would follow me to eat them on receiving news of my success.   Where he had been lately encamped on the mountains was only just over the brow, near which they had killed the two I had heard about ; and he would, he said, on no account go down the slopes on the western side.   The reason he gave for his objection to visiting that region was that it was infested with man-eating lions ; and he told me the following story as proof of this, and to account for his aversion to that part of the country.   I give it just as he told it me.

When he was a young man, he was once wandering there with a companion in search of honey—the usual occupation of these people.   While pursuing their quest, he was suddenly sprung upon by a lion, which seized him by the head and began dragging him away.   As it passed, with him in its mouth, close to a thick bushy tree, he (according to his own account) managed to get his head among the branches and thus delay his captor's progress, at the same time calling to his companion for help.   The latter let drive an arrow into the lion, which then transferred its attentions to him, letting go Lesiat.   Lesiat, after having had his head in the beast's mouth, did not care to pursue the controversy further, so ran away shouting and left his friend to be eaten.   The lion, he explained, did not die. In proof of his story he showed me the scars on his head, which were plain enough.   I pointed out that this must have happened a great many years ago, as he was now an elderly man ; but he maintained that the man-eater was still haunting the neighbourhood, and that it was not the only one that preyed on human beings in that part.

CHAPTER XI

FROM EL BOGOI TO LAKE RUDOLPH

A trying march—A Swahili yarn—Shoot an uncommon gazelle—The "high veldt"
—A jackal claims relationship—A curious episode—Thomson's gazelle and
Jackson's hartebeeste—My "lucky camp"—A new branch of obstetrics—A
land flowing with honey—My ivory store—A welcome sight—Disturbing a
siesta—A gardener's opportunity—Death of a favourite—A photographer's
disguise—Our route to Lake Rudolph—A providential escape.

ON 9th October I climbed the range, accompanied by Baithai
and two Ndorobo youths, and of course my usual little party
of nine or ten men carrying my hunting equipment. We had
a terribly trying march. Baithai took us straight up the
almost precipitous mountain side, where there was no track of
any sort. After struggling through dense thickets at the base,
we found the lower part of the ascent covered with a thick low
growth of brushwood, very disagreeable to get through, and
above that the dry grass was as slippery as ice. This on such
an excessively steep gradient made the long climb a most
arduous and trying one in the broiling heat. When, at last,
the pleasant cool shade of the forest was reached on the
summit, the relief was unspeakable, after the fierce glare of the
burning sun on the steep hillside to which we had been
exposed all the morning while laboriously mounting step by
step some 3000 feet. Once on the top, our hard work was
over. We could walk with comfort among the stems of tall
trees, there being but little undergrowth except in the valleys,
and had a welcome rest by a little stream (the head of El

Bogoi) which we soon came to, in whose clear cold water my thirsty men were glad to slake their thirst.

I soon pushed on, and reached the camping-ground Baithai recommended soon after 2 P.M. ; but most of the porters had stopped behind and lost our trail, and were not brought in by the Ndorobo sent in search till near sundown. It was a picturesque spot by a little, open, grassy glade, below which in a hollow, the head of a ravine, was a spring whose water flowed westward. The whole of the tops and western slopes of this range are clothed with forest, cold and damp and gloomy, the trees (which in some parts are of considerable size, attaining occasionally to perhaps even 100 feet in height) festooned with mosses, and every hollow with its swampy stream. It is a dismal and depressing place, and strange creatures emit weird and melancholy cries all night ; sounds which puzzle one as to whether they are produced by bird, beast or reptile.

Squareface and Baithai had gone on ahead in the afternoon to look for spoor, and found some quite fresh not far off, and also heard the elephants, so in the morning we went to look for these. The night had been fine, without even a mountain mist, but there was a heavy dew and the still air of the early morning was chilly. It is needless to recount all our tedious windings on this day, as it proved another blank. We followed fresh spoor, which we picked up near where the elephants had been heard the afternoon before ; but they had wound about and separated, and must afterwards have got our wind, for though we persevered assiduously till well on in the afternoon, through many steep and slippery kloofs, and even once heard them, we could never come within sight. Then the tracks became involved and difficult to puzzle out ; it was thundering and beginning to rain, and our guides said that if we followed farther they would not be able to find the way back to camp, so I turned back heavy-hearted and empty-handed once more.

It was hard work, but the forest was beautiful and interesting. Where fairly level, as on the ridges, the ground was tolerably open among the tall, straight tree-trunks ; but in the steep kloofs of the streams and numerous little boggy tributaries (all eventually joining a branch of the Seya) there was much undergrowth. Everywhere were signs of elephants frequenting the forest, but, except here and there a little rhino dung, of no other game. Pigeons were numerous, and the wings of the plantain-eaters lit up with flashes of crimson the sombre grey-beard moss with which many of the trees were draped, or streaked the green canopy of foliage as one looked down over ravines resounding with their noisy but pleasant cries. There was a long, heavy shower in the evening, and the night was cold and misty.

I had been working pretty hard for some time now, with no success to stimulate me, on a not very wholesome nor nourishing diet (namely, beans and wild green stuff), and often getting insufficient sleep, so that I felt a bit slack ; and knowing how this is apt to affect one's nerves and through them spoil one's shooting, I concluded that a day's rest would do me no harm. So that the next day (11th October) I stayed in camp and pottered about in the forest, where there was plenty to interest one, catching butterflies or admiring beautiful little tree-frogs and rare birds ; while Squareface and Baithai went out in one direction, and Juma with another Ndorobo in the opposite one, to look for spoor.

In the afternoon I was strolling about in the forest not far from camp when I met Squareface returning laden with fresh elephant meat. As I had not fired a shot the day before, I wondered how he had procured it, until he explained that he had shot a small cow himself. He said that he had got in among a herd without knowing it, and that this one had charged him, and declared that he had only fired one shot. I knew the Swahíli character better than to believe this yarn, and did not feel at all pleased, being sure that he must have

driven the herd away. Still, the meat was acceptable and I
did not upbraid him. It transpired long afterwards, though,
that he had used a number of cartridges. My fears about the
elephants leaving the neighbourhood were also verified, as will
presently appear. He knew that I never allowed him to use
his rifle, which he carried merely as a weapon of defence ; but
I expect he was tempted to try his hand by coming upon the
elephants in open forest, where it would be easy to get near
and obtain a clear shot from the safe cover of the trees. Juma
brought no news of any use. He was out till sundown and
saw the spoor of three travellers only, going south.

The day had been cloudy and showery and the night was
cold and wet, and it still rained in the morning when I started
out again myself with Juma and one Ndorobo, Squareface with
one or two more of my men going to fetch the teeth of his
elephant and some meat, while Baithai was off to summon his
family to the feast. We took a long round, crossing the deep
valley of the main stream draining this part of the range (from
the crest on the opposite side of which I got a fine view over
the open country beyond for a long distance), and then descending to where the valleys join the level country and begin to
open out into green, grassy savannahs. I determined to come
and camp in this pleasant borderland between the forest and
the open plains ; and I hoped still to find elephants somewhere,
though it was clear the herd Squareface had disturbed had
shifted its quarters, since the only fresh tracks we could find
were those made in its retreat. Still there was plenty of
recent spoor everywhere, and anyway it would be interesting to
see something of the country on this side of the range and find
out what game it contained.

So the next day we moved down, camping in a little glade
close to the edge of the open country, on the banks of a strong
stream. The descent on this side of the mountains, though
sufficiently difficult with loads, is nothing like so steep as their
eastern face, and the plains here must be much higher than the

country on the El Bogoi side.[1]   In the afternoon I took a stroll into the open and shot a brace of Grant's gazelle.   I found that they differed from those on the other side of the range (and everywhere else I had been) in having longer hair and dark bands on the sides, while the shade of the back is also deeper than in the common kind.   I brought home a skin of this variety and it is now in the British Museum.   I am indebted to Mr. Oldfield Thomas for the following description of this variety which has appeared in the *Annals and Magazine of Natural History*, November 1897.

Gazella grantii, notata, subsp. n.

Similar in all essential characters to the typical *G. grantii*, but distinguished by the greater length, breadth and intensity of both the dark and light lateral bands.   The former is nearly black, the latter pale buff, and succeeded above posteriorly by a second dark band, lighter than the main lateral band, darker than the centre of the back.   Pygal band black and strongly defined.

Habitat, W. slope of the Lorogi Mountains, British East Africa.

Collected and presented by Arthur H. Neumann, Esq.

This handsome Gazelle has since been obtained in the same region by Mr. H. S. H. Cavendish.

I remained here from 13th to 19th October.   I never succeeded in coming up with elephants, which seemed to have been thoroughly scared by Squareface's escapade, so that his small cow probably cost me the loss of several pairs of tusks.   We found plenty of evidence of their frequenting the district in numbers, and once or twice came upon fresh spoor, but only of travelling parties.   Nevertheless I much enjoyed my stay in this beautiful district.   Its character is totally distinct from that of the other side of the range, and the game is also mainly of different species.   Just at the foot of the mountains, where the forest and grass land meet, is a charming

---

[1] Having no instruments to determine altitudes, I can only make guesses; but I should judge the respective heights to be about as follows :—Country at foot of range on eastern side, about 4000 feet ; Lorogi Mountains, from 7000 to 8000 feet; plains on western side, 5500 feet.

bit of country, well watered and verdant, which struck.me as a most desirable locality.   The grass, kept green by the frequent rains which the mountains attract (it rained, often with thunder, almost every day I was there), is not rank, and, while timber is abundant on the adjacent slopes, the open country has the character of what is called "high veldt" in South Africa, and gives one the idea of capital grazing, suggestive of horses and sheep.   The climate, too, seems healthy, with cool nights and not very hot days, while the air is clear and fresh.

Being anxious to see something of the open plains, and particularly to make the nearer acquaintance of some large antelopes I had seen in the distance once or twice, of whose species (though apparently a hartebeeste) I could not be certain, I gave up a day to visiting a small lake, called by the Ndorobos "Kisima," which I had heard of.   On the way I succeeded in stalking two young bulls of the hartebeeste whose species I was anxious to identify, and shot them both. One dropped on the spot, and proved to be Jackson's harte-beeste ; the other went off slowly, lying down at intervals. After waiting a little while I followed, and, when it ran, set " Pice " (my tiny terrier, about eight months old only) after it. He chased and brought it to bay, bravely ; but, when I got near, he suddenly left it and fled back towards me.   I could not make out why, at first, but as he came nearer I saw a jackal running after him.   I had sat down to avoid alarming the hartebeeste when its attention was no longer occupied by Pice, so that the jackal came within a few yards before it noticed me and retreated.   No doubt it had recognised a relative in my dog, and wished to make its acquaintance ; indeed, I had once before had the opportunity of observing similar advances to a dog of mine on the part of a jackal. I then encouraged Pice to take up the chase again ; but now a big bull of the same species as the one I was in pursuit of, coming from a herd we had passed near, took up the running, and jealously chased my wretched wounded buck.

SCRATCH PACK CHASING WOUNDED HARTEBEESTE (*Bubalis jacksoni*).

On coming over the next rise no hartebeeste were visible ; but soon I spied my terrier and two jackals, standing not far apart.   I feared that Pice, having overcome his first terror, had got interested in these, and given up the pursuit of the antelope ; but, on getting near, I found it lying down close to him.   He sometimes lay down, and then would run round to have a look at his quarry, the jackals waiting a little way off (evidently for the buck to succumb), while vultures hovered over the poor brute, in expectation of the approaching end.   It was altogether a curious episode, and, except that I was sorry for the sufferings of the hartebeeste, almost worth making an indifferent shot to witness.   However, calling up the men, we soon caught and despatched it, though it was just on the point of death.   I had left a man to skin and carry in the first buck, which was near our camp, and this one I protected from vultures with a white handkerchief fluttering in the breeze, according to my usual custom, and left till our return.

As we got farther away from the hills the country became drier and drier, showing how very local are the rains, and there was hardly any game, it being attracted by green grass near the forest edge.   The lake I found to be a sheet of stinking, greenish water, of no great size, very salt and quite undrinkable.   Its surface, and some little islets of whitish rock, were covered with ducks and other water-fowl—a most interesting sight, reminding one of Naivasha on a small scale.   On our way back we picked up the hartebeeste meat.   In this district I also found Thomson's gazelle, one of which I shot, for purposes of identification, and brought the skin and skull to England.   This is the only point on the whole of my journeys between Mombasa and the north end of Rudolph where this gazelle and Jackson's hartebeeste are met with, and hence appears to be the extreme northern limit of their range. Thus the Lorogi Mountains here form a distinct line of demarcation in the geographical distribution of certain species.

I saw no Grevy's zebra here, but large herds of one of the

varieties of the smaller class, of which Burchell's is the typical
species.   I shot one, and carefully noted its characteristics, as
well as those of others which I had the opportunity of observing
at short range through my glasses ; but I unfortunately did
not bring home a skin, as I was disappointed in my expectation of procuring a specimen on my return journey.   The
peculiarities, as noted in my diary, are : " Stripes black and
very broad, and ground colour white in *all* (both mares and
stallions)."   They also struck me as being unusually small,
but in this I might be in error through my eye having become
accustomed to the upstanding form of the splendid animal
called Grevy's zebra.   The measurements of the one I killed
(an adult male) were : height at withers, 3 feet 11 inches ;
length of head, 1 foot 9 inches ; ditto, from between ears to
root of tail (straight), '5 feet 7 inches ; tail (without tuft),
1 foot 5½ inches ; girth, 4 feet 10 inches (measured just after
death and entered on spot).   I subsequently came to the
conclusion that these zebra did not differ from those of the
Burchell type which I met with elsewhere on this expedition
(though, as I had not kept the skin of the one just described,
I could not compare them side by side), for one which I shot
to the eastward of the Lorogis (also an adult male) measured
exactly the same in height.

As I knew that Abdulla might be expected to arrive at
El Bogoi any day now, I wanted to be at hand.   Accordingly,
on 19th October we started to return, crossing the mountains
by a different and much better route.   We followed a good
elephant path, with a comparatively easy gradient, most of the
way to the top, and camped for the night close to Lesiat's old
kraal, near the eastern summit and overlooking the low country.
It was a pleasant march, through fine shady forest, in some
places the trees of considerable size.   The juniper is chiefly
on the western slopes, but not, as a rule, very large.   The
huts in this Ndorobo encampment in the forest (now deserted)
were thatched with leaves, as there was no grass there ; they

were built among the tree-stems, with no attempt at a clearing.

In the morning we descended, early, the almost perpendicular face of the range by a fairly well-beaten path to my old "lucky camp," as I called it, in a glade at the foot, whence I had hunted the year before and bagged several fine bulls. On the way we passed through the present abode of Lesiat's

NDOROBO ENCAMPMENT IN THE "SUBUGO" FOREST ON THE LOROGI MOUNTAINS.
(From a Photograph by the AUTHOR.)

clan, in a romantic gorge near the mountain's base, the funny little untidy huts picturesquely stuck here and there where space could be found among great rocks and trees. A bevy of comely "dittos" (damsels) greeted me with friendly hand-shakes. Lesiat himself, the "laigwanane" (or headman), as they called him, was out. However, they all told me that elephants were about again and had been seen the previous day—news which Lesiat himself confirmed in the evening.

The much higher temperature here to what it is where we had come from was very noticeable.

It proved true enough that elephants were in the neighbour-hood again, but my bad luck still pursued me. At this time there was hardly any wind, and what there was used to come in eddying currents, rendering it almost impossible to approach game in these difficult jungles without its getting your scent. Only once during two hard days did I succeed in getting a snap-shot, and then failed to score.

On the evening of this second day, after returning dis-appointed to camp, Lesiat and his wife came down, bringing me mead. It was very good, and they seemed to have found it so themselves, for they were unusually talkative. He had often pressed me to give his wife medicine to enable her to bear him another child. He now declared that she had one in the small of her back, where it had been a year, but could not get it into the proper position to be brought forth, and that God refused to allow her to be delivered. He put her hand in mine and implored me to give him some charm, that he might have additional offspring. Though I did not want to seem to make light of his distress, I could not help laughing, in spite of my own dejection. He admitted that she had already had five children ; but, on my delicately hinting that this was surely no despicable family for one woman to have borne him, he scouted the idea and declared that she wanted twenty ! I then ventured to vaguely suggest that, as she already shared his affection with another lady, perhaps she would not resent a third (and younger one) being received into the partnership and accorded another small slice of his heart. But to this he replied dejectedly that Ndorobo girls would have nothing to say to an old man. I had always told him I was ignorant of this branch of medicine, but he refused to believe me, and on this occasion was determined not to be put off with excuses and promised me fabulous ivory if I would help him. Seeing that he was in a particularly impracticable mood to-day, I persuaded him to defer all our business till I got back to my main camp, whither I meant to return in a day or two.

In the meantime I visited his kraal and paid my respects to Mrs. Lesiat (that is, the principal Mrs. Lesiat, for there were two) in her own hut. Though mere shelters of the most primitive kind, and not even weather-proof, unless where a skin may have been thrown over the roof, these huts are not dirty inside, nor do they seem to harbour noxious insects. The people themselves, too, appear to be clean in this respect, and do not, like most of the South African races (the Swazies, for example), improve every spare shining moment in examining each other's heads. They also compare favourably in other ways—in appearance, manners, and liberality—with those greedy, stingy, untaking people. Indeed they are the pleasantest natives I have come across, and far less grasping and objectionable than most Africans. They are also healthy, clean-skinned, and free from loathsome diseases, and, though a small race as a rule, are wiry, active, and enduring. Their children always look sleek and well fed, showing what a wholesome food honey, which may be called their staff of life, is, and I saw none with skin diseases or pot bellies such as disfigure the children of the agricultural tribes.

The Ndorobos live on what they can pick up. To call them a race of hunters is hardly correct ; for though they, or rather a few individuals among them, slay an elephant or two and an odd rhinoceros now and then, with poisoned harpoons either thrown by hand or suspended in heavy shafts as traps over paths, they kill but little other game. Their mainstay is honey. This is a great country for flowers, and bees are very plentiful ; and, besides constantly hunting for the wild nests, like some other tribes they put up tubs made of hollowed logs in the trees for the wild bees to hive in, and when the season is favourable the land flows with honey. But they are as often as not in a state of semi-starvation, supporting life on roots, berries, and old hoarded pieces of dry rhinoceros hide. In times of famine the aged and weakly succumb, and this doubtless tends to preserve the stamina of the race. The price of a wife among them is ten bee-tubs, as going concerns ; but Lesiat explained, when asked why, since he was so anxious for more progeny, he did not marry another (for they are not restricted in the number they may wed), that the girls can choose their own husbands and only marry young men.

The Ndorobos of the present day are a mixed race. You see quite different types among them. Some are black, with negro characteristics, others comparatively light-coloured and have the better features and hair of the Masai. This is explained by information I got in the course of interesting conversations I had with Lesiat and others of themselves.

Originally there were small, cattle-owning tribes in this country, akin to the Wakwavi and Masai, but weak and disunited. The sites of some of their former kraals have been pointed out to me and are still discernible. The Wakwavi, who then frequented the pasture land west of the Lorogis (which are, in fact, the north-eastern extremity of the region commonly called Leikipia), where their former cattle-tracks can be even now plainly made out, raided all their cattle, and were subsequently themselves driven out by invading Masai. Row-row's people—now living under the eastern side of Kenia—are the remnants of the former, while the nearest Masai are to-day at the western base of that mountain. But the survivors of the petty tribes of this district, who had lost their live stock, joined the original Ndorobos, who from time immemorial had lived as these do to-day, and took to their mode of life. One old man (of genuine woolly-headed, negroid type) was pointed out to me as a specimen of the pure old Ndorobo stock.

Since Abdulla and his men had left on their second trip to Mthara, ill luck had invariably attended me, with the result that either through unfavourable conditions or my own clumsiness, or a combination of both, I had not killed a single elephant. We had, indeed, picked up, during my week in the Lorogis, one passable pair of teeth and one or two very small ones ; but these were a poor reward for all our efforts.   I may in passing— apropos of the finding of tusks in the forest—take the oppor- tunity of pointing out that the statements sometimes met with in books, to the effect that there is some mystery about what becomes of the remains of elephants that die in the forests, are erroneous.   I have often and often met with their skulls and bones in the course of my hunting, and, if they are not more commonly seen, it is because travellers do not generally spend their time, as I did, in traversing these in all directions.   That the tusks are not so often found is obviously because they have already, at some previous time, been appropriated by natives ; but I have, in the course of my experience in Central Africa, come across a good many, at one time and another.

I now began to get very impatient for the return of my caravan ; for I was eager to be off northward into new hunting- grounds, where I hoped to find the odds not quite so long against the hunter as they are in this impracticable dense scrub. The elephants seemed to have left our neighbourhood, too, now, and I did not care to make any more lengthy excursions, so I occupied myself with adjusting loads and completing, as far as possible, my preparations for continuing my journey.   I had a large pit dug, in a suitable spot among some trees hard by, and buried all my ivory, taking care to injure the creeping plants which covered the ground as little as possible, so that after a shower or two of rain all traces of the ground having been disturbed would soon be obliterated.   I, however, showed Lesiat and Baithai the spot, so that, on my return, should it have been tampered with, they might not be able to disclaim responsibility.

They often visited me, and kept me well supplied with honey.   I sometimes gave Lesiat as many beans as his wife could carry away ; but he did not now seem to care much for any food I gave him except meat, which is always welcome to an Ndorobo.   The fact was, honey was very abundant at this time—"like water," as Lesiat himself expressed it,—and when that is the case they will not trouble about anything else. The bush was white with the blossoms of a black-barked tree with hooked thorns, common in this part, and the air fragrant with their scent, giving the bees an ample harvest ; and Lesiat assured me that they could tap their bee-tubs twice a month.

By the end of October Abdulla had still not returned, though he had now been away thirty days instead of the twenty we had agreed upon. I therefore determined, though rather reluctantly, to go on ahead as far as Mount Nyiro and wait for him there. I hoped I might find elephants in that district now, and, at all events, it would be less monotonous than waiting longer at El Bogoi, where it was troublesome even to procure meat. So on the 30th, as there was still no news of the caravan, I started, taking all but two men, whom I left in charge, with my own personal baggage and a couple of donkeys carrying food, leaving orders that Abdulla was to follow with the whole outfit as soon as he arrived.

Owing to there having been much rain in these parts during the past wet season, there was more grass and tangled weeds than when I went through the year before, making our progress slow and arduous, so that it was noon on the second day when we got near the Barasaloi. But what a difference on coming within sight of it ! Instead of dry burning sand, a welcome silver stream was visible through the green mimosas as we approached ; a sight which made me thank God fervently. On the march I had shot a Grant's gazelle for meat, picking out the ram, for the sake of my men, on account of its much larger size ; although, when shooting purely for my own larder, I generally chose the tenderer venison of the doe—nor do I see that there is anything unsportsmanlike in making such a selection in a wild country where one has to live by one's rifle, and where mine was the only one that ever took toll of the game. Not but that I wanted meat myself, too, now ; but my plodding

porters were always my first consideration when travelling, and
I was well satisfied to take a bit of whatever I found it most
advantageous to shoot for their benefit.

Strolling through the green bush bordering the stream in
the afternoon, accompanied only by Pice, a short way only
from camp, I saw a rhinoceros cow with a calf. But as, with
the few men I had, we could not carry more meat, I left her
alone. When on my way back, Pice, as was his wont, ran
under a shady tree just ahead ; and before I knew anything
about it, out charged the rhino with the calf after him. The
dog made straight for me (I was only a few yards off), pursued
by the irate cow whose siesta he had disturbed, and I had to
bang off my rifle hurriedly in her face to turn her, which it
fortunately did. Lions roared during the night, and mosquitoes
made almost as much, and a more disagreeable, noise.

In the morning we had but a short march to the other
branch of the Barasaloi, called the Suya ; and it is remarkable
that whereas on my previous journey, the year before, the
Barasaloi was dry—not a sign of moisture to be found even by
digging,—while this spruit had plenty of water, now the former
was running strong all over its sandy bed, but here there was
much less water than there had been then, and in the afternoon
it almost ceased to flow. This is an illustration of how very
partial and uncertain the rains are in this country, and shows
how dangerous it is to calculate on finding water even a short
way ahead (though you may have got plenty there formerly)
because there happens to be no scarcity in one part.

I stayed over another day here in order to have a look
down the valley in case there might be any elephants about,
and took advantage of the delay to send a couple of men ahead
to hide a bucket of water some four hours' march along the
route we should have to pass (the next being a very long stage),
so that the men might have a good drink, in addition to what
they could carry themselves, on our road to Ongata Barta. I
found nothing but old spoor, proving there were no elephants

near now, so took a round over the hills, and shot a couple of
Grant's gazelle for meat.

Ongata Ndamez, as this locality is called by the Ndorobos
of the adjoining districts, has the appearance of being a very
sporting country. It looked much drier now than when I was
here before, but the numerous well-worn paths leading to the
water, all freshly trampled with rhinoceros and other footprints, suggested abundance of game, though it seemed to range
far afield in search of more succulent food than the withered
herbage (resembling scraggy heather covered with fine sharp
thorns) afforded. The rhinoceros "scrapes" were numerous
and full. What I mean by a "scrape" is a wide saucer-shaped
hole, which it is the peculiar habit of the black rhinoceros to
scoop out in the ground before depositing its droppings. The
same holes are used regularly, and other animals, such as zebras
and gazelles, often add their contributions, so that accumulations
of manure are formed. They made me think of "the old man
with the muck rake"—as in my childhood we used to call the
ancient rustic who, with barrow and shovel, collected in the
village road fertilising material for his allotment. Here he
might fill not only his barrow but a cart, often, at a single
"scrape." The thoughts of the potatoes and cabbages that old
fellow's garden would produce made one long for something
more than the dinner of bitter herbs that is one's contentment
here! In connection with these same "scrapes" I may point
out that the furrows it is this animal's habit to draw, sometimes
for several yards along the ground, from the spot where this
natural process has been gone through, are not made, as is
sometimes supposed, with its horn, but with its feet.

The plateau between the Lorogi and Mathews ranges has
been much cut up by the valleys of the Seya and its tributaries,
of which the Barasaloi and the Suya are the principal. Their
main valleys are worn to a considerable depth and bordered by
much denuded hilly ground with a gravelly soil, from which
many conspicuous white quartz reefs crop up in parts. The

high koppie called Murkeben is not, as appears on the maps, part of the latter range, but the highest point of an isolated rocky ridge half-way between the two.   Knowing our way and the distance before us, we had no difficulty—by starting about noon, marching till sundown, and on again at 4 A.M.—in reaching the water at Ongata Barta a little before noon the following day.   The water I had taken the precaution to have

CAMP UNDER MOUNT NYIRO.
(From a Photograph by the AUTHOR.)

planted on our line was much appreciated ; fortunately, too, the weather was not very hot, so none suffered.

We reached the stream which flows out of Donyo le Nyiro (that is, Mount Nyiro) early on the 6th November, and camped in a pleasant open lawn on its banks.   When I came on here I expected my main caravan under Abdulla to catch me up any day, and hoped to be able to continue the march with the whole party in ten days or a fortnight at most.   But, through a series of untoward events, we were delayed altogether about twice that time, and my patience was nearly worn out when, at length, nearly a month after my arrival, we were able to march once more. Abdulla was much longer in following than I had expected, and, when he at last arrived, it turned out that on reaching El Bogoi he had found that the men in charge there had lost the donkeys, with the result that when, after several days' search, they were recovered, they had almost perished from thirst and one died in consequence. Then the two that I had brought on had to be sent back for some loads that had been left, and on the way one was killed, one dark wet night, by a lion. This one was a great favourite of mine and the handsomest and best I had, as is sure to be the case when any evil befalls one of your animals. I was particularly grieved about these mishaps to my cherished donkeys, which I had cared for almost like children. But one must take all misfortunes, annoyances, and delays philosophically in Africa, especially trying though they be when brought about by carelessness.

On this visit I succeeded in getting in touch with the natives inhabiting the mountain, and got some of them to come to my camp. They call themselves the Sambur tribe (not Samburu, as it is generally spelt). They live entirely in the mountains, other communities of the same tribe inhabiting the not distant heights of Kulale and Marasambiti. These people have been able to keep their live stock in spite of raids, thanks to their mountain fastnesses. They live solely on the produce of their cattle and do not cultivate. They do not differ much in type from the Masai. One old man, whom I saw a good deal of, was a particularly handsome specimen, with regular features. I did not find them satisfactory people to deal with. They had been accustomed to Swahili traders, whose custom it is to give presents to any native who tells them pleasant news, the consequence being that they are constantly fooled by the false reports which they have paid for.

I learnt that a party of Wakamba, from south of the Tana, had been here two or three months ago hunting elephants, and

I saw the skeletons of some they had killed. They hunt in large parties, using bows and poisoned arrows and wound a great many besides what they kill. I could find none, though I tried in all directions except on the mountain-top. That was covered with heavy clouds during the whole time I was in its neighbourhood, for the weather was very stormy. I was told there were elephants in the " subugo " forest on the summit, but as it was always raining there I did not attempt to climb the mountain. It was bad enough below, the wind rushing down with terrific force on to a camp I had for a day or two close under the western face, where it is very precipitous, seeming to come straight down the cliffs like a waterfall.

Nyiro is neither a peak nor a range ; but rather a block, with apparently a considerable extent of mountain forest on its top. Owing to its isolation, surrounded by waterless plains and cut off by wide uninhabited tracts from other districts, the cattle plague which devastated East Central Africa several years ago seems not to have reached these islands in the desert. I gathered that the Sambur natives owned considerable herds of cattle, though they keep them out of sight in the ravines of the mountain. I noticed, too, the spoor of small herds of buffalo once or twice, a rare sight now in Central Africa.

Though I got tired of waiting here so long and met with no elephants to reward my exertions in examining the neighbourhood, it was as pleasant a place to be delayed in as any on the route : a fine open country, a good stream of clear, cold water, game enough within easy reach to keep the larder supplied, and a healthy climate. One day I shot an ostrich, but, though a cock, its plumes were damaged. There were a good many about, and once or twice I saw large flocks of chicks. Something must prey on these, or ostriches would be much more numerous than they are. When the skin of my ostrich was dry, I made an attempt to utilise it as a disguise (*à la* Bushman) for the purpose of photographing living Grant's gazelle.

With my camera in one hand, a stick supporting the bird's head in the other, and the skin over my shoulders and back, I approached in a stooping attitude, trying to look as much like an ostrich as possible.   But though the gazelles were evidently puzzled by such a curious mixture of feathers and garments, and allowed me to get nearer in their surprise than would ordinarily be easy, all my blandishments and ostentatiously unconcerned peckings at the ground failed to persuade them to let me get within less than about fifty or sixty yards.   I found it very hot and uncomfortable under the greasy skin ; and finally, after persevering in defiance of perspiration and back-ache as long as my endurance could hold out, I had to abandon the attempt with no other result than a couple of abortive snaps.

I had to decide about the route to take before starting on for the lake.   The natives advised going round the eastern side of the mountain, but I had not confidence enough in their trustworthiness to rely on their guidance, and would not risk marching with a loaded caravan through country unknown to us without certain information about the water ahead.   I therefore sent a few good men on, under Squareface, to explore as far as the lake, but chose the western side of the mountain as probably the best-watered, and likely to lead us more directly to the shores of Rudolph.   After an absence of several days they returned with a favourable report, in so far as that there was sufficient water, though they found the country very rugged and stony.   Better by far, though, to have some difficulties we knew all about than to go a road none had tried and trust to the doubtful guidance of unreliable savages ;[1] so I determined without hesitation to follow this route.

A day or two before leaving this camp I narrowly escaped being bitten by a very venomous snake, which I nearly sat on in the grass.   Luckily, when on the point of doing so, some-

[1] I had learned by sad experience, in years gone by, what disastrous consequences to a caravan might result from such a course.

thing that looked like a toad caught my eye, beside my boot. Thinking I had inadvertently trodden on a harmless reptile, I was about to move my foot in compassion when I noticed a black, forked-looking tongue darting viciously close to my right foot, and, looking more carefully, saw that what I at first took for a toad was in reality the villainous triangular head of a large puff-adder, on whose neck I had set my foot, its body swollen out as big as my thigh. By so providential a chance had I held it fast in this way that it could not move its head to strike. Having my rook rifle by me, I put the muzzle to its head and sent a bullet through its brain. It measured 4 feet 8 inches long. Such lucky coincidences suggest to one that, though we suffer many misfortunes, dangers are doubtless often escaped unconsciously.

CHAPTER XII

LAKE RUDOLPH

ON 2nd December I made a final start for the lake, feeling that at last Reshiat was within my reach ; for I had sufficient food for all hands to last, with care, two months. For the first two days the going was comparatively easy, and water plentiful. The western face of Nyiro, under which our course lay, is almost precipitous and very grand, topped with dark forests and cut by narrow, giddy-looking gorges flanked with red cliffs, and here and there hang waterfalls from the mountain side, filled with the outpourings of the heavy clouds which often cap the summit. But all these clear, cold, rushing streams which pour out of the mountain disappear as if by magic in two or three miles. Occasionally gaps in the ridges to our left afforded glimpses of a wide valley beyond, in which a small lake could be seen shining far below. This is in fact, I suppose, the connecting portion of the "rift" stretching southward (or rather south by west) from Bassu in the direction of Baringo.

We were now entering among rough, stony hills, which would have been hardly passable in places but for a capital elephant path which we followed. It had probably been used for ages, and in some parts was worn down into the solid rock like a little cutting.   Farther on we had to leave it, as it kept too much to the right, probably leading to Kulale, and our difficulties became greater.   Constantly descending, we got among still more terribly rugged hills, full of kloofs and chasms, the tops flanked by red precipices and the valleys full of boulders from top to bottom.   The formation is a marvellous jumble of different kinds of rocks, chucked about in chaotic confusion.   By the third day we had reached a very much

FIRST PEEP OF BASSU FROM THE SOUTH.
(From a Photograph by the AUTHOR.)

lower level, and it was getting much hotter, while the vegetation became scantier and drier.   We had to climb over dividing ridges and through narrow ravines, picking our way among the fallen rocks, which caused much trouble to those in charge of the donkeys, overthrowing loads, and cutting their packs.

At last, on the afternoon of 4th December, on getting on to a rough, irregular sort of plateau, we came in sight of Bassu (Lake Rudolph) ; and a fine sight it was, looking blue like the sea.   Beyond the island, near the south end, its waters stretched dimly northward until lost in haze.   In one or two places about this part I noticed a number of circles of large stones, about three yards in diameter, evidently arranged by human hands.   These must have formed the ground-plan of some sort of rude huts.   But who made them, or what they could have been doing in this desert, and why they should camp, even if travelling, where there was no water, is a puzzle.   These circles of stones on bare ground are quite distinct from the heaps of broken lava so often seen in a volcanic country, and which, though they present the appearance of having been piled up artificially, can only be due to natural causes.   These "blows" of rock (as I call them) I have always supposed to have been caused by huge bubbles in the molten lava; but whether I am right or not I leave to more scientific travellers to determine. For a while the going was easier ; but just at sundown we came above a quite impassable descent for loaded donkeys, so bivou- acked for the night in sight of a place where our pioneers told us water was to be had, some two miles ahead, in another valley.

This had been a hard day, but we had seen the lake and hoped to reach it on the morrow.   But it proved farther than it had appeared, for there was much broken ground between which had not been visible from the plateau, as we had looked over it to the water far out from the shore, and a great drop had yet to be made before we could reach its brink. During this day's march I had seen some koodoos (the large species) among the hills and noticed a good deal of their spoor. Though I had shot many in South Africa in former years, these were the first I had actually seen myself in Central Africa, where they are, as far as my own experience goes, very uncommon. Few signs of other game were here ; an occasional zebra spoor and a little old rhino dung now and then was all the evidence I noticed.   I observed a few of the rare glossy starlings of the beautiful crested species (*Galeopsar salvadorii*), of which I had obtained a specimen near Murkeben on my former trip ; but even birds are scarce in this barren region.   In the morning I got all the donkey-loads carried down the declivity by sunrise, and we

then went on to the water.   It was necessary to halt for some
time there for the men to cook, and to allow all to rest a while.
We then had more climbing over rocky hills, and it was not
till afternoon that we began the final descent towards the lake,
which was now really not far off.   But we still had many steep
and difficult ridges of broken lava to negotiate, and at dusk we
were compelled to bivouac again without having reached the
shore, and to sleep once more without water, under a cliff
which gave a little shelter from the gale that was blowing.

At last, early on the morning of 6th December, we came
down the last step and reached the shore, and I had the satisfaction of drinking and bathing in the bitter water of Lake
Rudolph.   It is a desolate and forbidding land, but with a
wild grandeur of its own which had a great charm for me.
Rugged hills of bare, broken lava of all-sized chunks and every
kind of volcanic product, with hardly a vestige of vegetation,
rose all around from the water's edge.   One perfect crater was
visible at the south-west corner of the lake.   It may be
Teleki's volcano, but I saw no signs of activity.

We struck the lake at the south-east corner, and what we
had to do was to follow its shores round the eastern side to
its northern extremity.   I knew that, though we might have
difficulties, we could not lose ourselves nor want for water, and
of food we had ample supplies, so I felt confident of reaching
Reshiat.   We did not go much farther that day, but camped
on a pleasant bay where a deep gully came in.   There were
some mimosa trees, lots of firewood, and good pickings for the
donkeys—all desirable attributes of a camping-ground, and by
no means everywhere to be found in this inhospitable region.
The ground was all stones, of course,—there is nothing else
there,—but I pitched my tent by tying the ropes to boulders.
It was necessary to make all securely fast, as a violent gale
blew unceasingly day and night now.   The men caught lots of
fine fish of several kinds and enjoyed themselves immensely,
for Swahilis are very fond of fish and fishing.   One of them

showed me a curious little fish he had caught, covered with a
sort of prickles and marked with greenish stripes, which had
the power of blowing itself out.   He said a similar kind was
found in the sea on the east coast.   One of the fish I had for
dinner and found it good.   The only game I saw, besides a
hippo or two, were a few grantii.   Cormorants were numerous,
and an odd pair or two of Egyptian geese might be seen, but
not a duck of any kind.   The lake has every appearance of
being deep at this southern end, the shores sloping steeply
down for the most part, so that you may get out of your depth
close to the bank.   One or two dead trees of some size, standing in the water where it was now pretty deep, showed it to be
considerably fuller now than it must have been for many con-
secutive seasons a number of years ago.

For a day or two more we plodded on, following generally
the windings of the shores and occasionally cutting a corner
over a promontory, through country of the same character—
a succession of black (or rather dark reddish-brown) ridges
composed of loose lumps of rough lava rock running down
into the lake with difficult gullies, all full of stones, between.
Sometimes the donkeys got into difficulties and their loads
had to be carried past an awkward corner by hand, or one
toppled over, burden and all, into the water, all causing delay;
but, strange to say, not a man nor a donkey got lame, sick, or
sorry.   The gale continued the while with unabated violence,
especially at night, making things very uncomfortable.   It
seemed to come down like an avalanche from the mountain,
rushing into the deep basin of the lake, sometimes in terrific
gusts.   At times it was difficult even to stand, and cooking
and eating were conducted under disadvantages.   Nothing
would stop on the table, the very tea was blown out of one's
cup, while black sand and small stones got into the food and
filled one's bed at night.

At the same time the lake was beautiful, with many charming little bays, suggestive of convenient anchorage for a boat.

My longing for one was, however, tempered by the contemplation of the seas this furious wind raised out in the open water of the wide channel between us and a large, barren-looking island, which rose high out of the expanse of waves opposite. Beyond again, a steep and rugged range of forbidding-looking hills, forming the western shore of this end of the lake, seemed to come sheer down into the water.

Being almost devoid of vegetation, this district has naturally little animal life—a small troop of the ubiquitous grantii here and there, and rarely a few oryx, was all I saw in the way of game. It was difficult to shoot anything, as these were singularly wild and the high wind made it hard to hold a rifle steady, while the country was a bad one to get about in ; but I managed to get a gazelle on the evening of our second day on the lake, by making a careful stalk up one of the lava ridges. The men continued to catch plenty of fish, though, of various kinds, some very large. A goose also fell to my rook rifle.

The conditions had not improved on 8th December ; the going was as bad as ever, and the hurricane, which had never dropped for a moment for days, still blew, giving one no rest and making things thoroughly uncomfortable. What with the desolate surroundings and the uncertainty as to how far this sort of thing would continue, I confess I was feeling a little bit low-spirited, and a curious sight we came across rather tended to depress me more, though I admit the folly of allowing oneself to be affected by such influences. Alongside a rocky gully, right on the lake side, a patch of the black lava debris was covered thickly with bleached bones. From a distance it looked like snow, and I wondered what in the world it could be ; but on getting close I found it to consist of the whitened bones of camels. Hundreds must have perished here, all huddled in one little corner. What could be the history of the catastrophe ? In a country, too, where now is no sign of human inhabitants and which seems uninhabitable.

Happily, just after this we came out into more level ground and a little grass began to appear in dry tufts here and there, while ahead the country looked more promising, and my cheerfulness returned.   Mount Kulale could be seen to the eastward, even now capped with heavy clouds though with us the weather was bright and dry.

The next morning the wind gradually abated, to our infinite

CAMEL BONES IN DESOLATE COUNTRY ON EDGE OF LAKE.

relief, and at last dropped altogether.   I felt thankful for a little peace, and, though the sun was excessively hot, I revelled in the calm.   We had now got into more level country, with comparatively few stones.   It seemed perfect comfort marching here, after the awful ground we had lately traversed, and the caravan came along famously in consequence.   Another treat we enjoyed was a drink of fresh water out of a little running stream, evidently coming from Kulale, which we crossed where

it entered the lake.   We had by this time got used to the lake
water, though not exactly to like it.   It is perfectly wholesome,
and food cooked with it requires no salt.   But it differs from
all other brack water in that it contains some property (perhaps
soda) which brings out the strength of tea made with it, so that
only half the quantity of leaves is needed, otherwise it will be
too black to drink ; whereas the saltish water so commonly met
with in Africa will not make tea.

With the flatter shores a corresponding change in the
character of the lake washing them followed.   Shoal water in-
shore, with weed and water grass, and wide shallow bays were
now its features, as contrasted with narrow little coves of deep
clear water and abrupt rocky banks, such as we had been
accustomed to.   As a consequence of the more favourable
conditions, there were more geese and a much greater variety
of fish-eating fowl and waders ; pelicans, storks, ibises, etc.
To-day my tent could be pitched with pegs once more, the
camping-place I chose being bare smooth ground close to the
shore of a bay, in which was an islet with some huts on it.
We were obliged to choose a spot with a few trees near, so
that we might obtain firewood, the country being for the most
part without a stick ; but an additional inducement to halt here
was the wish to make the acquaintance of the fisher folk, whose
huts we had seen on the islet, and some of whom were paddling
about opposite in canoes.   After a little hesitation they drew
nearer, and three men and a woman got out into the water and
waded towards us ; but it was only after a good deal of parley-
ing that they could be persuaded to come ashore.   I gave
them beads and received some fish in return, and the men
bought a quantity, both dry and fresh (one very large), for iron
wire.   While the bargaining was going on at the water's edge
I was able to get an interesting snap at them with my hand
camera, and it is one of the few photographs I took that has
not been utterly spoiled either by light getting in or from the
effects of the climate on the plates.

EL MOLO FISHER-FOLK.

"A harmless timid people, subsisting solely on fish."

These are the true El Molo. They are far from numerous, and always live on the little islands not far from the shore which occur here and there in this part of the lake. A harmless timid people, subsisting solely on fish, which they catch with nets in the shallow bays, with the rare addition of a hippopotamus once in a way, their lives are purely aquatic. I was able to communicate with them through my interpreter, as one of them knew something of the Ndorobo dialect, though their own language is totally distinct ; but I could get no information out of them about the country or elephants, as they said they live in the water and only land to procure firewood. Even then, they declared, they never go beyond the shore ; a statement which I believe to be true. Their canoes are constructed each of several small logs, fastened together side by side ; no trees are to be had with trunks large enough to make the usual type of dug-out canoes. After bartering to their satisfaction, our friends (the first natives we had seen since leaving Nyiro) became reassured and visited our camp.

A hippo was seen grazing on the bank by one of the porters who had wandered along the shores on fishing intent, but it had disappeared by the time he had called me ; and the few gazelles I saw were very wild, as, strange to say, all game seemed here. During the night, which was very hot, some noisy birds (storks, I fancy) were holding a great " shauri," with much loud altercation and unseemly commotion, in the water close to our camp ; the uproar combined with the heat banishing sleep.

After a few more outlying lava ridges—the farthest outposts of the volcanic formation—the country assumed a more uniformly level aspect, with a sandy soil, and travelling became easy ; though since we had got beyond the influence of the gales, which seem to be generated by Nyiro and Kulale, the heat had become very great, both day and night. Our routine of marching could now be evenly regulated in convenient stages. Calling the donkey-men and my boys at 4 A.M. (my cook never needed rousing), I dressed and got some breakfast while the animals were being packed and the tent, etc., struck and tied up. It took an hour and a half to pack the asses, and by 5.30 it was light enough to march ; for we could not start earlier in an unknown and pathless country.   By noon we were generally camped at some suitable spot where a few trees or bushes furnished firewood ; our trusty friend the lake supplying water and securing us from all anxiety on the score of thirst—that most-to-be-dreaded of all calamities in African travel.

In spite of the arid, barren nature of the country, there was a charm about the lake shore, and I enjoyed travelling along it, and always found something to interest me.   There were the birds, in astonishing numbers and great variety,— pelicans sitting sleepily on the water and shoals, secure from crocodiles (for I watched one swim through a flock), or flying in skeins to and fro ; flocks of gulls and terns ; storks, herons of various kinds, ibises, egrets and many other small waders, with countless cormorants in two sizes ; besides numerous Egyptian geese, where damp lawns bordering the shore afford them grazing, but duck and teal singularly scarce.   Game, too, was a little more plentiful, and I began to notice zebra spoor and occasionally an old rhino " scrape " again.   We passed more islets with little settlements of El Molo in the many bays formed by this part of Bassu, until we rounded the bight of the lake where the shore suddenly trends for a spell, towards the west.   Here the coast is exposed to the swell raised by the prevailing southerly and south-easterly winds, and the conditions are less favourable to both natives and birds.   As we travelled along this part I noticed old beaches of various heights.   Sometimes we would march along one far above the present level of the water, like a well-kept, wide, gravel carriage drive, at another part one ran along like a barrier reef, separated from the present shore by a lagoon.   On these beaches the surf sometimes roared like the sea.   After cutting across the promontory terminating this reach, whose extreme cape is

tipped with a picturesque rocky headland, more sheltered bays
are reached, where the shore again takes a northerly trend.

Toward noon on the 12th, I went ahead as usual to look
for suitable camping-ground, and had just shot a granti when
I discovered a good-sized collection of huts on a sand-spit.   I
did not know what the inhabitants, who seemed numerous,
might be, so took the precaution of disposing my camp in a
defensible position.   Then I went on with Squareface to make
our presence known.   On seeing us, a woman, who was the
first to notice our approach (for they had not heard my shot),
ran in to give the alarm, and there was considerable commotion
in the village, the men rushing out spear in hand.   At first
we shouted to them from a distance (that is, my man did in
Ndorobo), and when our mutual distrust was allayed, we met
some of the leaders and interchanged greetings and explanations.   It appeared that they were a community of Ndorobos,
akin, they told us, to some living at Kulale and Nyiro, but had
taken to the same mode of life as the El Molo, depending
chiefly on fish, though they also hunt.   But the two races are
quite distinct, though living amicably side by side.   The El
Molo, who are the aboriginal fisher-folk, are much blacker, and
their language is quite different ; that of the Ndorobos, as elsewhere, being similar to Masai.   The latter seem to capture
the fish by spearing them from canoes in the shallow water of
the bays.   None of the fishing natives know the use of hook
and line ; and, strange to say, my men could no longer catch
any.   Whether owing to the shallowness of the water or what
I don't know, but certain it is, that though the water was stiff
with them, the fish, except an occasional " barber," would not
take a bait any more.

I could not wonder at the preference of these people for the
lake with its inexhaustible wealth of food, so much more easily
obtained than the precarious living of those who hunt land
animals.   Simply marvellous is its fertility in fish.   What
immense quantities must be consumed daily by the armies of

birds preying upon it, not to take into account the crocodiles (also very numerous) and the colonies of fishermen! But, in spite of all, so prolific is it that the water fairly teems with fish. These natives are less timid than the El Molo, and as soon as we had made friends quite a crowd followed me to camp. Their headman presented me with a fish or two, and I gave him a few strings of beads and the skin of the buck I had shot (a thing they prize, and cannot easily obtain themselves), and then a brisk trade went on with the porters, who bartered whatever trifling ornaments they had for the heaps of dried fish brought by the natives for sale. I noticed that all these fish-eating people looked sleek and plump ; thus rather seeming to controvert the opinion I have read that an exclusively fish diet causes skin diseases. Famine must be unknown among them.

During the morning's march we had passed a not very old camping-ground, with quantities of camel and cattle dung in the "boma" (enclosure of cut branches). At first I was puzzled, wondering whether it could have been a party of Bworanas or Randilis ; but further investigations soon revealed tell-tale evidences of Europeans, in empty cartridge-cases, torn paper coverings, and such like. I then concluded (from the proof of the presence of camels) that it was a caravan from the Somali coast, and what I gathered from these natives confirmed me in that conclusion. They said, however, that there was only one white man, and told me that he had come up some other way, through the Bworanas, and had been to Murli, at the north end of Bassu, passing here on his way back, and had been guided by them to Kulale instead of following the lake to the south end, whence we had come. They also informed me that he had fought with some tribes and captured much cattle, goats, etc., some of which he had given them. This was, of course, Dr. Donaldson Smith's caravan, though at the time I did not know who it could be, and thought perhaps it might be Mr. Chanler again. I wished I had been a little quicker coming up, so that I might have had the pleasure of meeting a European in this far and lonely desert.

In reply to my inquiries about elephants, I was told that I should meet with some farther on, when approaching the northern extremity of Bassu, where Reshiat was situated, which they declared they had visited. Thus I seemed to be getting at length within reach of the rather mysterious country which was our present goal, and I had every reason to feel thankful that all was so propitious ; for we seemed to have overcome the greatest difficulties of the journey. The going was now first-rate, the ground level, with hardly any stones. The hills had fallen back, and were now a considerable distance off to the eastward, a wide plain bordering the lake. Here and there were belts of mimosa bush, generally about dry watercourses ; and in front, beyond a large bay, was a hilly headland which I took to be the one which Teleki and Von Hohnel cut across, as shown by their map. This map was very useful, and enabled me, though without instruments, to tell approximately what part of the lake I had reached.

Arid and barren though the country still was, there was a little more vegetation than farther south, in the shape of sparse and withered grass and a few stunted thorn bushes scattered here and there, rendering it more suitable to game ; and as a consequence I noticed a good deal of zebra spoor of both the large and small species, also a few fresh rhino tracks as well as a new " scrape " or two, while gazelles seemed more numerous than hitherto. During the day's march I had bagged several geese with my rook rifle, so that my own larder was well supplied ; but my men had not had much meat lately, so I determined to make an effort to obtain a good supply that afternoon.

My experience is, as the result of many years of observation in Africa, that meat is a most important addition to the food of porters on the march. Its value in keeping them strong, healthy, and contented is inestimable ; and I think a conclusive proof of this is that I hardly ever had a case of even trivial sickness during the whole of this journey, and never any that a pill or two or a few opium tabloids would not cure. My men carried far heavier loads than is customary (or even lawful, according to present regulations!) in Europeans' caravans; yet not only did they never complain, but with, as far as I can remember, the single exception of a case of gripes or stomach cramp, lasting half an hour or so, and one of lameness at the very end of the return journey, not a porter was ever unable or unwilling to shoulder his load in the morning and bring it in smiling to the camping-ground for the day. I think I may say that this evidence contrasts favourably with the descriptions of the " sick-roll," etc., so often met with in accounts of African travel. At the same time, meat *alone* will not do; and, for men accustomed to a farinaceous diet, is less desirable even than grain alone.

To return to my progress on this 13th December '95. I found a pleasant spot in which to camp, beside a little creek, just about the right time, with a thorn-tree to pitch my tent under; and after seeing everything in order and having some tea and a snack, I went off with one attendant to hunt. I took up the gradually rising ground towards the east, the wind being favourable—that is, in my face—and before going very far sighted four or five Grevy's zebras feeding on an open ridge. It was not an easy place to approach them in, but I was determined to do my utmost to get a shot. I succeeded better than I had hoped for even. Taking advantage of some little hollows, which I managed to reach unobserved by making a circuit, I crawled alone to near the brow of the low ridge on which they were, unconscious of danger, without showing myself. Then, waiting prone till they were turned away from me, I got into a sitting position on ground commanding a clear view of them; shot one as soon as it turned sufficiently to afford an aim at a vital spot, and, before the others knew what was the matter, had given a second a bullet, each, after a short spasmodic rush, falling dead. They were two large mares, in fine condition.

Swahilis are very fond of zebra meat, especially when fat (and they do get very fat), so there was great rejoicing in camp at the news of my success, and more so still when I announced that in consequence of this windfall we would rest a day here. This would enable the men to partially dry a quantity of meat, so that they could carry much more, as in the dry air the strips soon part with a large proportion of their moisture and become very much lighter. As it was not very far from camp, and in the perfectly open country the place would be easy to find, I had left Juma (who had been with me) to begin skinning while I brought word myself ; and on my calling for volunteers nearly every one set off eagerly in the direction I pointed out. The meat was all brought in by sundown and soon distributed among the various " messes." (For it is always better to have this done by the headman, in camp, to avoid quarrelling and unfair division.)

In the morning a strange Swahili turned up at our camp. This was a surprise, as Swahili caravans hardly ever visit this region (the few that have reached Reshiat went round to the west of the lake, and only very large parties venture so far). Our visitor explained that he belonged to a small party of Swahili traders who were on their way back from the north end of the lake, and were then encamped a short distance away. They had heard my shots in the afternoon, and he had come on to see who it was. Later the whole caravan arrived, and camped near us. There were only some thirty of them, and it appeared that they had followed us from the coast with the intention of asking my permission to travel in company with my caravan ; but while we were at El Bogoi they had passed up by another route and come on, supposing us to be in front of them, until they met Dr. Donaldson Smith's party, and had then followed his track back to Kéré and Magu, up the river which runs into the lake from the north. They were now on their way to the coast. They said their trading had not been a success, but gave us a lot of useful information about the country ahead, and told me there were plenty of elephants about the north end of the lake, though they had seen no signs of any along the shores in this direction.

The man who had first come to meet us now said that he would like to turn back with me, as he had some trade goods left which he wanted to try to barter for ivory, though he had been obliged to come away, as the other members of the caravan would not wait. He said that if I would allow him and two or three of his assistants to join my caravan, and would supply them with food, of which, as well as the where-withal to buy more, they were short, he would guide me and assist me in every way in his power. To this I gladly agreed, thinking it a most happy stroke of good fortune to obtain such valuable help from a Swahili who knew the way and all about the natives in the country where we were going. Nor had I ever reason to regret my decision ; for Mnyamiri (such was his name) was of the greatest use to me both as guide and interpreter, being a proficient linguist in many African languages and thoroughly at home in Masai and its kindred dialects, which were the only means of communication we had with the tribes among whom we were going.

It seemed an especially fortunate coincidence that I should have met with this man here, anxious to accompany me, just where we needed a guide, having reached a point whence we ought to strike across country, leaving the lake for a time, and make a short cut to Alia Bay. I took the opportunity of writing some letters to send to the coast by the returning caravan. I expected they would take months on the road, but knew they would get there some day and that the news of me would be welcome to my friends. I found out, in the course of conversation, that these traders had, on their up journey, taken the route to the eastward of Mount Nyiro, where they had suffered much from thirst, some of their donkeys perishing from want of water. On hearing that we had experienced no sufferings from that cause, they concluded that ours must be the better route, in spite of the rough hills and stony going. So altogether I seemed to have been most happy in my choice.

Saying good-bye to our trader visitors bound for Mombasa, we resumed our march next morning, our newly-acquired guide trudging importantly ahead.   We cut across a cape, but came down to another bay beyond, the last point of Bassu we should touch before striking inland for a spell.   For here a range of rough stony hills juts out into the lake, so that not only is it a great saving in distance to leave it to the left, but if the shore were followed at this part progress would be most difficult.   Game-tracks were becoming more numerous as we proceeded, the grass making a better pretence of covering the now sandy soil, and that night I heard lions roaring, a sure indication that game is not scarce.   I also noticed a good many rhino spoors.   I was most anxious to meet with rhinos here, as Von Hohnel (whom I had the pleasure of meeting in Mombasa, and who had most kindly given me much valuable information about the country) had told me that those found on the eastern side of Lake Rudolph were possibly a distinct species.

From this point we traversed a wide flat valley between two parallel ranges of hills, the one bordering the lake, the other inland ; the valley—cut up by denudation of the friable soil into many little ridges and gullies—made rather tiresome going.   Water was scarce, the sun burning hot, and the marches long and trying, and I sighed for our dear old lake ;—a good friend had it been to us.   Never had we had any worry about water or the distance to camp since we had struck it. Now, no sooner did we leave its shores than our trouble began : anxiety as to whether there would be enough for all, the tedious process of watering the donkeys out of buckets, scooping up the reluctant fluid by cupfuls out of holes in the gravel (myself standing in the stifling heat of the river-bed, exposed to a burning sun, to see that each one got its turn), stinted allowance for washing, and all the inconveniences of a short supply.

It was not till the third morning after leaving its shores, that, with delight, we found ourselves once more beside the ample bosom of our dear old friend. We were now on the large bay of Alia or Lalia. The water here is very shallow for a long distance out, and there is much water-grass growing in it. We camped early, under some bushy thorn-trees giving real shade, a by no means common feature of the trees in this country, but particularly grateful in the torrid heat. The opportunity of resting in comfort was especially welcome, as I had got a touch of fever from the trying ordeal of seeing the donkeys watered the day before. Opposite was another fishing village on a small island, the natives from which soon brought quantities of fish for sale. I sent word that I should like some freshly caught, and some of them went out and speared a lot in quite a short time. There were some Reshiat people, too, here, who had come for the sake of the fish on account of famine in their own country. All are excessively black.

I saw a good deal of game ; and, in addition to the usual oryx and grantii, now, for the first time, " topi." I shot one of the latter in the afternoon, but had to fetch Pice to assist in its capture, and it gave us a good chase before it was done, not-withstanding that I had hit it right in the shoulder, though an inch or two low if anything. It seemed wonderful how it could live and run after such a shot. This was the first antelope of the kind I had ever shot, though I had seen some years before in Sotike (a district in the direction of the Victoria Nyanza, but south of the ordinary route to that lake). They remind one strongly of the bastard hartebeeste (*Damaliscus lunatus*) of the south. I am not sure whether this variety is identical with the " topi " of the east coast, or whether, as I think very likely, it is an intermediate form between that and the " korrigum " of the west, in the same way that the oryx agrees entirely with neither beisa nor callotis.[1] It was here, too, that I noticed

---

[1] Probably the " topi," " korrigum," and " tiang " are all three mere local varieties of one species.

flocks of white spoonbills for the first time. I also saw some
of the birds which in South Africa go by the name of the small
locust bird.

Our progress was now smooth and pleasant in spite of the
great heat, over great flats with a sandy soil, varied sometimes
by low ridges of rotten ground with stones, where the pace was
slower, the hills far away on our right and the lake more shoal
than ever, with water-grass a mile or two out to sea. More
fishing kraals on islands were passed, whose inhabitants were
always ready to sell fish, both fresh and dried. I saw, too, a
few duck at this part, and, all along, the various water-birds of
the kinds already mentioned, with others not enumerated, were
in astonishing numbers. Hippos are not common, and the few
seen mostly far out from the shore, but land game plentiful,
especially "topi" (which did not seem very wild), sometimes
in large herds, as well as the usual kinds, including considerable numbers of the smaller zebra, Grevy's being also
present.

Three or four Ndorobos from the large settlement we had
passed several days before had been following us with the
object of selling some ivory they knew of, which was concealed
on the lake shore at this part. It proved to be two very large
bull tusks, but they had evidently lain here for many years, and
were nearly rotten. However, Mnyamiri was very pleased to
acquire it, as he was able to buy it for a small quantity of
goods. It seemed folly to me to carry such comparatively
worthless stuff such an immense distance to the coast; but
Swahili traders refuse nothing in the shape of ivory, however
much damaged, and even buy rhinoceros horns, undeterred by
long and difficult land carriage.

I had hoped to begin to meet with elephants in this part,
as Count Teleki and Captain Von Hohnel had told me that
they had found numerous herds along this coast, all the way
from Alia northward. But there can be no doubt that, at the
period of their visit, a succession of seasons of exceptional

drought must have caused all the water in the surrounding country, far back in every direction, to dry up, thus forcing all the elephants to resort to the lake shores.   This is also shown by the obvious proofs I have noticed of the lake having filled up very much of recent years.   I could see no signs whatever of elephants having frequented the neighbourhood for a long time back, the only evidence of their ever having done so being, besides the ancient tusks above mentioned, an old skull and a few very much decayed bones.

Though I had kept a careful look-out for rhinoceros all along the coast, and occasionally noticed their tracks, it was not till 21st December that I met with the animal itself.   On that morning, a couple of hours after starting, I saw one ahead. As already explained, I was particularly anxious to get one here to examine, and obtain a specimen of the supposed small variety said to be peculiar to this region.   At the same time an abundant supply of meat for my men would be most acceptable ; so I halted the caravan, took my Lee-Metford magazine rifle, and went after it.   The wind was not un-favourable, blowing from our right, while the rhino was advancing slowly towards us but diagonally across our line of march.   The ground was perfectly open, not a stick or tuft a foot high anywhere ; and as I went forward towards the left, in the endeavour to cut it off, it seemed to see me.   But when it looked in my direction I kept still, and it appeared reassured and fed as it went, for on raising its head again from the ground I could see it was chewing.   Pice was at my heels ; and on my giving him a caution in a hoarse stage whisper, the rhino looked up towards us.   But it came on again, and I got right in front of it.   Its attendant birds alarmed it a little by flying off, but it still came unconcernedly on.   I had sat down —my favourite position for a steady shot,—and when our friend got within thirty yards and still continued to advance straight for me, with nothing but a little rough grass between us, I thought it time to try to make him halt, my attitude not being an altogether dignified one in which to receive, at close quarters, so august a visitor ; so I gave a slight whistle between my teeth.   He stood still, and held his head well up with his ears cocked, looking hard towards me and exposing his breast. I at once, being in readiness, gave him a bullet in the throat, just above the chest (the chest itself is too low to aim for a front shot), and, as he swung round and started off, another in the ribs.   He galloped about fifty yards, just managed to get through a little gully, though his action was getting laboured, and on to the stony farther bank, where he stood for a second, half turned round, and toppled over on to his side ; then kicked his legs into the air a couple of times, and, after a squeal, lay still.   Pice was soon smelling at his nose, and, on my getting up to him, though his little eye still blinked, he breathed no more.   Even half a minute or so later, on putting my finger to it the eyelid winked again ; but it was only the muscles working automatically, for he was dead.   Cutting him up delayed us an hour and a half ; but it was well worth it. He was fat, and the men loaded themselves in great glee with the meat (much beloved of Swahili) on top of their burdens—one would have thought to the breaking point, and so they would have said, had it not been to fill, first their pots, and then their own stomachs.

Before allowing him to be touched I had examined him critically, and carefully measured him with my tape-line, and, though I could detect no structural difference whatever, he certainly was, although evidently a fully mature bull, so much smaller than the average "faro" of farther south that on comparing his measurements with those of my large El Gereh specimen he seemed quite a pygmy.[1]   I hid his whole head under a heap of stones.   The horns were not long.   Fortunately it was rather cloudy with a nice breeze, so that we did not feel the heat as usual, and in spite of this delay and

---

[1] These measurements, together with others, will be found in the table given on page 425.

another halt to let the men drink, we were able, by keeping at it later, to do about our accustomed distance.

While waiting for the men to drink, I was interested in watching, through my glasses, a party of spoonbills feeding in the shallows. They reminded me forcibly of mowers moving slowly in a row, some fifteen or twenty abreast, in open order with measured steps, their heads down and the points of their long bills under water swinging regularly with a sweeping action from right to left. This was evidently their method of feeling for food on the muddy bottom. Some white herons and egrets of various sizes accompanied the spoonbills. There was also a clump of stately pelicans on a low island near, and beyond a large flock of gulls resting on a mud-bank, besides the usual assortment of storks, herons, etc., etc. I wished I could get near enough to photograph the scene, but all my attempts to take snap-shots at the lake birds have resulted in failure.

We found a nice spot for our camp again to-day, with shady thorn-trees, near two more fishermen's villages on low islands. There was also a high island opposite, far out, not marked on the map I had with me. The lake here is ugly but still interesting — as how could it fail to be with its abounding bird life? Game too was plentiful, and a hare would now and then get up under one's feet and scuttle away (an animal which, though I have not mentioned it before, is occasionally met with all along the lake). There are also great numbers of small black crows all along here. They may be seen among the huts on the little islands occupied by the El Molo, picking up the fish refuse; in this way no doubt useful to the islanders, who do not molest them. Hence they become very tame and sometimes a nuisance; there were flocks always about our camp, and they would venture right in among us and were constantly trying to steal the strips of meat spread about to dry.

Once more we had, on the 22nd, a series of stony volcanic

BIRDS ON LAKE RUDOLPH.

ridges (though of no height), coming right down into the water, to get over, reminding us of the south end of the lake.   This kind of margin is much more picturesque than the low swampy parts, the water being clear and deepening rapidly.   Both south and north of the lava ridges are sandy flats.   We got through the difficult ground in one good day's march.   There was a fairly distinct path running along the sides of these rocky hills parallel with the shore ; indeed it is generally the case wherever the ground is covered thickly with stones, if there is game in the country, that paths are formed by any animals passing through, owing to their naturally following the line of least resistance, and so a beaten track is made and kept open by constant use.   Where the ground is unobstructed and presents no obstacle to progress in any direction, paths are not so likely to be formed.

We found another dry river-bed with trees to camp in.   On this day I saw a small school of hippos, the first I had seen together on the lake, though I had occasionally seen scattered individuals.   In the night I heard a leopard grunting, and the geese were so noisy as to disturb one's sleep.   From here there began to be a good deal more bush, though still scattered, mainly "suaki" near the lake and farther back low-spreading thorn bushes.   The "suaki" is a bushy, evergreen shrub or low tree with small, round, light green leaves.   It is the sticks of this bush that are used by Swahilis as tooth-brushes.   I presume the name Suakin (which merely means "at the suaki" in Swahili) is derived from this tree.

There was great abundance of game at this part.   I had not seen it so plentiful for many a long day.   There were zebra of both kinds, oryx, topi antelope, Grant's gazelle in plenty, and a good many Waller's gazelle ; I also saw a troop of waterbuck—the first I had met with on the lake—but my glasses being behind, I could not be sure of what species.   There were numbers of rose-coloured bee-eaters here, and I saw one large green one which seemed unfamiliar to me.   It was here too that

I first observed a rather curious thing which afterwards became a
common sight. It is the habit of this rosy bee-eater (*Merops
nubicus*) to ride on the back of the large crested pauw (*Eupodotis
kori*), which is common about the north-east extremity of
Bassu. It sits far back, on the rump of its mount, as a boy
rides a donkey. The pauw does not seem to resent this liberty,

PAUW (*Eupodotis kori*) AND BEE-EATER (*Merops nubicus*).

but stalks majestically along, while its brilliantly clad little
jockey keeps a look-out, sitting sideways, and now and again
flies up after an insect it has espied, returning again after the
chase to "its camel"—as Juma not inaptly called it. I have
even seen two bee-eaters riding on one pauw. I have also
noticed this pretty little bird sitting on the backs of goats,
sheep and antelopes, but the pauw seems its favourite steed.

I imagine it gets more flights in this way at game put up by its bearer, which also affords it a point of vantage whence to sight and pursue its prey in a country where suitable sticks to perch on are few.

During this day's march I came upon the carcase of a Grevy's zebra foal which had been freshly killed by a leopard, but the latter had slunk away, no doubt warned by the men's voices.   Later I happened upon a walleri fawn only just born and not yet dry, and moved it out of the path of the caravan lest any of the men should hurt it.   In one place I noticed no less than five old bleached rhino skulls within a short distance of each other, though there seemed but little fresh spoor about, and I wondered what could have killed them, as there are now no hunting natives anywhere near.   Possibly they may have been shot by Count Teleki when he passed this way some eight years previously.   Jackals are common all along here, and— as might be expected where game is plentiful—hyenas and vultures are numerous ; for though I met with no lions, they are sure to be there to provide pickings for these scavengers.

Another frequent and disagreeable accompaniment of abundant game was a fly, two specimens of which I caught, that I have always taken for the female of the "tetse," though in this I may be in error.   It is larger than the typical one and of a uniform brownish colour with no markings, but in other respects exactly similar both as to appearance and habits, and I have always before noticed it associated with the smaller striped variety, though I saw none of the latter kind here. Whether this kind is poisonous or not I am not sure.   My donkeys never suffered from having passed here ; but then they can stand a *few* "fly," though where the "tetse" is numerous they soon succumb.   It was here that I was at last cheered, for the first time since reaching the lake, with signs of elephants having been about not long since, leading me to hope that our perseverance would soon be rewarded.

I have had occasion to mention before that the liver of the

rhinoceros is esteemed a delicacy by Swahilis. For my own part I never thought much of it, and the only part of this animal I usually ate was the tongue, though rhino tail is very good stewed (it takes about twelve hours' boiling to render either tender); but my cook on this occasion concocted a dish which converted me and which I can recommend as an entrée. He made me some rissoles of pounded liver and tongue (both previously boiled), flavoured with the herb of my own discovery to which I have previously alluded. These, nicely fried, are first-rate. Feruzi called these triumphs of his skill " cartrets," and I eventually came to the conclusion that he was trying to say *cutlets* (though of course that was the wrong term for them), but I would suggest that the dish may be called " paté de faro " on the menu.

On 24th December I bagged another rhino. We had just had our usual short rest in the middle of the march, and I had already shouted the order to " bandika," when, as the men were beginning to take up their loads, I heard " Fau, fau ! " (an abbreviation of " faro," the Swahili for rhinoceros), and looking up saw a small and very thin rhino with long horns sauntering very slowly across to windward of us. It had evidently not heard us, though quite near, thanks to a stiff breeze that was blowing. Telling the men to sit down again and keep quiet, I took my .303 and went towards it, followed by Pice. I saw it was hardly worth shooting for meat ; but as it had a fine pair of horns and looked very small I was anxious to get its head as a specimen of the Bassu variety. With a high and favourable wind and stunted bushes between, I easily got close. Then it, I suppose, heard me, for it turned, and I at once gave it a shot. On receiving the bullet it waltzed round and round once or twice, and as it was moving away I put in a second by way of making doubly sure. It then got behind some scrub, and I set Pice on. His bark and its snorts showed me it was close by, and I got up just in time to see it totter and fall into a lying-down position, from which it never moved. I then photographed it and measured it carefully.   It was a cow, considerably smaller than the bull of the other day and the thinnest I had ever shot, though its horns did not seem as if it were extraordinarily old.   Its front horn only measured 26½ inches, though, owing no doubt to the very small size of the animal itself, it looked much longer.   The porters took meat in spite of its emaciation, while I cut off the horns and buried the skull, having avoided chopping the bone at all.

DEAD RHINOCEROS COW OF THE SMALL VARIETY (*Rhinoceros bicornis*).
(From a Photograph by the AUTHOR.)

There was here much stunted bush, though not thick ; the country was very flat and the soil like dried mud, which it undoubtedly is, namely, lacustrine deposit ; and all along this part were many tall chimney-like ant-heaps.   The usual kinds of game were observed, with more Waller's gazelle than I had seen anywhere.   For a day or two past I had noticed that the lake water was getting fresher and at the same time less clear, and now it had lost its salt taste altogether and become muddy, looking quite red out to sea.   This was of course caused by the large river running in from the north, now only a short way ahead, for Mnyamiri assured me we should reach the first kraals of Reshiat early the day but one after. Fringing the lake margin were beds of tall, dark-green rushes, contrasting picturesquely with the numerous white herons and egrets.

I went out in the afternoon to try to shoot a granti for my own larder ; but the sun and wind were together—that is to say, the sun getting low and the wind also in the west, a most unfavourable combination—and I could not get near them, though numerous. The most favourable conditions for approaching game are a low sun on your back and the wind in your face. Then the hunter is in shadow, the game conspicuous, and the wind from the latter to the former ; reverse these conditions and the chances are all against him.

The next day I had the opportunity of examining through my glasses some waterbuck (the second lot I had seen), and made out that they were not the ringed sort, but a variety (probably " defassus ") with white patches on the stern in place of the elliptical mark characteristic of the common east-coast waterbuck. This is the only part of the lake where any are seen. Here the shore was fringed with " suaki " jungle, with bushes in the water too, which was now very muddy but quite sweet. We camped close by a very big old elephant skull—perhaps a victim of Count Teleki's.

Bethinking me that this was Christmas Day, I got out my rook rifle and shot a goose, deeming that as suitable a dish for the occasion as I could command ; for I had no fresh meat, and it seemed a shame to have dry biltong for my dinner. Luckily it proved a fat one, and, though so freshly killed, was a success on the table. I had no delicacy to bring out as a treat in honour of the festival ; no " medical comforts " whatever, my one grub box containing nothing but tea, salt, soap, matches, a little coffee, and a few candles (the latter kept as a stand-by in case of sickness), besides some cartridges to make up the weight. Nevertheless I enjoyed my dinner, though the accompaniments of the "roast goose" (really boiled first and then fried a bit in a pot) were only millet porridge instead of vegetables, a small millet-meal cake for bread, and porridge again with honey by way of pudding ; while, for drink, coffee sweetened with honey had to satisfy me : and I thought it all first-rate.

I had been feeling a shade low-spirited, the effect, perhaps, of the contrast the day suggested between my loneliness and the convivial associations usually considered appropriate to the season. But Abdulla cheered me up by his hopefulness. A good man, Abdulla, who always took a hopeful view of things. I often used to have a chat with him in the evening by the camp fire over my after-dinner pipe, and he invariably maintained that our prospects were bright. "Inshallah, Bwana, tu ta pata ndovu tele !" (Please God, master, we shall get plenty of elephants). He always identified himself thoroughly with the undertaking, and took the greatest interest in the serious business of the expedition. He often amused me vastly by his contemptuous way of speaking of those who went merely to "tembea" (that is, to take a stroll for amusement) in the "bara"—namely, scientific travellers, etc.

Our march the next morning was really only about two hours' actual going; but, though starting as usual, we did not get to the kraals of Reshiat till 9.30, owing to delay over a Grevy's zebra I shot on the way. It was a single old stallion. I was very anxious to get some meat to make the men happy at the end of the long desert journey, and had been rather regretting not having halted a day among the game for the purpose of shooting them some, for we seemed to have got out of it now. So, seeing this fellow standing some way off watching the caravan, and knowing we had only a short march before us to-day, so that the waste of time would not matter, I determined to try hard to get a shot at him, and happily succeeded. There were clumps of "suaki" about, favouring my chance, so that I was able, by taking advantage of their cover, to get within shot while his attention was taken up watching the distant caravan, which I had allowed to go on.   When I fired he galloped off, and I lost sight of him behind bushes; but I had heard the bullet strike and seen, by his tail-on-end race away, that he was hard hit, so followed, though I could see no blood on his spoor. On rounding a clump of "suaki," behind which he had dis-appeared, to my joy I saw him lying dead close by.   I piped my signal on my empty cartridge-case (which I always carry in my pocket as the most convenient call) with a thankful heart, and felt as pleased as the men seemed when they came up. I had him cut up and divided on the spot and then went on.

We soon reached the first kraals, and camped close by under shady thorn-trees.   The natives were friendly, but not trouble-some—as Africans too often become when their friendliness is too demonstrative.   They had a good many goats and a decent little troop of cattle, besides a number of donkeys.   I had an extra ration of meal served out to the caravan as a treat, to celebrate our safe arrival in Reshiat.   The leading porters thanked me for having brought them all safely through—their manner of offering congratulations.   Nice of them, this, I thought.   Every one seemed in good spirits, and I myself had quite recovered my cheerfulness.

CHAPTER XIII

A SOJOURN AT RESHIAT AND KÉRÉ

Among artless savages—Scene of a massacre—Egrets and their hosts—Myriads of
mosquitoes—A satisfactory morning's work—Good out of evil—A new antelope
—A revolting disfigurement—The metropolis of Kéré—Exchanging greetings—
Waifs from a European expedition—New Year's Day—A melancholy event—
Pacifying a chief—A consequence of lavish expenditure—Exorcising a marauder
—A model in ebony—Getting rid of a nuisance.

HAVING reached once more a country with settled inhabitants,
the first thing to be done was to make their acquaintance. I
had an interview with the head of the kraal, which was
satisfactory so far as it went. He brought one of his wives,
who knew the Masai language, as his interpreter, while I
employed Mnyamiri, who spoke it fluently. I found these
satisfactory people to deal with : it is a treat—and a rare
one nowadays even in Africa—to meet with simple, unspoiled
savages. They cultivate nothing but "mtama" (millet), and
even that only to a very limited extent, just along the damp
margin of the lake. The crops there were in ear and looking
splendid. It appears that the uncertain rainfall deters these
not at all energetic cultivators from extending their operations,
though the soil is alluvial and probably fertile all over these flats.
It often struck me, while sojourning in Reshiat, that the lake
water might be used for purposes of irrigation by means of
windmills, for there is generally a good strong breeze blowing
from a south-easterly direction. Hills were now visible to the
northward over the intervening flat country and beyond the

end of the lake, and across its northern extremity the low shore could be made out. Throughout the whole length of Bassu, with the exception of one part—the only one where there is a water-horizon to the westward—hills are visible across the lake, the land on its western banks being for the most part high, though of course the actual shore is nowhere visible, until it narrows at the north end where hills no longer border it.

Until the last day or two I had never, during the whole journey along the lake, heard a mosquito ; since then a few had been in evidence, but here they swarmed. No doubt the water, impregnated with soda (or whatever the right name for its saline property may be), did not agree with them, but here, in the swampy border of the lake, where it is fresh, they find a congenial habitat.

I had heard a good deal about Reshiat, when making inquiries about this country before leaving the coast, from the few Swahili traders who had visited it. The name is used by them to designate generally the inhabited region at the north end of Bassu, and I had pictured a populous and extensive district. My surprise, then, was considerable when, after one short march from its commencement, Mnyamiri told me that we had reached the last kraals or Reshiat proper ; the whole comprising but a few small villages scattered along the shore.[1] It is rather a pleasant bit of country (comparatively so, at all events) ; some sandy ridges rise from the shore, fairly well grassed, with open plains behind and open water in front.

I saw a good many hippos here, and herds of "topi" grazed sometimes quite close up to the kraals. I did not interfere with them during the march, but after camping among some clumps of "suaki" bush went out to procure meat. I first bagged a ram Grant's gazelle (though not without some

---

[1] I afterwards learned that there is another district of the same name at the north-western corner of the lake.

trouble, as the wind and sun were again together, the former pretty strong and blowing the brim of my flabby old hat constantly into my eyes) ; and then, after a good deal of manœuvring and dodging, succeeded in getting a shot at a " topi." She (it was a cow) ran some distance, notwithstanding that she had got the bullet fairly in the ribs, and disappeared among some bushes. But I could tell by her flurried scamper off that she would drop, and soon found her lying dead. She was very fat indeed. All hands got meat again and were happy. The topi, when in good condition (and nearly every one I shot in this country was fat), furnishes splendid meat, and is one of the very best of the larger antelopes for the table ; thus resembling, in this respect as well as in appearance, the " bastard hartebeeste " (though, for the matter of that, all the hartebeestes are good eating).

The guinea-fowls here are of the species having a stumpy horn and short thick beak with a little brush over its base. A little farther south I had met with both the common horned kind of East Africa and the vulturine guinea-fowl, also near the lake. Flocks of crowned cranes frequent the cultivated strip fringing the lake shore in this and the adjoining districts. Their loud and rather musically plaintive note, while reminding one strongly of the South African species, differs sufficiently from the latter's cry to proclaim them distinct even before the divergence in appearance is noticed.

While out hunting I came across a rather disagreeably suggestive sight ; numbers of bleached and grinning human skulls were scattered about over the ground, betokening some bygone fight or slaughter. One account I heard attributed these to a Swahili caravan, said to have been massacred by natives ; but whether that was the true version, or whether they marked some battle of the inhabitants with raiding Bworanas, I am not sure.

I, as usual, made the acquaintance of the owner of the kraal near which we had camped. He was one of the tribe which the Swahilis call Wakwavi, a pastoral people who formerly lived side by side with the Masai (to whom they are akin), and by which race of marauders they were, after long fighting, dispersed.   They are now scattered far and wide over East Equatorial Africa, and members of the clan may be met with living among the different tribes in the most distant parts.   They are useful as affording means of communication with the peoples among whom they have settled, and whose languages they have acquired, for every caravan has some men with more or less knowledge of Masai.   There are, of course, drawbacks to passing all one has to say and the answers through two interpreters (one is bad enough, even if efficient), and no doubt the meaning is often altered or turned upside down ; but in these remote parts, so seldom visited even by Swahili traders, one may think oneself lucky to be able to communicate at all, however imperfectly, with the inhabitants.

Lekwais (such was my present interviewer's name) told me that around Bumi, the next district, which we should reach on the morrow, were many elephants ; and that some had been seen that very day by a boy who had come from there. One herd, he told me, had its retreat by day in bush growing *in* the lake itself, but might be found outside in the early morning ; others were in the habit of coming down to drink during the night, and retreating to the back country for the hours of daylight.   It was from him that I first learnt that there was only one river entering the lake, from the north (as Dr. Donaldson Smith found and has now made known), and not two as had been supposed.   Lekwais called this river the Warr, but said (as I afterwards myself found) that it had a variety of names.

This elephant news was indeed encouraging ; and I could not help thinking continually how very fortunate I had been to reach this country so successfully and easily ; my men and donkeys all safe and sound, not one having been seriously sick or sorry since leaving Nyiro.   All through this wide wilderness we had been able to travel quietly and comfortably without any hardships or privations worth speaking of. Hard *work* we had had some of among the hills and rocks and stones of the south end of the lake, but no insurmountable obstacles nor serious accidents. Above all, the lake had always been near to give us water and guide us on our way without risk of thirst. Everything had seemed in our favour, and happened most propitiously for our journey.

We were now close to the extreme northern end of the lake, and the shore we were following was in reality that of its most easterly inlet running in that direction. As we proceeded on the following morning (28th December) along the extensive low flats studded with " suaki " bushes, which at this point border the lake, the part of the latter we were skirting assumed almost the character of a mangrove swamp. The shallow water is thickly filled with bush extending far out ; indeed, from the low bank, except a lane here and there, little open water can be seen, and it appears as if the whole width of the gulf were of this nature.

I soon noticed quite fresh elephant spoor along the path we were now following, and some distance ahead a flock of white egrets attracted my attention, hovering about one spot at the edge of the marsh and anon settling, apparently on the bushes. On getting nearer I made out a herd of elephants just outside of this swamp bush. I stopped the " safari " and went towards them with only my gun-bearers. There might be thirty of them : I could not see them all at once. They were moving slowly along, feeding here and there as they went, accompanied by the white egrets, which perched on their backs and heads and bespattered them with white splashes, the pure white plumage of the birds contrasting picturesquely with the dark bodies of their great hosts, who seemed to have no objection to their attentions. Why, then, I wondered, do the tick birds never haunt elephants as they constantly do rhinos and other animals ? I have always supposed that elephants

ELEPHANTS AND EGRETS.

(From a Drawing by J. G. MILLAIS.)

"The pure white plumage of the birds contrasting picturesquely with the dark bodies of their great hosts."

resent such liberties, and, being provided with far-reaching trunks, are able to make it unsafe even for such active and persevering little hunters, to get rid of whom the tormented donkey rolls in vain. Whether or not elephants harbour the right sort of parasites to suit the taste of these little birds I cannot say ; but the egrets appear to accompany animals, not for anything to be found on their persons, but for the sake of the insects disturbed by their feet as they move about.

By the time I got near them the elephants were entering the swamp, some already in the mud and water, which—full of pits from their feet—was impassable for us. A few stood still on the edge, and I might have reached them and shot probably one ; but I thought it better to leave them alone, as, though I might kill one, I should disturb the herd and could not follow it, while interfering with my chance for the morrow. So I satisfied myself with feasting my eyes on the spectacle, standing on an ant-heap glasses in hand.   It was a grand sight ! There were some good tuskers among them, though, owing to their being turned away from me and already among the bushes, I could not get a view of the ivory of most, but the massive size of those I could see showed them to be bulls. One, a fine young male with beautiful white, symmetrical teeth of perhaps 60 lbs. apiece—egrets sitting on his back,—stood picking a mouthful or two of leaves off a shrub outside after the others had entered the water.   They slowly plodded, with much splashing, through the deep mud, and disappeared into the mangrove-like swamp.   The wind, and everything except the mud, had been favourable for shooting, and I was filled with hopes of success for my hunting in this region.

I returned to the caravan and we continued our march to Bumi, the next little settlement ; which consists, like Reshiat, of a few kraals scattered at intervals along the lake.   A continuous narrow strip of cultivation runs along the shore.   The people of both these little districts live from hand to mouth, beginning to eat the green millet as soon as the grain is formed ; so that, though they keep on planting crop after crop as each is reaped, not only have they none to spare for sale, but they are themselves often in straits for food ; for the area under cultivation is so small that the produce of one crop is finished long before the next is fit to eat. The inhabitants of Bumi belong to a totally different tribe from those of Reshiat, and speak a different language. Their tribal name is El Gume (akin to the Suk), and they are, I gathered, immigrants from west of Bassu. They own little live stock—a few goats only—but snare game, while their next-door neighbours of Reshiat have no skill in hunting or trapping in any shape or form. The latter are mainly pastoral by nature, though now their cattle are but few ; and, like all pastoral tribes, they are a good-looking, well set-up race, both men and women mostly very tall though of slender build. The El Gume are far inferior in these respects.

I camped near one of their kraals a little distance back from the lake, where I had found a small tree with creepers over it to give me a little shade. The heat here is tremendous, as great as on the coast, and it is generally rather a relief when the fiery sun disappears ; but no sooner was it down than the air became thick with mosquitoes, simply in millions, and I had to finish my dinner in great discomfort. I had a smoky fire lighted just behind my tent, so that the wind blew the smoke in ; this helped a little, and, though half choked, I managed thus to hold friendly converse with the owners of the kraal. But I was soon glad to take refuge under my mosquito-net ; and, in spite of a few of these assiduous insects that found their way in with me, should have slept tolerably well had it not been for the row the poor men were making all night, who could get no rest, and spent most of the time walking about flapping themselves with cloths.

As soon as light enough to see, I started to hunt the elephants we had passed on our way here the day before. We soon found fresh spoor ; then warm dung ; then heard a great splashing and saw one in the water, and, just after, sighted the herd standing close to the edge of the swamp at about the same place as yesterday. It seemed a herd of bulls, chiefly at any rate ; there were a few I took for cows, but I incline to think they may have been young bulls, and that they and their tusks seemed so small by contrast with the monsters. The herd may have numbered perhaps twenty or thereabouts ; it did not seem a large one. In order to get up to them I had to skirt the swamp and pass through some mud—the wind being favourable that way, while there was just enough cover to allow a near approach, with caution. The sun had but just risen behind the elephants, its horizontal rays thus shining right in my eyes ; and, to add to the difficulties, no sooner had we got to the edge of the swamp than the mosquitoes attacked us in myriads. It was useless to attempt to combat them : one saw them hanging from one's eyelids ; they got into my ears, down my neck, even into my mouth, and bit me all over, through clothes and everything. But I had to disregard them, as far as possible, and concentrate my attention on my game.

I crept up behind some low bushes to pretty close quarters to the herd, which stood in a clump. One big fellow, with fine tusks, was nearest me, just the other side of this slight screen. He came forward a little, giving me a good side shot, and, fearing they were about to enter the swamp, I seized the opportunity and gave him a shot in the shoulder. There was but a very slight breeze blowing in my face, and the volumes of smoke, from 10 drams of the abominable old black powder, hung in the heavy morning air, so that I could not use my second barrel at once. However, the elephants seemed uncertain at first which way to run, and, opening out a little as they moved about in confusion, allowed me to make out two or three real monsters (though nearly all were large bulls) ; so, picking out two of the others with the biggest tusks (having by this time reloaded my right barrel), I sent a bullet into the ribs of each. The herd then swung round and set off at a run, describing a semicircle so as to get into the swamp behind

us, one, however (probably the first I had fired at), going off
alone slowly, evidently very hard hit, in the opposite direction.
Running across with my magazine rifle in my hands, I was
able—though not in time to cut them off—to get in two or
three shots at the wounded ones, with the result that another
turned out and walked back across the flat.

By this time the main body had entered the swamp, but I
noticed the bull with the longest tusks of all, and which I was
particularly anxious to kill, behind, and getting along apparently
with difficulty.   I had the .303 still in my hands, and as he
stood for a moment on the edge, before following the rest into
the swamp, I had a fine chance, and aimed for his temple in
hopes of dropping him.   But the confounded rifle had got on
half-cock in the mysterious way it has the knack of doing at
the most inopportune moments, and by the time I had got
hold of the 10-bore the elephant was off after the others ;
however, I gave him a couple of stern shots and he came to a
standstill.   I could see he was done, so watched him.   Another,
that looked like a cow, waited a little for him, but then went on,
and I did not interfere with it.   I had left Smiler behind to
give me warning should the wounded ones come back.   After
watching the huge fellow standing up to his belly in the swamp
a minute or two, and being satisfied that he was done, I
turned to go and look after the others, but, just as I started,
he made an effort to move, and then fell over on his side in
the water, one tusk and half his body, but very little of his
head, visible.

Leaving him now with confidence that he was safe, I went
out to where Smiler was on guard.   I found that he had heard
rumblings only a short way ahead in the direction the first
wounded bull had taken.   I climbed a high ant-heap to get a
view, and soon made him out lying down but with his head up.
I felt sure he could not get away, but was considering whether
to go and give him a shot in the brain, when I saw several
other elephants a good way ahead.   Some four or five were

moving slowly along the edge of the swamp away from us, but one giant stood behind alone. I now started after them. As we passed opposite the one that was down, I saw that it had fallen over on its side. Going on, we found much blood on the spoor of the big bull standing alone, which was thus proved to be my third wounded one, and, getting within glass-range, I could make out a bullet-hole in his left shoulder. I noticed he seemed standing as if lame in both shoulders, and when I got pretty near he turned round, and I could see that there was also blood on the opposite side. I now crept up, and, taking the cripple-stopper, held for a steady finishing shot, but two cartridges snapped, and I had to take my .303 again. He was moving towards the swamp again now, and more or less away from us, so that it was not easy to bring him down suddenly ; but, after receiving two or three bullets in quick succession, he staggered and pitched on his front knees, resting his tusks on the ground for support, his lofty hind-quarters still standing erect, and, after remaining for a brief space in this curious position, lurched backwards, and finally rolled over on his side. Thus I had my three bulls—all huge fellows—down. This last had massive but not long tusks. I measured him carefully at once. The elephants that had been in front of him had now disappeared into the swamp, so we retraced our steps towards the other dead ones.

On coming within sight of the other, which lay in the open, I could see its upper tusk gleaming in the morning sun like a great white crescent, concave side downwards. When I came up to it I was indeed pleased to find its tusks were both long and thick—much bigger than any I had yet shot. They girthed 1 foot $9\frac{1}{4}$ inches just outside the lip. My gun-bearers congratulated me with pleased smiles. I believed the one in the lake, though, to be the best of the three, but when I came to measure the tusk above water (the right) I found it was not quite so thick. At the same time, I knew that an elephant always falls with its heaviest tusk down ; besides, I had a good

view of its left—now under water—which had been next me
when it passed, and it had particularly caught my eye, being
long and of a yellowish colour.[1]   Anyway, I felt that I had
done a satisfactory morning's work.

Several natives had now turned up, and I told them to
follow me to camp and I would then give them leave to take
the meat.   Taking another look at my prize in the water as I
passed, I soon reached my tent—no great distance—and had
a bath and some food, while Squareface went with some porters
to cut out the fat and choose an elephant for my men (Swahilis
are prejudiced generally against eating elephant meat, but
many of mine had overcome their scruples while in my service,
and learnt to appreciate it), and make over the other one on
dry ground to our neighbours here, while that in the water was
to be for Lekwais's people.   But when I got there later I found
that the natives had already cut up all three.   I reached the
one in the water by being pushed through the intervening space
in a dug-out, but only the skeleton was left of the upper half,
and they were even cutting off the meat under water.   When ex-
postulated with for this unseemly haste, they declared that they
meant no harm, but explained that they had been accustomed
to follow about the white man, who had been here lately, when
he went out shooting antelopes, to pick up the carcases left
lying on the veldt.

Abdulla (my headman) was in great spirits at the news of
my success, and I felt I had made a good beginning towards
my ivory heap.   My intention was, though, to push on till we
reached a district where food could be bought, as I knew the
importance of doing so while we still had a good store in hand,
and then, after making a standing camp and seeing the food
trade fairly started, to return with a few men to hunt.   But as
the people at the kraal here were very keen to show me a large

---

[1] The elephant which fell in the swamp eventually proved to be slightly the best.
The weights of the tusks when got out were—113 lbs. and 111 lbs.; 112½ lbs. and
108 lbs.; and 76½ lbs. and 66 lbs.   Of course they subsequently lost a little in drying.

herd of elephants which, they said, were in the habit of drinking every night at the lake close by, and returning into the extensive bush, which here stretches from the open ground near the shore over all the gently-rising country behind, to pass the day, I determined to stay over one more day. I was sorry for my men, who could get little sleep ; as for me, though this Egyptian plague of mosquitoes destroyed all comfort, I could take refuge under my net, while they were unprotected from the merciless foe. I wondered how the natives could live in such a place, and, on inquiring, was told they slept in rows with fires between each two ; but my men declared fires to be of no avail against these mosquitoes, so I can only suppose the inhabitants had become to some extent inured to the venomous swarms.

My next day's hunt was rather a failure. My native guides proved to have little skill in venery, and took me careering about the bush without any method, apparently on the chance of running up against elephants. Like children, they fancied that where they had lately happened across the herd, there we were sure to find it now, and were astonished not to see the elephants waiting for us. Thrown upon our own resources, we pursued more systematic tactics, with the result that we at length found spoor. It led us a long chase over a series of low, gravelly ridges covered with fairly thick, though not dense, bush, and at last to a herd of cows and calves. I was not keen on shooting cows here, where I knew there were bulls to be found, and circled round the herd in hopes of discovering some. I could see none, and one large cow, with very fine teeth, was in the centre of the herd, and I could not get near her without alarming others I should have to pass. The upshot of it was that, the wind being shifty, some of those on the outskirts, which I had passed very close to before I saw them, got my wind, and the whole troop stampeded ; and, though I followed a long way, all I could get a chance at were two small cows, which I shot with my .303. I killed these for the sake of the natives near whose kraal we were camped, as they had been forestalled by outsiders at yesterday's bulls, and were very eager for meat, and I wished to encourage their friendliness to us.   The tusks, though good, were thin and light.

We had a hard and rather disappointing day, and our weary tramp back was made longer by our getting somewhat out of our course—for our guides had long since disappeared ; it was cruelly hot, and my gun-bearers were worn out by the mosquitoes and burnt up with thirst.   But even out of these evils good came ; for, in some rather open bush country we passed through before reaching the lake (which we afterwards struck too far north), I saw some large hartebeeste of a species not only new to me, but which seemed to correspond exactly with none of which I had read.   There was a little herd of them, and I had a good look at one (apparently the bull) which brought up the rear, through my glasses, and became much interested, feeling certain this would prove to be an undescribed species.   For, although a mere hunter, my love of the subject had led me to acquire some general superficial knowledge of African antelopes, including the hartebeestes.   Its action and general appearance corresponded with that of other members of the genus, but it struck me as resembling most, both as to size and in other respects, the "tora."

I did not get near enough to have a good chance to shoot one, and, though no doubt I might have succeeded had I followed, under the then circumstances I was not very anxious to kill a specimen, feeling sure that I should be able to obtain some before leaving the country.   And so, fortunately, I did, in spite of subsequent difficulties, and the curious fact that I met with this hartebeeste nowhere but in this particular neighbourhood.   My inquiries of the natives elicited only confirmation of my own observations in this respect : they all declared that only in that circumscribed locality was this animal known.   The explanation probably is that this is the extreme limit of its range in this direction, the area of its distribution projecting in a narrow point, as it were, so as to

approach Lake Rudolph only at this particular part. For the
natives themselves do not penetrate any distance into the back
country, as was shown by their conduct on this day. I had
supposed that they turned back from fear of the elephants, of
which they undoubtedly stand in great dread ; but they assured
me they were afraid to go far in that direction lest they might
meet with some of the Batshada people, with whom they were

A NEW HARTEBEESTE (*Bubalis neumanni*, ♂ and ♀).

not on speaking terms. It shows how risky it is to lose a
chance of getting any desirable specimen when opportunity
offers, in the hope—which may and often does prove vain—
of meeting with plenty more farther on. In this instance,
however, I was luckily not disappointed, and was able to bring
back with me to this country the skulls and scalps of a male
and female, as well as a flat skin. Subjoined is the description
of this new species of hartebeeste from the *Annals and
Magazine of Natural History* (ser. 6, vol. xx. October 1897).

NOTE ON A NEW ANTELOPE

By the Hon. WALTER ROTHSCHILD

Bubalis neumanni, sp. n.

Mr. Arthur H. Neumann, during his recent travels in some of the most interesting parts of Africa, on the east shore of and to the north-east of Lake Rudolph, met with a hartebeeste which I cannot refer to any of the already known forms, and which I wish to name after its discoverer. I have before me two skulls with horns of a male and of a female, and the skin of the body of one.

The horns differ widely from those of *Bubalis major* (Blyth) of West Africa, and *B. buselaphus* (Pall.) of Northern Africa and Arabia, in being slenderer and in their tips being inverted, instead of pointing outwards or straight behind. The nearest ally seems to be *B. tora* (Gray) of Upper Nubia, Abyssinia, and Kordofan, which, however, has more slender horns, with more distinct rings, reaching almost round, a broader forehead, and a generally paler coloration. The horns also diverge much more in *B. tora*, as shown at a glance by the distances between the tips of the horns, as recorded in Rowland Ward's *Horn Measurements*. *B. neumanni* has evidently nothing to do with *Acronotus lelwel*, Heugl. (*Reise N.O.-Afr.* ii. p. 124), in which the tips of the horns point straight outwards. Matschie has referred *A. lelwel* to the West-African Bubal, but Sclater and Thomas have more correctly placed it among the synonyms of *B. buselaphus*. However, a query should be added to the name, the description not being exact enough to make out what the name means. The type is not in the museum at Stuttgart, according to kind information of Professor Lampert, nor can it be found elsewhere at present.

The horns of *B. neumanni* measure as follows :—

Circumference at base, ♂ 273 millim., ♀ 183 ; total length along the curves, ♂ 420, ♀ 345 ; tip to tip, ♂ 206, ♀ 249.

The rings of the horns are not very prominent, and do not reach all round.

Breadth of skull at forehead, ♂ 100 millim., ♀ 80 ; length of skull from base of horn to upper lip, along the side in a straight line, ♂ 430, ♀ 403 millim.

Colour of hair fulvous fawn, much richer on the back, where there are also some darker spots, which may be stains or natural ; below, very much paler. Chin blackish, tip of tail black. The male is brighter and darker in colour than the female. There are also on the back some patches with longer, thicker, almost whitish-buff hair, perhaps remains of the winter fur.[1]

---

[1] There is no winter in Equatorial Africa.—A. H. N.

I was anxious to get on to Kéré, where Mnyamiri assured me we should be able to buy plenty of " mtama " grain, in order to make a standing camp and depôt ; moreover, the discomfort every one experienced here from the nightly plague disposed me the more to push on without further delay at present. The mosquitoes seemed, if possible, even thicker than ever that night, and even I, under my net, could get little rest. It can be understood, then, that it was with no reluctance that the caravan left Bumi, where the men had all been so miserable from lack of sleep, and proceeded on its journey.

About an hour's march took us to the extreme point of the most north-easterly horn of the lake. Here we were to leave the lake and strike across for Murli, a little distance up the river ; so, having been told it would be rather a long march, I halted the caravan to allow the men to fill their calabashes. About here we crossed a great deal of elephant spoor, the creek being a much-frequented drinking-place, and even saw two, one with a calf, crossing an open glade on the far side towards thick forest, which stretches uninterruptedly from there to the mouth of the river. On turning our backs upon the lake we passed first over pleasant open ridges dotted with trees, where was a good deal of game, mainly " topi," and I took note of suitable camping-ground, two or three miles from the water, where I hoped we might be comparatively free from mosquitoes, to pitch my tent in on my return for systematic hunting after establishing a market.

Murli [1] did not prove so far as I expected. After topping the highest part of the gentle rise between the fork of the lake and the river, a winding belt of tall, dark-foliaged trees could be seen marking the course of the great affluent ; and thence the descent was through thick scrub, for the most part, until the cultivated ground in the neighbourhood of the villages

---

[1] The letter " r " is pronounced with a strong roll in all names in which its sound occurs in this region. Thus this might give a better idea of its true pronunciation if written " Murrli." The " u " is, of course, similar to our " oo " in sound.

is reached.   The settlement consists of several large kraals
near the river.   It is not a pleasant place, as there are no trees
at this point on the left bank ; however, as I knew of no better
near, after searching in vain for some more suitable spot, we
camped on the high bank overlooking the river.   The latter is
deep, broad, and dark-coloured, with a slow current, and looks
navigable here, but the natives only seem to use their few dug-
outs for ferrying across.   Numbers of crocodiles are always
visible in mid-stream, floating lazily with more or less of the
upper part of their heads above water.

These were the least attractive people I had seen ; very
black, ugly, and not too civil, though at the same time not
offensive.   The women are disfigured by way of ornament, in
the most ghastly fashion.   The lower lip is separated from the
mouth by a slit extending from corner to corner, and into this
gash a section of the thick end of a cow's horn, two or three
inches long, is inserted, the severed part of the lip being stretched
over the edge of the upper opening of the horn (of oval section),
the hollow of which is closed by a saucer-shaped piece of wood
fitted into it, while the rest of the horn depends in front of the
chin.   They are a most revolting sight to look upon ; and they
appear to be conscious of it themselves, for I have often seen
one put her hand up in front of her mouth to hide the disgusting appearance from our astonished gaze.   Nothing I had
ever seen brought home to me so emphatically that we had
indeed penetrated into the heart of savagedom.   Some even
have a similar ornament, though on a somewhat less exaggerated scale, in the upper lip as well.   Some of the men
affect a miniature horn-like ornament attached by perforation
of the centre of the lip just above the chin ; but this does not
distort the mouth.

There were cultivated lands of some extent in the vicinity
of these villages ; but the only ones now under crop were the
low narrow terraces on the immediate brink of the river.
These, naturally irrigated when the river is high, grow magnifi-

cent millet (now nearly ripe) in their rich alluvial mud.
Though one would have thought the natives here must have
plenty of grain, nothing was offered to us for sale with the
exception of a few green ears—like bunches of small grapes—
for which an exorbitant price was asked.

At last, on 1st January 1896, we reached Kéré, which I
intended should be the end of our long journey, at all events
for the present, and our headquarters for some time to come.
The march was through dense scrub most of the way, but there
was a passable path which was parallel with the river, at times
close to the bank or skirting one or two large lagoons which
border its course.   After about five hours of this, the scrub
ends abruptly, and, emerging into the open, the metropolis of
Kéré, a large fenced village, is before us on a slight rise overlooking the river, a few smaller villages, constituting the
kingdom, not far off.   The vicinity of the town did not look
inviting as camping-ground : behind and around open veldt,
yellow with dry grass ; in the immediate environs bare baked
ground, sending up clouds of dust under the frequent passage
of flocks of goats and little herds of cattle ; not a tree to give
shade from the glaring heat.   I resolved to seek a cooler,
cleaner, and more secluded camp on the river-banks, where
groves of fine and shady trees presented an inviting contrast.

But first we had to exchange greetings with a party of
young warriors—fine, tall, well-made fellows many of them, but
black as the ace of spades,—who had come out, spears and
shields in hand, to see who the intruders were.   " Beni ! " (friend)
would cry one, to attract your attention ; of this a responsive
grunt is the correct acknowledgment.   " Na ! " shouts he :
" Faya ! " you reply.   He—" Na ! " you—" Faya ! " " Na "—
" Faya," " Na "—" Faya "—ad lib.   To be polite, you must
now accost your friend with " Beni ! " and, after his " nn," take
up the " Na ! " while he chimes in with " Faya ! " and so on
" Na "—" Faya," " Na "—" Faya," etc., as before.

I had some trouble in finding a suitable camp.   The

enticing groves of forest trees proved to be across the river ; but I got a satisfactory spot at last under a large tree alongside a patch of bush, conveniently near the river and not too close to any kraal.   Every one has his own ideas as to what constitutes a good site for a camp.   Swahilis always take up their quarters close alongside of, or even in, the village.   They like the natives constantly crowding about and in their tents ; and do not regard the other conditions, such as want of cleanliness, distance from water, etc., as discomforts.   I prefer a little privacy with clean ground, and look upon proximity to water and, if possible, shade as desirable concomitants.

I have advisedly styled the little district of Kéré a " kingdom," for it was the first tribe I had come in contact with in all the country from Mombasa to here which recognised a chief.   In the afternoon I sent up Abdulla and Mnyamiri (the latter of whom was already known to him) to present my salaams to Labugo (such was his name) and report my arrival officially.   He sent word in reply that he would visit me in the morning.   No presents passed so far.

A young fellow, to all appearance one of the inhabitants of the place (except that he was not quite so black), and like them, in common with the males of all the tribes of this part of Africa, stark naked, came out and made himself known to me as a member of Count Teleki's caravan, having been left in Reshiat sick, as a boy, some eight years previously, and lived with the natives as one of themselves ever since.   He seemed pleased to see me, and said he would like to accompany my caravan on our return to the coast.   To this I had, of course, no objection, and thought Hamisi (his Swahili name) might prove useful as interpreter while we remained here, though he certainly seemed rather out of practice with his mother tongue. In reply to my inquiries why he had never returned to the coast with trading caravans, one or two of which I knew to have visited the country during the intervening years, he said that he would not trust Swahilis, and preferred remaining here,

where he was kindly treated, to being enslaved. I afterwards
learned that there was another waif from the same expedition
living at Bumi, whom Mnyamiri claimed as a kinsman ; but he
would have nothing to say either to his would-be cousin or any
of us, having become so thoroughly habituated to the savage
life that he had no desire to revert to one less wild. Indeed
he would not acknowledge that he was any different from the
natives of the place, nor was he distinguishable from them by
any one but Mnyamiri, who professed to know him by certain
marks, which he himself also carried, characteristic of a particular clan.

I had recollected that this was New Year's Day, and thought
we were happy to have reached a place of rest on such a propitious date. I little knew what was in store for me ; for a
terrible event happened towards sundown. On my arrival here
about mid-day I had bathed in the river, standing up to my
waist in the water, which was deep close in to the bank, in spite
of the crocodiles to be seen in the middle ; for both I and the
men had been in the constant habit of performing our ablutions
in the lake, where these reptiles were in plenty, and so had
come almost to disregard them, though I never went out of my
depth, or even far from the bank.

Late in the afternoon I went down for another bathe, with
Shebane (my servant) as usual carrying my chair, towels, etc.,
and did the same thing again. It is a large river and deep,
with a smooth surface and rather sluggish current ; its water,
dark-coloured and opaque, though hardly to be called muddy,
deepens rapidly, so that a step or two in is sufficient at this
point to bring it up to one's middle, while the bottom is black,
slimy mud. As we descended the bank towards the low
muddy shore, a native who was tending his crops said something to us, but knowing nothing of the language we could not
understand him. Having bathed and dried myself, I was
sitting on my chair, after putting on my clothes, by the water's
edge, lacing up my boots. The sun was just about to set

CROCODILE TAKING POOR SHEBANE.

"I was sitting on my chair by the water's edge, lacing up my boots . . . when I heard a cry of alarm, and, raising my head, got a glimpse of the most ghastly sight I ever witnessed."

behind the high bank across the river, its level rays shining full upon us, rendering us conspicuous from the river, while preventing our seeing in that direction. Shebane had just gone a little way off (perhaps a dozen yards) along the brink and taken off his clothes to wash himself, a thing I had never known him do before when with me; but, my attention being then taken up with what I was doing, I took no notice of him. I was still looking down when I heard a cry of alarm, and, raising my head, got a glimpse of the most ghastly sight I ever witnessed. There was the head of a huge crocodile out of the water, just swinging over towards the deep with my poor Swahili boy in its awful jaws, held across the middle of his body like a fish in the beak of a heron. He had ceased to cry out, and with one horrible wriggle, a swirl and a splash all disappeared. One could do nothing. It was over; Shebane was gone. The men soon came swarming down (some one having given the alarm) to see, some with guns; one fool asked for boats. There was nothing to be done, but sadly to pick up the ownerless clothes. I felt truly sad and sorry for my servant, and the dreadful incident had an insupportably depressing effect on me. A melancholy New Year's Day indeed!

Shebane had been my "boy" for two years, having accompanied me in that capacity on both my journeys into this region. He had learnt my ways and was a good and cheerful servant, so that it can be understood how much I missed him. I now learnt that it was no uncommon thing here for a native to be taken off the banks by these loathsome reptiles, and a man was actually so taken while we were in Kéré.

The next morning Labugo came to see me, but brought no interpreter, so we could do little but look at each other. My first impression of him is thus described in my diary :— "He is a very tall man; does not seem intelligent, no expression, looks neither pleasant nor surly, merely apathetic." There was nothing chiefly about his bearing, nor did his people seem to regard him with awe nor treat him with much respect. He

brought me no present, not even food. In the afternoon I
sent for him again, and, having got hold of Hamisi to interpret,
had a great " shauri," he being now attended by some of his
principal retainers.

It now transpired that there were two grievances, which,
trifling as the circumstances may appear, were troubling the
minds of Labugo and his people. First, why had I camped
here, in the bush, instead of alongside of his town ? I pointed
out to him that, as a European, I had my own customs and
ideas, which differed from those of Swahili traders, and tried to
explain how miserable I should have been, exposed to the
fierce sun and the clouds of dust raised by the frequently
passing cattle, with crowds of gaping natives continually round
my tent, not to mention the din they made night and morning ;
at the same time, I declared that this was equally his kraal
where we were. The second source of offence was that we
had fired no guns on arriving. As to this, I asked him whether
there had been any attempt at concealment about our arrival ;
any sneaking in at night, or round some back way ? Had we
not rather come at mid-day, right past his town ? And did
I not send envoys specially to announce my advent ? As to
letting off guns, I said that I was not in the habit of wasting
cartridges for nothing, after the manner of Swahilis ; I kept
mine for elephants or enemies ; and by way of a final clincher,
which I knew would tell (and I could see by their looks, did),
I promised him that, should any hostile tribe attack him while
I was here, he should hear my guns fast enough. I then took
him into my tent and gave him a present of assorted treasures,
handing him in addition some beads for his followers. His
own he left in my charge till the evening, being afraid of having
the whole begged from him by his loving subjects, should they
catch sight of it. Labugo promised food trade for the morrow,
and said he would come himself to arrange about the price.
He also said there were elephants in the neighbourhood, and
that I should have guides to show me their haunts whenever I

liked.   He gave me small offerings of food, and a day or two after brought a large, but not very fat, "billy-goat."   I was pleased with this attention (notwithstanding that the animal did not promise to make good meat), as showing a good feeling towards me.   I therefore accepted with thanks, and made him another present (which seemed to catch on) in return, giving also soft words.

The market question proved a troublesome one, and it was two or three days before any understanding was arrived at. This did not surprise me, as I had often been had that way before ; and I congratulated myself on our having twelve full loads still in hand of the food we had brought so far with us, to live on while the dead-lock in the food trade continued. It was a serious question to us, and called for much tact and patience as well as all my arts of diplomacy ; for we needed large supplies, and it was most important to obtain them at reasonable rates, lest our stock of beads, etc. (the currency of the country) should run short before our return to the coast. Swahili traders are singularly improvident in this respect, and often get into dire straits in consequence.   " Exploring " caravans, too, are generally a source of inconvenience to the humble traveller coming across their track who needs to economise his goods and get his supplies of food cheaply.   As a rule, money is no object to the leaders of such expeditions, whose headmen are allowed, unchecked, to lavish goods from their abundant stores with reckless profusion and disastrous results to prices (which, once raised in Africa, can never be lowered again) and to the sorrow of those who may follow.   I am bound to give Mr. Astor Chanler, at whose boma I was camped for some time near Laiju in the Kenia region, credit for being an exception to this rule.   He not only did not spoil the market there, but put it into good order, though the Swahilis have since made it worse than ever.   Thus it was some time before I could come to any terms with these people, and then food was dear and came in only in driblets.   They

explained, however, that, until the crops now ripening should
be ready to gather, grain was scarce.

In the meantime I had a hut built for myself and a shed
to store my goods, food, etc., in.   It was a great comfort to
have a roof and walls, a bit more substantial than canvas, to
shelter one and rest in ; for the weather was excessively hot
notwithstanding that, being north of the line, it was now really
the coolest time of year here.   During this delay I sent some
men back to Bumi to extract the tusks of my elephants, now
loose through decay, and bury them in the kraal there.   I
never *chop* out ivory now, unless in a hurry, as that is a
laborious process and the ivory is often chipped ; whereas in a
few days natural decomposition causes the tusks to slip out
without trouble and uninjured.

One night at this time a hyena carried off and chewed up
Mnyamiri's powder-horn, which had been hanging from a bush
right over its sleeping owner.   His own account of it was that
the " fisi " (as they call it) had intended to seize him, but had
made a bad shot.   The next day he offered up a goat in consequence, and went through a religious ceremony in connection
with the sacrifice to protect him from wild beasts.   I was
pleased to accept a bit of the goat, as it was a meat famine
with me at the time ; but I had my doubts as to the efficacy
of exorcism against marauding animals.   That night my own
ration of beans was carried off from Feruzi's (my cook's) camp,
and the bag containing it rent open by the " fisi."   This might
be, of course, because it was the portion of an unbeliever ; but
unfortunately for the success of such an explanation, the
following day a leopard chased a native cur out of the bush
right up to and nearly over Mnyamiri himself, in broad daylight, nearly frightening him out of his senses.   I myself heard
the yelping, very suggestive of intense fear, made by the flying
pariah.   This additional proof of the boldness of the beasts
here rather upset Mnyamiri's confidence in his charm, and I
think he almost regretted having grudged a bit of his goat as

bait for a gun which I had offered to set. By this time it had all been eaten, so I was unable to lay a trap then.

Bawdo, a younger brother of the chief and a friend of mine, brought word that afternoon that elephants were damaging the crops on the other side of the river ; so it was arranged that he should come first thing next morning to take me to hunt for them. Accordingly at sunrise I started with him and my usual attendants. I did not like the ferrying in a crank and wobbly canoe : I am no sailor, and confess.I do not feel safe in such a craft, with my clothes and boots on, and over a deep and dark river below whose smooth surface I know lurk monstrous crocodiles in numbers, voracious and hungry. But Bawdo was expert with his pole, used either to punt or paddle according to the depth of the water. He was a fine athletic savage, tall and lithe, and looked quite a model in ebony as he stood in the stern of his dug-out, pole in hand, plying it vigorously, now on this side and now on that. Our quest was fruitless as far as elephants were concerned. We followed the spoor of a small herd of cows a long distance, but then found the footprints of some natives following it ahead of us, so it was useless going farther.

On the way back we came across a small herd of topi antelope. I got a nice shot and knocked over two (bull and cow) with my .303. Bawdo, who had never seen anything shot before, was much impressed at seeing each tumble over a few yards from where it had received the bullet, and examined the tiny holes (particularly those of egress) with evident emotion. I was glad that he, an important and noted warrior, had witnessed this practical demonstration of the power of our weapons ; because I had heard that some of the young men of Kéré had made contemptuous remarks about firearms as compared with spears for fighting purposes, and did not doubt that his report would have a salutary effect. We pulled the two " topis " under a tree, and I left a man to commence skinning, while we returned to camp and sent others to carry in the meat. It proved nice and fat and was welcome, giving my men a fine feast, which they evidently appreciated, as shown by the noise they made in the evening. But Bawdo, who had patiently ferried it all over, together with the porters, in his canoe, to my surprise turned up his nose at it, though he asked for a skin. It seemed the people of the Kéré tribe proper do not eat game, though the El Gume, of whom there were plenty too here living in small communities in villages of their own side by side with them, eat anything and everything. The latter keep donkeys, a large herd of which I had seen to-day, for the sake of both their meat and milk. Prizing them highly as food, they cannot be induced to sell any, being indifferent to trade goods.

I was now able to set a gun for the hyena which had made itself a nuisance, and hoped even to get the leopard, as I have often caught this animal too by such means. The latter, however, never came ; but while I was having my evening smoke in bed, bang went the gun, and I went, accompanied by several excited volunteers, to see the result. It was our friend the " fisi." For a wonder he was not quite dead, and, though unable to run away, was still on his legs—as we could make out, on getting close up, by the light of a wisp of dry grass used as a torch—and staggering about in the gloom. I had brought my revolver in my hand on the chance of a weapon being needed, and soon despatched him with a couple of shots from it, and the men dragged him out and made merry over his corpse in camp, after I had put a fresh cartridge in the set gun. It was worth the trouble of setting it even to give the men so much amusement. I now went to bed and to sleep, and slept till about 3 A.M., when I was awoke by the gun going off again. But I did not turn out till it got light, and then, on going to see, found it was another " fisi," this one dead on the spot, as is usually the case when a gun has been properly set. I chaffed Mnyamiri a bit, telling him my charm was more powerful than his. It is exemplary of the different methods of the European and Swahili that, though Mnyamiri was only too glad of an excuse to kill a goat, nominally as a sacrifice, really for a feast, he grudged giving a small piece of meat to trap the animal he was praying to be preserved from ; while I, though going through no incantations, soon put our unwelcome visitor beyond reach of doing further mischief.

Though I have seen descriptions of the setting of guns in books, I have never seen advocated the best method of contriving the means by which they are to be fired ; it may therefore be useful to set forth the system I find most successful, and at the same time the simplest.   But as I shall have occasion later on to describe and illustrate my plan of setting guns for lions, which is done on a different principle, it may be better to give both methods then.

CHAPTER XIV

RETURN TO LAKE RUDOLPH

Back to Bassu—Vigilant guards—A miraculous escape—Acute sufferings—Native
solicitude—An exultant tribe—Rare luxuries—A long illness—An anti-slavery
tribe—A chief's prescription—Longing for a change—A relapse—My "convalescent camp"—Start a poultry-yard—Breeding-time of topi—Native trappers
—A curious phenomenon—Fabulous elephants—Arrival of ivory traders—A
happy coincidence.

EVERYTHING being now in order here, and as Abdulla was
able to buy sufficient food to keep us going and a little over,
with the prospect of a better supply later on enabling us to
accumulate a store as soon as the fine crops of "mtama," now
nearly ripe, should be reaped, there was nothing to keep me
here longer.   The men I had sent to extract and stow away
the ivory of the elephants I had shot on the way here had
returned from Bumi after accomplishing their errand, and
reported that elephants were still drinking nightly at the corner
of the lake, though nothing had been seen of the troop of bulls
since I had attacked it.   I therefore made my preparations for
a hunting trip back to Bassu in the first instance ; and on 9th
January started with fifteen men, taking my tent and other
necessaries, and a supply of food to last us some time, as well as
ammunition, etc.   Before leaving, I commended my people
whom I left behind to Labugo's care, and enjoined upon
Abdulla and those under his charge to on no account fall out
with the natives.

Starting, as was my usual custom, about 5.30, we marched

to the neighbourhood of Murli ; but instead of going right on
to the villages, we halted at a charming camping-place I found
under fine shady trees by the river-bank about half an hour
short of the settlement, and rested there about 2.30. These
grateful groves of tall, dark-foliaged trees, which fringe at intervals the river-banks, form a refreshing contrast, pleasant to
the eyes, to the thirsty-looking stunted scrub with which the
greater part of this arid country is covered. They are frequented by the beautiful colobus monkey, whose cry may often
be heard in them, though the animals themselves keep out of
sight in the leafy tree-tops. Then going on again we bivouacked
at sundown on the open ridges half-way between Murli and
Bumi. I found plenty of mosquitoes even so far from the lake,
and had to get up in the night and pitch my net ; but there
were not enough to trouble my men much.

The next morning we went on down towards the lake
and formed camp under a tree about half an hour's walk
short of its nearest point. I then sent on to Bumi for my
two native friends. On arriving they said there was a large
herd on the edge of the lake near here, but that it was now in
the dense bush which stretches from the other side of this bay
towards a place called Murthu, near the mouth of the river.
They came prepared to sleep in my camp, ready for hunting
on the morrow. In the afternoon I went out and shot a " topi "
for meat, not far from camp. There were great numbers of
them about.

This was 10th January. Just before the entry for that day
I find the following note in my diary :—" Up to this I wrote
regularly in my diary each day the doings of the day before.
Meeting with a serious accident on the 11th, I was unable to
keep on this practice for the time : nor did I feel certain whether
I should ever be able to pick up the thread again, not knowing
how my illness might end. I therefore kept count of the days
and events on note-paper in pencil only, and it was not until
27th January that I felt able once more to open this book ; be-

ginning by copying in my rough notes for the intervening days."
And the entry for 11th January is headed by this note :—
" This account was written two days after the event. I need
hardly point out that if it is not very lucid, a consideration of
the circumstances under which it was written may cause its
weak points to be pardoned." Nevertheless, though the word-
ing is terse and abrupt, the description of the details of that
disastrous hunt is sufficiently clear to bring vividly back to me
the memory of every incident and of some particulars even
which I had forgotten. With its help I will endeavour to give
an intelligible account of what happened.

We were off betimes, then, on the morning of this eventful
day. Striking straight across the open, we made a tangent to
the farther edge of the bay and soon entered the thick bush
which, from a little beyond it, stretched over the whole country
along the shores, and even into the lake itself, right away to the
river, and back towards the path we had come by the day before
from Murli. Our friends took us first to an isolated patch of
cultivation on the border of the swamp in which the lake here
terminates. The owners, a man and one or two women who
belonged to the district of Murthu beyond, were standing on
high platforms constructed on lopped trees so as to command
a view over their little field of millet—nourished into luxuriance
by the damp alluvial soil. The sun had but lately risen, and
the mosquitoes were still unpleasantly active, though the natives
seemed not to notice them, their attention being taken up by the
birds, flitting hungrily about the little clearing, at which they
shouted and slung stones. Their task was one of unremitting
care ; for they were compelled to sleep on their elevated look-
outs in order to endeavour by shouting to scare the elephants
from their crops. These latter were apparently not much in
dread of the guards or of their noise, for we learnt that they
had been heard close by that morning, and were even now
probably not far off.

Entering again the encircling forest, we proceeded along

the muddy margin of the swamp. Here the bush was dense and leafy ; farther out into the swamp the trees seemed dead, but no open water was visible, while farther back the cover was in parts a little less continuous and varied here and there by narrow grassy glades. We soon came upon fresh spoor on the elephant paths—which cut up the thicket skirting the swamp, and wound in and out, sometimes through mud, at others over sandy soil. The footprints were of cows and calves, and there appeared to be a large herd. I wanted bulls ; but, as our informant in the garden had told us there were some of these also, I went on in hopes of finding them.

We now heard much splashing ahead, as of many elephants tramping slowly through the marsh. They seemed to be moving along in front of us, in the direction we were going. The wind was most troublesome and perplexing, blowing sometimes in our faces and again coming from behind, so that it was difficult to decide how to act. Under the circumstances I decided to push on and chance it. We soon overtook the rear-guard, as we could tell by the splashing opposite us ; and shortly after saw a little lot of cows enter the path ahead of us, coming up diagonally from the swamp. They must have got our wind, for they were evidently aware of our presence ; but they did not seem alarmed, and continued to saunter slowly along in front of us, occasionally standing for a little. I could only get fitful glimpses of them as the windings of the paths allowed, but I saw enough to show me that they were all small cows with comparatively light tusks. I was therefore not anxious to shoot them ; but followed for some distance with my Lee-Metford (as the most suitable weapon, anyway for this class of elephants) in my hands (not wishing to use any of my big cartridges on such small fry), on the look-out for one with rather better teeth.

As they seemed all about the same class and I was afraid they would re-enter the swamp and escape us altogether, I increased my pace so as to overtake them, with the idea that even smallish tusks were better than no ivory. As I did so, they halted again. I could see only bits of one or two through the foliage, and was hesitating what to shoot at when one of them decided the matter by coming towards me. I fired for her chest, and she fell at once and never got up again. The others continued their way, and I hurried after them till one of them, a cow with small tusks, turned and chased us a short way ; but we had a good start, and when she got unsighted she turned back after the others. I did not want to shoot her, for her ivory was poor and she had a calf with her. Following again, I got a chance at another cow, with teeth a little better than those of the first. A single .303 bullet disabled her also, passing diagonally through her shoulder. As she plunged about a good deal in falling, I gave her a shot in the brain from the Martini in passing, by way of making sure, and hurried on without bestowing another glance at my second victim. Just after this a large elephant crossed the path in front, pausing a moment opposite me. I seized the opportunity it thus gave me, and, though it passed on to the right after receiving the shot, I felt sure it was fatally hit. I did not pause then to look for it, and later we had other things to think about, but some days after, when my men came to fetch the ivory, they found it lying dead close to where I had fired at it (a young bull with tusks of about 50 lbs. the pair).

More than once this morning the next cartridge had refused to go into the breech of the magazine rifle after a shot, in one case spoiling a good chance at another elephant ; and I said and felt that I was not safe with this weapon in my hands, in spite of its marvellous shooting powers—to say nothing of losing elephants through the best chance often passing. Nevertheless I kept on with it without giving the matter another thought. Without a moment's delay after firing at the young bull (whose short, white, thickish tusks I had mentally noted), I pushed on along the narrow path which continued parallel with the swamp, through dense jungle, in pursuit of the still slowly retreating elephants.   I may say parenthetically here, in explanation of the behaviour of these elephants, that, though there are, I believe, some natives across the river who hunt them and sometimes kill a few, the inhabitants generally all round this part stand in great fear of these animals, and run away whenever they happen to come across any. Hence, I fancy, the elephants have become accustomed to this treatment, and, regarding human beings with contempt, are inclined to be aggressive and so exceptionally dangerous.

Advancing hastily thus, on the look-out for another shot, I came suddenly on two or three round a corner of the path. Among them was the vicious cow, and she came for me at a rush.   I say *the* vicious cow, because, from her short stature and small tusks, I believe she must have been the same that had made the short charge earlier in the day ; I could also see that there was a large calf following her as she came.   I stood to face her, and threw up my rifle to fire at her head as she came on, at a quick run, without raising her trunk or uttering a sound, realising in a moment that this was the only thing to do, so short was the distance separating us.   The click of the striker was the only result of pulling the trigger.   No cartridge had entered the barrel on my working the bolt after the last shot, though the empty case had flown out !   In this desperate situation I saw at once that my case was well-nigh hopeless. The enraged elephant was by this time within a few strides of me ; the narrow path was walled in on each side with thick scrub.   To turn and run down the path in an instinctive effort to escape was all I could do, the elephant overhauling me at every step.   As I ran those few yards I made one spasmodic attempt to work the mechanism of the treacherous magazine, and, pointing the muzzle behind me without looking round, tried it again ; but it was no go.   She was now all but upon me.   Dropping the gun, I sprang out of the path to the right and threw myself down among some brushwood in the vain hope that she might pass on.   But she was too close ; and,

"Kneeling over me she made three distinct lunges, sending her left tusk through the biceps of my right arm and stabbing me between the right ribs, at the same time pounding my chest with her head and crushing in my ribs."

turning with me like a terrier after a rabbit, she was on the top
of me as soon as I was down.   In falling I had turned over on
to my back, and lay with my feet towards the path, face upwards,
my head being propped up by brushwood.   Kneeling over me
(but fortunately not touching me with her legs, which must, I
suppose, have been on each side of mine), she made three distinct lunges at me, sending her left tusk through the biceps of
my right arm and stabbing me between the right ribs, at the
same time pounding my chest with her head (or rather, I suppose, the thick part of her trunk between the tusks) and
crushing in my ribs on the same side.   At the first butt some
part of her head came in contact with my face, barking my
nose and taking patches of skin off other spots, and I thought
my head would be crushed, but it slipped back and was not
touched again.   I was wondering at the time how she would
kill me ; for of course I never thought anything but that the
end of my hunting was come at last.   What hurt me was the
grinding my chest underwent.   Whether she supposed she had
killed me, or whether it was that she disliked the smell of my
blood, or bethought her of her calf, I cannot tell ; but she then
left me and went her way.

My men, I need scarcely say, had run away from the first :
they had already disappeared when I turned to run.   Finding
the elephant had left me, and feeling able to rise, I stood up
and called, and my three gun-bearers were soon beside me.   I
was covered with blood, my clothes were torn, and in addition
to my wounds I was bruised all over ; some of my minor
injuries I did not notice till long afterwards.   Squareface, on
seeing the plight I was in, began to cry ; but Juma rated him
for his weakness and he desisted.   I made them lead me to a
shady tree, under which I sat supported from behind by one
of them sitting back to back with me ; was stripped as to
my upper parts, and my wounds bound up.   I then told
Juma to run back to my camp as fast as he could for help
to carry me in.   The elephant had trodden on the stock of

my gun, indenting it with her toe-nails, but otherwise it was uninjured.

I could not blame my gun-bearers for leaving me ; though they had loaded rifles in their hands. It was through no fault of theirs that I was caught this time. It is true that I did think that Squareface, who had my big double in his hands, might have fired a shot, considering that he had shown himself able to kill an elephant when he was not wanted to ; but it is not a service that one expects of Swahilis, and it might probably have done no good. They had never left me in the lurch without occasion, but had many times stuck by me well at critical moments ; and as for poor Squareface, he has since fallen a victim to a still worse fate himself, as will appear later on. They declared, very likely with truth, that they had not even known I was caught. It was a most fortunate circumstance for me that this accident had occurred beside the lake, where water was close at hand to appease my feverish thirst, cool my wounds, and pour over my head. Camp was a considerable distance away ; but at last, in the afternoon, the men came, cut a pole, and carried me carefully in a ground-sheet slung on it. On the way back we had to pass close to part of the herd of elephants, which were still about. I could hear them quite near, and dreaded lest the men should throw me down and bolt. But they carried me past safely, shouting occasionally as a precaution, and we reached my tent at sundown. Then I had to be washed amid clouds of mosquitoes.

There is no need to describe my sufferings. That they were intense is self-evident. Still, I felt from the first that I had a good chance of recovery. By the most happy good fortune, though several of my ribs were broken, no limb was fractured ; and, by almost a miracle, the tusk had neither severed the artery of my arm nor penetrated my lungs. Thus I had every reason to feel thankful for having got off so easily. In following this pursuit one must reckon with the risks ; and I always knew that there was a probability of an accident happening some day.   In fact, if one only keeps on at it long enough, sooner or later he is bound to be caught.   For in hunting elephants in the dense cover in which, for the most part, they have to be sought in Equatorial Africa, any little hitch or mischance at a critical moment, such as tripping up, or a difficulty with one's gun similar to what occurred in my case, is sufficient to turn the scale against one's chance of escape ; and, once caught, the odds are overwhelming that the hunter upon whom the tables have been turned will not live to tell the tale.   Just retribution, perhaps you will say ; and, for my part, I harboured no ill-will against the elephant for avenging its kith and kin.   It was the fortune of war.

The next day I sent word to Abdulla to come with more men to carry me back to Kéré, that I might be laid up in my own camp.   They arrived the morning after, and made a stretcher under my directions ; and early on the third I was carried back half-way.   At this halting-place I caught a severe chill, through lying naked on wet sheets all night.   I made my men pour water over my wounds to cool them, and no one had the sense to see that I should suffer from this treatment, while I was too weak to take much notice.   The result was severe fever, which added greatly to my sufferings.   But details of these would not make edifying reading.   My men carried me with the greatest care and gentleness back to Kéré, and the journey was less painful than I had expected.   I thought it well to give Abdulla a short letter to take back to the coast in case I should not recover, explaining what had happened, and testifying to their good behaviour.   One and all vied with each other in doing everything in their power for me ; they gave me no trouble, and their behaviour was in every respect most praiseworthy, while their solicitude for me earned my sincere gratitude.

Though my men's exemplary conduct gave me no cause for disquiet, I felt considerable anxiety during this long period of helplessness and pain.   My camp at Kéré was, as I have explained, within a short distance of Labugo's large stockaded village. His people had recently been successful in routing a neighbouring section of their tribe which had attacked them, and had afterwards burnt the villages of the aggressors and captured their cattle, and were exultant and inclined to be boastful ; and as I lay during those long weary nights of suffering, unable to sleep, I used to listen to them singing and dancing half the night and fear lest they might be tempted by my own helpless condition and the smallness of my little party to think our belongings would be an easy prey. But they never molested us nor stole a thing all the time we were there. Their weird and rather tuneful singing, mellowed by the inter-vening distance, was in itself rather pleasant and helped to pass the dragging hours ; and I always felt grateful for the commotion heralding the earliest streaks of dawn, as the inhabitants bestirred themselves preparatory to hieing to their fields, before the birds began their forays on the heavy red clusters of ripening grain. Then as the light began to come I would be put outside on my camp chair, while the air was yet comparatively cool, to watch the wedges and undulating lines of storks and pelicans winging their way across the placid sky—against whose pale, greenish blue background, lit up with faint streaks of crimson, their rhythmically gliding forms stood out, though below it was still dusk—before the fiery sun should make all one glare, up or down the river as they changed their feeding-grounds between the various small lakes near its course.

The days were less tedious than the dreaded nights. Among other sources of distraction I used often to question Hamisi about his experiences among the people of Kéré. He described to me the battle, before alluded to, in which he had taken part. All the inhabitants were collected in the town on the news being brought in by a woman of the approach of the attacking force. The fighting men, armed for the fray, waited till the enemy, advancing in battle array, were within a stone's throw of their gates ; then, having proclaimed to his warriors that their day had arrived to do or to die, Labugo, spear and shield in hand, led the charge upon the confident foe with such effect that the assailants were put to flight with great slaughter. This account raised Labugo very much in my estimation, proving him to be as different in character as he was in appearance from the orthodox type of obese, self-indulgent African monarch, cruel and cowardly ; and though he resembled others in his rapacity for presents, by which he worried me a good deal, I could not but feel a respect for this tall, active, and redoubtable savage.

Hamisi also introduced to me an affable old man whom he called his father, with whom I had an interesting chat through his adopted son's interpretation. I found out from him that these people know little or nothing of the country beyond their own immediate neighbourhood. The petty detached tribes with which it is so curiously peopled are mostly at enmity, and always distrustful of each other, so that there is little communication except within the narrowest limits. He told me that they believed that there was a tribe of cannibals living to the northward, but the only evidence they had was the testimony of a woman who had run- away from there and found her way to Kéré, where she had since made her home. She described how they bound their victims, he explained, while he demonstrated the method for my edification by drawing up his legs as he sat on the ground, his knees against his chin and his calves touching his thighs, at the same time clasping his arms round his doubled-up legs. In this position they were put alive into huge pots, water poured in, and fires lighted under them. I told him I thought the tale was probably invented by the woman out of spite against the people she had escaped from ; but he evidently believed it. He also gave me an account of a great flood which had occurred on the river, when the water reached nearly to their kraal, which is on pretty high ground, bringing down huts, cattle, and human bodies.

The men, including this old gentleman and even Labugo himself often, used to go out daily with the cattle to protect them from marauders while grazing. They owned a good many, thanks partly no doubt to their recent victory over their invading neighbours and the consequent raiding of the vanquished enemy's stock. This was indirectly advantageous to me, as I was able to buy milk, a rare luxury in Central Africa, the only nourishment I could take for about the first month of my illness ; indeed, if it had not been for that, I do not see how I could possibly have pulled through.

I found it necessary to procure special calabashes for my portion to be milked into, or I could not drink the milk. The universal method of cleansing the utensil into which a cow is milked, among most Central African tribes, is by turning it upside down over a lighted stick of a particular kind, thus confining the smoke, which is peculiarly pungent, and causing the vessel to absorb it. It then imparts its pungent flavour to the milk, which sometimes, after this treatment, fairly burns one's throat. The owners of the cows objected to milking them into any tin or dish of European manufacture, declaring that their milk would dry up ; but I got over the difficulty by procuring new calabashes, which were sent with the payment for the milk always at milking-time and afterwards washed. Another luxury I was able to buy here was coffee ; and very good coffee, too. It is not grown here, but procured from some natives living in the hills not far off, with whom those of Kéré were on visiting terms. It cannot be grown very far away, because it is so cheap ; when any was brought for sale a string of beads would buy almost as much coffee as millet. It is dried in the cherry, but my cook easily cleaned it by pounding in a wooden mortar. The natives of all the little tribes around the head of the lake are very fond of it, though what pleasure they can get out of drinking it in the way they cook it I cannot imagine. The coffee, just as it is in the dry cherry, is boiled,

without roasting, for hours and hours, and the hot decoction
drunk. I suppose it must have some invigorating property,
but it tastes like dirty water.

I took particular pains to find out whether slavery is
practised, or any slave trade carried on, by the people of
Kéré and the adjoining districts. But all the information
elicited by my inquiries, made in various directions, went to
prove that none of the tribes round about the head of the
lake have any such customs. I was assured on all hands that
they do not enslave even their enemies, and was led to believe
that they disapprove of bartering human beings. I think that,
were there any such trade carried on, I could not have failed to
hear of it, as I have done in other parts of Central Africa—
even to being myself asked to buy sometimes. But what
seems the strongest proof that not even domestic slavery
obtains here is the fact that Hamisi was free and well treated.
Having been left in Reshiat some eight years previously, as a
small boy, he had wandered on, under pressure of famine, till
he found an asylum in Kéré. Here he had been adopted by
the old man already mentioned, who had not only fed him, but
treated him with uniform kindness, as if he had been his own
son, from that day until my arrival.

Labugo sometimes came to see me. He rather bored me
when I was ill, as he generally came to beg. Had he been
entertaining, I should have been glad of his company, as I
was grateful for anything to pass the time ; but he was not
communicative and never smiled. However, I always tried
to be agreeable to him, as it was important to keep on good
terms. He showed a certain amount of interest in my progress, and the first time he saw me after the mishap he
strongly advised that I should have a sheep or goat killed and
drink the blood as medicine. As I believe blood is a purga-
tive, it may be useful in that way, failing any other remedy ; but
I thought I could obtain the same results with less disagreeable
drugs, so declined to avail myself of his prescription.

In the absence of any surgical aid, the healing of my wounds had to be left to nature, acting on a healthy constitution and seconded by cleanliness and water-dressings, while my ribs had to set themselves. For weeks I hardly slept, and it was two months before I could lie in any position except on my back. Sometimes even that caused me such agony that I had to be propped up all night in a sitting posture ; but without any pillows or cushions, or an easy-chair, I soon got too sore to endure that either. Still the healing process went on gradually ; the hole in my arm had closed without any trouble, and though the muscle did not join quite evenly, through the severed parts being somewhat displaced, it was well by about the middle of the second month. My side was more troublesome, the internal injuries causing suppuration with much discharge and all the disagreeable consequences, rendered particularly trying by the sweltering heat, day and night, which increased as the year grew older.

By the end of the first month I was so sick of the shut-in camp at Kéré, and had such a longing for a change of scene, that, feeling so far better as to be able to stand being carried, I determined to be taken back to the lake. On my journey hither I had noticed, in the Reshiat district, a sandy ridge with a few scattered trees, overlooking the lake at a part where it was open water, and I longed to be there, in the more airy situation, with the sea prospect and the birds and game to interest me. Besides, I hoped soon to be able to pot something, if only doves ; for I began to feel the need of something more substantial than a milk diet to recuperate my wasted strength and fill out my shrunken limbs. I explained my plans to Abdulla, and told him I had confidence that I should pull round much more quickly if I could only get back to the shores of Bassu ; so a stretcher was prepared, and twelve of the best porters told off to carry me in relays, two at a time, in it slung from a long pole. They performed their task most zealously and ably ; leaving on 5th February, we reached the place where I intended to camp early on the morning of the 8th. The bulk of the caravan was still to remain at the Kéré camp.

At first I felt so much better that I was able to walk slowly without assistance, and even managed to shoot a few doves with my rook rifle, a performance of which I felt immensely proud. I then, presuming on my strength, attempted a more ambitious task, and early one morning, attended by the faithful Juma carrying the .303, managed to get within long range of a topi, and even succeeded, at the second shot, in killing it, much to my delight. But the exertion was too much for me, and I had a relapse. I was living in my tent again here, with only the indifferent shade afforded by a small tree from the scorching sun. Worse fever than ever ensued, accompanied by violent dysentery, throwing me back another whole month. But by about the end of the second from the accident, I was again well on the road to recovery. By this time I had got a good airy hut built for myself on the highest part of the rise, with other little buildings near ; one for my cook, another to use as a bathroom, and a shed for the stores, which were to be gradually moved from Kéré.

I called this " convalescent camp," for here I steadily progressed without any further serious relapse ; and I was really very comfortable in it in spite of some drawbacks, notably mosquitoes and other insect pests. During the hours of daylight the flies gave one no peace, and no sooner did it get dark than mosquitoes put in an appearance, except when there happened to be a stiff breeze blowing, though this had an unfortunate knack of generally going down with the sun ; then if I ventured to have a light on my dinner-table, the food soon became filled with minute flies and little round yellow beetles. All these insects were bred in the swampy margin of the lake. The land was poor in insect life, owing to the dearth of flowers ; there were very few butterflies, and those only of the commonest kinds, and not a bee to be seen. As a consequence of the absence of the latter, this country of course produces no honey, though I did manage to get a little of very inferior quality, which came, I was told, from the hills.

But, notwithstanding these little discomforts, I was happy enough during the two months I spent in this camp. I was able to get milk daily even here, though I was forced to give corn brought from Kéré in exchange for it, as these people do not care much for trade goods, and are generally, as already explained, short of food. The bones which strew the ridge for a mile or more in the neighbourhood of their kraals testify to the number of their cattle before the dire plague of some six years ago had decimated the herds of Central Africa. Another luxury I had here was eggs. There are only one or two kraals (in Bumi) where the natives keep a few fowls, and I bought up all I could get and started a poultry-yard of my own with about ten tiny hens and a cock. These kept me supplied with their funny little eggs, and afforded me a certain amount of interest besides. They never laid more than ten or a dozen eggs each before wanting to sit, but soon began again when prevented from indulging this instinct ; but what attracted my attention most about them was that, as a rule, they never cackled after laying, in fact there was only one that ever did so. I had every opportunity of observing this peculiarity, because many of them used to lay in my hut. This seemed to me a rather singular fact, and may go to prove that these little fowls are more nearly related to the wild progenitors of the race than our European breeds. The cock became dear to me from his cheery crow, 'announcing the near approach of the welcome dawn and the end of the tedious, oppressive night.

During the time that I was here there were several heavy thunderstorms. I supposed these to be the heralds of the wet season, which *ought* to arrive about April ; but they were about all the wet season we experienced that year. Probably this was an exceptionally meagre allowance of rain, even for this country ; but there can be no doubt that the climate is a

very dry one, as is proved both by the appearance of the
country and the poverty of its vegetation, and also by the fact
that the natives find it does not pay to cultivate except in the
damp ground close to the water.

These thunderstorms of which I have spoken brought out
a tinge of green grass over the open ground surrounding my

TOPI HARTEBEESTE ♂ (*Damaliscus jimela*).

camp—" the country sweated green," as a Zulu would have expressed it.   There was a broad level valley behind, overlooked
by my ridge, and in this the topi antelope used often to collect
towards evening or in the early morning.   They were sometimes
literally in thousands, the flat for a mile or more being covered
with them, collected in one enormous herd.   During March all
the cows seemed to have calved, and I used to enjoy watching
the gambols of the troops of light fawn-coloured calves, racing

fleetly up and down, and chasing each other in and out among
the herd. Once or twice I had the opportunity of witnessing
a fight between two bulls. Between the rounds they stand a
little apart, pretending, as it were, to take no notice of each
other ; then, suddenly, as if instinctively impelled by some
simultaneous impulse, they rush together, going down on their
knees as their heads clash. At night the topi used to come
quite close up to my camp, and I have seen their footprints in
the morning within fifty yards of my hut, and often heard them
grunting and sneezing in the night. There were also a good
sprinkling of Grant's gazelle about, and a few zebra. The
latter were seldom to be seen during daylight, but on moonlight nights I could sometimes make out the clouds of dust
they raised in rolling, and the bray of Grevy's zebra was constantly to be heard then. The gazelles drop their fawns a little
later than the topi, apparently.[1] A few giraffe are also found
(absent all along the lake southward), and I often saw a little
lot of ostriches when taking a stroll in the cool of the evening. The sound made by the cock ostrich is commonly called
a roar ; but to my mind "drumming" is a more appropriate
description of it, and my men used to say that the ostrich
was "striking its drum" ; it has some resemblance, on an
exaggerated scale, to the drumming of a cock turkey. I could
trace no resemblance to the voice of the lion, which was not
wanting for purposes of comparison, being audible almost every
night at this time. Another familiar sound, which often added
its volume to the nocturnal music here, was the sonorous bellow-
ing of the hippos in the lake.

With game so near, I was able, as I gained strength, to
procure meat, even within the limited range of my early morning
strolls, the length of which I was gradually able to extend,
starting with the first streaks of dawn and usually getting back
before the sun became very hot. Thus I could generally shoot

---

[1] If I am not mistaken, the breeding-time is different south of the line, but in this I
am open to correction.

a grantii for my larder, and a topi or two for my men whenever
I wanted. It was wonderful what a strengthening effect the
meat diet had on my lowered system, with almost magical
rapidity. I had tried in vain to buy a sheep or a goat from
our neighbours ; so little do they value the articles of commerce,
usually dear to savage hearts (or indeed any personal adorn-
ments whatever), that they could not be induced to sell one,
though they possess considerable numbers.

I dared use no other rifle now than the .303, for fear of the
recoil of black powder—even my trusty old .450 was now
permanently laid aside—and I came to value the wonderful
powers and pleasant shooting of this minute bore so much that
I never wished to use any of my others again. The absence
of recoil and smoke is such a comfort, and the deadly effect of
the long, thin bullet, propelled with such tremendous velocity,
so all-sufficient for any animal, that I never wished to go back
to the noise and other unpleasant habits of the old-fashioned
weapons. Its one drawback is the tricky mechanism of the
magazine. Of course I could not carry a rifle myself, and
could only shoot from a sitting position ; but the trusty Juma
always accompanied me, and even when creeping up for a shot
crawled at my heels, ready to put it into my hands at the last
moment, after I had got within range. It is true he used to
try my temper severely by his unconquerable habit of handing
gun or glasses wrong end foremost, or left-handed, which is
particularly exasperating when one's eyes are riveted on the
buck, and hurts the more that one cannot relieve one's feelings
by strong names, under such circumstances ; but he was free
from one most annoying fault of many gun-bearers, he never
lagged behind.

Another benefit I gained by being able to kill game again
was in the matter of light. There were one or two among the
members of my caravan who could, on occasion, the conditions
being favourable, manage to kill a sleepy, unsuspecting rhino ;
but wilder game, especially in the open, was seldom within

their powers of marksmanship. Consequently, during my long illness, the supply for my primitive lamp had run short. Now the topi were always fat, and Feruzi, after a few experiments, acquired the art of making their hard suet into candles, using a large, hollow reed, split lengthwise, as a mould. Beeswax, where obtainable, is also suitable ; but it is not easy to get, even in honey districts, as the natives always swallow it.

I obtained several fine heads about this time ; and although I never allowed myself (nor would it be any pleasure to me) to shoot anything which was not wanted, the exercise and diversion of keeping up the supply of meat occasionally, and at the same time procuring trophies, was a welcome change to the monotony of my life here during the slow process of recovery, and I could not have been camped in a better situation for the purpose. It was during the period of

A NATIVE GAME-SNARE.

convalescence, too, that I was so fortunate as to secure specimens of my new hartebeeste. I had hopes of getting a young topi alive, to bring to the coast, as the El Gume snare a good many with nooses ; but, though I offered any price for one, they never could make up their minds to forgo the feast whenever a victim was caught. The snare is made of twisted strips of hide, laid up exactly like the " neck-strop " used to yoke bullocks in South Africa, with a running noose at each end. A contrivance like a little wheel without a nave, with an inordinate number of spokes (sharpened at the end pointing to the centre), is laid over a circular hole dug in a path or crossing much frequented by game, and on the outer edge of this the loop of one end of the snare is laid, a log being attached to the other. On an antelope treading on this trap (which is covered over with grass, etc.), its foot goes through the centre of the wheel ; the converging spokes hold fast to its fetlock, preventing the noose from slipping off until the latter is drawn tight. Then it sets off with the log dragging and

NATIVE BOXES MADE FROM ELEPHANT TUSKS.

bumping beside or behind it, alternately making short bursts and turning to face the log, which it cannot shake off, until, tired out, it falls an easy prey to the trapper. These people do not seem to fish ; and the only kind of fish my own men ever caught here was an occasional barber. One monster of this kind weighed 38 lbs. and was 3 feet 6 inches long.

A curious phenomenon often drew my attention while

living here.   The prevailing wind on the lake, as before noticed,
was from the south-east ; but whenever it changed to the north,
as it occasionally did for a day, bringing squally weather and
the thunderstorms already alluded to, the lake became dotted for
miles with floating islands of various sizes, some of them with
tall grass or rushes growing on them.   These are evidently
masses of water-weed, detached by the strong northerly breeze
from great beds of floating vegetation formed about the mouth
of the river.   They present a most curious and picturesque
spectacle drifting southward over the broad expanse of water ;
but, on the return of the prevailing southerly winds, they all
get backed up again at the northern extremity and leave the
water open once more.

One of the natives who had accompanied me on my ill-
fated hunt of 11th January was an Mkwavi, though living
among the El Gume people at Bumi.   He was rather a nice
fellow, and often came to see me and professed great friendship.
He said that his father had been a friend of Count Teleki's,
when that great traveller was here on his memorable journey
during which he discovered and named this lake, and he considered it a duty he inherited to be " the dog of the white man,"
as he expressed it.   Lekwari (such was his name) confirmed,
by his own evidence, what I had already gathered from the
testimony of the dead trees and bushes standing, more or less
submerged, in the lake, some of which are visible at a great
distance from the shore.   He said that at the time Teleki was
here a great part of this corner of the lake was dry, and that
what was cultivated land in those days is now under water,
thus restricting the area of moist ground suitable for growing
crops.   This accounts for the difference between the present
configuration of this end of the lake and Von Hohnel's map of
the part.   During our chats he used to tantalise me with tales
of fabulous elephants with tusks to which those I had shot near
here on my way up were as nothing !   He compared their
thickness to the girth of his chest, and pointed to the central

posts supporting the ridge-pole of my hut as indicative of their length, declaring that the owners of these monstrous tusks were unable to lift their heads from the ground for their weight, or even to run ! Although I hardly credited these tales, it may well be imagined how I chafed under my imprisonment when plied with such enticements and assured that these and countless other elephants now thronged the banks of the lake, just south of Reshiat. A few elephants even passed close to my camp one moonlight night. My men wanted me to shoot at them ; but I said that I was not yet strong enough to tackle elephants again, and that when I was I should prefer attacking them by daylight on my first attempt. Two were still grazing on the flat when I went to bed.

As a matter of fact, although for a time I had impatiently looked forward to getting to work again before long, I had at last reluctantly realised that all my schemes for penetrating farther into the unknown regions north and west of Bassu must be given up for this trip ; but so much in earnest was I, and so little discouraged by my reverse, that I used to amuse myself by laying plans for another on a larger scale and making lists of articles to be provided for the next expedition. Such occupations helped to pass the time, which often hung rather heavily, as I had little to read—and what I had had been read over and over again. But I found a good deal to interest me, even without leaving my hut, in watching the birds to be seen from my door. Flocks of the little, long-tailed, bearded doves were fond of feeding about on the ground outside, some coming close up to the very door when I kept still. The rosy bee-eaters, whose habit of riding on the great crested pauw I have already referred to, were very numerous, while their " camels " were common enough. One day I wrote thus in my diary :—
" Saw a bird that is new to me, apparently a stork. A pair of them are hunting about in front of my hut. They are jet black with white belly. One of the rose-coloured bee-eaters made use of one as a steed in the same way I have often seen them do

with the large bustard ; it tried the other once, but it would not submit to be ridden." A flock of the beautiful sacred ibis frequently fed about my hut, and egrets often attended my donkeys when grazing.

So time went on, and I almost began to think the wound in my side would never heal ; but at last, three months after my accident, it so far improved that I determined to make a start southward, whole or not. With great difficulty Abdulla had accumulated a sufficient store of food to carry us through the desert. He had in vain tried all the surrounding districts : not a ration was to be obtained anywhere else, and even at Kéré the supply had so fallen off that we could hardly keep pace with the consumption. Under these circumstances, if we delayed longer we should soon be reduced to eating our stock, so that it was important to start while that was still intact. Accordingly, I had the whole of our belongings brought over from Kéré, the ivory dug up, and set about making all ready for marching once more. The food and ivory were weighed and made up into loads of suitable size for porters and donkeys (a donkey carries two men's burdens), and all other necessaries were adjusted for carrying, while the donkeys' pads and other pack gear were overhauled and mended.

The difficulty of completing our food purchases had been considerably increased by the arrival of a large Swahili trading caravan from the Turkana country west of the lake. Kéré being practically the only market in the neighbourhood, these traders had to repair there for supplies, and the district being so limited, their competition at once caused scarcity and higher prices. Fortunately we had already a good store in hand, and needed but little more. On the other hand, Abdulla was able to buy from them some splendid donkeys for me, which were most useful to supply the place of some we had lost and supplement our troop of pack-animals. These donkeys (of which they had a large number) had been bought in Turkana, where they are plentiful. They are of a light yellowish colour and very strong and enduring, but many of them extremely wild and troublesome to pack. They are, no doubt, a near relation of the wild ass. Their own country being a very dry one, they do not suffer soon from thirst ; indeed, they seem to drink less water than other donkeys, and understand digging for it in the sandy river-beds with their feet.

This caravan was under the leadership of a Beloochi, and had been away from the coast about two years already. Such caravans are made up of a number of traders, each with his own goods, porters, etc. They combine together for mutual help and protection on long expeditions. The ivory trading is carried out by the leader, each trader putting in goods in proportion to his wealth into the general stock, the proceeds being afterwards divided in like proportions. One of these men, who had formerly been an askari in a caravan of the I.B.E.A. Co. which I had been with years before, and who remembered me, sent me a present of a fine fat goat. This was the most disinterested present I ever received from an African, for the giver knew there was no possibility of our meeting and consequently that he could receive no return.

By the most happy coincidence the last trace of the aperture in my side—which had obstinately refused to unite so long as the internal wound remained unhealed—finally closed on the very day that Abdulla arrived with the last instalment of our possessions from Kéré ; and, to my intense relief, a little more than three months after receiving the injuries, I became externally whole once more. I was still weak, and my battered chest and side sore and stiff ; but I felt so far sound, that not only did I feel confident of being able to walk to the coast, but I determined to go on a few days ahead, while Abdulla waited here with the main body, to have a look for Lekwari's monster tuskers.

Giving my headman instructions, then, to remain until he should get word from me, in readiness to follow at once with

the caravan, I started at length from my convalescent camp—
not without a certain amount of regret at leaving its accustomed
comforts—on 17th April.   In spite of many drawbacks, I had
enjoyed many advantages there, and felt grateful to the now
familiar spot where I had so far recovered my strength.

CHAPTER XV

RETURN TO LAKE RUDOLPH (*continued*)

Adjustment of caravan—Desertion and disappointment—A school of hippos—" A
day of humiliation "—My clumsy specimen—A problem for scientists—An
elephant hunt—The reward of patience—Rapacity of a vulture—Shooting a
veteran—The tusk of a patriarch—Planning of transport—A diverting study—
Preparation of " biltong "—A triumphant show—Settling a point of honour—
A mistaken hardship—Treatment of carriers—Arrival of caravan.

MY expedition, small as it was, had been equipped with a view
to being away at least two years ; hence I had some surplus
supplies of beads, cartridges, etc., which it would be useless to
carry back to the coast. These superfluous loads I left in
charge of Lekwari, building a little hut for the purpose of
storing them in his kraal and telling him not to expect to see
me back again under two years. By reducing my impedimenta
to what I considered necessary to see us down, including
possibly two or three months' delay at El Bogoi, I was able to
have several spare porters after allotting all the loads. Our
food supplies, consisting of some thirty odd loads of meal, and
the smaller ivory, as well as beads and ammunition, could all
be packed on the donkeys, leaving only the heavy tusks, my
own personal belongings and specimens, etc., to be carried by
the porters. Of course, had not my hunting been brought to
a sudden end and my journey cut short, I might have accumulated more ivory than we could transport. But in that case I
should have had to make some special plan to get it carried
down, such as two trips to some point south of Bassu where a

depôt might be made and whence help could be sent for to
the coast, or some such scheme.   Although, unfortunately, no
such satisfactory difficulties had to be met, I was anxious at
least to take as much as my little party was capable of ; that
is, to have no men " empty hands " (as it is called) nor carrying
anything that was not necessary.   What I am driving at is,
that in order to render my caravan as usefully laden as possible,
it would be necessary to procure several more loads of ivory.
This deficiency I determined to make an effort to supply.

Lekwari's yarns had not been without their effect upon me,
exaggerated though I knew they must be ; and I was keen to
see for myself how much substance there might be to warrant
his highly-coloured pictures of phenomenal tuskers.   It had
been a great source of satisfaction to me that I had obtained
two or three very fine tusks (well over 100 lbs.) before the
mishap stopped my hunting ; for I had sold all the ivory shot
during my previous trip, in the confident expectation of getting
even better on this expedition, and it would have been a
grievous disappointment to have had to return to the coast
without a single really fine tusk to keep as a trophy.   But
although such an ignominious failure was already obviated, I
entertained a lingering hope that I might even yet acquire
still finer specimens.

It was a bad augury for the truth of Lekwari's enticing
tales of marvellous elephants just beyond Reshiat, that in
passing the last kraals, only two hours after starting, he gave
us the slip and we never saw him again.   Two other guides,
whom we procured there, were equally disappointing ; for,
having accompanied us a little farther and taken us somewhat
out of our direct course, they failed either to show us any fresh
tracks or to give us any information as to the game we were
in search of.   The fact is, these people are no hunters : being
unable to kill game themselves, they take little interest in, and
are little or no use in its pursuit, though they are ready enough
to eat it when killed.   I therefore allowed these two to go

about their business, and determined to continue along the route we had followed on our up journey in the hopes of striking spoor farther on. I noticed a good many of the smaller species of pauw, similar to the common pauw of South Africa, during this day's march—a bird I have seldom met with in Equatorial Africa.

The next morning we regained our former track in about half an hour, and after following it for about two more I saw a school of hippos in shallowish water near the shore of the lake. As my men were keen for meat, that of the hippopotamus being highly esteemed of Swahilis, and my cook importunate for lard, I determined to try and shoot one. The wind, blowing off the lake, favoured me, and I was able to creep up under cover of some rushes growing on the bank. In the confusion that followed my first shot I could not tell whether I had killed or no, and so fired at and wounded a second. I was sorry afterwards that I had done so, for when the rest had made good their escape, the first was seen lying dead. I was compelled, then, to finish off the other, both on account of its being wounded and because it stood close to the dead one, so that the men dare not go to the latter. They proved to be bull and cow, but unfortunately neither fat. In order that the men might have the full benefit of the meat, I camped close by ; and they enjoyed themselves to their hearts' content, rolling the carcases over and over up the gently shelving shore to the water's edge, and there cutting them up. When they had taken all they wanted, the onslaught of the flocks of vultures, of two or three species, that had collected, mingled with a good few marabouts, was a sight to see ; nothing could be seen but a confused mass of dingy feathers and flapping wings heaped up over the spot, with here and there a grotesque marabout, tall and solemn, standing pompously by with inflamed and distended throat.

As soon as I decided to camp, I had sent Juma on to reconnoitre ahead, for we had seen some yesterday's spoor along our path, and I thought it likely there might be elephants not far on, of which he would be sure to find traces if in the neighbourhood. After an absence of only about two hours, he returned with the news that he had actually seen the elephants themselves, feeding and drinking in some tall water-grass growing at the edge of the lake. In accordance with my instructions he had avoided approaching ; but from a distance had counted five, of which the nearest to him he could see to

ROLLING HIPPO TO SHORE.

" In order that the men might have the full benefit of the meat, I camped close by ; and they enjoyed themselves to their hearts' content, rolling the carcases over and over up the gently shelving shore to the water's edge, and there cutting them up."

(From a Photograph by the AUTHOR.)

be a bull with good teeth, and there might be more beyond hidden by the long grass, etc. Though I had stood the walking well, so far, I felt that I had done enough for my strength that day, what with the march and standing about with my camera taking shots at the men rolling up the dead hippos, so I decided to leave the elephants for the morrow.

April 19 is headed " A day of humiliation " in my diary.

I had decided to pack up and march with the whole of my outfit, as usual when travelling, instead of merely taking my gun-bearers, as when hunting with the intention of returning to the same camp.   My reason for this was, that, being still so weak, it was important to camp as near as possible to the scene of action ; and as it would be necessary in any case to follow along the shore till either the elephants themselves or the place where they had drunk should be found, I thought it better to have all my belongings with me in the meantime, so that I might have as short a walk as possible after the hunt. We started at five o'clock, which is about the hour when the first glimmerings of dawn become manifest in that latitude, and in half an hour, while still dusk, saw an elephant looming black in the water near the shore of the lake, ahead of us.   I took the caravan a little way back, and left them among some " suaki " bushes with strict injunctions to keep quiet, while I went after the elephant with Juma carrying the .303 and Squareface with my camera.   I never got a shot with the latter, and the one I had with the rifle was a failure !

The elephant—we could only see one, a big bull—had by this time come up from the lake and was strolling slowly through the open bush, a party of white egrets riding, in picturesque contrast to the dark hulk, on his neck and head.   When we got to where he had entered a patch of thicker bush and become hidden, we took his spoor.   The sun had just risen and was in our eyes ; it was my first attempt at elephant since my mauling and consequent long illness, and I was not as cool as I was wont to be, and as one ought to be to kill this game. These preparatory excuses are leading up to the confession that when we caught sight of the bull again, although the bush was not very thick compared with what I had thought nothing of before, I was in too much of a hurry to shoot, without waiting for a good chance or getting nearly so close as I had always been in the habit of approaching before firing.   The consequence of all this was, that, though I thought at first that he was fatally hit, the result proved that I must have made a bad shot.

The elephant ran straight into a large patch of jungle which extended along the shore, at this part, from just beyond where he had been drinking.   Now this was that peculiar kind of dense cover already described in an account of a hunt in the valley of the Seya, mainly composed of a plant which grows in low, damp situations where the ground is salt, which forms an impenetrable and almost solid mass of vegetation.   I was not in the humour to rush into thick cover, but by working round the edge we were able to get along between the water and the thicket.   The jungle was not very high, but there was not a tree of any kind to get a view from ; however, finding a spot where there was a slight knoll or rise in the ground, I got on to Juma's shoulders and was able to see over the cover, and there my bull stood in the middle, the top of his back and head showing above it.   He was standing alone, but farther on I could see the foreheads or back ridges of some twenty others, perhaps more, standing in a clump, evidently on their guard, facing outwards and frequently trying the wind for suspicious odours with their uplifted trunks.   I tried every way to get a shot at the solitary bull, which I took to be the same I had shot at, without actually crawling to right under it, but could see nothing but the top of its forehead, even when I had entered the jungle by a path running parallel with the shore and got quite near it.

I felt ashamed of myself ; it was ignominious to be beaten. At last I mustered up courage, and, though I didn't like it—I confess I did *not* like it a bit—crept through a narrow little overgrown path, at right angles to that we had come along, to within certainly considerably under ten paces of it.   The wind was right, and though it had nearly died away about sunrise, was blowing pretty steadily now.   I sat down in my tunnel, and could see the elephant's hind feet and a little of the leg above, but no other part of it.   I determined, since nothing else was possible, to try and disable it, and fired at the near hind leg just above the foot joint. No sooner had I pulled the trigger than, as by inspiration, with an activity I had hardly thought myself capable of now, I whipped round, and, half scrambling, half running through the tunnel, was in an instant tearing down the path in the instinctive endeavour to get out of the way, in case it should come. It was lucky I lost no time ; for it turned and came straight for me, my shot having failed, evidently, to break its leg. Looking over my shoulder as I ran I saw the huge beast coming at a run right along the path behind me. Weakened as I was from my accident—my wound but just healed over, and my right side still sore and stiff—I felt unable to run hard ; but I made the best effort I was capable of, and turned sharp to the right along the track we had come. As I did so, I heard that awful shrill, harsh trumpet behind me, so suggestive of impending swift anni-hilation, which seems to come down upon one as the doom of irresistible vengeance ; and, throwing my gun to one side to be out of harm's way, I ducked behind some brushwood, stumbling as I did so, and hid there for a minute till I found I was safe. The elephant had turned to the left when coming into the main path and gone off in the direction of the herd. My men turned up as I was picking up the rifle, and we went back to hunt for my hat.

It appeared that on seeing what was happening from where they had remained behind when I crawled through the tunnel, they had been able to get out of sight into a little opening in the brake, which walled in the path on either side, while the elephant passed in my wake. There was no blood on the spoor ; but that is nothing remarkable with so small a bullet, and I still hoped that we might eventually find the elephant—whether the same or not—which I had first fired at. But though I sent back more than once during the next few days in hopes the vultures might show us the carcase, nothing was ever found. Of the rest of the herd I could not get a view to give me any sort of a decent shot, from any point I could reach without either giving them our wind or going right up to them. The latter alternative I was determined not to adopt again to-day ; my nerves were not in the form for that now, nor do I think it would have been anything but foolhardiness, in my then state, to tempt the fates by any further attack on so difficult a position.

Crestfallen, and not a little ashamed of my discomfiture, I retraced my steps to where I had left the caravan. After making a stupid hash, one is apt to try and console oneself with excuses. Was not allowance to be made, I asked myself, for the failure of my first attempt since rising, but the other day, from a sick-bed, where for three solid months I had been suffering from the wounds inflicted by one of these beasts ? This was the hardest morning's work I had yet attempted, and I was of course somewhat exhausted by the time (not far short of noon) I had established myself under a " suaki " bush —swarming as usual with little black pesty ants, but a welcome screen from the hot sun. A hot swill down and some food did more than any attempts at self-justification to put me in a better frame of mind, and the fact that I felt no ill effects and was able to enjoy a hearty dinner of hippo heart in the evening went far to restore confidence in my powers of endurance.

On the following day I made only a short march, and camped close to where I had buried the skull of the rhino cow on our way up. It was untouched, and now quite clean. It was too heavy for us to carry, so I had it tied in a tree to be brought on by the main caravan. I was determined to take it to the coast, no matter at what cost, thinking that it might be of interest to the natural history authorities in England, owing to what Von Hohnel had said about this small variety ; and I took considerable trouble to get it transported. Those only who know the difficulties of carriage in Central Africa, where no wheeled vehicles can be used, can appreciate the difficulties of carrying such heavy and clumsy specimens so far, especially through foodless country. It rode on top of one of the pack-donkeys between its two loads of meal, where it was carefully tied every morning, all the way to Mombasa, and eventually reached this country safely. As, however, it was not thought of any particular interest in London, while I myself rather valued it, I did not think it worth while presenting it to the British Museum. As already pointed out, I am convinced that this rhinoceros is merely a small local variety ; and, more than this, I am as positive as an unscientific observer can be—who has merely studied animals in an amateurish way in their native lands and is not qualified to critically examine the portions of their tissues to be found in museums—that there is only *one* species of rhinoceros in all East Equatorial Africa. The skull of the particular individual above alluded to is figured in conjunction with others. The photograph also illustrates strikingly the various angles at which the horns slope in different specimens.

It naturally occurs to one to inquire why the rhinoceros of these parts should be, as it certainly is, so much smaller than those of the same species farther south ? At first I was inclined to attribute the difference to the greater sterility of this arid region affording less nutritious food. But why, then, should it nourish such enormous elephants ? *They* are not an under-sized race ; on the contrary, I believe them to be among the largest, both in bulk of body and weight of tusks, of their kind to be found in Africa. Thus it would almost appear as if the conditions affected these two animals in inverse proportion. For, judging by the dimensions given by that reliable observer and renowned hunter, Mr. Selous, the rhinoceros of South Africa (I refer, of course, only to *Rhinoceros bicornis*) attains a greater size than even the largest of the equatorial representatives of the species, while (on the same authority) the elephants of the south are undoubtedly of smaller average stature. Here is a problem which our scientific authorities, through their knowledge of the structure of bones, may be in a position to kindly elucidate for us.

Half an hour after starting the next morning, and a little before sunrise, two elephants were seen by some of the men behind, at the edge of the lake. We in front had not noticed them ; perhaps they moved so as to become visible only after we had passed the spot whence they could be seen ; at all

RHINOCEROS SKULLS AND HORNS.
The longest horn of the three measures 40 inches on front curve.

events, we had unluckily already reached a point from where the wind blew dead towards them. I sent the "safari" back a little way, and went towards them with my two gun-bearers. The elephants—two big bulls—had by this time come up from the water, and by the quick step they went off at along the shore, in the direction we were going, I could tell that they had got our wind and were in full retreat. We had some distance to go, and long before we cut their spoor they had disappeared among some big thorn-trees which grew on the banks of a dry water-course just beyond. Finding that, after crossing the spruit, they had taken away from the lake and were making off into the bush, I sent Squareface back to bring on the men, pitch camp under the shady trees, and then go on to see whether there were any signs of more elephants on ahead, while I and Juma followed on the spoor of the two bulls.

I was rather glad to have only Juma with me to-day, for the other man sometimes rather flurried me, and as I never took more than one gun now (the .303), a single gun-bearer was sufficient. I was not feeling very hopeful, and as we trudged along I thought what a contrast my present frame of mind was with the confidence I should formerly have felt in a case like this. We went up one long slope, and then, after topping the rise, descended into a broad, shallow valley, in which were some considerable patches of pretty dense and very thorny scrub. I expected our game would stand in these, and we had not yet got down to the flat when I caught sight of a reddish-brown prominence visible over the similarly tinted scrub. Had I not been on the look-out I might not have noticed this, or mistaken it for an ant-heap; but looking at it carefully, I now made out that it was the ears and upper parts of our two elephants, which were standing close together in the middle of a thicket of stunted thorn bushes a good many acres in extent. After reaching the level of the valley we could no longer see them, and failed to find any possible way of approach anywhere on the leeward side of the scrub. I was determined not to enter this; for, though dry and leafless and consequently not difficult to see through for a short distance, the bushes of which it was composed were of a kind armed with such villainous hooked thorns that to move, except with the greatest deliberation and care, would be impossible, inside.

I imparted to Juma that my fixed resolve was to hunt " poli-poli " to-day—that is, cautiously and gently—and he entirely

concurred in the desirability of such procedure. We then
retired to one of the chimney-like ant-heaps so common here,
standing a little back from the edge of the thick scrub, from the
shoulder of which we were able to observe the elephants, and
waited. As they had not been very much alarmed, and were
quite unconscious of our presence, I hoped they might move by
and by into a more favourable position. Soon they began to
move about, and I could see that one was considerably larger
than the other ; but both seemed, from the glimpses we got, to
have equally good, though not exceptionally massive, tusks.

At last, after moving backwards and forwards several times
inside their retreat and exercising our patience a good deal,
they approached the limit of the brake on our side, and finally
came just outside and walked along skirting its edge. I
refrained from shooting while they moved, but got near and
followed along parallel with them, until, before they had gone
far, my patience was rewarded by a good chance. They stood ;
and I got up to the base of an ant-heap from whence I could get
a good clear shot. I gave the larger a bullet in the centre of the
right shoulder, and as they were making off I disabled his
mate with a shot into his hip, crippling him. The first ran
back to near their original position, and stood for a minute ;
but while we looked, it started to run full speed in our direction, and suddenly fell over, in mid career, rolling on to its
back with its feet kicking up into the air. Even then, as we
were congratulating each other, it got up again and stood.
What had happened was undoubtedly (I have seen the same
thing in other cases) that my shot had fractured the bone high
up ; so that, though it did not break at once, it caused the
limb to snap when it was running, thus bringing about its
sudden collapse. Both were now at my mercy, and I was not
long in giving them their quietus. The first probably needed
none, but the .303 bullet makes such a tiny wound that it takes
some time to kill a big bull, even though in a mortal spot.
They both had fine tusks, which I estimated to be a full load

apiece; those of the smaller bull were rather the thicker, the length averaging about the same.[1]

Juma and I were in great glee at our success; and I was kept from feeling fagged, on the way back to camp with our two tails, by the elation of a thoroughly satisfactory hunt. I was especially glad that no refugees were left to scare any elephants there might be ahead. Ours was a particularly pleasant camping-place, too, to-day; so that I was able to enjoy in comfort the rest which the feeling of having done a good day's work makes so delightful.

In the big thorn-tree under which my tent was pitched was a goose's nest. I had noticed the goose in it on our way after the elephants; but now, on my return, I saw a vulture in possession. I suspected what this meant, and, on sending a man up to inspect the nest, the explanation proved to be as I had feared. The vulture had breakfasted on the egg—there was but one—of the goose, which our camping here had scared from the protection of its home. Whether the nest was made by the goose itself, or was an old one of some other bird — vulture or eagle—which it had made use of, I am not sure, but the empty shell was undoubtedly that of a goose's egg. This nest was in the fork of a big bough high up from the ground. A few days later I came across another goose's nest, on which also the bird was sitting until I disturbed it. This one was on the bushy top of a low, flat-crowned thorn-tree, in such a position that we could not get at it, and just too high for me to see into from Juma's shoulders; but I should say that it, at any rate, was in all probability built by the goose itself. Farther southward, though, along the lake, trees are scarce, while Egyptian geese are in many parts very numerous, so it seems hardly likely that they can all nest in trees. I suppose they must keep guard over their eggs constantly from the time

---

[1] These teeth, when got out, weighed 86 lbs. and 83½ lbs.; and 84 lbs. and 81 lbs. It is curious—and it has happened three times in my experience—that bulls are often found in pairs whose teeth weigh almost alike.

they are laid, to preserve them from the rapacity of the vultures.

The distance to our elephants not being great, I sent Juma back with another man in the afternoon to get me some fat and a piece of the heart of one. I told him I thought the smaller of the two was the fatter ; but he found it to be in poor condition, while the big one was fat. I doubt if any one can tell, without opening it, whether an elephant is fat or not ; as a matter of fact they never look so externally.

Squareface had brought word that he had found the spoor of an odd bull or two near one of our former camping-places, some distance on, and also that the herd, at which I had so bungled my chance, had drunk near here during the previous night. Knowing him to be an indifferent judge of spoor, I did not put much faith in the latter piece of information ; but I decided, at any rate, not to move camp again until I had made sure that we were leaving no elephants in the immediate vicinity. So, as I did not feel much the worse in the morning for what had been a rather hard day's work for me nowadays, I started off about 5.30 with Juma and Smiler to look for fresh spoor ahead, sending Squareface in the opposite direction on a similar errand. We went nearly to our next camping-place, but found no spoor, even of the day before, barring that of the two bulls already accounted for ; so I came back to camp early, feeling that, failing any news of elephants near, I needed some rest to-day. As Squareface, who did not return till about 1 o'clock, reported that our herd had gone right back to its former haunts, I spent the rest of the day quietly in camp. Having already sent instructions to Abdulla to follow with the caravan, I decided not to move back in the direction of Reshiat again, but to go on to the camp where I had arranged to wait for him, and hope to pick up another bull in that neighbourhood, so as to be ready to continue our journey when my people overtook me.

During this last night here there were noises and reports

as of snapping trees, and splashing in the edge of the lake; so in the morning, after packing up, I sent my gun-bearers along the shore to see if there were any fresh elephant tracks. There were no signs of such, though, so I concluded it must have been hippos disturbing my rest. In consequence of this delay we did not get off till rather later than usual, but it was not a long march to where I intended camping; and when within a mile or so of the place, we crossed the spoor of three elephants, a little distance apart, going down to the water, two being large bulls, the third a cow.

I had succeeded so well on my last hunt, attended by Juma only, that I determined to pursue the same tactics to-day, in the hope that our luck might continue; so Square-face was given command of the "safari," with orders to form camp at the spot agreed upon and make all snug against my return. We found, on taking up the spoor, that the elephants, after drinking, had returned from the lake and made away inland. The tracks seemed quite fresh; and, after following them a short way, we came to where the elephants had stood and dusted themselves at the foot of an ant-heap. Looking beyond, over pretty open country, we caught sight of them, far ahead, on the top of a low, open ridge, apparently feeding. There were four of them, standing out like huge sphinxes on the sky-line. The wind was then blowing from us to them, so we started to make a long circuit, in order to get round to leeward of them, though at present they were too far off to scent us; but soon it became shifty, and sometimes died away, and we stopped to see which way it would settle down to blow from. After a while it came up—in gusts first, but finally as a good, stiff, steady breeze—from the usual south-east quarter. This was exactly favourable for us, so we went on, and got within two or three hundred yards without any difficulty or risk of alarming our game, and waited again to reconnoitre.

Up to this point there had been sufficient thin bush to

screen our approach, quite enough to obviate any risk of our
being seen at that distance by such short-sighted creatures.
I had never before, during all my elephant-hunting in Central
Africa, seen any in such open ground ; and it was the first
occasion in my experience when a horse might have been
used.   The elephants were now standing still, nearly in a row,
one behind the other, but at right angles to us.   I surveyed
them through my glasses.   The three bulls were all big
fellows, with fine tusks.   Those of the first were long and
white ; the second, which had a very old look about the face,
seemed to have even longer tusks, though not so white ; the
third was the cow, with insignificant ivory ; while the fourth's
teeth appeared the thickest of all, though shorter than the
others.

The ground between us and them was so open and devoid
of anything to cover one's approach, beyond a few very scraggy,
thin, and low bits of stunted bushes, that I thought we could
not get within easy killing range, and hoped they would move
on to more favourable ground.   But as, after waiting some
time, they still remained stationary, I decided to try and get
near, lest the wind should fail or change ; for the weather
looked unsettled.   Taking advantage of a slight hollow, and
crouching low, I succeeded, by using the greatest caution, in
reaching successfully a little screen of bare, semi-transparent
sprays, whence nearer approach seemed impossible unobserved.
What I could see now of the tusks of the second bull increased
my ambition to possess them.   Partly veiled though they were
by a thin shrub just in front of them, I could trace the outline
of the one nearest me, and it seemed to reach the ground !
But after trying to get a good aim from this point I felt
dissatisfied, not wishing to wound and lose, so crawled on
hands and knees, in spite of tiny thorns innumerable, to
within perhaps fifty yards.   Thence I got a good view ; and,
having. still avoided detection by keeping close to the ground,
while availing myself as much as possible of such sticks and

tufts of grass as served, the chance of discovery, as long as I kept still, and the wind held true, was past.   The old veteran, on whom I had set my heart, now offered a good mark, broadside on, but slightly turned towards me.   Taking steady aim, I gave him a shot right through the shoulder.   He ran but a little way, getting another bullet as he retreated, and then came down, never to rise again.

This was very satisfactory.   The others, being unhurt, and not knowing what was up, stood again just beyond his prostrate hulk, beside some good-sized leafy suaki bushes.   I risked the fallen bull getting up again—a not unlikely chance—and crept up under cover of his carcase.   Luck was with me : the very one I wanted—that, namely, which I believed to be the second best—moved out from the trees, just sufficiently to give me my opportunity.   As he stood sideways, I recognised him at once to be the one which had stood foremost, when I had first taken stock of them, and he also got a fatal wound ; but I could not give him another as he decamped, owing to the rifle getting on to half-cock again—as is its aggravating wont at inconvenient moments, though I have never succeeded in making it do it in cold blood.   However, I had hardly got it to rights before we saw him fall, heels in air, amidst a cloud of dust, in a little, bushy hollow just beyond.   He got on to his legs again, but was evidently done, and Juma wanted to follow up the other two at once ; but I said no, let us stick to our motto of " poli-poli," and see these two safe first.   He soon lay low, though, for the last time, and we went on after the remaining two, of which there was only one left worth shooting.

Taking their spoor over another slight rise, we found they had entered a shallow valley with some thickish patches of bush, but of no very great extent.   I did not feel keen about following into thick cover ; however, we kept on for a while, and, having ascertained which direction they had taken, I went up on to the low ridge skirting the valley to look over it.   I soon made out an ear in a thick patch under a big " suaki," but, even as we looked, they moved on again. Going along parallel with the valley, we by and by caught sight of them again, from one of the little knolls which commanded a view, standing once more in a similar position under another suaki tree. They had chosen the centre of a particularly thick part of the scrub, with tall, close-growing, leafy bushes all around. It was not far from open ground on the farther side, but I could see from my point of vantage that it would not be possible to get a shot without crawling close up. Compared with cover I used formerly to thread unhesitatingly, this was not bad, the bushes composing it not being of a thorny nature. But now " my hearts were two "—as the Zulus would say. One raised objections ; but the other— animated by the eager spirit of the hunter, still strong within me—would not let me off. I finally went through to the other side of the valley, farther back, and entered the bush again opposite the place I had marked.

On getting near, my old form reasserted itself, and my interest became keenly concentrated on the exciting pursuit. The bush inside was not so bad as it had appeared from without. My luck still held. I caught sight of the bull through openings in the scrub ; but from the first spot whence I tried to get a shot I could not obtain a clear enough view to satisfy me. I was determined not to fire any flurried, uncertain, or bungling shots to-day, so crept nearer till I could get an unimpeded view of the big brute's left shoulder, into the middle of which I sent, at close quarters, one of my tiny, slate-pencil bullets. I got in a second from behind as he turned, and in a few seconds we heard him fall with a crash. Going cautiously forward I made out the side of his great belly sticking up as he lay. He got up again though, and after falling a second time was on his legs once more ; so, though I knew it was only the smallness of the bullet that made him— such a huge beast—so long in dying, I thought it kinder to hasten his end.

I did not stay long admiring this last prize after Juma had cut off his tail.   He had fine tusks, of fair length and thick ; the thicker of the two measured 1 foot 8¼ inches in circumference just outside the lip.   Then we went back to the first two, which we had hardly glanced at yet.   They proved about as I had judged.   The one with the whitest ivory (the second killed) had teeth hardly as thick as the last, but about on a par otherwise.   The old fellow had very long tusks, though slightly thinner than the others, the right a good deal worn down, but his left the longest I had ever shot.[1]   He had no hair on his tail : evidently a patriarch.   Then I was not sorry to make for camp—luckily not very far off—for I was tired and sore, and the sun was extremely hot.   I felt very pleased with my morning's work.   I had accomplished it in what I considered a workmanlike manner ; not wasting many cartridges nor letting my game go far after being struck, and, above all, wounding none that escaped.   The fourth elephant I had no desire to harm.

I had now killed five more bull elephants of the largest size, whose ten heavy tusks would require as many of my best porters to carry them—a good many more than I had " empty hands," as the loads were at present arranged.   It would therefore require a good deal of scheming and contriving to enable us to take these ; and to take them I was determined.   The problem how to make two dozen porters carry thirty loads would obviously have defied my mathematics, had it not been for the fortunate circumstance that I had a number of spare donkeys.   Even thus it was not so simple as it may seem ; for donkeys can only carry suitable loads and cannot possibly bear large tusks ; moreover, pads, etc., are needed.   However, the difficulties were eventually overcome, so as to leave sufficient

---

[1] This tusk weighed 117½ lbs., and only lost 1½ lbs. in drying.   Its present weight is thus 116 lbs.   It measures exactly 9 feet.   Its fellow weighed, when got out, 109 lbs. Those of the other two weighed 117 lbs. and 104 lbs. ; and 96 lbs. and 95½ lbs.   An outline of the first is shown, together with others of my finest tusks, in the drawing, p. 422.

men to carry all the heavy ivory, though in the end it resulted
in a box of cartridges having to be buried under a heap of
stones. But as these were encased in lead, I look forward to
finding them still in good order on my next trip; and I am
quite sure no one else will ever find them.

In order to provide material for making extra "sogis" (a
sort of pliable panniers), I went out the next day to endeavour
to procure some skins. When we passed here, outward bound,

ORYX ANTELOPE (*Oryx beisa*).
(From a Photograph by the AUTHOR.)

game swarmed; but owing to the veldt being now very dry,
while farther back there was young grass, it had shifted its
range, so that there was hardly any in the neighbourhood at
this time. However, I managed to get what I wanted. A
very short way from camp I shot a single oryx bull, which
proved to be the finest specimen I had ever bagged. The horns
measure 36 inches and $36\frac{1}{2}$ inches, which for this species of
oryx is very good, especially in a male. But the hide of an
old bull is too thick to make a good "sogi"; so, after calling
men to skin and carry in the meat, I went on in hopes of

getting something more suitable. Farther on I saw four
young " topi " bulls, grazing in the open. Luckily, though,
there was some thin bush within shot of them on the leeward
side; and by making a detour I was able to stalk them
successfully, and before they had made up their minds definitely
which was the safe direction to finally run away in, I had three
of them down within less than fifty yards of each other. The
fourth I let away as not wanted.

I had three men with me, so with one working at each
buck the skins were soon removed and sent back to camp by
one of them, while I went round by the first of my elephants
of yesterday in the hopes of getting a shot with my camera,
which I had brought for the purpose, at vultures and marabouts
at work on the carcase. However, they had not yet been able
to effect an entrance through the hide, and so were only
soaring about and waiting for decay, beasts of prey, or man
to enable them to begin their feast. Great numbers of them
had been attracted to the vicinity, though, and the display
of meat drew many round our camp, as well as flocks of
crows and several kites. The kites were constantly swooping
down upon scraps, and the crows caused my men much
annoyance by their audacity in making raids on the garlands
of biltong spread about to dry.

These last afforded me a good deal of amusement by their
droll ways. Like all crows, there is a comical seriousness
about their actions most diverting to study. One, bolder
than the rest, would advance by alternate hops and steps to
within an inch or two of a piece of meat ; make a feint ; look
about knowingly ; open his wings in false alarm ; drop again
in front of the alluring morsel, and finally stretch out his neck
and seize it with a sudden effort of resolution. Then the
others, who had been watching this adventurous individual
from close by, would pounce down eagerly, encouraged by his
success, and a regular scramble would ensue, until a stick
hurled among them by the indignant owner of the meat

would send all flapping off to wait a few yards away till
another volunteer should summon up courage to renew the
attempt.[1]

On the 26th I sent for the tusks of the first two bulls.
They had been shot five days, and I knew that the ivory would
come out easily ; and as the caravan ought to arrive in a
day or two, I wanted to get all together in readiness. For
that reason it was necessary to extract the teeth of the other
three on the following day, so that there might be no needless
delay later. Being fresher, and so large, these took some
chopping to get out ; but they were all brought in in triumph,
and when laid out side by side at the foot of the tree in front
of my tent these ten magnificent teeth made a fine show.
Abdulla and his party had only heard of the bagging of the
first two elephants ; so when the "safari" came in early on
the 28th, the row of splendid ivory caused quite an excitement,
and they were examined and lifted with eager interest, while
Abdulla himself was in great glee.

I should explain that all the best porters take a pride
in carrying the biggest ivory, and it is a point of honour with
all the leading ones to have a heavy tusk apiece assigned to
them, these always being given precedence at the head of
the caravan. Thus if one of the best men was not entrusted
with such a burden he would consider himself slighted. In
this way my "kilangozi" or leading porter (a most important
personage [2]) had immediately taken possession of the heaviest of

---

[1] The proper way to cure meat as "biltong" is to hang it in the *shade*. It then dries by
the action of the wind, if the weather be suitable, while remaining sweet. Made of good,
tender meat, it is first-rate, when successfully cured, either roasted crisp on the embers or
pounded, moistened and fried, or may even be eaten raw. Swahilis, however, like more
tasty food (as any one may tell who has passed near a shop where the dried fish they
particularly affect is exposed for sale) ; and they designedly spread their strips of meat
on the ground in the fierce sun. Treated thus it acquires a relish which was rather a
trial to me when the porters carrying my box or furniture had tied any, during the march,
on top of their loads.

[2] Much depends on the "kilangozi," and it is policy to keep him in good humour.
Mine I always conciliated by conferring little favours—such as a small special present of
meat when it was scarce, or an occasional bit of calico (such trifles are highly prized in

the Bumi tusks as his right ; while one of the strongest among
those who were accustomed to follow him in the van had been
somewhat aggrieved at not being allotted one from the first.
I had told him then that I hoped a tusk worthy of him would
yet be found, and so it was with considerable satisfaction that
I now conferred the coveted favour upon him by pointing to
the biggest of all—a few pounds heavier even than the yellow
one carried by the "kilangozi"—as his burden, amid general
laughter.

I think this shows what nonsense it is to talk of the
cruelty of using men as beasts of burden, and the absurdity of
restricting, by vexatious regulations, the weight of a porter's
load to fifty or sixty pounds or some such ridiculous limit.
Here were my men competing eagerly with each other for
my permission to shoulder tusks weighing about a hundred-
weight apiece, and the disappointed ones asking me in injured
tones where was their "pembe" (horn).   This, knowing that
there was a journey of some seven hundred miles before us,
the greater part through pathless tracts, over rugged hills
strewn with sharp rocks, among thorny scrub and thick grass,
often for long stretches with no water, and all under the fierce
heat of the equator.   They get no extra pay for carrying these
heavy tusks ; and the only little privilege they enjoy is never
being asked to carry their own rations, as the others have to
sometimes for several days, and perhaps getting the preference
in the matter of meat.   Their chief reward, to which they look
forward during the whole long journey, is the proud moment
when they enter Mombasa, decked out gaily with flowing red
cloths (their customary perquisite), and march through the
streets with their glistening white burdens, showing off before
the admiring crowds.   Men who are not able, without any
strain or inconvenience, to carry a far heavier burden than

the "bara"). He has much to do with regulating the pace of the caravan, and has great
influence with the other porters ; so that keeping him contented and cheerful tends to
make things work smoothly and counteract any possible friction.

the authorised Government load are not, in my opinion, worth their "posho" (ration) as porters.[1]

That it is no hardship to good ones to do so, with the addition of gun, cartridge-belt, and sometimes several days' rations, as well as their own odds and ends, is proved by what I have stated above, and also by the fact that I had mostly the same men on the second expedition who had been with me before. The hardship will be rather when they lose their occupation; for they engage in it voluntarily, in preference to other work, and I had several mechanics in my caravan—a stone mason, a cobbler, etc.—who preferred the free life of a caravan porter to working at their trades.

That porters are sometimes cruelly used by unprincipled Europeans when beyond the influence of public opinion is true enough, but such employers will not get Swahilis to engage with them a second time nowadays; and injustice and harsh treatment often bring their own retribution by causing the failure of the expedition. For my part, I do not believe in excessive strictness. I find I can always get more out of men by treating them with consideration, and it is much pleasanter when a kindly feeling exists. Of course if any one is so unfortunate as to get a bad lot of men, severity may be necessary; but mine never gave me any trouble, and I don't believe there are any Africans that will follow one so faithfully and patiently into remote regions as these Swahilis, or Zanzibaris, or whatever you may please to call the mixed lot of men who constitute the regular caravan porters one gets in East Africa. As to punishments, I rarely have occasion to inflict any; and flogging I never resort to except in the most extreme cases, such as looting from natives or grossly insulting one's headman, proved by ample evidence. A punishment for minor offences I found most suitable was adding some article

---

[1] Of course with a heavily-loaded caravan it is necessary to travel slowly. If a quicker pace and longer marches are desired, the loads must be reduced by nearly one-half.

to the load. This makes the culprit do useful work—for there is seldom a time when something is not in want of means of transport, such as a newly-acquired specimen, for example—and the fact of its having been added as a penalty has a great effect upon him, though the actual weight may not make any material difference.

A rule I never depart from, and to which I attach the greatest importance in dealing with Africans, is to allow one's men free access to oneself to lay their grievances before their master. If the complaints are frivolous, I point out to grumblers their groundlessness ; it relieves their feelings to have had their say, and thus a little " shauri " often removes discontent. Above all, never allow a headman to punish nor give him uncontrolled sway over the men ; such a course surely leads to favouritism and cruelty, however good a man he may be.

I felt so sure that the caravan would come in that day that I went out early on the morning of 28th April on purpose to get some meat for the men. Those who had been with me here had always had more than they could eat, but the others could get none while I was away, and, as they were now carrying heavy loads, deserved some. I shot two " topi," and the " safari " came in all safe and sound just as I got back. As it was yet early, we were that day able to get completed all the additional preparations and disposals which the newly-acquired ivory rendered necessary, and everything ready for starting in earnest with the whole outfit, on our return journey, the following morning. Every one was in high spirits, not excepting myself, for I had every reason to feel thankful for my recovery and for the many fortunate circumstances which had combined to make things smooth for me and to render my expedition far from an absolute failure, in spite of my serious accident and consequent loss of three months and upsetting of my plans. Men are always pleased at the prospect of returning to the coast after a long trip ; and happily we had an ample supply of food to see us through, anyway to El Bogoi, so that I saw no cause for anxiety ; in fact, everything seemed favourable once more. The only thing I dreaded was that the heavy rains, which according to generally received notions were now overdue, might give us trouble and impede our progress. As a matter of fact, though, we never experienced anything that could be called a wet season at all that year.

CHAPTER XVI

EN ROUTE FOR EL BOGOI

Easy stages—Astir betimes—A regretful shot—Diversity of zebra—A blessing in disguise—A salutary lesson—Implementing a promise—A spider and its prey—A gladdening feast—Lacking a handy camera—A curious coincidence—El Molo mode of fishing—Stalking zebra—Departure from Lake Rudolph—Mount Nyiro—A dispensation of Providence—A scene of carnage—El Bogoi camp—Hearty greetings—A test of affection—Disappointed hopes.

THE 29th of April saw us once more fairly on the march southward. For the first week or so it was necessary to travel by very short stages, till the men should get accustomed to their new loads. Tusks are carried on the shoulder, and not on the head as other articles are. The latter part can be protected by a long cloth, wrapped round and round so as to stand up from the top of the head and form a thick pad, hollow in the middle, for the load to rest on ; but over the shoulders only a loose cloth, like a mantle, is worn as a protection to the skin. Hence it is only gradually that the porters' shoulders become hardened to bearing such great weights ; and in the meantime one must go easy with them. When thoroughly accustomed to them, my men would often march for four hours on end before ever putting their loads down to rest. It is a rather pretty sight to see a string of men, each with a big white tusk on his shoulder glistening in the early morning sun, marching along in single file, all carrying on the same side ; and then, when they want to change over, all with one accord—the word having been passed along—

swinging the long logs of ivory round behind their backs on to the other shoulder.

Fortunately, at this time there was a morning moon (that is, it was on the wane), so that, knowing our way now, we could start as early as we liked ; and with a " heavy safari " nothing is so important as to get as much of the march as possible in the cool of the morning. When the sun gets high overhead, every quarter of an hour tires the men more than an extra hour before sunrise. So I used to get the ivory party off by 4.30 or even 4 A.M., as long as the moon lasted. This meant being up by 3, or soon after, myself, as the donkeys had to be loaded (a longish process), and I did not like to leave them far behind.

On the second morning I was compelled (most regretfully) to shoot a rhino ; I say regretfully, because it was early in the morning, and we could not afford to waste time over it, nor was it desirable to let the men pile meat on top of their heavy loads with the march before them. So I would gladly have left them alone (there were two), had they not come blundering towards the caravan. No one would have been hurt, in all probability, had I allowed them to come on ; but the loads would all have been chucked down and very likely something broken. Besides, it damages ivory to throw it down on stones or even hard ground, and I have had tusks splintered and chipped so through a " faro " scare. I therefore felt constrained to administer a .303 bullet to the leading one, which turned them both and brought the one which had received it to the ground in a few strides, and, after a squeal or two, to its last breath. It was a young cow, adult, but very small, and after examining and measuring it I had to leave it—with much sorrow for having been driven reluctantly to cause its useless death—to the vultures and hyenas.

My custom was not to attempt to shoot anything during the march ; to do so would delay us, and we had quite enough to carry already. But I did my best to procure meat for the caravan, and during this part of the journey—that is, before we had reached the rugged country at the south end of Bassu—kept up the supply pretty abundantly, shooting something about every other day. Starting so early and making only short marches, there was plenty of time to hunt after camp had been pitched. In this way zebra of both kinds, oryx, etc., were shot, an odd hippo, and once a solitary cow buffalo (an animal I had not set eyes on for years, and which quite reminded me of old times).

Whether the zebra of the small species are absolutely identical with those already mentioned as occurring in the neighbourhood of the Lorogi Mountains, it is impossible to be certain without seeing them side by side ; but I incline to believe that those in this locality, at any rate, may be found to differ somewhat from the variety described as *Equus grantii* by Mr. de Winton. I noted of one obtained in this part that " the black stripes are wide and the white narrow, *particularly on the neck,* and along the back are spots or blotches instead of distinct stripes." But it appears to me that all the varieties of this zebra, such as Chapman's, Grant's, etc., are but local forms of Burchell's, with which they are all specifically identical, though differing slightly as to details of colour and markings.[1] In all their general characteristics, whether of form, appearance, habits, paces, or voice, they are indistinguishable, while equally separated from the totally distinct Grevy's zebra by a wide gulf.

I am not partial to zebra meat myself, but the tongue is good, and rissoles made of the liver (always supposing the animal to be young and in good condition) are not to be despised. Generally, though, I prefer venison ; but my first object always being quantity, for the sake of my hungry porters, I commonly neglected gazelles and devoted my

[1] In a fœtal skin which I have obtained a little north of the Tana, faint "shadow stripes" are apparent between the dark bands on the thighs, though these clearly-defined dark bands continue right down to the hoofs.

attention to the larger animals first. Moreover, the Grant's gazelle were not in good condition at this time, and one young specimen I shot was rendered unfit for food by large dark-coloured warble grubs, of which its back was full just below the skin.

Early on 6th May the extreme south-east point of the bay of Lalia was reached, whence our route struck inland for several marches. I felt some uneasiness about the water-supply when the lake should be no longer within reach, for the weather had been so excessively dry of late that the country was more burnt up than ever. I therefore took the precaution to send messengers to ascertain whether any was to be found at the camping-places between. On their return, the middle of the next day, we learnt that the pools half-way across the isthmus still contained sufficient for our needs, but at the intermediate camp it was all dried up. This would make the stages very long, and I was not without anxiety about the severe marches over heavy ground that would have to be undertaken in face of these rather trying conditions, the heat being intense. However, it had to be faced ; but, just before we should have started, what was very nearly resulting in a catastrophe, but which in the event proved the best thing that could have happened, occurred, in the shape of a sudden flood.

About this part many very broad water-courses enter the lake ; indeed, sometimes one walks for considerable distances through what seems one broad, shallow river-bed, though all as dry as any bone. It is in such situations that trees are found, and on this occasion, as on many others, we had camped in one. A storm came on to-day, and must have been far heavier up the course of our sand river, for in the midst of the shower a wide stream of muddy water came rushing down upon the camp, and in a twinkling tent, loads, and all were flooded. Luckily the water did not rise much above ankle deep, but at the time things looked serious. It was not easy even to find a safe spot to retreat to, but we managed to get our dripping belongings carried to a slight elevation—a sort of bank of gravel—over which, luckily, the inundation did not rise, all hands working with a will. It was not a cheerful sight to see the water surging around the stack of precious food (the ivory could not be hurt) and through my tent, while our belongings were hastily transported anyhow in the pouring rain. However, the damage proved less than at first sight appeared ; only a few loads of meal were soaked, and though the mishap caused us a day's delay and a good deal of trouble to dry everything, no food was really spoilt. As often happens, what at first threatened to be a calamity was in reality a most fortunate occurrence for us ; even the flood turned out a blessing, for we now had an abundance of water where thirst had menaced us. Thus the favourite Swahili formula when travelling— "Omba Muungu" (Beg of God)—seems, on occasion, something more than a mere form of words.

As showing how porters appreciate one's efforts to get meat for them, and prize such an addition to their regular food ration when obtainable, I may mention a little incident that occurred about this time. I had been rather annoyed about something that had been going on in the caravan, and had purposely abstained from shooting any game for a day or two in consequence. The men knew the reason, and the pressure thus brought quietly to bear had a salutary effect. One evening, after I had lain down, and while having my last smoke, Abdulla came into my tent, and after squatting down and turning his head about (to the accompaniment of sundry little preliminary coughs) in his usual nervous manner when he had anything in the nature of a favour to ask—a sort of bashful smile on his face, lit up by the flickering fire outside,—said that the men were bemoaning the meat famine, and had asked him to express their regret for having caused me annoyance, and to beg that I would hunt for them again. It being against my will to deny them, I let him please them by a promise to try and shoot something on the morrow. This produced quite a cheer and chorus of thanks, and the camp, which had been unusually hushed, was now cheery again with their talking. This was a relief to me, as I always like to see the men happy. At the same time it was as well to let them be reminded that I was incurring a good deal of fatigue, which in the weak state of my health was no small strain upon my strength, for their benefit, in my desire to add a liberal supply of meat to the customary ration of grain to which they were entitled, and which is all they would get in most caravans.

After this I felt it to be a point of honour to kill something the next day, which happened to be the one on which we reached the lake again, and once more camped on its now familiar shores. The country seemed to have little game in it, but after making a round I espied with my glasses an oryx grazing near the shore, and on getting nearer saw that there were two Grevy's zebra with him. The place was bare, but there was an odd shrub or two on the way to them. Leaving Juma, I made a very careful stalk, taking every precaution, as I was specially anxious to be successful. I crawled most of the way, waiting patiently prone whenever they were turned in my direction, and at length, by care and luck, reached the last bush, which was within easy range of the three, all pretty close together. But as I edged round to get a shot, the wary oryx twigged me and set off, the zebras following. Exhausted by my crawl and out of breath, I missed a running shot at the foremost of the latter; but a chance for a rather long shot which the other gave me, by standing for a moment farther on, I made better use of, the bullet going right through both shoulders, with the result that he staggered and fell. It was just sundown, but luckily camp was not far off; so the plentiful supply of meat was soon brought in and distributed, in fulfilment of my promise, to the delight of both the men and myself.

My side was pretty sore next day as the result of my crawl,

but it did not matter, as there was no occasion to hunt.   While resting during the march, I was interested in watching a tiny gray spider with black stripes—one of the jumping kind— pounce upon a big yellow ant, and kill it in no time by biting its waist while sticking to its back.   I knocked it off twice with a bit of grass, but it returned to its victim after a short pause both times.   The second time, however, it met some small dark red ants, which had discovered the prey, and backed away, seemingly afraid of them.   The relative proportions in size of the predatory spider and its victim were about those of a lion to a camel.   I once noticed, when bathing in the El Bogoi stream, one of these little spiders, of a somewhat similar kind, swimming.   It was on the bank when I saw it first, and deliberately put out into the stream when I went near, making a circuit and returning to the bank lower down, a performance it repeated each time I disturbed it.

On the 13th we camped near the big fishing village, halting earlier than usual, by special request of my leading porter, that the men might have the amusement of bartering fish and the advantage of additional rest.   Swahilis dearly love fish ; even when meat is plentiful they are always eager to get fish too, if they can.   Knowing their weakness, and also that they could have little of their own to exchange for their favourite delicacy, I gave Abdulla orders to buy all that was brought with some spare beads I had among my own things, which I had kept there as a reserve in case any might be needed on the road, to save opening a load.   In a very short time a big heap of dried fish, besides a quantity of fresh, was accumulated ; and as I afterwards went out and shot three oryx, meat enough and to spare was added ; so altogether there was a feast for all hands to rejoice the porter's heart—for he loves his "tumbu" (stomach).   Glad I was that they should revel in plenty while they could, for I knew it would not always be so.   Truth to tell, I was not sorry to camp early myself that day, for I was feeling very sore and stiff in my side and hardly able to keep

up even with the slow pace of the caravan, though later on
this wore off and I was able to hunt.

Where we had stopped to rest this morning during the
march was a party of flamingoes. I watched them through
my glasses (they were not far off), and was much interested
in observing their curious method of procuring their food.
They were in very shallow water ; putting their heads down
and beaks in the mud, they worked their feet about with a
dancing movement, their knees swinging outward and together
again alternately after the fashion of a " Punch and Judy "
man clapping his cymbals with his elbows, the while waltzing
round and round, the head acting as pivot. When they fly,
the scarlet wings show with beautiful effect, the immensely
long necks being stretched out to their full extent. There
were many pelicans about, too, as well as other water-birds of
various kinds. On such occasions I always thought what a
pity it is one cannot have a camera that would photograph
what one sees through a good pair of field-glasses, and as
handy to use as they are. It is not possible to get near
enough to wild creatures to show anything distinct enough to
have any value in a picture taken with an ordinary hand-
camera ; and even if it were, one capable of taking a negative
of sufficient size to be of much use is comparatively clumsy,
troublesome to carry, and difficult to get out at a moment's
notice. A day or two later I came across wonderful armies of
these birds and attempted a snap-shot ; but the result was, as
usual, a failure.

The last sentence in my diary under this date (13th) runs
as follows :- " Just as I had finished writing the above entry
there was a distinct shock of earthquake." It is a curious
coincidence that this was, almost to a day, the date of the
rather severe earthquake experienced on the coast the year
before.

Two days after the above occurrence we took a short cut
across a hilly promontory which I had noted on our way up,

thus saving (as in a smaller degree at other points) a good deal in distance through our knowledge of the country. At this part the lake is extremely wide, and when viewed from an elevation looks lovely—deep blue flecked with white wave-crests.

On the broad, sheltered bays which terminate this most easterly gulf of Bassu we met with our El Molo friends again, now no longer suspicious of us. One afternoon I had the opportunity of watching their mode of netting fish. The fishermen passed my tent in procession on their way to the part of the bay they intended to try, each with a coil of net, skewered on an oryx horn, slung behind his back, knapsack fashion, one or two women accompanying the party. Unwinding their pieces of net, each several yards long, on the bank, they waded in till the water was about up to their chests or necks, and then separated, holding the nets between them, till they had formed a circle. They did not close in much, but the fish that were encompassed, being frightened, dashed about, leaping out of the water, and some over the nets, in their efforts to escape, and many were caught. Then the women took out the captives and threaded them on a cord—first killing each by piercing the head with one of the sharp oryx horns, thus preventing trouble from its flapping about when suspended to her waist in the water—while the men began to wade off for a fresh haul farther on. When a shoal was enclosed the scene was a lively one; the water would fairly boil for a few moments within the circle, the silvery fish glinting in the bright sunshine as they leapt into the air, amidst great excitement and jabbering. The fish caught in this manner were very handsome; they were deep and narrow, and some of considerable size, and when fresh from the water were very good eating.

How little trouble it is to procure abundance of food of this kind here is shown by the fact that, after about an hour's amusement in the comparative cool of the late afternoon, the party returned with quantities of beautiful fish. The numbers of pelicans and fish-eating fowl of every possible kind, too, show these bays to be a great resort of the fishy world of Bassu. In the evening the dead bushes in the water are simply laden with cormorants, herons, etc. I also observed cormorants' nests containing young on a dead tree in the shallow water.

I continued to hunt almost daily, devoting my attention chiefly to zebra, and was pretty successful. In this perfectly open country it is by no means easy to get within shot—then sometimes a long one. It is often only to be accomplished by a long and careful stalk—laborious and trying under a blazing sun and over baked bare, stony ground, but rendered the more interesting by these very difficulties. Thus, after sighting a pair of zebra from a rocky hill, standing motionless in a bare valley a couple of miles away, in an apparently unapproachable position, and then working one's way arduously along little rough gullies, crawling under partial cover of some slight inequality of the ground—watching the while the tips of their ears with strained eyes as you wriggle along among the stones and the little thorny plants which are almost the only vegetation the barren ground supports, regardless of the tiny hair-like spines penetrating hands and knees—it is satisfactory to attain at length the point previously noted as within striking distance, and floor both before sufficiently recovered from their alarm at the sudden apparition to get out of range. And when an experimental incision over the plump, wide quarters, grooved like a ripe peach, and as sleek, shows a layer of yellow fat— beloved of porters—half an inch or more in thickness, the thought of the glee with which your straining men will carry in the meat makes the tramp back to camp happy with the anticipation of their joyful smiles. Having propped the round carcase with stones so as to lie on its back, and tied a fluttering white handkerchief to one of the up-sticking hind feet[1] (for there is most likely no stick near), you know it will be safe

---

[1] As illustrated in the photograph on p. 211.

from the vultures. This expedient for protecting game from birds I have not seen recommended. Others may have adopted it, though I have not come across any mention of it myself. I found out the dodge some twenty years ago, in South Africa, and have never known it fail if properly carried out, adapting it to the situation by such various devices for attaching the flag as circumstances may dictate.

We were now close to the rugged black lava hills, already described as characterising the country at the southern end of the lake, where I knew game to be scarce ; and glad was I that the men had been having a good time with meat galore, so as to have strength in reserve for the hard work ahead. Our last comfortable camp was on the charming little stream which comes from Mount Kulale. How beautiful is running water in this arid land ; and how sweet it tastes after the nasty stuff of bitter old Bassu ! Thence it took us a week's hard toil to get through the terrible country already described—country which a Zulu would say (and truly) had been "badly hurt." As before, terrific gales made things unpleasant for us, and the work harder : it being sometimes hardly possible to stand, and out of the question to attempt to pitch a tent or use a table, while nothing was safe without stones on it. But one may get, in a measure, hardened to almost anything ; and I came to take less notice of the discomforts the unceasing wind entailed than formerly. By steady plodding we got through all the difficulties without mishap. Of meat we got none ; I could not even get a chance at one of the Grant's gazelle, a few of which are to be found even there.

It is perplexing, at first sight, why these buck, which can hardly ever see a human being, should be much wilder than those in inhabited parts. Being unaccustomed to man certainly produces no shocking tameness here. The explanation seems to be, that where there are natives who are practically unable to harm them, they get used to seeing people about ; whereas these, having an in-bred fear of man, the inheritance of ages,

CARAVAN MARCHING; NEARING THE SOUTH END OF BASSU.

dread the unwonted apparition.   Where the inhabitants do not
hunt, the game may be said to become partially domesticated
to a slight degree.   Deer in parks are somewhat more so ; a
tame one becomes even offensive through excessive familiarity.
On the other hand, cattle, left to themselves, soon get wild ;
showing the same natural fear of the lord of creation.   Where
persecuted, animals are, I suppose, still wilder than where un-
associated with mankind—though I confess I often wonder
how little difference it seems to make to their approachability.

It was not without a certain regret that I finally turned
my back upon the lake.   Viewed as a whole, Bassu resembles
the Red Sea in many respects, though of course on a smaller
scale.   Its long narrow shape, barren shores, and hot dry
climate, all remind one of that arm of the ocean ; while the
high ground on the eastern shore to a certain extent bears out
the comparison, and the bare rocks of Aden are not unlike the
style of country at the southern end (though those here are
much more broken up).   But, though I had become attached
even to this not altogether entrancing lake, when, two or three
days later, we reached a higher level, with a colder climate,
near the base of Mount Nyiro, I felt reconciled to the separa-
tion.   As we rose and entered the zone influenced by mountain
showers, the vegetation became quickly more verdant.   It was
indeed pleasant once more to camp among fresh green leaves,
grass, and flowers, by a cool, clear, trickling spring, and to hear
the cheerful notes of familiar birds ; the fresh, chilly, early air
was an invigorating treat not felt for months past, while the
sweet, cold water seemed the most delicious beverage possible.

Early on the 26th we got out into the high open plateau
near the southern end of Mount Nyiro.   About 6.30 I noticed
a rhino with a big calf away to our left, under the spur or
buttress of the mountain which forms its south-eastern corner,
which we were just about to round.   Had she remained where
she was I should not have gone out of my way to interfere
with her so far from our next camp, notwithstanding that we

had had no meat for nearly ten days ; but she came along diagonally in our direction, as it were to cut us off, though she was evidently quite unconscious of our presence.   It shows how blind these creatures are, that she never saw the caravan with its row of gleaming white tusks marching right across her right front.

When near meeting her, the men put down their loads, and some bolted for shelter in a little gully, while I took my rifle and sat on a slight prominence to await my chance, determined, since providence had sent a supply of meat into our very hands, to take advantage of it, notwithstanding that it was still a long march to our camping-place for the day. When she got within about a hundred yards or less she seemed to see me.   Probably my rifle-barrel glinted in the sun, which had just topped the hills.   She turned nearly facing me, and stood with her head up, trying to make me out, giving me the opportunity to plant a .303 bullet at the root of the neck.   On receiving it she turned and galloped perhaps two hundred yards ; but I could see by her laboured action, and the way she threw up her forelegs, that she had got enough.   Then she stood and tottered about, lifting her forelegs out straight in front of her with a peculiar dancing action, and fell over dead.   I wanted to let the calf go, but, as usual, it would not, and the men begged for its meat ; so, as I wanted them to get a good feast after their hard work and short rations, I let it have a bullet just in front of the point of its shoulder, as it stood diagonally head on to me, and it shared its mother's fate after running some hundred yards from her.

The cow was fat, and the men cut up the meat in high glee and piled it on to their already well-laden shoulders, or heads.   I waited for them nearly two hours before I could get them to leave the carcases ; and it was wonderful how little there was then left but hide and bones.   The donkey-men, who were sometimes out of it when anything was shot *en route*, through being behind, were, this time, to the fore with the rest in the scramble. When a beast is killed on the march, I let the men help themselves ; there is not time to have it cut up and divided, as it is always best to do with meat that can be carried straight into camp. The scene of carnage under these circumstances beggars description—such hacking and struggling and tearing ; one can liken it to nothing but the vultures' carnival, only with men instead of birds. The meat supply was most welcome—to myself as well as the men.

Just south of Nyiro the country was much drier than when we passed up ; but a little farther on we got quite suddenly into fresh green grass, showing that a good deal of rain had fallen there recently, further evidence of which was a pool of water and the unusual quantity running in the Barta spruit. But no sooner did we leave the latter than we got as suddenly into dried-up country again, showing that it was only one of those narrow storm-paths, I have before noticed, that we had been crossing. Quantities of game, attracted by the young pasturage, were congregated at one part of this green belt, where the grass had previously been burnt, reminding me of the Transvaal " High Veldt " in old times, though the species here are different. I took toll of them in passing, just before we reached our Barta camp, and was successful in picking out a very fat *E. grevyi* for my victim. We found a party of natives of the Suk tribe here, living on game which they snared in the manner described as practised by the El Gume. I had never seen a human being in this part before, and fancy they were wanderers beyond their usual range. They all cleared out under cover of the night, evidently suspicious of our intentions, probably through a consciousness that they were intruders in this region.

We got through the long dry march to the next stream splendidly, doing a great part of it by night, the ivory-men having by this time become thoroughly accustomed to their tusks, and able to carry them with ease for hours at a stretch, and with less fatigue than some of the porters carrying lighter loads.   There was no running water in the Suya now, and the quantity of fresh spoor on the numerous game-tracks leading to the pools showed that there was none at all away from the river.   At the Barasaloi plenty was still to be had, a little below the surface, by digging in the sand, and that deliciously cool and much better than at the last stream, no doubt because this one rises in the high "subugo" forests of the Lorogi Mountains.

On nearing El Bogoi we almost felt as if the worst of our journey was over, although it is really only about half-way to the coast; but the rest of the distance to the coast was through comparatively familiar ground, and even the El Bogoi camp seemed quite homelike now.   Before getting in, a couple of Ndorobo youths belonging to Lesiat's clan overtook us as we were threading our way through the bush in the early morning. They had been lying in wait by one of the game-paths traversing the jungle, in the hopes of getting a chance at a rhinoceros, which they had noticed was in the habit of using it on his way to or from the water, and had their harpoons with them.   Rhinoceroses are scarce here, as a consequence, no doubt, of the vicinity of this community, and the chances of getting one by these means must be infinitesimal; indeed, how rarely these hunters meet with success was illustrated at the time by the fact that the principal item of news they had to give us, in reply to our inquiries, was that one of these animals had been killed during our absence (about seven months), and another wounded, but lost.

It was cheering to be greeted with friendly smiles and handshakes, indicative of genuine pleasure at meeting us, by these careless children of the forest.   They accompanied us for some distance, asking many questions about our experiences, and looking with admiration at our fine show of ivory.   On hearing of my accident they showed much interest and concern, and finally—somewhat to my confusion—insisted on my stripping to the waist and showing my wounds, which they examined with evident sympathy. They then ran off to carry word of my return to their people.

I was a good deal dismayed on reaching our little stream to find its bed dry, as I feared we should be compelled to go and camp higher up its course in a less convenient spot, nearer the mountains, where I knew it never ceased to flow; but we found a little trickling rill still running on the surface for a few yards, a little below where we crossed and close to my favourite camp, just sufficient to supply the donkeys as well as ourselves with water. We were soon comfortably installed in the old spot; and it was a source of no small satisfaction that we had reached here once more safely, and if myself not altogether sound, all the rest—both man and beast—well, not a porter lame nor a donkey with a sore back. Of those who went up with me, Shebane alone was missing; and his sad loss was brought vividly to my memory here by the absence of flowers from the table, when spread in my favourite "bower" dining-room.

Soon more of our Ndorobo neighbours, including Lesiat himself, turned up, some bringing me little presents of their delicious honey, and all welcomed me as an old friend, and seemed as pleased to see me as I was to see them. Then I was importuned to exhibit my scars again, and received many kindly condolences. Lesiat at first told me that he had been compelled by hunger to eat two loads of beans of mine, which had been left in his charge, owing to one of the donkeys that had been sent back for them from Nyiro, when we were on our way up, having been killed by a lion. I told him that it was of no consequence, he being my friend, and that I could not quarrel with him on such an account. Fortunately, we were in no straits for food; although in such a place, so far from any source of supply, it is, of course, very valuable. Having been assured of my forgiveness, he forthwith declared that he had

only been testing the strength of my affection for him, and
that the food was safe and intact in a cavern, where he had
carefully stored it, barricading the entrance. And so it proved
to be : he had hidden it in this dry cave, a secret retreat of
his, the entrance to which could only be approached with
difficulty, hidden as it was in dense scrub. I said he might
eat one of the two loads now, in that case, as he told me that
he and his people were suffering from famine (he certainly
looked thin), and I also rejoiced his heart with the promise of
a donkey.

But the most unsatisfactory news he had to tell me was
that there was not an elephant in the whole country now, nor
had been since my departure. This was disappointing, as I
had planned to stay some time here, while I sent to Mthara
for more food, and to the coast for help to carry down our
ivory ; and hoped to add a little to the latter in the interval,
by hunting during the delay.

The pit in which I had planted what I had shot in this
neighbourhood on our way up was not only untouched, but
so overgrown with weeds that it was not possible for any one
to see the ground had ever been disturbed. We could not
carry its contents along now, even with the spare donkeys,
without great difficulty, although we still had sufficient food
to take us to Ukambani. Moreover, I feared the Tana River
might be impassable, and I had no objection to another month
or two in this district before proceeding coastwards. I had
therefore determined to send to Mthara as before for additional
supplies, while I remained here, at the same time sending
messengers to the coast to bring up some additional porters
to meet us at Mtiya's (across the Tana), whither we would in
the meantime transport our loads, in two journeys, after the
return of the food caravan. With this idea I had been writing
letters, for several days past, to be ready to send to the coast,
and I devoted the next day to the same duty while my men
were getting a rest.

Having completed that task, I determined to give the caravan one more day to recruit its strength before setting out on the journey to the foot of the Jambeni range—which would have to be accomplished by forced marches ("empty hands," of course) so as to economise food,—in order that I might try and shoot them some meat. I accordingly went out early, with Baithai, on the second morning after our arrival; and, luck being with me, I killed two giraffe, with one bullet each, out of a small troop I had stalked. I gave my Ndorobo friends one, and the "safari" the other, which provided abundance of meat for all hands, and made every one happy. The extra day's delay gave me time to make some additions to my batch of letters for the mail, while the goods shed was repaired, the donkey boma strengthened, and our ivory buried. The camp was full of Ndorobos, and the men were very noisy; but, though rather disagreeable, I put up with that, as I like to hear them in good spirits.

CHAPTER XVII

CAMPING AT EL BOGOI

A vexatious disablement—A drastic cure—Man-eating lions—Juma's lion story—A diary under difficulties—Predatory lions scared—Loss of pack-animals—Precautionary measures—Setting a bait—A tragic scuffle—An exciting moment—A magician's failure—Cheering prospects—A novel Excuse—The lions' den—An effectual trap—My treacherous gun—The last of the besiegers—A joyful moment—Anticipation and realisation—Methods of setting gun-traps.

WE had reached El Bogoi on 3rd June, and on the 6th Abdulla left with the bulk of the men for Mthara, a few only remaining with me, together with all the donkeys (except two or three which he had taken). I was waiting for Lesiat to bring me news as to whether any elephants could be heard of in any of the country round about, he having promised to send out messengers for the purpose of obtaining information. But hardly had the caravan left, than my right hand became inflamed and swollen and extremely painful. I had got a thorn in it one night when putting wood on my fire just before our arrival here ; and whether it was that there was anything poisonous about that particular thorn or the needle with which it was extracted, or what the cause was, I could not tell, but in a few days it became so bad that I did not know what to do with it. Thorns and scratches are such a matter of course in one's hands when hunting, that I never took any notice of them nor ever felt any ill consequences from their attentions ; in this case, however, something in the nature of blood-poisoning ensued, resulting in my having the most frightful hand, from which I suffered agonies.   I believe it was made worse by my allowing one of my men to cut into it ; but the pain was so excruciating and continuous that I was ready to try anything, and would have almost submitted to have it cut off at one time.   Thus, by another stroke of ill-luck, this originally trivial affair disabled me again for fully a month, during which I suffered greatly and was of course a prisoner in camp.   At the same time I thought myself extremely lucky not to be compelled to march while my hand was in this state.

Lesiat used to come frequently to see me, and kept me supplied with quantities of honey ; indeed he considered it his own peculiar privilege to keep my honey keg full.   He used to eye my galvanised iron buckets with admiration, and often begged me to leave one with him on my departure for the coast, together with my enamelled wash-hand basin as a cover for the same, promising that I should find it full on my next visit.   He explained that wooden utensils with skin covers were liable to be damaged by insects, and declared that one large receptacle of the kind, which he had hidden full of honey in the forest against my return, had been eaten by a hyena. One day, when I was at my worst, he brought me about a quart of the most lovely honey, like olive oil, extracted from pure, white virgin comb, telling me to drink it all like water before going to bed, with the assurance that it would do me good like medicine.   I did not feel equal to following his advice literally, though I have little doubt that the effect could not have failed to be pretty drastic ; at the same time, I hold strongly the opinion of the sage of old, exemplified as it is in the Ndorobos of to-day, that honey is " health to the bones."

Elephant news was not much use to me under these circumstances ; but I learnt that there were some on the western slopes of the Lorogis.   This information had been gained from a neighbouring community, some of whom had been with me formerly on my excursion down the Seya valley. It appeared that several of these people had been on a honey-hunting expedition in the "subugo" forests there—owing to the dryness of the season having caused a dearth on this side, while these conditions were favourable to the bees' harvest in that moister climate. But their operations were suddenly cut short by a tragedy: one of their number had been carried off and devoured by a lion, which had sprung upon the unfortunate man while he was engaged in digging out a hive from a hole in the ground, in broad daylight—so at least the affair was described to me. In consequence of this, none of these people would venture over the mountains again, although they declared that honey was in abundance there, while here, on their own side of the range, it was now so scarce.

Another disaster of the same kind occurred shortly after to a member of Lorgete's family. They had only just returned from the Gwaso Nyiro River, where they had been hunting and trapping for some time; and, not having yet heard what had happened, two or three of them went over the "subugo" to reconnoitre, with a view of camping on the far side of the range for a time. It is the habit of these natives, when starting out in the early morning, to carry two or three burning brands, drawn from the fire, in one hand; and when the air is chilly—as it always is in the "subugo" until the sun gets high—the bearer puts his fire-sticks on the ground now and then, and, blowing them up, sits cowering over the blaze, his skin cape drawn round his shoulders, to imbibe the warmth. In this position one of the party was pounced upon by the man-eater, as witnessed by his terrified companion from a little distance, and became its easy prey, just as in the case already mentioned.

It seemed a remarkable corroboration of Lesiat's dread of the lions of that part, against which he had formerly warned me when narrating his own adventures with one there in his youth. Events which transpired later seemed to show, though, that these animals were unusually daring and dangerous this year; and I believe the explanation to be that, owing to the drought, the country was exceptionally bare of grass, making game much more difficult of approach and capture by beasts of prey. The latter, unable to satisfy their wants in the ordinary way, were thus rendered desperate by hunger, and became proportionately bold and aggressive. I have observed the same thing in South Africa; there, the grass is universally burned during the winter or dry season; and it is invariably in the early spring, when all the country is devoid of cover, and before the new grass has begun to grow, that lions wander from their usual haunts in the uninhabited bush tracts, where game is their prey, into the neighbourhood of the border kraals, and make raids upon the natives' cattle. I have myself lost cattle in this way—always at that particular time of year. There, however, the depredators seldom live to continue the habit. The alarm is at once raised, and all the men from the surrounding district muster up and hunt out the intruder, whom they seldom fail to make pay the penalty of his temerity. The scattered Ndorobos, on the other hand, whether from timidity or want of cohesion, make no attempt to avenge the death of one of themselves; and, as a consequence, the lion, once having overcome his instinctive fear of man, repeats the attack whenever hunger prompts and opportunity offers.

Soon after my hand first became bad I had sent Juma with another man to follow Abdulla to Mthara, with a message about my mail. On their return he, too, had a lion story. He said that one evening when they had halted for the night on the banks of the Gwaso Nyiro, as his companion was cooking their food a lion had sprung at him, but, missing the man, had landed in the fire and upset the pot. Whether his majesty was too much disconcerted by this failure and the burning of his paws to follow up his intended victim, or whether the latter had already made good his retreat aloft, I am not clear, but at all events both the messengers returned safe and sound, arriving back on the 22nd. They declared, though, that they had always slept in trees after this scare. About a week before this I had heard a lion roaring one night not very far away, a very unusual thing here ; indeed I don't think I had ever heard one before near El Bogoi.

My hand had been in such a state that I began to fear mortification ; it was swollen out of all shape—the swelling extending up my arm and the pain into my side—and turning black ; but about this time it took a more hopeful turn, great quantities of matter were discharged from both palm and back, with corresponding abatement of pain. But it was the mere wreck of a hand, undermined about the base of the fingers with tunnels penetrating from front to back, through which daylight could be seen—an utterly useless member so far as grasping power was concerned—and the arm, now the swelling had abated, shrunken to half its natural size. During the whole of this time I wrote my diary with my left ; and so quickly can one adapt oneself to circumstances, that, whereas the first few days are hardly legible, in three weeks I had attained such proficiency as to be able to write almost as neatly as with the right, though of course not so fast.

I was in this crippled state, then, when, a few days after Juma's return from Mthara, I sent him with two or three others to collect moss in the " subugo " for stuffing donkey-pads. The distance to the top of the mountain was considerable, and as it would take some time to gather sufficient moss from the trees in the forest, they could not get back till the succeeding day ; so that I was left with only three or four men in the camp.

I slept in a shed, open at one end, behind which was the one containing our stores, and a few yards beyond that again the kraal or " boma," a circular enclosure of thorny branches, in which the donkeys (some two dozen) were shut up every night ; a little to one side were the cook's shanty and two or three huts belonging to the other men. One of my principal donkey-men and " askari," named Maftaha, who was in charge of the stores, and whose duty it was to count the donkeys every night and see them shut safely into their "boma," slept in the goods shed.

On the night in question, namely, that of 25th June, about 9.30, I had just gone to sleep when I was awakened by the sudden rush and rumble made by the troop of donkeys breaking out of the kraal and stampeding. In the "bara"[1] one acquires the habit of sleeping, as it were, with one eye (or, at all events, one ear) open, so that any alarm or commotion arouses you in an instant and you instinctively spring out of bed and seize your rifle. From bitter experience I had learnt the advisability of having mine ready to my hand, and always placed it (loaded and with cartridges in the magazine) on two upright forked sticks—driven into the ground between my bed and the tent wall—so that it lay horizontally in a position to be handily grasped at once, alongside of me. On hearing the commotion, I knew at once it must be a lion, and ran out with the rifle in my left hand. The moon, somewhat past the full, had lately risen.

Maftaha, not realising the situation, had gone out empty-handed, with the usual Swahili stupidity; and as I got round he was just going to look into the kraal, but on getting opposite the gate he started back with a cry of "Ah! Simba!" at the same moment that the lion gave a growl. The men were all gaping, no one thinking of his gun till I rated them for their idiocy. I, the while, was fumbling with my game hand at the breech of my Lee-Metford, and making a hash of trying to get a cartridge into the barrel (I had moved the bolt as I came out with the idea of making quite sure that the cartridge was in the breech all right this time; and, owing to my right hand being maimed, it had flown open and the cartridge out). I could hear a donkey kicking on the ground in the kraal, and

---

[1] This Swahili word is said to be derived from the Arabic one signifying coast. It is, however, used to denote the wild interior as distinct from the civilised maritime region, and its resemblance to the Zulu word "ibala" is at least a curious coincidence. The latter is often used in much the same sense; thus the locative form "obala" (Zulu) or "ebaleni" (Swazi) means "in the open or uninhabited country."

moaning in its death struggles ; but there was now no other
sound.   Then, just as I had managed to get my gun in order
and was going to the gate of the kraal—having motioned
Maftaha to follow me—with the intention of trying to loose off
at our enemy, the fool let drive at random into the bush from
behind a bank of weeds—fancying, I suppose, he was safe there
because he could see nothing—scaring the lions (he declared
there were two), and our chance of immediate revenge was lost.

The dead donkey (a small one) was merely killed by bites
in the throat and back of the neck, but not touched otherwise,
except for scratches in the struggle.   Had it not been for my
maimed hand I could hardly have failed to shoot a lion in the
kraal, for it was bright moonlight and the dead donkey was
plainly visible from opposite the gate.   We kept watch all
night, but the enemy returned not.   Three donkeys came back
into camp during the night, and were secured and tied to trees
among the huts.   There happened to have been two Ndorobos
sleeping in camp, so in the morning I sent one of these with
the donkey-herd to try to follow up the spoor of the frightened
pack-animals, while the other went to Lesiat's to get more help.
A few volunteers soon turned up, all wishing to assist in the
search for the lost asses.   One was found close by, slashed, but
only skin deep, with claw-marks, and three more, unhurt, were
found during the day ; yet another trio came home by themselves about sundown, but there was no news of the rest.

In the meantime it had been necessary to keep the few
men I had here hard at work making a new " boma " close to the
goods shed ; the other had been too weak, and in the shadow
of trees, with scrub right up to the back of it.   The camp was,
indeed, most villainously situated in this respect, surrounded by
thick cover, favouring the approach of predatory beasts ; but
this was unavoidable here, the whole country being one continuous jungle, and as nothing had ever happened before—
though the donkeys had been here for months in charge of only
two or three men,—no special precautions had been taken this

time to make the kraal secure. Of course, with so few hands, it was not possible to remedy this defect in one day, especially as Juma and his two men did not get back till the evening ; however, it was made as strong as could be managed under the circumstances, in the hope of keeping the donkeys in ; and, at sundown, those that had been recovered were put in and the entrance closed, as securely as could be contrived, with big thorny boughs.

I could, of course, do nothing myself but look on and encourage my men. To attempt to look for the lions would, even had I been whole, have been quite useless without dogs (even Pice had died in Kéré) in the thickets that surrounded us in every direction. Had I been able to shoot, I might have posted myself in some position whence I could watch the dead donkey all night, after securing it in some way to prevent its being dragged, so as to ensure as far as possible the lions remaining by it, should they come at all, until the moon rose, which would not be till after ten that night. Even that might not have been successful, as the night proved cloudy and dark, while the place where the kraal had been was overshadowed by trees ; but, as it was, I did not, of course, attempt anything of the kind.

We had been obliged to use all the branches of which the "boma" had been made for the new one, cutting more to add to them ; and, even working their hardest all day, my few men (including cook and all) could not construct such a fence as to make me feel much confidence that the panic-stricken donkeys could not burst through, if frightened again, formidable though the barricade of branches looked. Hence there was no time to build any barrier round the carcase, to allow of my setting a gun in the only way it can be usefully done over a kill ; and the only thing I could do to-day was to set one baited with meat in the way I always adopt with success when the depredator whose end it is wished to compass is a hyena. Having done that, I thought it best to remove the dead donkey, so that there would be a better chance of the bait proving an attraction.

There happened to be some Ndorobos from a distance at my camp, in addition to Lesiat and a number of his people ; and these strangers asked permission to eat the donkey, having no prejudices against the meat such as Lesiat's tribe professed to entertain ; so I allowed them to cut up and remove it, and I then set my gun just beyond where it had been, supposing that to be the direction from which the lions would be likely to come should they return. Not that I felt sure they would come again at all, seeing that they had been disturbed before getting even a mouthful of their victim and had not attempted to return during the night on which it had been killed, although that had occurred so early in the evening. As the event proved, they did come again ; but not past my gun at all. There were a considerable number of Ndorobos in my camp that night, and Juma and his men had returned, so we were quite a large party.

Having done all that could be done, and not expecting anything to happen, at all events for some time, as soon as it got quite dark I sat down to have my evening porridge (I could no longer dignify the meal with the name of dinner now that meat was an unknown quantity on my board, owing to my being unable to hunt). The camp was quite astir with men and natives sitting talking as usual about their fires. Hardly had I got seated, and before I could take a second spoonful, the donkeys suddenly burst out of the new " boma " ; and immediately after, amid shouts from the numerous occupants of the camp, there was the sound of one of the poor brutes being choked by our enemy, not fifty yards from my hut. I was standing just outside, rifle in hand, and all crowded round me. Aided by their judgment (their ears were better than mine, though not their eyes), I calculated the exact direction whence these ghastly sounds were issuing ; to *see* anything was out of the question, for not only was it very dark, but the scuffle was going on among some brushwood.

Though I could not grip my rifle with my right hand, I could hold it up with my left and put a finger of the damaged one on the trigger, and in this way, aiming for the sound, I fired a shot. Instantly a light-coloured animal dashed out of the scrub within a few yards of us, made visible by the light of the fire that always burned outside my hut. Those around me nearly knocked me down in their alarm, rushing back into my hut under the impression that the lion was upon us; and I confess that at the first moment of catching sight of it I thought it was one myself. But it turned behind my hut instead of coming on, and was, in fact, the donkey which the lions had dropped on my firing the shot.

At the time I supposed that the whizzing of the bullet close past had made them let go for a moment, but it proved afterwards that this shot had actually hit one of them; the donkey, moreover, was in the end recovered, and eventually got over its wounds. This by the way: I did not know then that I had done any good, though I knew I had hurt my hand; and my impression that it was to no purpose was confirmed by another donkey being caught at once, as was proved by similar sounds of a struggle coming again from close to the same spot as before. Neither shots fired by the men nor firebrands thrown had any effect, and after more struggling, panting, and groaning, the donkey was killed and then dragged farther off, amid horrible gurglings and gruntings. I concluded it was useless to attempt to do any more in the pitch dark, for, even had we succeeded in making the lions drop the present victim, another would have certainly been caught, since all the donkeys were out in the bush; better, then, let one be eaten, and endeavour to concoct a plan to make its sacrifice a means of revenge. In the meantime I finished my interrupted meal.

Lesiat rather annoyed me by talking idiotically. I fancy, though, that he was even more disappointed in me; and I must have fallen lamentably as a magician in the estimation of my Ndorobo friends on this occasion, in that my magical powers—

powers that they insist on imputing to one in spite of himself
—were unavailing to prevent the lions playing havoc with my
donkeys. Subsequently, I believe, I recovered their good
opinion, but, unfortunately, not all my donkeys. Explanations
of my inability to see in the dark were considered inadequate,
and any allusion to my crippled hand was coldly received ;
some manifestation of supernatural powers was clearly expected
of me.

But what I most objected to, and was at last constrained
to protest against, was Lesiat's wild statements about the
danger we were in, calculated as they were to increase the
uneasiness of my already frightened men. He asserted that
the lions were certain to attack us, and held out the cheering
prospect of our all being eaten eventually, one by one ; escape
would be impossible, since we should be followed up remorse-
lessly whithersoever we might attempt to retreat. At last, out
of patience with his unmanly conduct, I told him I could do
no more that night, but that I was prepared to make an effort
in the morning, and asked if he could spoor the lions by
daylight. To this he replied that he would unfailingly track
them to their hiding-place and show me where they were. No
doubt he did not expect me to ask him to fulfil this promise.
At all events, when, as soon as day had dawned, I turned
out with my rifle and sent Juma to summon him, he flatly
refused to move a step in the direction in which the carcase
had been dragged, declaring that he was going to look for the
other donkeys. His line of argument was similar to that of
a formerly well-known character among South African gold
prospectors, of whom it is told that, when asked to join in a
lion hunt in a remote part of the Transvaal bush veldt, where
the prospectors' pack-donkeys were being preyed on, he declined
on the ground that " He hadn't lost no lions." Even of
searching for the lost asses Lesiat made but a poor pretence,
he and his men returning in a short time to make a formal
declaration that none could be found, and then going their ways

to their own quarters, glad to be quit of us and our disquieting troubles.

Starting from the scene of the tragic scuffle, where the ground was marked all about with deep hoof-prints, Juma and I had not far to follow the plain groove in the laid grass indicating the track of the dragged carcase.   It led into a little " donga " or gully not a hundred yards from camp, and under a drooping bushy thorn-tree surrounded by brushwood which grew in the very bottom close under the opposite bank.   The entrance to this cavern-like lair was through a little dark opening, like the mouth of a cave, into which the carcase had been dragged.   Peering into this den, half the donkey could be discerned in the gloom, lying in the centre, its head bent under the neck.   There being no signs of the lions, we entered, and found that the whole of the hindquarters had been eaten, while the front half was still entire.   Just outside the den was a heap of rubbish, evidently scraped together, and under it was buried part of the animal's intestines.   This we threw to the vultures, in order that the only attraction left might be the half-eaten carcase inside the den.

My men worked hard all day at strengthening the " boma " still more, piling on thorny boughs all round so as to make the fence both high and wide, and, if possible, impregnable. It was even more important to prevent the donkeys getting out, than lions in ; for they were so panic-stricken that the least thing was enough to stampede them, and Maftaha declared, and I believe truly, that it was the mere scent of the lions prowling about that had caused them to break out again last night, carrying the mass of thorny branches, forming the boma, before them in their mad charge.   I meanwhile braced myself to the task of setting a gun at the entrance to the den in the gully ; for I felt that it was imperative to use every effort to compass these marauders' destruction, in spite of the difficulties I worked under owing to my crippled hand (made still sorer by handling my gun).   Fortunately I knew, from long experience, how it ought to be done ; and when, immediately after sunset, I went down to put the cartridge in and cock the gun (it was one of the porters' Snider carbines), I felt that the trap was well laid.   The place was a most suitable one for the purpose, as there was hardly another opening, and such as there were we had endeavoured to block up.   Only two donkeys turned up that day, and these we tied to trees instead of putting them in the kraal.

The camp was hushed that night ; not an Ndorobo was there, and my men were very quiet.   It was again cloudy and dark ; but nothing happened till about 3 A.M.   Then the stillness was suddenly broken by the loud explosion of the gun in the gully, followed almost simultaneously by savage growls and horrible groaning roars.   At first the outburst of angry sounds was appalling, but though the noises continued with slight pauses for a considerable time, by degrees they became fainter and the intervals longer, until at last they died away altogether.   There could be no doubt that one of the lions had shot itself ; and what made me hopeful that the result had been fatal was the fact that all the uproar proceeded evidently from one spot, and that close to where the gun had been set.   From the time when it ceased up to daybreak, the only sounds that could be heard there were occasional low grunts and the crunching of bones.   These I supposed were produced by hyenas, which had been howling about, and one of which I saw, as soon as it got light, slinking off with distended belly, but it proved otherwise.

As soon as it was fully light I went to see what had happened, followed by two or three of the men with their guns. On reaching the bank of the gully, which on our side sloped gradually (the opposite one being steep), so that I could over- look the narrow grassy space between our edge and the thicket under the tree where the gun was set, I caught sight of a lion's ear sticking up among the grass.   Though it did not move, I thought it best to make sure, so fired a shot into the spot where I calculated its owner's chest must be ; but he had long been dead. I afterwards found that my bullet would have finished him had he needed it. But, just as I was going down to him, Feruzi drew my attention to sounds, as of tearing, which could be caught proceeding from inside the den ; and, on our drawing nearer, some animal was heard breaking through the cover on the far side, and two of my men banged off (of course fruitlessly) as it scrambled up the bank. On the top was a little open space which it would have to cross, and I stood ready for a shot. It was the other lion, and it gave me a beautiful broadside shot as it cantered across the few yards of open before it reached the bush beyond. I felt I was dead on, and hoped to see it go head over heels ; but my treacherous gun played me false once more, sticking at half-cock, and to my disgust the chance of laying the two marauders side by side was lost. However, it was something to have been avenged on one, and we carried him up in triumph. The bullet had got him in the loins as he was entering the lair. He was one of the small maneless lions, a mature male, and proved very thin. The brutes were evidently rendered bold by hunger.

During the day the kraal gate was made very solid, and I thought the whole thing was now so strong that it would be impossible for the donkeys to break out or a lion to get in. Search was also made for the donkeys, and about half were found, though ten were still missing. Of course I reset and loaded the gun again. That evening, as I was lying on my bed, smoking my last pipe before going to sleep, having already been round with the men to make up a big fire of logs, which we had lighted on the far side of the kraal, the gun went off again. I jumped up and stood outside to listen, and some low, gurgling growls followed from the same spot, which sounded exactly like a lion's dying gasps, and were certainly made by no hyena. After a few prolonged groans the sounds died away, and all was still for the rest of the night, except for an occasional slight chuckle of one of the latter animals crunching the bones of last night's lion, whose carcase had been thrown out for them to eat ; and I rested with a relieved mind, confident that in the morning we should find our remaining scourge lying dead beside my trap.

And so it proved ; for, on going to see the result of the shot, there lay the other lion, dead, just inside the den, from which he had been coming out.   He had got the bullet in the head and dropped on the spot, under the gun.   This one was rather larger than the first, but of the same type ; both were full-grown males.   In skinning the last, a .303 bullet, very much knocked out of shape, was found in his upper lip.   This was the shot I had fired in the dark.   It had hit the large upper canine tooth right in the very centre of its point, smashing the tooth to atoms and indenting the nose of the bullet. The lion must have had his head on one side, holding on to the donkey, to have received the bullet in such a way.   It shows how keen he must have been, that even that could not deter him nor even spoil his appetite.   That morning the donkey which this shot had rescued was brought in.   It had some deepish claw gashes on its hindquarters, but had not yet been caught by the neck when let go.   What astonished me about this experience was the difficulty these lions had in pulling down a strong donkey, and the time it took them to kill one. I no longer wondered at zebra often getting off with scratches— I have often shot them with long scars made by lions' claws.

We could now sleep in peace once more, except for the rejoicings of hyenas, which could do us no harm, over the bones of the lions.

Lesiat and Co. looked with astonishment at seeing two lions' skins pegged out, and thought after all I must have some powerful charms.   As for my donkeys, we eventually found all but four ; they were scattered far and wide, and the last of those we recovered were not brought in till a month after. Donkeys differ from horses and cattle in this curious respect, that when lost they wander about aimlessly in any direction, not going back the way they came nor heading for some part they know, as would other animals, but becoming hopelessly lost.   On the other hand, they never stray gratuitously, and in this way are infinitely less trouble.   Indeed they are rather a nuisance from the perversity with which they persist in poking about inside the camp and getting among one's tent-ropes.

The day after the siege of our camp had thus been raised, by the death of the last of the besiegers, Abdulla returned from Mthara.   He was evidently proud of having had no casualties among his donkeys in passing through the district where lions were numerous, across the Gwaso Nyiro, and believed this immunity to be due to a charm which he possessed.   Though too polite to express his feelings in words, his self-satisfied smile was indicative of conscious superiority in this particular respect. He left again a day or two later, with the first instalment of ivory for Ukambani, where it was to be deposited at Mtiya's. It was not till some days later, though, that the men with my mail, which had been fetched from the German mission station at the coastward end of the above country, arrived.

I had, of course, had no letters or papers, nor any communication with the outside world, since I had passed through there just about a year before ; and it may be imagined how anxiously I looked forward to getting news, especially after being laid up so long with nothing to read.   It was, then, a joyful moment when I heard one of the men exclaim that the long-expected messengers with the mail were close by, and a glad sight to see Squareface come round the corner, followed by his mates, and deposit a sackful of letters and papers at my feet.   But, as often happens in such cases, the realisation does not bear out the anticipation.   After reading hard half the night, one's head, now so unaccustomed to this form of excitement, gets in a whirl, which prevents much sleep during the other half, with headache to follow next day.   Moreover, I have generally found that letters that have been waited for so long, and so much looked forward to, are to a large extent disappointing. Many friends cease to write when you are far from regular reach of post ; others write perfunctorily, as an irksome duty, and probably tell you about the weather ; some even say disagreeable things, not taking the trouble to think how unpleasant it will be to read such productions in the loneliness of the remote African wilderness.

All this has a depressing effect on a sensitive traveller, with the result that the reaction, after eager expectation, almost makes him wish he had not read these disillusioning epistles. Newspapers are, at all events, interesting ; there is nothing personal about them, though they are cold comfort to the

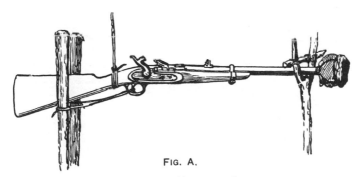

FIG. A.

BAITED TRAP FOR HYENA OR LEOPARD.

solitary exile. But there are other letters which it really does him good to read ; some have thought of the wanderer, and written so kindly, and with such evidently genuine good feeling, as to bring a grateful glow to his heart. But such are few and far between. From the rest he turns with relief, to listen once more to the familiar tongues of the never ill-natured trees, to study the rare books, and wish himself better qualified to profit by the sermons of the stones.

Fig. A represents the best method I know of for setting a gun for a hyena or leopard. This trap is baited with a piece of sinewy meat, tied firmly over the muzzle of the gun (I have used a Snider carbine for the purpose), which should all but, though not quite, pierce the centre of the bait. It is best to suspend the butt, as shown, so that it swings freely and may be pulled forward without any effort. The two posts driven into the ground, one on each side of the stock, keep it in position, and should be just far enough apart to allow of its sliding easily between them. The trigger being attached by a string to these posts, the animal, on taking the bait, and with it the muzzle, into its mouth, shoots itself neatly. A convenient way of judging the right height for the gun is to go down on hands and knees in front of it, thus impersonating the hyena. Thorny branches must be placed all round it, to prevent the animal approaching from any direction but straight in front,

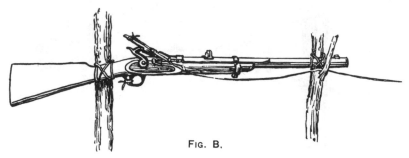

Fig. B.

LION TRAP FOR GAP IN FENCE.

and there a little path should be left, exactly opposite the muzzle, with a thorny barrier on each side. All can be made ready during the afternoon, and the cartridge slipped in and gun cocked last thing in the evening.

Fig. B shows the best way of setting a gun at an opening in a fence, as where an animal has been killed by lions and every other entrance blocked except a narrow one in front of the muzzle. The gun is securely tied to posts (or convenient small trees may often be utilised both in this and the previous method) and the trigger tied back to the guard, so that the hammer works freely up and down without cocking. A piece of light, hard wood is then cut, of the shape shown in the drawing, to support the raised hammer, its base resting beside the nipple or striker. A string from its upper arm is carried across the path, and should hang a little slack, so that when the animal's chest comes against it, the gun will not be fired until its shoulder is about opposite the muzzle. For lions, about 2 feet 3 inches is the right height from the ground for the barrel, which in both cases should be about horizontal. This latter plan of effecting the discharge of the gun is much preferable to any arrangement of levers acting on the trigger. The stick supporting the hammer must, of course, be carefully adjusted so that the trap be set "tickle." This can be tested before the insertion of the cartridge.

CHAPTER XVIII

EL BOGOI TO MOMBASA

A mountain excursion—A troublesome lion—My gun-bearer's tragic end—Three-horned giraffe—Grevy's zebra—Varieties of oryx—Suggestion for British Museum—Equatorial elephants : their size, tusks, and peculiarity—Dimensions of rhinoceros and zebra—Ndorobo conception of the Deity—A native's expectation—Description of country—Parting with Ndorobos—Skittish pack-animals—A compulsory action—Ikutha—Wakamba raiders—Wasanya hunting weapons—A long march—Entering Mombasa—A picturesque procession—Payment of carriers—Valedictory retrospect.

I HAVE not much more that can interest to relate of this journey. My hand had gradually healed ; so that, though the fingers were still stiff and interfered somewhat with my command of the trigger, I could shoot once more, if not quite up to my previous form. The return of the mail men made it possible, now that the lions were disposed of, for me to make another excursion, to fill up the interval before the return of the caravan from Ukambani should allow of our making a final start for the coast. The second visit which I now made to the western side of the Lorogis, the main purpose of which was to procure some specimens, with the chance also of obtaining a little more ivory, was even more fruitless than the former one, and need not be further alluded to were it not for a calamity which overtook us there, in the loss of my gun-bearer Squareface. Baithai, with another Ndorobo, accompanied me. He unfortunately took us somewhat out of our way on the second morning, after sleeping in the mountain forest on the summit of the range ; so that we did not reach the stream on which I meant to camp, in the open just outside the forest, till noon. My intention was to make a strong " boma " round our camp, believing that, with proper precautions, we should be able to sleep safely ; and that, as soon as an animal for bait could be killed, we might trap the lion which had caused the neighbourhood to be dreaded by the defenceless Ndorobo stragglers who sometimes wandered hither. At the same time, I did not believe that our party would be in much danger.

Unluckily, heavy rain came on (during which it is impossible to keep Africans at work), still further delaying our preparations, so that when the evening closed in, cloudy and threatening, the fence was only half built. The grass in the open country was now yellow, and about the stream a good deal of it was old and rather long. My men were camped at the foot of a single tree which grew on a little knoll, my tent being a few yards away. When the young moon went down, it became very dark and showery, and I confess I did not feel very happy, thinking about the man-eating lion and our exposed position.

There was a fire, as usual, in front of my tent, and the men had collected plenty of wood and had made several all round them, beside which they sat talking till near midnight ; but with their usual carelessness they had all gone to sleep about the same time, so that when I went outside once more, a little before one o'clock, after some fitful and uneasy sleep, all was quiet and only Baithai was still sitting up. I had just awoke from a troubled slumber and a disagreeable dream about a lion invading my camp, and felt uncomfortable. I lay down again, however, and had just gone off again into a light sleep when I was suddenly aroused by the commotion of an attack—this time, alas ! too real—from the lion we had heard so much about. Its growls — such familiar sounds to me now, the meaning of which I knew too well—were mingled with shouts and cries of alarm from the men, and the scuffling noise occasioned by its and their movements. Seizing my rifle, I rushed out; but the lion had already disappeared into the darkness. I fired a shot in the direction it had taken, as its growls had indicated, and two of the men fired off their guns immediately after; there was another growl not far off in response, and it evidently shifted farther away, for the other shots produced no reply and we heard no more of it. I knew what had happened without being told—of course it had taken one of my men; all I asked was, " Who is it?" and received the answer that Squareface had been carried off. I looked at my watch; it was 1.15.

I will not attempt to describe what my feelings were; they were the more unpleasant that I felt to blame for having exposed my men to the risk after being warned. The whole thing was ghastly, and I felt helpless. The men came to my fire, and we sat there for the rest of the night. At last the morning dawned, and I followed—Juma alone accompanying me—the horribly suggestive trail, faintly discernible along a glade in the edge of the forest; and we soon saw, by the vultures and ravens already settling, where the remains were. This was also a proof that the lion had gone. I will not give further details of the revolting sight, I could hardly bear to look at it myself. The lion had evidently been gone some time, as his track was not visible in the wet grass; he had apparently entered the forest close by, but no spoor could be seen.

Returning, we found the dejected porters anxious to be off. I felt it to be degrading to leave without any further attempt to avenge my man's death; but it was clear that the men would not stay. Nor could I ask them to sleep another night there (without which there was nothing to be done), for it was my duty to consider the safety of my living followers more than the memory of the one already dead. It was true, as they pointed out, that we had no tools with which we could make, in one day, any safe structure in which they could sleep. Juma endorsed their protest against waiting: " We shall all die, master! What can we do for him who has finished dying?

It is God's command." Such were their arguments. Could I
have seen my way to remain without risking their lives, and
have convinced them of it, I made no doubt that by staying a
few days I could compass the death of that lion and avenge
my gun-bearer's tragic end ; but the means were wanting, and
I felt constrained to yield to their importunities, for I could not
risk losing another man. My things had been already packed
during my absence, and we returned sadly to El Bogoi. I
asked Bathai that night if the lion was a big one. He spoke
no word in reply, but pointed to the trunk of a big tree.

The morning after our return to El Bogoi some Ndorobos
from a distance brought in four more of my long-lost donkeys.
They were some of my very best, too, and were rejoiced over
the more that we had despaired of ever finding them again,
and had given up the search as hopeless. They had been
found in the open country between the Seya and the Mathews
range, grazing in company with zebras, and were looking as
sleek as their late companions do and seemed almost as wild
at first. The finders were liberally rewarded. There were still
four missing, and these I never recovered ; doubtless they were
eaten by lions.

I was expecting my caravan to return again before very
long now. I could get no news of elephants in the surrounding districts, and there was not time for any lengthy excursion,
as I was anxious to be ready to start for the coast immediately
Abdulla should arrive. So I devoted myself to preparations,
and my shooting was for the purpose of obtaining skins for
lashing up loads of ivory, specimens, and meat. Among the
specimens was the head of a young bull giraffe, and the skull
and skin (entire for mounting) of a Grevy's zebra stallion.
These I took some pains to preserve and convey to Mombasa
and England with a view to presenting to the Museum, thinking they might be of interest. The former was eventually
accepted ; the other I found was not needed. I chose a not
quite fully adult giraffe for this purpose, on account of the

difficulties of transport, and even it was no slight addition to our impedimenta. However, when anything proves of value one is repaid for the trouble involved in bringing it to the coast; and this was found to be of some interest, as illustrating points of distinction between the northern and southern species. By kind permission I am enabled to reproduce the engraving of this head, from the *Proceedings of the Zoological Society of London*, and quote from Mr. W. E. de Winton's Remarks on the subject.

EXTRACTS FROM REMARKS ON THE EXISTING FORMS OF GIRAFFE

By W. E. DE WINTON, F.Z.S.

From the Proceedings of the Zoological Society of London

There seems to be some doubt among naturalists in regard to the specific relations of the Giraffes of Nubia and the adjacent countries to those of Africa south of the Equator; the almost total absence of wild-killed specimens of the northern form during the last half-century, until within the last year or two, is no doubt the reason for the nomenclature of the two species being left in a very unsettled state.

The exhibition of the skin of a Somaliland animal by Mr. Oldfield Thomas, on behalf of Messrs. Rowland Ward & Co., at a meeting of the Society on 20th February 1894, made me look into the literature on the subject. Since then the British Museum has been fortunate in augmenting the older material by heads of both species received from the actual collectors—Mr. H. A. Bryden having presented a head of the southern form brought home by Khama, killed in the North Kalahari; and Mr. Arthur H. Neumann a head of the northern form, killed a little to the east of the Lorogi Mountains and north of the Gwaso Nyiro (about 1° N. lat.); besides which, others have been acquired by purchase.

"Northern Form," Thomas, *P.Z.S.* 1894, p. 135; Matschie, *Säug. Deutsch-Ost-Afr.* p. 103 (1895).

The ground-colour varies from white to fawn; the dark polygonal markings vary from orange-red to red-chocolate, the edges being even and sharply defined; the spaces between the dark patches are generally narrower, and always far more clearly defined in aged animals than in those of a similar age in the southern species. The legs below the knees and hocks are white. The males have a third horn in the centre of the forehead just above the eyes, cylindrical, from 3 to 5 inches long ; in the young animal this position is occupied by a prominent tuft of black hairs.

Inhabits Gallaland from the Tana River northward, Somaliland, Abyssinia, Kordofan, and probably ranges right across Africa to Sene-gambia, in suitable localities, from the Equator to about 15° N.

It will be seen that with the material I have been able to collect, some dozen skins [1] and thirteen skulls of both species of all ages, I cannot give more than a general outline of colouring. The adult

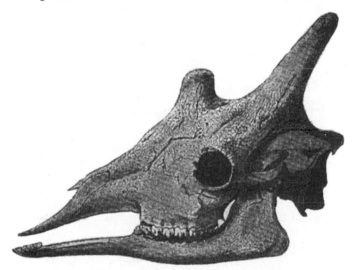

THREE-HORNED GIRAFFE SKULL (*Giraffa camelopardalis*)
(From *P.Z.S.*, February 1897.)

Southern Giraffe has the general effect of a dirty white animal covered with brown blotches, with wider light spaces between them, the lower legs mottled, and upper face grizzled. The adult Northern Giraffe has clearly defined polygonal patches, the light intervening spaces narrower, the lower legs white and upper face roan.

The horns of the northern species are longer, more massive, and slope backwards more than those of the southern species. I have never seen the two horns of equal length in either species.

Mr. Selous tells me that he has never seen a bull Giraffe with a third horn in South Africa, and Mr. Neumann says the same.

Noticing the great difference in the weight of the skulls of the two

[1] Since writing the above, Messrs. Rowland Ward & Co. have shown me about a dozen scalps and neck-skins of the southern form, and they all show the same characters, though the light intervening spaces vary in width.

sexes, I was curious to put them on the scales : taking the dried skulls of two wild-killed Abyssinian animals, I found that of the male weighed 19 lb. 8 oz., while that of the female only weighed 7 lb. 6 oz. The bones of the skull of the female are very smooth and thin ; the whole of the upper

YOUNG FEMALE GIRAFFE OF THE NORTHERN SPECIES
(*Giraffa camelopardalis*).
(From a Photograph of a Mounted Head.)

side of the skull of the male is covered with a rough superficial osseous growth, which has its centre in the three horns, gradually enveloping the whole of the upper parts of the skull, forming lumps on the supraoccipital and supraorbital bones, and covering the face to the end of the nasals and the cheeks, so that all the true bones are completely hidden.

Mr. Arthur H. Neumann—to whom I am much indebted for loan of specimens and help in working out the distribution, being well acquainted with the two forms, is perhaps the only hunter who has killed the Two-horned Giraffe both in South and East Africa, and also the Three-horned species, having formerly killed Giraffes in South Africa when they were much more plentiful than they now are, and extended farther southward— tells me that on a journey from Mombasa as far as Usoga, on the route to Uganda, none were noticed but the southern or blotched kind, and that no Giraffes were seen west of the Naivasha Valley, the route taken from Naivasha to Kavirondo being more southerly than that at present followed by caravans.   And writing to me on his recent successful hunting expedition to the northern shores of Lake Rudolf, Mr. Neumann says :—" I only observed the southern variety in the neighbourhood of the Athi or Sabaki River ; I had a good view of one a little south of that river.   The northern species I found from the Tana River northward as far as I went, namely, to the north end of Bassu (Lake Rudolph) ; I mean, of course, the kind with the defined polygonal pattern.   Whether or not there are any of this kind south of the Tana I do not know, but I feel sure that in the direction I went it is the only sort to the north of that river.   In some parts, particularly about the Gwaso Nyiro, it is very plentiful, far more so than I have ever seen the southern type anywhere.   From a little north of the Lorogi Mountains, I met with no more Giraffes until near the north end of the lake, where I noticed a few in one locality."

With regard to the possible use of this massive head, I was anxious to find out whether the horns are used in fighting.   Mr. Neumann says of the Three-horned species the nearest thing to fighting he has seen was two young males playfully butting one another with their heads ; he has seen Giraffes pressed by dogs keeping off their pursuers by kicking with their *hind feet* in rather a cowish fashion.   Mr. Selous, on the other hand, says he once witnessed the following very pathetic incident—a newly-born calf lying in the grass was seized by two Leopards, the mother Giraffe at once coming to the rescue, fought with such effect with her *fore feet* that she succeeded in driving off the Leopards, but, unfortunately, one blow aimed at the Leopard struck the calf in the back, breaking it.   On seeing this the hunter went up and put the poor little beast out of its misery.   All hunters agree that the Giraffe never uses its head in self-defence.

Grevy's zebra is now well known, so far as regards its markings, as many skins have come from Somaliland, but it strikes me that the descriptions our naturalists give of the animal itself are not altogether accurate.   As an unscientific observer, I have had great experience of this animal, and numberless opportunities of comparing it — both alive and dead—with the form of Burchell's (I think called now Grant's)[1] inhabiting the same region, the two species ranging side by side, not only in the same country, but often associating in the same herd ; and I am therefore, perhaps, qualified to judge of the outward appearance of these animals in the flesh.   Mounted specimens are of very little value as a means of estimating the size and shape of animals, unless accurate measurements have been taken of the beast when freshly killed, as a guide to the operator in the difficult process of mounting.   The skin shrinks out of all shape in drying, and when relaxed may be stretched to anything ; there is nothing more pliable and easily adaptable to any size or form, by suitable manipulation, than a slack hide.[2]

I find it stated that *Equus grevyi* is a slight, slender beast, approaching to the true or mountain zebra[3] in build.   I have never seen the latter, but have always understood that it is the smallest of the zebras.   Now Grevy's is far and away the biggest.   So far from being of slight build, it is an immensely powerful upstanding animal, at least twice the size of its small congener.   I think the measurements I give are sufficient to prove this.   It is more horse-like in its appearance and action than the smaller species, though, curiously, its cry has more resemblance to that of the ass and its ears are larger (the difference being more in width than length, though) than its neighbour's.   The hoofs illustrate the difference in type as well as anything.   Their paces are also characteristic.   The small zebras, when alarmed, start off at a short donkey canter,

---

[1] I am inclined to think, though, that it differs from that variety (the type of which came from farther south) just as Grant's does from Chapman's.

[2] I would suggest that travellers should take careful measurements of rare animals, whose skins they intend to bring home for the purpose of being mounted, immediately after death.   Without such aid it is impossible, even for such a skilful and artistic naturalist as Mr. Rowland Ward, to produce a life-like image—true to nature in every proportion—in the case of animals unrepresented in the Zoo.

[3] (Never found, I believe, anywhere except in the extreme southern end of the continent.)

the legs appearing to be kept very upright, and unless hard
pressed do not "lay themselves out" at all. Grevy's starts
off at a trot, with free, high action, and its movements recall
those of the horse rather than the ass. Its head is held
high, too, while the other keeps a more horizontal position
of the neck. I have read that the trot is an acquired pace,
peculiar to the domestic horse and not natural to it in its
wild state. If so, the paces of Grevy's zebra correspond more
with our civilised horses' than can those of their nearer wild
relatives'.

I have often been asked, when mentioning the fact that

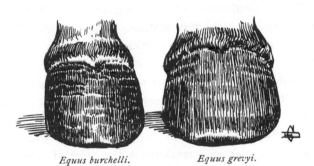

Equus burchelli.   *Equus grevyi.*

ZEBRA HOOFS.

the two kinds of zebra are frequently found consorting
together (it being especially common to see a single stallion
grevyi in a troop of the smaller species), whether they do not
cross breed. In reply to this question I say, certainly never.
Wild animals of distinct species do not interbreed in a state of
nature—unless, perhaps, very rarely, under quite exceptional
circumstances; and then, probably, only owing to artificial
causes, such as one kind being almost wholly exterminated by
man. Even in the few recorded cases, the hybrid animals are
often doubtfully so, and may be erroneously called by that
name. I do not believe the females allow any such intercourse.
That they graze together is nothing extraordinary; many
totally different kinds of herbivorous creatures are in the habit

of feeding in company harmoniously ; indeed, they have a
particular predilection for such companionship—it tends to the
common safety. Thus, giraffe, zebra, antelopes, and even
rhinoceroses, may sometimes be seen in close proximity, and
(with, perhaps, the exception of the last) clearly do so from
choice, with the object of getting warning from each other of
approaching danger ; and—apart from carnivora—wild animals
seldom or never resent the mingling of those of other varieties
with their herds. But I fancy that, in most cases where a
single Grevy's stallion is noticed in company with zebra of the
other kind, the latter are all males. Like all such polygamous
beasts, the weaker males consort together in separate herds,
turned out by the strongest stallions from among the mares.
The large male grevyi whose skin I brought to England,
and which I had shot among a troop of the small zebra, had
his neck all scarred with recent wounds, evidently inflicted by
the teeth of a rival, just as horses or donkeys bite each other
in fighting.

Another animal on which it may be worth while to take
the opportunity of here remarking is the oryx of these regions.
I had always regarded it as the ordinary " beisa," but Messrs.
Rowland Ward have pointed out to me that the specimens
which I brought home resembled in some respects " callotis,"
though having no sign of a tassel to the ears. The ears seem
somewhat more pointed than those of the Somaliland oryx,
the stripe on the cheeks is more defined and descends lower—
in some cases meeting the dark patch on the throat,[1]—and the
animal itself is considerably larger than the typical " beisa,"
albeit resembling the latter in the shade of its general colouring.
Thus this may be an intermediate form, differing slightly
from both these accepted species, just as we find a gradation
of varieties of the smaller zebras from South to North Africa.
It would not surprise me to find that the " topi " of Bassu

---

[1] There is a certain amount of variation among individuals as to the throat-markings.
In one specimen which I have, the dark line down the dewlap is absent altogether.

occupied a similar position in reference to that of the east coast and the western Senegalensis or " korrigum."

I am convinced that our good friends of the Museum need very much more extensive series of specimens to enable them to judge of the limits and relations of species. Single individuals are not much to go upon, they differ among themselves to a certain extent in the same locality (I am speaking now not of any particular species), and age is a factor that has to be taken into account, immature specimens being often very misleading. If I may venture to say so (though it is not without fear and trembling that I hazard any suggestion), I think it would be an immense enhancement of the instructiveness of our national collection if more specimens of the most interesting varieties of allied species were exhibited in the public galleries. It is true that the authorities are most courteous and obliging in showing any particular specimens to an inquirer; but, when they are stowed away in private rooms, it prevents any group being examined as a whole, by any one who wishes to study it at leisure without giving trouble. The idea that only representative specimens should be exhibited in the cases is, I think, a mistake ; the display should, I maintain, be made as comprehensive as possible, otherwise the collection can only be, generally speaking, for the benefit of a few savants.

A few of the conclusions which my experience of the elephant of Equatorial Africa has led me to may be worth recording. First, as to size. I believe that in the regions where I have been hunting he attains his greatest dimensions, both as to bodily bulk and weight of ivory. That renowned South African hunter and most careful observer, Mr. F. C. Selous, puts the average height of full-grown bulls at from ten feet to ten feet six inches. I will give the measurements of some I have measured myself, which, while among the largest I have killed, were not, as far as I know, in any sense exceptional, among fully matured bull elephants of these regions, nor even, perhaps, the biggest I shot. At the same time, there are undoubtedly larger specimens, as there are smaller ; for the individuals often vary a good deal among themselves. I would premise that to take very accurate measurements of the height of a dead elephant, lying on its side, is not altogether easy. Its feet are of enormous weight, and, with only two or three hands to help, it is by no means easy to keep the knee-joint straight. I can only say that I have striven to be as exact as possible, and aimed rather at being under the mark, and err, if at all, on the safe side, than to exaggerate.

Bull Elephant.	Height at Shoulder, in Straight Line.	Length from Root of Tail to Eye, in Straight Line.	Girth of Forearm below Elbow.	Circumference of Forefoot.	Long Diameter of Hind Foot.	Girth of Thickest Tusk just outside Lip.
Shot at El Bogoi (foot of Lorogi Mts.), 30th Sept. 1894	10 ft. 3 or 9 in. (at least)	12 ft. 6 in.	4 ft. 6 in.	4 ft. 8½ in.	1 ft. 9 in.	1 ft. 6½ in.
Shot at Bumi (Lake Rudolph), 29th Dec. 1895	10 ft. 5 in. ,,	12 ft. 6 in.	...	4 ft. 8½ in.	...	1 ft. 6 in.
Do. do.	10 ft. 9 in. ,,	12 ft. 8 or 9 in.	...	5 ft.	1 ft. 10 in.	1 ft. 9¼ in.
Shot at Janjai (near Kenia), 13th May 1894	10 ft. 6 in. ,,	...	...	...	...	...

These measurements are copied out of my note-book just as entered on the spot where they were taken. The three first were old bulls of the type found, as a rule, in separate herds. The last was a "herd bull" or breeding male.

I have already given the weights of several of my heaviest pairs of tusks. Those of the big bulls of the exclusive age (that is, old fellows who do not consort with cows) may be expected to weigh on the average about 70 lbs. or 80 lbs. apiece—say from 60 lbs. to 90 lbs.—while " herd-bulls' " teeth scale about 50 lbs. generally. Good cow teeth vary from 12 lbs. to 24 lbs. apiece. My heaviest pair of the latter weigh 36 lbs. each, but these are quite exceptionally large. The heaviest bull tusk I have weighs 116 lbs., and I got several elephants with tusks of about a hundredweight apiece. The

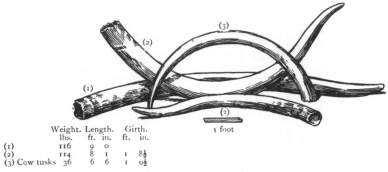

	Weight. lbs.	Length. ft. in.	Girth. ft. in.	1 foot
(1)	116	9 0		
(2)	114	8 1	1 8½	
(3) Cow tusks	36	6 6	1 0½	

MY LARGE ELEPHANT TUSKS.

amount lost in drying varies very much ; the one just mentioned lost only 1 lb., while another I have, which originally weighed nearly as much, lost 7 lbs. The ivory of very old elephants, I believe, loses less than that of younger animals, but I have found that, as a rule, the difference between fresh and dry only amounts to 2 or 3 lbs., even on a large tooth, in the country I write of.

Thus it appears that the elephants of the central part of the continent exceed those of both the northern and southern portions—judging from what one reads and hears—alike in stature and size of tusks.[1] I may add that I have never yet

---

[1] The heaviest tusks known of seem to have come from East Equatorial Africa—*e.g.* Sir Edmund Loder's record one of 184 lbs., measuring 9 ft. 5 in. along the curve (and I almost think an even more ponderous specimen was once brought to Zanzibar, though sawn in two pieces), and one of 165 lbs. which was presented to the Duke of York by the officials of British East Africa.

seen a tuskless elephant of either sex, and I doubt if there are any where I have hunted.

Another feature which I have noticed, as characteristic of the elephants of these equatorial regions (at all events, on the eastern side of Africa), and in which they seem to differ somewhat from those of farther north (I do not know whether the

THE BIG TUSK (8 FT. 7½ IN., 165 LBS.) PRESENTED BY THE OFFICERS SERVING IN BRITISH EAST AFRICA TO H.R.H. THE DUKE OF YORK ON THE OCCASION OF HIS MARRIAGE.

(From a Photograph by Mr. J. R. W. PIGOTT.)

same applies to the southern representatives or not), is the ear. I have been much struck with this difference when conferring with Mr. Caldwell (the artist who has drawn many of my elephant pictures with such painstaking care) on the subject of illustrations for this book ; and from my descriptions and measurements, in the illustration on page 97, he has succeeded most faithfully in showing this peculiarity. I mean the shape of the upper part of the ear. It will be seen that this curls over backwards in a curve or arch at the top, and hangs behind as a loose flap. Now the elephant in the Zoo (which, I am told, came from North Africa)—and it is, I fancy, from this or former occupants of those stables that most of the illustrations in books are modelled—I say, this familiar representative of elephantine Africa has ears lying on the top of its neck, with a small, flat crease turned over *outwards*, as if ironed like a collar, on to the front or inside surface. I have never shot an elephant with ears like that; and I was so much impressed with the difference that I asked the keeper (to whom I am indebted for much interesting information about the animals in his care) whether anything was done to these, but he replied in the negative. The following dimensions of the ear of one of the bulls I shot will exemplify what I have been saying :—

Depth of ear from tip to top of curl . . . 4 ft. 6 in.
Depth of ear from tip to extreme end of flap . . 5 ft. 3½ in.

It will be seen from this measurement that there are 9½ inches of flap hanging over behind, from the top of the curl. This never lies on the neck as in the Zoo specimen, but hangs loosely between the back of the ear and the neck.

While on the subject of measurements, I will give those I made of rhinoceroses and zebras. The dimensions given of the former animals illustrate the smaller size of the local variety found on the east of Rudolph, while those of the zebras show the great contrast between *E. grevyi* and the form of *Burchelli* (perhaps *Granti*) found in the same region. It will also be noticed that the difference in size between the male and female rhinoceros is much more marked in length than in height, the male being longer in proportion to his height than the female in both varieties. These measurements were all carefully taken, and entered on the spot in my notebook.

Rhinoceros bicornis.		Total Length without Tail, in Straight Line.	Height at Shoulder, in Straight Line.
Common kind.	Bull shot at El Gereh (Lower Seya), under Mathews Range (7th Sept. 1895)	10 ft.	5 ft. 3 in.
	Cow shot under Mount Nyiro (26th May 1896)	8 ft. 8 in.	4 ft. 10 in.
Small variety.	Bull shot on eastern shore of Bassu (Lake Rudolph), near northern end (21st Dec. 1895)	9 ft.	4 ft. 9 in.
	Cow shot in same locality as above (24th Dec. 1895)	8 ft. 3 in.	4 ft. 7 in.

All the above were old animals.

Zebra.		Height at Withers, in Straight Line.	Length from between Ears to Root of Tail, in Straight Line.	Girth behind Shoulder.
Grevyi.	Stallion shot near R. Seya (7th August 1894)	4 ft. 11 in. (full).	6 ft. 8 in.	5 ft. 9½ in.
	Stallion shot near Mount Nyiro (17th Nov. 1895)	4 ft. 10 in.	...	...
	Stallion shot near R. Seya (27th July 1896)	4 ft. 9½ in.	...	5 ft. 6 in.
	Mare shot near R. Seya (26th July 1896)	4 ft. 5 in.	...	...
Granti (?) = local form of Burchelli.	Stallion shot near R. Seya (26th July 1896)	3 ft. 11 in.	...	...
	Stallion shot at western foot of Lorogi Mountains (16th Oct. 1896)	3 ft. 11 in.	5 ft. 7 in.	4 ft. 10 in.

All these were adult animals.

Before closing my account of this district, I should like to say a word or two more about the Ndorobo people. Were I a missionary, these are the natives I would choose to labour among. Not that I wish to advocate their being taken up, because our missionary methods tend, too often, to spoil interesting and unsophisticated African races. However, I think there is not much fear of this particular tribe being exploited by us in that way—there would not be enough to show for it.

To my own sympathy the Ndorobo ideas of the deity strongly appeal in their simplicity. In contrast with the natives of Southern Africa, who cannot be said to have any notion of a Supreme Being, these have a distinct belief in God, and ascribe all events to His ordering. Asked what they know of Him, they told me: "We only know that He made all things. If it rains, we say it is God; when the wind blows, we say here, too, is God; and when the white man comes, we say this again is God's doing." Thus:

> "The feeble hands and helpless
> Groping blindly in the darkness
> Touch God's right hand in that darkness."

When parting with my old friend Lesiat—in giving him, amongst other things, a rug off my bed, which I had promised him, when passing on my outward journey, should be his on my return,—I asked him if he would not let one of his sons accompany me to the coast; telling him that he would be able to learn much, and bring back wonderful accounts of all the marvels he would see, as well as many nice things. He replied that, if he were to give me a boy to go with me, he would expect me to show him the path to heaven, that he might see God and learn from Him how to put a new heart into his father!

This striking statement made a great impression on me at first, and I strove (through my interpreter, of course) to elicit some more precise explanation of his meaning. I regret to have to say that any idea of attaching a spiritual signification to his words was at once dispelled by Lesiat's avowal that he spoke solely of his carnal heart. He simply meant to say that he wished to be brought to life again if he should die. He said, too, that their sons were too useful in searching for wild honey, to be spared.

Notwithstanding the upsetting of the theory that this pretty little speech was a romantic appeal for religious instruction, Lesiat declared, in reply to my queries, that they would welcome a European to live among them, and that the women and children would come to be taught. There certainly seems an opening for useful work among such raw material. If only they could be induced to cultivate the rich soil at the foot of their mountains, where rain is frequent, the Ndorobos of Lorogi might always have abundance. But I fear me, when taught settled ways of living, they would lose their picturesqueness, and miss the romantic wild life as the forest Indians of Brazil and their little peccaries—reclaimed by the old Jesuit father— missed the shade of the primeval woods.

I am not one to give an optimistic picture of this or any other district in Equatorial Africa. There are suitable spots here and there at the foot of the Lorogis for stations, where brooks issue from the mountain—soon to sink into the earth, like all streams in this country, but sufficient to irrigate a little of the adjacent rich soil,—and the climate is not a bad one. At the western foot the country is more attractive, though the soil is less fertile ; and water is there more abundant, while the mountain forest (not like an African forest at all) is at hand with useful timber. But all such favoured spots are exceptional in Equatorial Africa—as I know it,—like islands in the desert; there is no extent of useful country. The streams will not flow any distance ; their waters evaporate or become absorbed by the soil. From the Jambeni range and Kenia northward, as far as Bassu and beyond, none of the drainage water ever reaches the ocean—at all events, above ground,—and such rivers as have a longer course flow for the most part through barren and unfruitful lands.

We travellers and pioneers are too fond of giving glowing descriptions of new lands—very lands of promise as they are often represented to be, with every possible advantage and beauty.   Probably the country has been seen after rains, when looking its best.   One is apt, too, to be captivated the more readily with any verdant belt, by contrast to the parched monotony which is the rule ; for even the most unpromising and arid scrub becomes beautiful and attractive after heavy rains.   Anyway, I have noticed that the newest district is praised invariably as the one most desirable spot on earth ; but no sooner is it annexed or occupied, and become familiar, than its ideal perfection vanishes, its drawbacks and disadvantages are then what are heard most of.   Perhaps this part of the continent has more than its share of waterless waste.   Some lovely bits of country there are, it is true.   But of how limited extent !   Moreover, as a rule, where well-watered, fertile, and healthy lands exist, they are densely populated already by natives, so that there is no room for colonists.   What Africa lacks are ranges of snow mountains to feed perennial rivers, such as would afford unfailing supplies of water for irrigation. With moisture, even the wilderness may blossom as the rose.

It was with much regret, and the hope of seeing them again some day, that I parted with these pleasant Ndorobo people.   Lesiat and other friends gave me abundance of honey for the journey, and invoked God's blessing upon us with pathetic earnestness.   I have not a doubt that he is hoarding honey for me now.

On our way down we found the country drier than I had ever seen it ; no running water where we crossed the Seya, and none between there and the Gwaso Nyiro.   Our donkeys —many of them half-wild Turkana asses—were restless and easily scared, and most troublesome during this part of the journey.   No doubt the terror of the lion attacks had upset them.   Sometimes they would stampede after game we passed near on the march, causing long delay and hard work before they could be turned and brought back.

Mnyamiri, who had preceded us, had, I afterwards learned, lost several of his altogether, which had followed a rhino that crossed their path.   He was so unfortunate, too, as to get all but one of the remainder drowned in the Tana, when attempting to follow my plan of pulling them through the rapids with a rope.   We lost none, but ours gave us little rest when bivouacking in the open, where there was no water and where we could build no boma.   They were constantly stampeding through the camp in the night, through taking false alarm. Then they would come and smell out my little store of precious water, and upset it, and even eat my allowance of coarse cake for my morning meal if left on the table.   But, thanks to our knowledge of the country, we never suffered, to speak of, even this exceptionally dry season, for lack of water.   Our march was uneventful and free from any misfortunes, or even inconveniences except of a trivial character.

One afternoon, when passing round the end of the Jambeni range, and within a few hours of the first stream on the Tana side, I was reluctantly compelled to shoot two rhinos within half an hour, for which we had no use.   It caused me real pangs of sympathy to take their lives thus ; but each was so close to our path that there was great risk of their causing a stampede of my skittish donkeys, as well as among the porters, though little actual danger to ourselves.   For the wind was from them to us, and, unless warned by scent, these blind creatures are too stupid to get out of the way until the caravan is right upon them, when they are likely to cause a scare. Abdulla had experienced such a one on his journey with the first batch of ivory from El Bogoi, with the result that many tusks were thrown down on the stones and several more or less damaged ; Mnyamiri, too, had lost some of his donkeys from the same cause.   The .303 bullet was as deadly in the case of these two as I have always found it; for these animals especially it seems almost infallible. One sufficed for each. Luckily we met a party of Wakamba just after, to whom the meat was a windfall. They were evidently hungry, as they had just been rescuing from the vultures some zebra bones left by lions ; so the rhinos were not wasted.

In passing through the Tana bush I saw very few " fly " (tetse) this time (end of August), and in consequence lost only three donkeys on the journey down. From that time on to November or December is the safest to travel with animals through " fly " country, when it is barest. All the rest of mine reached Mombasa in splendid condition and perfect health. It always pays to give special attention to one's animals ; and whether trek oxen in South Africa or pack-donkeys in Equatorial Africa, I have ever devoted much care to mine and been repaid by their keeping fat and fit.

We crossed the river without mishap—this time the impassable channel by a bridge—and, meeting fresh men from the coast at Mtiya's with my messengers, were able to continue our way with the whole of our effects from there. At the little German mission station of Ikutha—the first outpost of civilisation reached—though my kind old friend, Mr. Sauberlich, had gone to Europe for a well-earned holiday, I met with a not less hospitable reception from his successors, Mr. and Mrs. Hoffman, than he had always given me, and the most obliging and valuable assistance in obtaining supplies to last us to the coast. I could not take the direct route through the desert from the Athi to join the Uganda road at Samburu, near the coast, as the water had all dried up ; but, having travelled in former years all along that river, I knew that, by following it farther down, I should get a path with water every day to Mombasa, though a little longer ; and it is well worth while going several days round, rather than risk suffering from thirst, and possible disaster, with a heavy caravan.

In following this river route—one little used—down the

Athi (or Sabaki, as it is more commonly called in its lower course), I met with two instances of the predatory tendencies of the Wakamba, even so near the coast.   One day a party of Giriama natives, returning from Machakos, where they had been on a little trading expedition of their own, with nine goats which they had bought (as was testified by the pass they bore, signed by the officer in charge of that station on the main road to Uganda), caught me up.   They had fallen in with some Wakamba, who were nominally hunting, but appear to have been in reality highwaymen.   These attacked them in the night and carried off their goats, wounding one of the owners as they fled into the scrub.   A lad, son of one of the latter, disappeared in the confusion, and though his companions sought him for a whole day, after the marauders had retired with their booty, he could not be found, and had to be left to his fate, to die miserably of thirst in the bush.   Once thoroughly lost in this flat scrub-covered desert, there would be little chance of a scared child ever finding his way back to the river, in a country strange to him.   For, as already observed, natives take no account of the points of the compass, nor observe the position of sun or moon in laying their course through the bush, but go by what they know of the lie of the land, or can remember as to the character of the trees, ground, etc.

   The second raid that came to my knowledge was made on a village or kraal of Wasanya.   These people are a tribe of degraded Galas, who live mainly by hunting.   They occupy the same position in relation to the stock-owning Galas as the Ndorobos do towards the Masai.   Two or three of them came into my camp one day, and told me that some Wakamba had lately attacked their kraal and carried off two women captive. This account was confirmed independently by a woman of the same tribe, whom I saw afterwards at the first Giriama village we reached.

   The Wasanya are remarkable for carrying immensely powerful bows, and most serviceable-looking arrows.   These weapons contrast strikingly with the short light bows and arrows used by most Central African natives.   It must require great force to draw one of these formidable engines properly ; and one can well understand that those skilled in their use, with the additional aid of poison on the missile, may kill—as they say they do—both elephants and rhinoceroses without much difficulty.   That both these animals frequent the river, especially during periods of drought, I had evidence in their tracks.   Once I came upon quite fresh elephant spoor ; but as it was only of cows and calves I did not follow it.   I might have done so, on the chance of finding a young bull or a cow worth shooting, but that I was lame at the time from my ankle (which had been sprained in my encounter with the elephant) having got worse again.

As proof of how thoroughly inured to carrying their tusks my men had become, I may instance the march we made the day we left the river, when the distance to the first water was considerable.   The entry for that day (26th September) runs as follows in my diary :—" Got up at 2 A.M. and started at 3.15.   After four hours' going waited for the ' safari,' but the men would not stop and we went on for another hour before resting, having thus done five hours' solid marching without a halt.   Then, after a fifteen minutes' spell, did three hours more ; rested half an hour and on to camp, which the caravan reached at 1.45.   Thus we did close on ten hours' clear marching, the greater part of the way through dense bush, the narrow path often a good deal overhung."

At last, on 1st October, we once more entered Mombasa ; and the men—decked in showy clothes, and headed by drummers hammering out, in perfect time, the regular " safari " beat—enjoyed the long-looked-forward-to parade through the streets.   And a picturesque sight it is to see a string of porters, with gleaming ivory arcs on their shoulders, threading slowly the narrow streets, thronged with dusky but cleanly-clad onlookers ; the leading men jumping up and dancing about with their hundred-weight tusks, to show off before their admiring female friends.   Indeed, it is often difficult to get them along at all, so proud and excited are they at entering their metropolis again after all the adventures of so long a journey ; and custom allows the " kilangozi " (or leading porter) to refuse to move until backsheesh of rupees has been sent to entice him to proceed with the caravan to deposit their loads at the custom-house.   That done, I give each man a rupee by way of " posho " for the day, and they disperse to make merry among their friends in the town.   A weighty bag

MOMBASA.
(From a Photograph by Major ERIC SMITH.)

of silver has to be ready for them when they reassemble at my quarters the following morning to receive their pay.   Careless, confiding fellows these porters ; they make no attempt to calculate how much is due to them nor ever think of counting over what they receive.   The one whose name is called holds out the corner of his cloth for the double handful of rupees, twists it up without a word, and off he goes — in most instances to squander recklessly the reward of a year or more's service.

I had no deductions to make from my men's wages, except for the advances they had before starting on the expedition ;

for I had felt that the least I could do in gratitude for their good behaviour and kindness during my illness was to give them such cloth as they required without—as is customary—entering it against them. Any extra presents, too, were much better appreciated in that form, given up country where little additions to their fare could be obtained by these means ; and though in particular cases one felt it a duty to add something to the amount actually due, as an acknowledgment of special services, the conviction that such liberality is thrown away destroys the pleasure of bestowing rewards of the kind, and I think to do so is really a mistake, and, so far from being valued, tends to lower one in the opinion of the average Swahili.

The time to give is when they have nothing : then they are capable of gratitude ; but ten, twenty, or fifty rupees more or less when their hands are already full of more than they can eat in the next week, they are incapable of feeling any concern about. Probably in a month the money will all be gone—a month of luxury and licence, as they know it : then one rupee will be thankfully received. By that time or a little later most of them will be ready to "write on" again for another expedition. One gets fond of one's men, and proud of them when they are good ones, as mine were ; and I was sorry not to be able to engage them again before they had drifted into other service.

I fear the fact that my journey was attended with so few serious difficulties or privations detracts from its interest to others ; but it is a source of considerable satisfaction to me to think that my men never suffered from either hunger, thirst, or disease ; that they got their regular ration daily, without our having ever raided or taken anything from the natives by force ; that they carried their loads willingly, cheerfully, and without suffering ; and that, with the exception of the two whose tragic loss I had to mourn, I brought them all back, safe, sound, and happy, to Mombasa. They on their part had

been as good as gold to me while I was ill, and I feel the
greatest gratitude to them for their kindly feeling towards me.
I tried to treat them as well as I could, and they amply repaid
me, and would, I know, follow me anywhere to-morrow.   I
only wish I could entertain the same confidence in regard to
my enduring reader!

APPENDIX

A LIST OF THE LEPIDOPTERA COLLECTED BY MR. ARTHUR H. NEUMANN

By EMILY MARY SHARPE

THE following is a list of the butterflies collected by Mr. Arthur H. Neumann on his journey to Lake Rudolph. They were collected in the country between Mombasa and the north end of Lake Rudolph, but the greater part were obtained around Mount Kenia, the Jambeni range, and the Lorogi Mountains, during the years 1894, 1895, and 1896.

Mr. Neumann was successful in getting three new species of butterflies belonging to the genera *Mylothris*, *Catachrysops*, and *Mycalesis*. The latter was first procured by Mr. F. J. Jackson in Kikuyu and Kavirondo, and Mr. Neumann has been kind enough to give a figure of it. A coloured plate of these species is given at p. 66.

FAMILY DANAIDÆ.

Tirumala petiverana.
  Danais petiverana (Doubl. and Hewits.), Kirby, *Synonymic Catalogue of Diurnal Lepidoptera*, p. 4 (1871).
Limnas klugii.
  Limnas klugii, Butler, *P.Z.S.* 1885, p. 758.
Limnas dorippus.
  Danais dorippus (Klug.), Kirby, *op. cit.* p. 7 (1871).
Amauris ochlea.
  Amauris ochlea (Boisd.), Kirby, *op. cit.* p. 8 (1871).
Amauris dominicanus.
  Amauris dominicanus, Trimen, *South African Butterflies*, vol. i. p. 61 (1887).

FAMILY SATYRIDÆ.

Melanitis solandra.

Melanitis solandra (Fabr.), Kirby, *op. cit.* p. 44 (1871).

Gnophodes parmeno.

Gnophodes parmeno (Doubl. and Hewits.), Kirby, *op. cit.* p. 43 (1871).

Mycalesis dentata, sp. n.   (Figs. 4, 4*a*, 5 on plate, p. 66.)

Both wings entirely dark brown on the upper side; a dull ochreous patch near the apical portion of the fore-wing, but not very distinct; two submarginal lines, one light brown and the second much darker, strongly marked on the hind-wing. The hind margin of both wings very much dentated, approaching *M. suassurri*, Dewitz, in appearance.

Under side : basal area very dark brown, ending in a wavy line which extends from the costa to the inner margin of the hind-wing, above the discoidal cell; the marginal border lighter in tint, suffused with ochreous yellow; a slightly sinuated line traversing the submarginal border, and a larger patch of the same colour near the apex.   Three distinct white-pupilled black ocelli, with a yellow iris encircled with dark brown, the outer portion again encircled with a violaceous gloss.   Of the ocelli near the apex, the lower one is very minute, the third being large and between the first and third median nervules.

Hind-wing very similar to the fore-wing, but with no ochreous shading.   A complete submarginal row of ocelli from the costal margin to the submedian nervure, varying in size, the smallest being between the second and third median nervules.   All these ocelli have the yellow iris surrounded with brown and a violaceous gloss as in the fore-wing; there is an additional ocellus, very minute on the inner margin, just above the anal angle.

Hab. ♂ Kavirondo.   Nov.–Dec. 1889.   Expanse, 1.7 inch.

The female is very similar to the male, somewhat larger, and paler in colour.   The ochreous-yellow apical patch on the under side is rather larger and a little deeper in colour (only one ocellus being visible near the apex), and has a minute spot above and below.   The submarginal row of ocelli on the hind-wing are not quite so large, and the two between the second and third median nervules and the discoidal nervule are almost obsolete.

Hab. ♀ Kikuyu.   Aug.–Sept. 1889.   Expanse, 1.9 inch.

Types in Coll. F. J. Jackson.

(My specimen was obtained in Embe on the Jambeni range. —A. H. N.)

Mycalesis caffra.

Mycalesis caffra, Wallgr., Kirby, *op. cit.* p. 88 (1871).

Mycalesis perspicua.
  Mycalesis perspicua (Trimen), Kirby, *op. cit.* Suppl. p. 707 (1877).
Neocænyra duplex.
  Neocænyra duplex, Butler, *P.Z.S.* 1894, p. 560, pl. xxxvi. fig. 1.
Neocænyra gregorii.
  Neocænyra gregorii, Butler, *P.Z.S.* 1894, p. 560, pl. xxxvi. fig. 2.
Ypthima asterope.
  Ypthima asterope (Klug.), Kirby, *op. cit.* p. 94 (1871).

FAMILY ACRÆIDÆ.
Acræa natalica.
  Acræa natalica, Boisd., Kirby, *op. cit.* p. 132 (1871).
Acræa neobule.
  Acræa neobule, Doubl. and Hewits., Kirby, *op. cit.* p. 130 (1871).
Acræa pudorina.
  Acræa pudorina, Staudinger, *Exot. Schmett.* p. 84, pl. 33 (1888).
Acræa bræsia.
  Acræa bræsia, Godman, *P.Z.S.* 1885, p. 538.
Acræa doubledayi.
  Acræa doubledayi, Guér., Kirby, *op. cit.* p. 131 (1871).
Acræa anemosa.
  Acræa anemosa, Hewits., Kirby, *op. cit.* p. 132 (1871).
Acræa cæcilia.
  Acræa cæcilia (Fabr.), Kirby, *op. cit.* p. 131 (1871).
Acræa mirabilis.
  Acræa mirabilis, Butler, *P.Z.S.* 1886, p. 760.
Acræa serena.
  Acræa serena (Fabr.), Kirby, *op. cit.* p. 132 (1877).
Acræa cabira.
  Acræa cabira, Hopff., Kirby, *op. cit.* p. 132 (1871).
Planema johnstoni.
  Planema johnstoni (Godman, *P.Z.S.* 1885, p. 537).
Planema monteironis.
  Acræa monteironis (Butler), Kirby, *op. cit.* Suppl. p. 719 (1877).
Planema montana.
  Planema montana, Butler, *P.Z.S.* 1888, p. 91.
Pardopsis punctatissima.
  Acræa punctatissima, Boisd., Kirby, *op. cit.* p. 132 (1871).

FAMILY NYMPHALIDÆ.

Lachnoptera ayresii.
    Lachnoptera ayresii, Trimen, *South African Butterflies*, vol. i. p. 196,
        pl. iii. fig. 5 (1887).
Atella phalantha.
    Atella phalantha (Drury), Kirby, *op. cit.* p. 154 (1871).
Atella columbina.
    Atella columbina (Cram.), Kirby, *op. cit.* p. 154 (1871).
Argynnis hanningtoni.
    Argynnis hanningtoni, Elwes, *Trans. Ent. Soc.* 1889, p. 558.
Pyrameis abyssinica.
    Pyrameis abyssinica, Feld., Kirby, *op. cit.* p. 185 (1871).
Pyrameis cardui.
    Pyrameis cardui (Linn.), Kirby, *op. cit.* p. 185 (1871).
Eurema commixta.
    Eurema commixta, Butler, *Ann. and Mag. Nat. Hist.* (5), vol. v. p.
        363 (1880).
Junonia cebrene.
    Junonia cebrene, Trimen, *t.c.* vol. i. p. 210 (1887).
Junonia clelia.
    Junonia clelia (Cram.), Kirby, *op. cit.* p. 187 (1871).
Junonia boöpis.
    Junonia boöpis, Trimen, *t.c.* vol. i. p. 217, pl. iv. fig. 2 (1887).
Precis gregorii.
    Precis gregorii, Butler, *P.Z.S.* 1895, p. 726, pl. xlii. figs. 7, 8.
Precis micromera.
    Junonia micromera, Butler, *Ann. and Mag. Nat. Hist.* (4), vol.
        xviii. p. 482 (1876).
Precis aurorina.
    Junonia aurorina, Butler, *P.Z.S.* 1893, p. 651, pl. lx. fig. 3.
Precis pelasgis.
    Precis pelasgis (Godt.), Kirby, *op. cit.* p. 190 (1871).
Precis elgiva.
    Precis elgiva (Hewits.), Kirby, *op. cit.* p. 189 (1871).
Precis natalica.
    Precis natalica, Feld., Kirby, *op. cit.* p. 190 (1871).
Precis amestris.
    Precis amestris (Drury), Kirby, *op. cit.* p. 189 (1871).
Precis sesamus.
    Precis sesamus, Trimen, *t.c.* vol. i. p. 231, pl. iv. fig. 3 (1887).
Precis calescens.
    Junonia calescens, Butler, *P.Z.S.* 1893, p. 652.

Precis cloantha.
Precis cloantha (Cram.), Kirby, *op. cit.* p. 191 (1871).
Precis pyriformis.
Precis pyriformis, Butler, *P.Z.S.* 1895, p. 726, pl. xlii. figs. 5, 6.
Precis taveta.
Precis taveta, Rogenhofer, *Ann. Hof. Mus. Wien,* vi. p. 460, pl. xv. fig. 7.
Precis cuama.
Precis cuama (Hewits.), Kirby, *op. cit.* p. 191 (1871).
Salamis aglatonice.
Salamis aglatonice (Godt.), Kirby, *op. cit.* p. 192 (1871).
Salamis anacardii.
Salamis anacardii (Linn.), Kirby, *op. cit.* p. 192 (1871).
Eurytela dryope.
Eurytela dryope (Cram.), Kirby, *op. cit.* p. 194 (1871).
Eurytela ophione.
Eurytela ophione (Cram.), Kirby, *op. cit.* p. 195 (1871).
Hypanis ilithyia.
Hypanis ilithyia (Drury), Kirby, *op. cit.* p. 196 (1871).
Hypolimnas misippus.
Hypolimnas misippus (Linn.), Kirby, *op. cit.* p. 225 (1871).
Neptis agatha.
Neptis agatha (Cram.), Kirby, *op. cit.* p. 242 (1871).
Euryphene cocalia.
Euryphene cocalia (Fabr.), Kirby, *op. cit.* p. 246 (1871).
Euryphene achlys.
Harma achlys, Hopff. *Ber. Verh. Ak. Berl.* 1855, p. 641.
Euryphene violacea.
Euryphene violacea, Butler, *P.Z.S.* 1888, p. 91.
Hamanumida dædalus.
Hamanumida dædalus (Fabr.), Kirby, *op. cit.* p. 249 (1871).
Charaxes neanthes.
Nymphalis neanthes, Hewits., Kirby, *op. cit.* p. 273 (1871).
Charaxes zoolina.
Nymphalis zoolina, Doubl. and Hewits., Kirby, *op. cit.* p. 273 (1871).
Charaxes saturnus.
Nymphalis saturnus (Butler), Kirby, *op. cit.* p. 267 (1871).
Charaxes candiope.
Nymphalis candiope, Godt., Kirby, *op. cit.* p. 268 (1871).
Charaxes brutus.
Nymphalis brutus (Cram.), Kirby, *op. cit.* p. 268 (1871).
Charaxes castor.
Nymphalis castor (Cram.), Kirby, *op. cit.* p. 267 (1871).

Charaxes kirkii.
  Charaxes kirkii, Butler, *Ent. Month. Mag.* xviii. p. 105 (1881).
Charaxes varanes.
  Palla varanes (Cram.), Kirby, *op. cit.* p. 274 (1871).

FAMILY LYCÆNIDÆ.

Axiocerces perion.
  Axiocerces perion (Cram.), Kirby, *op. cit.* p. 338 (1871).
Lycæna jobates.
  Cupido jobates (Hopff.), Kirby, *op. cit.* p. 349 (1871).
Lycæna lingeus.
  Cupido lingeus (Cram.), Kirby, *op. cit.* p. 350 (1871).
Lycæna trochilus.
  Cupido trochilus (Frey.), Kirby, *op. cit.* p. 357 (1871).
Lycæna palemon.
  Plebeius palemon (Cram.), Kirby, *op. cit.* Suppl. p. 765 (1871).
Lycæna gaika.
  Cupido gaika (Trimen), Kirby, *op. cit.* p. 362 (1871).
Lycæna knysna.
  Lycæna knysna, Trimen, *Trans. Ent. Soc.* ser. 3, vol. i. p. 282 (1862).
Lycæna stellata.
  Lycæna stellata, Trimen, *t.c.* vol. ii. p. 49 (1887).
Lycæna pulchra.
  Plebeius pulchra (Murr.), Kirby, *op. cit.* Suppl. p. 772 (1877).
Lycæna jesous.
  Cupido jesous (Guér.), Kirby, *op. cit.* p. 351 (1871).
Lycæna bæticus.
  Cupido bæticus (Linn.), Kirby, *op. cit.* p. 354 (1871).
Lycæna patricia.
  Lycæna patricia, Trimen, *t.c.* vol. ii. p. 20 (1887).
Catachrysops cuprescens, sp. n.   (Figs. 3, 3*a* on plate, p. 66.)
      Allied to *C. osiris*, Hopff., and wings rather more pointed; the blue basal area hardly visible, both wings being suffused with a coppery lustre.
      Costa and hind margins darker; two orange-yellow spots with black centres, near the anal angle on the hind-wing, between the first and second median nervule and the submedian nervure.
      Under side : similar to that of *C. osiris*, rather more heavily marked, the basal area of the hind-wing darker, with an extra black spot, close to the base, on the inner margin.
      The white discal band wider and not so hastate in shape ; the two orange-yellow spots having the black centres outlined with a metallic blue instead of green.
      Expanse, 1.1 inch.
      Hab. Lorogi Mountains (1894).

Castalius gregorii.
  Castalius gregorii, Butler, *P.Z.S.* 1894, p. 598, pl. xxxvi. fig. 3.
Castalius margaritaceus.
  Castalius margaritaceus, E. M. Sharpe, *P.Z.S.* 1891, p. 636, pl. xlviii. fig. 3.
Hyreus cordatus.
  Hyreus cordatus, E. M. Sharpe, *P.Z.S.* 1891, p. 636, pl. xlviii. fig. 4.
Spindacis ella.
  Aphnæus ella, Hewits., Kirby, *op. cit.* p. 404 (1871).
Iolaus bowkeri.
  Iolaus bowkeri (Trimen), Kirby, *op. cit.* p. 409 (1871).

FAMILY PIERIDÆ.

Nychitona alcesta.
  Pontia alcesta (Cram.), Kirby, *op. cit.* p. 439 (1871).
Nychitona dorothea.
  Pontia dorothea (Fabr.), Kirby, *op. cit.* p. 439 (1871).
Terias zoë.
  Eurema zoë, Hopff., Kirby, *op cit.* p. 448 (1871).
Terias regularis.
  Eurema regularis (Butler), Kirby, *op. cit.* Suppl. p. 791 (1877).
Terias orientis.
  Terias orientis, Butler, *P.Z.S.* 1888, p. 71.
Pieris boguensis.
  Pieris boguensis, Feld., Kirby, *op. cit.* p. 457 (1871).
Pieris severina.
  Pieris severina (Cram.), Kirby, *op. cit.* p. 457 (1871).
Pieris lordaca.
  Pieris lordaca, Walker, *Entom.* v. p. 48.
Pieris contracta.
  Glutophrissa contracta, Butler, *P.Z.S.* 1888, p. 75. n. 102.
Pieris zochalia.
  Pieris zochalia, Boisd., Kirby, *op. cit.* p. 457 (1871).
Pieris gidica.
  Pieris gidica, Godt., Kirby, *op. cit.* p. 457 (1871).
Pieris abyssinica.
  Pieris abyssinica, Lucas, Kirby, *op. cit.* p. 457 (1871).
Pieris thysa.
  Tachyris thysa (Hopff.), Kirby, *op. cit.* p. 464 (1871).
Pinacopteryx orbona.
  Pieris orbona (Geyer), Kirby, *op. cit.* Suppl. p. 793 (1877).

Pinacopteryx pigea.
   Pieris pigea, Boisd., Kirby, *op. cit.* p. 455 (1871).
Pinacopteryx simana.
   Pieris simana, Hopff., Kirby, *op. cit.* p. 456 (1871).
Mylothris agathina.
   Tachyris agathina (Cram.), Kirby, *op. cit.* p. 464 (1871).
Mylothris neumanni.   (Figs. 1, 1*a*, 2, 2*a* on plate, p. 66.)
   Mylothris neumanni, E. M. Sharpe, *Ann. and Mag. Nat.- Hist.* (6),
      vol. xvii. p. 125 (1896).
Mylothris jacksoni.
   Mylothris jacksoni, E. M. Sharpe, *P.Z.S.* 1891, p. 190, pl. xvi.
      fig. 3.
Eronia leda.
   Eronia leda, Doubl., Kirby, *op. cit.* p. 480 (1871).
Eronia buguetii.
   Eronia buguetii (Boisd.), Kirby, *op. cit.* p. 481 (1871).
Eronia cleodora.
   Eronia cleodora, Hubn., Kirby, *op. cit.* p. 480 (1871).
Eronia dilatata.
   Eronia dilatata, Butler, *P.Z.S.* 1888, p. 96.
Catopsilia florella.
   Catopsilia florella (Fabr.), Kirby, *op. cit.* p. 481 (1871).
Colias electra.
   Colias electra (Linn.), Kirby, *op. cit.* p. 490 (1871).
Teracolus calais.
   Teracolus calais (Cram.), Kirby, *op. cit.* p. 499 (1871).
Teracolus ocellatus.
   Teracolus ocellatus, Butler, *P.Z.S.* 1885, p. 767.
Teracolus castalis.
   Teracolus castalis, Staud., *Exot. Schmett.* p. 43, pl. xxiii. (1884).
Teracolus chrysonome.
   Idmais chrysonome (Klug.), Kirby, *op. cit.* p. 498 (1871).
Teracolus aurigineus.
   Teracolus aurigineus, Butler, *Ann. and Mag. Nat. Hist.* (5), vol.
      xii. p. 103 (1883).
Teracolus mutans.
   Teracolus mutans, Butler, *Ann. and Mag. Nat. Hist.* (4), vol. xix.
      p. 459 (1877).
Teracolus catachrysops.
   Teracolus catachrysops, Butler, *Ann. and Mag. Nat. Hist.* (5), vol.
      ii. p. 178 (1878).
Teracolus protomedius.
   Teracolus protomedia (Klug.), Kirby, *op. cit.* p. 500 (1871).

Teracolus puniceus.
Teracolus puniceus, Butler, *P.Z.S.* 1894, p. 573, pl. xxxvi. figs. 5, 6.

Teracolus phlegyas.
Callosune phlegyas (Butler), Kirby, *op. cit.* p. 500 (1871).

Teracolus imperator.
Callosune imperator (Butler), Kirby, *op. cit.* Suppl. p. 804 (1877).

Teracolus celimene.
Callosune celimene (Lucas), Kirby, *op. cit.* p. 504 (1871).

Teracolus hildebrandti.
Teracolus hildebrandti, Staudinger, *Exot. Schmett.* i. p. 44, pl. xxiii. (1888).

Teracolus phœnius.
Callosune phœnius (Butler), Kirby, *op. cit.* Suppl. p. 805 (1877).

Teracolus miles.
Teracolus miles, Butler, *Ann. and Mag. Nat. Hist.* (5), vol. xii. p. 105 (1883).

Teracolus omphaloides.
Callosune omphaloides (Butler), Kirby, *op. cit.* Suppl. p. 805 (1877).

Teracolus omphale.
Callosune omphale (Godt.), Kirby, *op. cit.* p. 502 (1871).

Teracolus ignifer.
Callosune ignifer (Butler), Kirby, *op. cit.* Suppl. p. 804 (1877).

Teracolus evenina.
Callosune evenina (Wallgr.), Kirby, *op. cit.* p. 502 (1871).

Teracolus minans.
Teracolus minans, Butler, *Ent. Month. Mag.* xviii. p. 229 (1882).

Teracolus sipylus.
Teracolus sipylus, Swinhoe, *P.Z S.* 1884, p. 444, pl. xl. fig. 11.

Teracolus heliocaustus.
Teracolus heliocaustus, Butler, *P.Z.S.* 1885, p. 768, pl. xlvii. figs. 8, 9.

Teracolus phillipsi.
Teracolus phillipsi, Butler, *P.Z.S.* 1885, p. 772, pl. xlvii. fig. 11.

Teracolus incretus.
Teracolus incretus, Butler, *P.Z.S.* 1888, p. 93.

Teracolus leo.
Anthocharis leo, Butler, *Ann. and Mag. Nat. Hist.* (3), xvi. p. 397 (1865).

Teracolus eris.
Idmais eris (Klug.), Kirby, *op. cit.* p. 499 (1871).

Herpænia iterata.
Herpænia iterata, Butler, *P.Z.S.* 1888, p. 96.

FAMILY PAPILIONIDÆ.

Papilio brontes.
> Papilio brontes, Godman, *P.Z.S.* 1885, p. 540.

Papilio nireus.
> Papilio nireus, Linn., Kirby, *op. cit.* p. 562 (1871).

Papilio jacksoni.
> Papilio jacksoni, E. M. Sharpe, *P.Z.S.* 1891, p. 188, pl. xvii. figs. 1, 2.

Papilio cenea.
> Papilio cenea, Stoll., Kirby, *op. cit.* p. 563 (1871).

Papilio dionysos.
> Papilio (?) dionysos, Doubl. and Hewits., Kirby, *op. cit.* p. 564 (1871).

Papilio mackinnoni.
> Papilio mackinnoni, E. M. Sharpe, *P.Z.S.* 1891, p. 187, pl. xvi. fig. 1.

Papilio colonna.
> Papilio colonna, Ward, Kirby, *op. cit.* Suppl. p. 812 (1877).

Papilio nyassæ.
> Papilio nyassæ, Butler, Kirby, *op. cit.* Suppl. App. p. 860 (1877).

Papilio policenes.
> Papilio policenes, Cram., Kirby, *op. cit.* p. 558 (1871).

Papilio demoleus.
> Papilio demoleus, Linn., Kirby, *op. cit.* p. 543 (1871).

Papilio phorcas.
> Papilio phorcas, Cram., Kirby, *op. cit.* p. 563 (1871).

Papilio constantinus.
> Papilio constantinus, Ward, Kirby, *op. cit.* Suppl. p. 812 (1877).

Papilio ophidicephalus.
> Papilio ophidicephalus (Oberth.), Trimen, *t.c.* vol. iii. p. 229 (1889).

FAMILY HESPERIDÆ.

Rhopalocampta anchises.
> Ismene anchises, Gerst., Kirby, *op. cit.* Suppl. p. 819 (1877).

Rhopalocampta forestan.
> Ismene forestan (Cram.), Kirby, *op. cit.* p. 581 (1871).

Rhopalocampta hanno.
> Rhopalocampta hanno, Plotz., *Stettin. Ent. Zeitschr.* vol. xl. p. 340 (1879).

Leucochitonea levubu.
> Leucochitonea levubu, Wallgr., Kirby, *op. cit.* p. 618 (1871).

Celænorrhinus biseriatus.
> Plesioneura biseriata, Butler, *P.Z.S.* 1888, p. 97.

Gegenes letterstedti.
 Pamphila letterstedti (Wallgr.), Kirby, *op. cit.* p. 599 (1871).
Pamphila inconspicua.
 Pamphila inconspicua (Bert.), Kirby, *op. cit.* p. 605 (1871).
Sarangesa pertusa.
 Sarangesa pertusa, Mabille, *C.R. Soc. Ent.* Belgium, 1891, p. 68.
Caprona canopus.
 Caprona canopus, Trimen, Kirby, *op. cit.* p. 634 (1871).
Caprona pillaana.
 Caprona pillaana, Wallgr., Kirby, *op. cit.* p. 634 (1871).
Cyclopides quadrisignatus.
 Cyclopides quadrisignatus, Butler, *P.Z.S.* 1893, p. 670, pl. lx.
  fig. 9.
Nisoniades djælælæ.
 Nisoniades djælælæ (Wallgr.), Kirby, *op. cit.* p. 630 (1871).
Nisoniades motozi.
 Nisoniades motozi (Wallgr.), Kirby, *op. cit.* p. 630 (1871).
Pyrgus spio.
 Hesperia spio (Linn.), Kirby, *op. cit.* p. 616 (1871).
Pyrgus diomus.
 Hesperia diomus (Hopff.), Kirby, *op. cit.* p. 615 (1871).
Pyrgus vindex.
 Hesperia vindex (Cram.), Kirby, *op. cit.* p. 615 (1871).

INDEX